THE VOICE OF TECHNOLOGY

THE VOICE OF TECHNOLOGY

Soviet Cinema's Transition to Sound
1928–1935

Lilya Kaganovsky

INDIANA UNIVERSITY PRESS

This book is a publication of

Indiana University Press
Office of Scholarly Publishing
Herman B Wells Library 350
1320 East 10th Street
Bloomington, Indiana 47405 USA

iupress.indiana.edu

© 2018 by Lilya Kaganovsky
All rights reserved

No part of this book may be reproduced or utilized in any form or by any means, electronic or mechanical, including photocopying and recording, or by any information storage and retrieval system, without permission in writing from the publisher.

The paper used in this publication meets the minimum requirements of the American National Standard for Information Sciences—Permanence of Paper for Printed Library Materials, ANSI Z39.48–1992.

Manufactured in the United States of America

Cataloging information is available from the Library of Congress.

ISBN 978-0-253-03264-5 (cloth)
ISBN 978-0-253-03265-2 (paperback)
ISBN 978-0-253-03266-9 (ebook)

1 2 3 4 5   23 22 21 20 19 18

For AWR, RAR, Н.И.П, А.Я.К., и О.И.П.

CONTENTS

	Acknowledgments	ix
	Note on Translation and Transliteration	xiii
	Prologue	xv
	Introduction: The Long Transition: Soviet Cinema and the Coming of Sound	1
one	The Voice of Technology and the End of Soviet Silent Film: Grigori Kozintsev and Leonid Trauberg's *Alone*	40
two	The Materiality of Sound: Dziga Vertov's *Enthusiasm* and Esfir Shub's *K.Sh.E.*	70
three	The Homogeneous Thinking Subject, or Soviet Cinema Learns to Sing: Igor Savchenko's *The Accordion*	108
four	Multilingualism and Heteroglossia in Aleksandr Dovzhenko's *Ivan* and *Aerograd*	138
five	"Les Silences de la voix": Dziga Vertov's *Three Songs of Lenin*	178
	Conclusion: Socialist Realist Sound	227
	Works Cited	243
	Index	257

ACKNOWLEDGMENTS

LIKE MANY BOOKS BEFORE IT, this one grew out of conversations with friends. Elena Mikhailovna Stishova brought Kozintsev and Trauberg's remarkable 1931 film *Odna* to William & Mary (with the help of Tony Anemone and the WGCTV), and that screening and the discussion that followed served as the impetus for this project. It was Yasemin Yildiz who first pointed out to me that I was already working on "sound" and, together with Michael Rothberg and, of course, Rob Rushing, over many meals shared together, helped me to articulate the stakes of this project. At one memorable ASEEES, over a drink, Masha Salazkina proposed that we edit a much needed collection on sound, music, and speech in Soviet cinema, and that collaboration, and the fantastic contributions of scholars from a wide range of academic fields—many of whom are cited in the pages that follow—deepened and informed my own work. And it was Michael Finke who noticed the plaque to Joseph Tykociner on the Illinois campus, connecting the history of the university and the invention of sound-on-film technology to the research I had undertaken.

Even more vitally, working on this book brought me in contact with scholars all over the world, many of whom became close friends. I cannot overstate the pleasure of lunchtime conversations with Emma Widdis, Susan Larsen, Joan Neuberger, Nancy Condee, and Julian Graffy, who listened, read, and always responded with great kindness and intellectual rigor, as I worked out the parameters of this work. In Moscow and Cambridge, at NIIK, VGIK, Gosfilmofond, and elsewhere, Nikolai Izvolov, Sergei Kapterev, Evgeny Margolit, and Peter Bagrov have been the best company and invaluable sources of knowledge of all things Soviet cinema, and without whom, this project would have been greatly diminished. Moscow and the UK were the two epicenters for research and writing on this book, and I am so grateful for the opportunities I had to live and work in Cambridge and Oxford, and for my many interactions with terrific colleagues in Slavonic studies at Cambridge—Rory Finnin, Jana Howlett, Rebecca Reich, and Alyson Tapp; at Oxford—Polly Jones, Catriona Kelly,

Dan Healey, and Andrei Zorin; and across England—Birgit Beumers (first and foremost), Sanja Bahun, Phil Cavendish, Connor Doak, Evgeny Dobrenko, Alexander Etkind, John Haynes, Jeremy Hicks, Stephen Lovell, Rachel Morley, Kristin Roth-Ey, Vlad Strukov, and the members of the UCL SSEES Russian Cinema Research Group.

Beyond the UK, my thanks go to Oksana Bulgakowa, Natascha Drubek, Sabine Hänsgen, Valérie Pozner, Dmitri Zakharine, and Eugénie Zvonkine, scholars and friends whose excellent work on cinema I return to over and over again. Of all the filmmakers I have worked on, Dziga Vertov proved to be the most difficult, the most contradictory and elusive, and I am deeply grateful to John MacKay for sharing his vast knowledge of all things Vertov, as well as to Robert Bird, Molly Brunson, Christina Kiaer, Michael Kunichika, Angelina Lucento, Joshua Malitsky, Anne Eakin Moss, Elizabeth Papazian, Gabriella Saffran, Libby Saxton, Nariman Skakov, and Yuri Tsivian, who, both through their scholarship and through dialogue, helped me to think through what Vertov might have been up to in the thirties.

And finally, I owe a great debt to my fantastic colleagues at Illinois, who have read, in whole or in parts, the many drafts of this book. In particular, I want to thank my wonderful colleagues in both departments, whose encouragement and support have been invaluable for making the University of Illinois a great place to work. The argument of this book was honed through many gatherings of the Russian *kruzhok*, over a glass of wine. I am particularly indebted to Harriet Murav, Valeria Sobol, David Cooper, Kristin Romberg, Mark Steinberg, Diane Koenker, and John Randolph, as well as the graduate students from Slavic, Comparative Literature, and History, for their enthusiasm and their questions, which helped me clarify my claims. Similarly, I am very grateful to Terry Weisman and colleagues in Art + Design, and to Julie Turnock and colleagues in Media & Cinema Studies, for their provocative and engaged responses to my work, as it took its final shape. But it is really to the members of my writing group, in its most stable iteration, that I owe the greatest intellectual debt: Justine Murison, Jennifer Greenhill, and Irene Small read, critiqued, questioned, and encouraged this project through sustained intellectual exchange (and the occasional dance party), and, through the example of their own excellent work, made it possible for me to complete mine.

Institutionally, this project was generously supported by the Illinois Center for Advanced Study, the Research Board, the Russian, East European & Eurasian Center, the Unit for Criticism & Interpretive Theory, and by the College of Liberal Arts & Sciences' Centennial Fellowship. Beyond Illinois, it was made possible by visiting fellowships at Trinity College (Cambridge) and University College (Oxford), and by the American Council of Learned Societies, together with the Social Science Research Council and the National Endowment for the Humanities. I am deeply grateful to these institutions for providing fellowships, release time, travel and research support for this project. Their generosity also provided funding to hire graduate assistants, whom I am very happy to be able to thank here: Alexandra Van Doren, Tatiana Efremova, Marina Filipovic, Anya Hamrick, Meagan Smith, and Oleksandra Wallo.

This book found a good home at Indiana University Press, and I am thankful to Raina Polivka for her initial interest in this project, and to Janice Frisch for seeing it through to its completion. I owe a great debt to Joshua Malitsky and the second anonymous IUP reader for providing incisive comments and suggestions for revisions, which I was happy to follow.

Intellectually and emotionally, this book would never have been completed without the love and friendship of the following people: Yasemin Yildiz, Michael Rothberg, Brett Kaplan, Justine Murison, Ericka Beckman, Dara Goldman, Nancy Castro, Gillen Wood, Manuel Rota, Nora Stoppino, Jim Hansen, Renée Trilling, Maggie Flinn, Patrick Bray, Valeria Sobol, David Cooper, Anna Stenport, Julie Turnock, Kristen Romberg, Amy Powel, Andrea Stevens, Ellen Solis, Gabriel Solis, Andrea Goulet, Jed Esty, Zachary Lesser, Polina Barskova, Masha Salazkina, Anna Nisnevich, Luba Goldburt, Michael Kunichika, Konstantine Klioutchkine, Serguei Oushakine, Evgeny Bershtein, Boris Wolfson, Tony Anemone, Eric Naiman, Anne Nesbet, Frances Bernstein, Eliot Borenstein, Emma Widdis, Susan Larsen, Joan Neuberger, Eugénie Zvonkine, Carola Hähnel, Philippe Mesnard, Maria Pilar Blanco, and David James. This book is dedicated to the memory of Catharine Theimer Nepomnyashchy, mentor and friend.

Most vitally, my life would be infinitely poorer without my family and the love that I have for them: more than anything, this book is for Rob, Sasha, Tolya, Natasha, and Lyalya.

Earlier versions of Chapters 1 and 3 were published in *Studies in Russian and Soviet Cinema* (volumes 1.3 and 6.3, respectively). Material from Chapter 2 originally appeared in German translation as "Elektrische Sprache: Dsiga Wertow und die Tontechnologie / Electric Speech: Dziga Vertov and the Technologies of Sound," in *Resonanz-Räume: die Stimme und die Medien*, edited by Oksana Bulgakowa; and in Russian translation as "Материальность звука: кино касания Эсфири Шуб / The Materiality of Sound: Esfir Shub's Haptic Cinema," in *Novoe Literaturnoe*

Obozrenie, vol. 120. An early version of the Introduction was published as "Learning to Speak Soviet: Soviet Cinema and the Coming of Sound," in *A Companion to Russian Cinema*, edited by Birgit Beumers. I am grateful to the editors and the journals for their permission to republish this earlier work here.

NOTE ON TRANSLATION AND TRANSLITERATION

THE TRANSLITERATION SYSTEM I USE in this book aims for readability in the text and accuracy in the notes. Russian names in the text are given in their conventional English-language spelling to render them more accessible (thus: Eisenstein, not Eizenshtein; Esfir, not Esfir'), while the Library of Congress system of transliteration is followed in all other instances. In translating titles of Russian films, I have also inserted articles where English fluency requires them. Unless otherwise noted, all translations from the Russian are my own.

List of Abbreviations

BFI	British Film Institute National Film Archive
Gosfil'mofond	Gosudarstvennyi fond kinofil'mov Rossiiskoi Federatsii (National Film Foundation of the Russian Federation)
MoMA	Museum of Modern Art National Film Archive
PFA	Pacific Film Archive
RGAKFD	Rossiiskii gosudarstvennyi arkhiv kinofotodokumentov (Russian State Archive of Film and Photo Documents)
RGALI	Rossiiskii gosudarstvennyi arkhiv literatury i iskusstva (Russian State Archive for Literature and the Arts)

PROLOGUE

Edison invented the motion pictures as a supplement to his phonograph, in the belief that sound plus a moving picture would provide better entertainment than sound alone. But in a short time the movies proved to be good enough entertainment without sound. It has been said that although the motion picture and the phonograph were intended to be partners, they grew up separately. And it might be added that the motion picture held the phonograph in such low esteem that for years it would not speak.
—Edward W. Kellogg, *Journal of the SMPTE*, June 1955

THE FIRST PUBLIC DEMONSTRATION OF sound recorded simultaneously with pictures on film took place at the University of Illinois Urbana campus on June 9, 1922.[1] Joseph T. Tykociner's double-feature motion picture included ringing a bell and reading the Gettysburg Address. Tykociner had been working on developing a system for recording and reproducing synchronized sound on motion picture film since 1918, and on June 9, 1922, he publicly demonstrated for the first time a motion picture with a sound track optically recorded directly onto the film. In the first sounds ever publicly heard from a composite image-and-audio film, Helena Tykociner, the inventor's wife, spoke the words, "I will ring," and then rang a bell. Next, Ellery Paine, head of the University of Illinois Department of Electrical Engineering, recited the Gettysburg Address. The demonstration was written up in the *New York World* on July 30, 1922.

Joseph Tykocinski-Tykociner (1877–1969) was born into a Jewish family in Włocławek, a town in the Polish territory then under Russian control.[2] Thus, we might say that from the very beginning, there was a connection between Russia and sound film. At the age of eighteen Tykociner first came to the United States to study science. In New York City he met Nikola Tesla and became an expert in shortwave radio. In 1901 he worked for Guglielmo Marconi in London at the time the first radio signal was

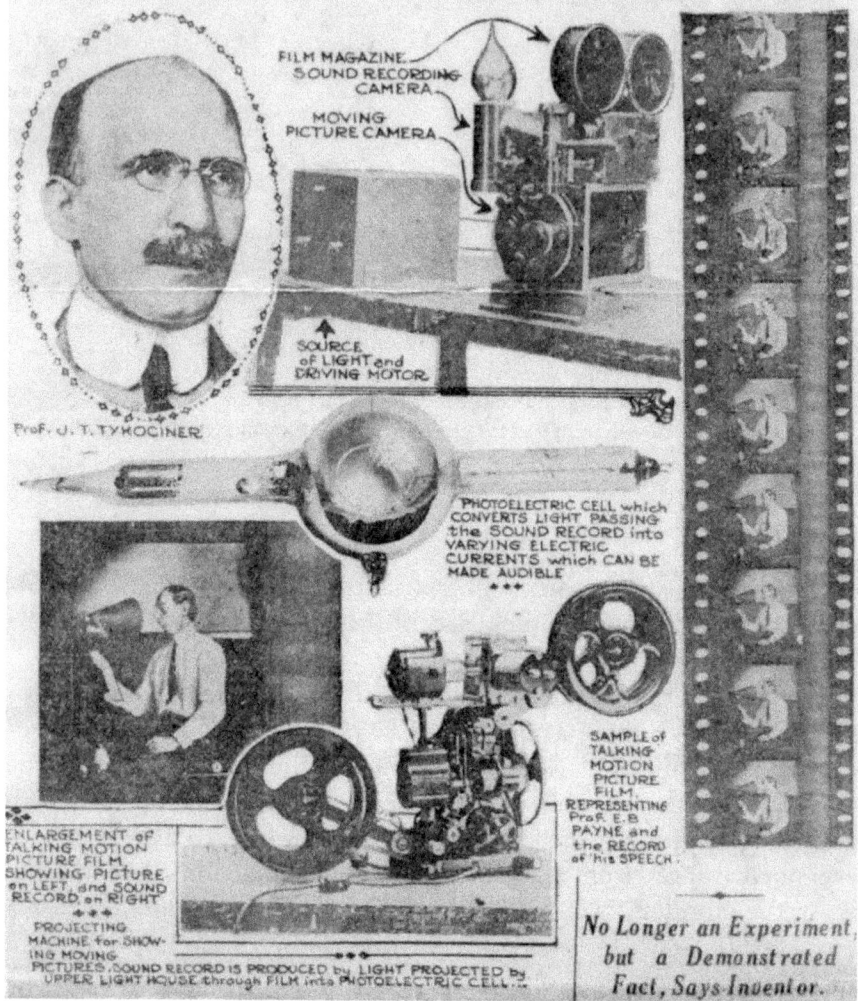

Figure 0.1. "Talking, Laughing, Singing Screen to Rival the Silent Drama Films" (Courtesy Joseph Tykociner Papers, University of Illinois Archives)

transmitted across the Atlantic, and then for the Telefunken firm in Berlin. In 1904, when war broke out in the Far East, the Russian government asked Tykociner to establish a radio communications system for their fleet. Tykociner became a pioneer in shortwave radio, helped develop a system to link the Russian fleets in the Baltic with those in the Black Sea, and was awarded a jeweled gold watch by Czar Nicholas II. He was also (apparently) at St. Petersburg's Finland Station when Lenin returned from exile in 1917.[3] After the Russian Revolution, Tykociner returned to Poland during the war for Polish independence. At the beginning of 1919 he proposed to the new Ministry of Post and Telegraphy a project to create a direct radio link between Poland and the United States.

In 1920, Tykociner again left for America and in 1921 he accepted a laboratory position as the first research professor of electrical engineering at the University of Illinois in Urbana. He worked in high-frequency measurements, dielectrics, piezoelectricity, photoelectric tubes, and microwaves, and devised a way of recording sound on film by using a photo-optical method of recording sound on light-sensitive celluloid by means of a mercury lamp connected to the electric circuit with a microphone. On June 9, 1922, he demonstrated the operation of this invention at a conference of the American Institute of Electrical Engineers in Urbana, Illinois. The first official demonstration of Tykociner's "talking motion picture apparatus" took place in the Physics laboratory in Urbana and was described in *SMPTE Transactions*,[4] but a dispute between Tykociner and then University of Illinois President David Kinley over patent rights to the process prevented its commercial application, and the patent was only awarded in 1926. President Kinley also told Tykociner that in order to stay at Illinois he would have to pursue other fields, and Tykociner obliged. He dropped his sound-on-film work and switched his area of research. In the mid-1920s he began to experiment with antennas, a precursor to radar development.

But it wasn't just a question of patents. In a recorded interview on May 3, 1965, Tykociner described his boyhood interest in sound recording, his dissatisfaction with the needle and cylinder, and his decision that sound "must be recorded photographically." In 1896–1897, when film was not yet known, he came to New York to see Edison's Bioscope displayed in a vacant store: "moving picture, but no sound." In 1920, he moved to the US and decided to work on sound pictures, but after one year with Westinghouse in Pittsburgh, he could not convince the laboratory director that there was anything in sound pictures. By 1922, working at the University of Illinois, Tykociner was able to demonstrate his invention, and the demonstrations made an impression; the public information director, Josef Wright, had clippings from 700 newspapers, and Tykociner received telegrams praising the invention. But specialists resisted the innovation; a "Hollywood man" said that the costs were too high, that "stars don't speak very well," they have poor diction, and "they drink too much." A psychologist said that "it was based on illusions of both sound and the eye." And an Eastman Kodak representative said "he wouldn't give a dime for it," explaining that "the public doesn't want it." As Tykociner notes, the first commercial film came six or seven years later, produced by Western Electric, with sound recorded separately on records.⁵

Thus the credit for sound-on-film technology went to Lee de Forest, who, by 1919, had already filed patents for his sound-on-film process Phonofilm, unaware of Tykociner's work. De Forest, working with Theodore Case, produced a number of short films in 1921 and 1922, and introduced Phonofilm at a presentation at the Rivoli Theater in New York City on April 15, 1923. Speaking of the future of sound pictures, de Forest gave a definite "no" to the question whether the existing type of silent drama could be improved by the addition of voice. But he foresaw the evolution of an entirely new type of dramatic scheme and presentations that would take advantage of the freedom that had been such an asset to the silent moving pictures as contrasted with the stage. The Phonofilm system was used in numerous theaters, with sound films made under de Forest's direction; but he did not succeed in selling the product more widely to American motion picture producers. Whether the imperfections of the system (defective film-motion, limited frequency range, loudspeakers that produced unnatural sounding voices), or the industry's prosperity, or the fact that perhaps the films demonstrated were uninteresting, sound film did not immediately catch on.

Case and de Forest had a falling out, and Case took his patents to William Fox, who used them to develop Fox Movietone. E. I. Sponable, who had been responsible for building several sound cameras in 1922, 1923, and 1924, joined the new company to design recording studios in New York and later in Hollywood. In 1927 he developed a screen that transmitted sound freely, permitting loudspeakers to be located directly behind the picture. The first public showing of Movietone recordings was in January 1927, and by March 1929, Fox stopped making silent pictures. The first commercial talking film, *The Jazz Singer*, released in 1927, used the Warner Brothers' Vitaphone system, which provided sound for pictures by means of phonograph (mechanical) recording. Tykociner's invention of the optical sound track was only later recognized, but it is still used for sound on film today.

Notes

1. Early work on sound in motion-picture film included, among others: Leon Gaumont, in France, who began as early as 1901 to work on combining the phonograph and motion picture; Ernst Rühmer in Berlin, whose work on photographic sound recording was first published in 1901; Eugene Augustine Lauste, who demonstrated his recording apparatus in 1911, during which

he produced what was probably the first actual sound-on-film motion picture in the US; and Thomas Edison, who in 1913 made a serious effort to synchronize phonograph sound with moving pictures, and whose talking-picture show ran for several months in Keith's Colonial Theater in New York. For a detailed history of the development of sound motion pictures, see the anthology of the *Journal of the Society of Motion Picture and Television Engineers, A Technological History of Motion Pictures and Television*, ed. Raymond Fielding (Berkeley: UC Press, 1967).

2. For more on Joseph Tykociner's biography, see Sławomir Łotysz, "Contributions of Polish Jews: Joseph Tykocinski-Tykociner (1877–1969), Pioneer of Sound on Film," *AAPJS Gazeta*, 13, no. 3 (Winter–Spring 2006). For archival holdings, see Joseph T. Tykociner Papers, 1900–1969, University of Illinois Archives.

3. Vladimir Lenin arrived at St. Petersburg's Finland Station by train from Germany on April 3, 1917, to start the October Revolution. The event is commemorated by the Soviet statue of Lenin dominating the square in front of the station.

4. The Journal of the Society of Motion Picture and Television Engineers.

5. Joseph T. Tykociner Papers, Box 18, "Biographical Tape Recordings—May 3, 1965, interview by M. J. Brichford."

THE VOICE OF TECHNOLOGY

Introduction

THE LONG TRANSITION
Soviet Cinema and the Coming of Sound

> Jean Painleve wrote that "the cinema has always been sound cinema." Jean Mitry specified, on the other hand, that "the early cinema was not mute, but quiet." To which Adorno and Eisler replied in advance, "the talking picture, too, is mute." Indeed, corrects Bresson, "there never was a mute cinema." Besides, André Bazin noted, "But not all of silent films want to be such," and so on. I throw out these few citations (out of context to be sure) to stir the waters of pat formulas; to this I'll toss in another stone of my own in stating that the silent cinema should really be called "deaf cinema."
> —Michel Chion, *The Voice in Cinema*

IN SOVIET FILM STUDIES, IT has been common practice to categorize the coming of sound to Soviet cinema as a moment of crisis and failure, the moment when the "Golden Age" of Soviet avant-garde cinema and the montage school came to an abrupt end.[1] A technological development that had profound consequences for the formal and aesthetic characteristics of cinema the world over, the introduction of synchronized sound coincided with and was subsumed by the massive cultural changes that were taking place in the Soviet Union from the late 1920s and into the '30s, making it impossible to separate the coming of sound from the chaos of the film industry, the consequences of rapid industrialization, and the new ideological precepts of Socialist Realism.[2]

Film historians such as Peter Kenez, Jay Leyda, Richard Taylor, and Denise Youngblood, along with many others, have documented the history of the Soviet industry's conversion to sound, often by emphasizing the Soviet industry's backwardness, its difficult assimilation of the new technology, and the political debates that surrounded the changes to the industry as a whole. As Youngblood notes, by 1930, the film industry had been almost completely disrupted, and as the times became more troubled, fewer and fewer movies were made. The drop in production was partially due

Figure 0.2. Alexander Shorin's sound camera on the cover of *Cinema and Life* [Kino i zhizn'] no. 14 (1930) (RGALI)

to the fears engendered by intensified political pressures, but also due to lack of raw materials and the "confusion over the future of sound." Artistically, writes Youngblood, "the silent era had ended, but due to technological backwardness, silent movies would continue to be made in the USSR until 1935."[3] "Soviet directors," writes Kenez, "had an opportunity to observe the birth of sound film from a distance, for the domestic industry could follow only with some delay. Technologically, the Soviet Union was backward. While in the West the first sound films appeared in 1926 and 1927, in the Soviet Union in the late 1920s the industry had only reached an experimental stage. At a time when the huge American industry had almost completed the transition, the Soviet Union was just producing its first sound film."[4]

Nevertheless, as Andrey Smirnov points out, the first practical sound-on-film systems were created almost simultaneously in the USSR, the US, and Germany. Pavel Tager began his experiments with sound in Moscow in 1926, and just a few months later, in 1927, Aleksandr Shorin started his own research on synchronized sound in Leningrad. The first experimental sound-on-film program—excerpts from the film *Women from Ryazan* (Baby riazanskie)—was demonstrated on October 5, 1929, in Leningrad in the Sovkino Cinema, specially equipped with Shorin's sound-on-film system. A few months later, on March 5, 1930, the first sound theater, *Khudozhestvennyi* (The Art), opened in Moscow, with a demonstration of a *Combined Sound Program No. 1* (Zvukovaia sbornaia programma N1), which included four films: a speech by Anatoly Lunacharsky about the significance of cinema, *March* by Sergei Prokofiev from the opera *The Love for Three Oranges* (Liubov' k trem apel'sinam, Op. 33), Abram Room's documentary *The Plan for Great Works* (Piatiletka. Plan velikikh rabot), and the animated film *Tip Top*, with music composed, among others, by Georgy Rimsky-Korsakov and sound design by Arseny Avraamov. In other words, while the conversion to sound certainly took longer in the USSR than in many other countries (with the notable exception of Japan[5]), the Soviet Union was nevertheless at the forefront of experimentation with sound—a fact that had consequences both for the theory and the practice of the new Soviet sound cinema.

In his seminal essay "Soviet Cinema: Making Sense of Sound," first published in *Screen* in 1982, Ian Christie writes:

> Looking at the frozen legacy of early Soviet cinema, inscribed alike in conventional and radical histories, the absence of any sustained treatment of the long transition to sound is striking. It is as if the brute industrial fact of sound, with its attendant aesthetic and ideological implications, constitutes a great *disturbance* for narrative history, or indeed, montage theory. Yet, the introduction of sound coincides with and helps to define the turning point in Soviet cinema. It is an example *par excellence* of the generally ignored intersection between the specificity of cinema and the histories—economic, technological, political, ideological—that determine and are in turn determined by it. Soviet sound cinema is effectively a "new apparatus" by the late '30s.[6]

Indeed, the common dismissal of the Soviet film industry as "technologically backward" is one of the ways the narrative of the transition to sound has been curtailed from the start, with scholars focusing on the problem of conversion as one of playing "catch up" with the American film industry.[7] A kind of "technological determinism" marks much of the scholarship on this period, with greater attention paid to the industry's failures than to the films themselves. Compare, for example, how differently critics write about the slow Japanese conversion to sound than that of the USSR:

One major factor in the Japanese film industry's successful survival of the transition to sound was its ability to convert to sound very slowly—over a ten year period—because of the popularity and strength of the indigenous variety of "silent film." Film in Japan was never experienced by the audience in silence; instead, the screening of silent films was accompanied by the live performance of narration and music in the theatre.... It was not until 1935 that a talkie film won first prize at the Kinema Jumpo annual critics' poll. In 1933, the four top awards went to silents (directed by Ozu, Mizoguchi and Naruse, respectively); and in 1934, an Ozu silent again won the top award.⁸

Of course, the discourse of Soviet "belatedness" is neither new, nor is it something invented by others to account for a messy period of transition. Soviet filmmakers and critics themselves felt that as the silent era came to a close, and with it, their preeminent position in world cinema, that they were falling behind the US and Europe.⁹ And while many of the avant-garde filmmakers of the twenties—Boris Barnet, Alexander Dovzhenko, FEKS members Grigori Kozintsev and Leonid Trauberg, Vsevolod Pudovkin, and, of course, Dziga Vertov—did make sound films as soon as they could, the most prominent Soviet director, Sergei Eisenstein, was not among them, and the film credit for the first 100 percent Soviet "talkie" went to a complete unknown: Nikolai Ekk for *The Road to Life* (Putevka v zhizn', 1931).¹⁰ Nevertheless, as I hope to show throughout this book, the films made in the USSR between 1928–1935, while Soviet sound technology was still in its infancy, represent something of a discovery. They are remarkable not only for their innovative, experimental, unexpected, and challenging uses of sound, but also for the way they reflect—by means of the new technology of sound—on the complexities of their historical moment, the transition not only from silence to sound, but from the twenties to the thirties, and from avant-garde art to Socialist Realism.

This book, therefore, aims to tell a different story from the usual narrative of Soviet belatedness. Rather, I argue that the "long transition" to sound gave Soviet filmmakers a chance to theorize and experiment with the new sound technology in ways that were unavailable to their Western counterparts, driven by market forces and audience demand. Many prominent Soviet filmmakers traveled abroad in the late twenties and early thirties, and early Soviet sound films were shown in countries such as the US, Germany, France, and the UK, in this way, forming part of the larger conversation about sound film that was taking place elsewhere. Moreover, Eisenstein, Pudovkin, and Vertov, among others, wrote extensively on the uses of sound in film—first theoretical, then practical—and their articles and pronouncements on the function of sound, music, dialogue, and noise effects circulated not only in Soviet cinema circles, but were also widely translated, and to this day inform the discipline of sound studies.[11] And while this book does not aim to be exhaustive, I do hope to show how the Soviet film industry's transition to sound was handled by a number of different filmmakers, using a variety of genres, formats, and techniques, and what these early experiments with sound—many of which remain unknown—can tell us about this period of cultural upheaval, as the Soviet Union moved from the Revolutionary Twenties to the Stalinist Thirties.

The Coming of Sound

How did the coming of sound change the cinema industry? What was made possible and what was foreclosed when Soviet cinema began to "talk"?[12] The 1927 release of *The Jazz Singer* (dir. Alan Crosland, USA) radically altered the art of cinema. Despite the many sounds—narrators, piano players, organs, etc.—that had been audible in the movie theater, the "silence" of silent film had been perceived as integral to the very art of cinematic expression, its distance from theater and literature in which the audible word predominated, its reliance on techniques of editing and montage, gestural language and the close-up (which brought to the forefront the full "encyclopedia of facial expressions," as Béla Balázs would have it[13]). Everywhere, the coming of sound to cinema at the end of the twenties meant a thorough rethinking of cinematic technique, production, and distribution. Everywhere, cinema industries had to be reorganized to convert the silent screen into "talking pictures."[14]

But in the Soviet Union, the introduction of sound coincided with a cultural, political, and ideological break of the period known as the Great Turning Point.[15] Stalin's First Five-Year Plan (1928–1932) began with a massive industrialization campaign that led, among other things, to a complete restructuring of the Soviet arts. Industrialization and centralization of the cinema industry altered the way movies in the Soviet Union were made, while the introduction of sound radically altered the way these movies were received. The coming of sound changed the Soviet cinema industry by making audible, for the first time, the voice of State power, directly addressing the Soviet viewer. The films of the transition all mark this ideological shift; each film stages its relationship to the technology of sound as a relationship to power. Looking closely at early sound films and the debates that preceded and accompanied the Soviet industry's transition to sound allows us to understand how Soviet filmmakers handled the double bind of working with new technology within equally new ideological parameters. In doing so, these filmmakers created films that were utterly unlike anything that had come before (during the Golden Age of Soviet cinema in the 1920s) or after (during High Stalinism, 1935–1953). More vitally, early Soviet sound directors also made movies that were very different from what was being released in the US, Germany, Britain, or France—or indeed, in any other country whose transition to sound was driven by consumer demand and capitalist modes of production.

It is important to note that even the American transition to sound, while it was accomplished very rapidly, was never smooth, and the narrative of that transition has been told in a number of (often conflicting) ways. Donald Crafton, for example, offers a revised and very detailed history of Hollywood's transition to sound, whose coming he sees as mainly a by-product of the different advances in electricity—what he refers to, using one of the terms common in the twenties, as "a new form of *electrical* entertainment."[16] Electric companies, along with studios and the popular press, argues Crafton, helped to create a climate of acceptance for the coming of sound cinema. They helped organize a discourse around sound, about progress and modernity, that made sound cinema appear not as a "natural" development from silent cinema, but as a "new and completely different product," a product of a new era of technological change. In contrast, David Bordwell, Janet Staiger, and Kristin Thompson argue that sound cinema "was not a radical alternative to silent filmmaking; sound as sound, as a material and as a set of technical procedures, was inserted into the already-constituted system of the classical Hollywood style."[17] Moreover, Douglas Gomery has dismissed any notion of an upheaval during the transition, arguing instead that rather than chaos, "the transition to sound by the US film industry monopolists was fast, orderly, and profitable."[18]

Yet, as James Lastra has argued, not only did Hollywood waver in its allegiance to representational modes during the transition, moving between discursive and diegetic forms, "but the mode of representation understood to be characteristic of the very technology of sound was likewise up for grabs":

> Was sound an effect? Was it narration? Was it clarifying commentary? Should it function as an added form of omniscient or restricted narration? Was it realist or spectacular in nature? Even its technical nature was in dispute. Was it closer in form and purpose to the phonograph, the telephone, or the radio? Each device, while useful for grasping some aspects of the sound film phenomenon, validated different techniques and implied different representational norms. So, before "sound as sound" could be "inserted into … the Hollywood style," it had to be determined just what sound "was" and what its appropriate functions were.[19]

The received idea that "sound hit Hollywood like a bolt of lightning" with the premiere of *The Jazz Singer*—as exemplified by such classic films as *Singin' in the Rain* (Stanley Donen and Gene Kelly, 1952, USA), as well as memoirs of prominent Hollywood studio executives—has been, in the last three decades, put under pressure by media scholars and historians. And it is clear that the transition to sound in the US was likely neither as earth shattering nor as smooth as the different accounts would have it.[20] Furthermore, other countries, such as Britain, France, Germany, and Italy (to take only the European examples) all experienced the conversion to sound at their own pace and none could accomplish the transition as quickly as was possible for the United States.[21] The effects of conversion were not simply aesthetic or psychological (audiences clamoring for "100 percent talkies"), but also financial. Hollywood's retrofitting for sound may have cost approximately $10,000 per theater, in addition to exorbitant millions spent on sound stages and new theaters nationwide.[22] Gomery suggests that the total investments might have ranged from $23 million to $50 million.[23] For the Soviet Union, caught in the Cultural Revolution and the First Five-Year Plan, without a native film production industry, and having severed its economic ties with the West, such costs would have been prohibitive. Indeed, had viable sound-on-film technology become available in the West only two years later, it is not clear that either the US or Europe would have made a successful conversion before the stock market crash of 1929.[24]

The transformation of American cinemas from almost all silent to almost all sound, as Crafton, Gomery, and others have shown, took about a year and a half, and by the time of the stock market crash in October 1929, "out-of-the way theaters and those servicing poor neighborhoods were the only ones still waiting for amplification."[25] Europe took longer, with the UK moving fastest, followed by Germany and France (UK exhibitors were 63 percent wired by the close of 1930; Germany did not top 60 percent until 1932; and France moved even slower).[26] Trying to stave off the Hollywood "talkie invasion," Germany developed its own sound-on-film method that became known as Tri-Ergon, but was not successful in integrating it into German theaters until the spring of 1929, when two different companies merged to form Tobis-Klangfilm, and successfully sued for the sole right to sound film patents within Germany.[27] By 1930, when the USSR declared its independence from Western economic relations and trade, the Soviet film industry was already lagging behind the US and Western Europe in the conversion to sound. Beset by a lack of resources, massive bureaucratization, and rapidly shifting ideological imperatives (which greatly affected script production and approval, among other things), the conversion to sound took until 1935, with silent versions of feature films still being released as late as 1938.

There were many reasons for this. For Soviet cinema, the conversion to sound coincided with a complete restructuring of the Soviet film industry; what had been in the twenties a fairly loose assembly of studios and artists was transformed during the First Five-Year Plan into a centrally organized and administered body. As Vance Kepley Jr. has noted, during the NEP period (New Economic Policy, 1921–1928), Soviet cinema was generally heterogeneous, with a number of regional and national film organizations participating in a growing film market. By 1927, the Soviet film industry included some thirteen production organizations with a total reported capital of 21,238,000 rubles.[28] Moreover, under NEP, each national republic maintained considerable autonomy of its national film market. Each republic was allowed to create a native film organization, with a monopoly on film distribution within the borders of that republic, which helped to prevent "colonization" by larger distributors like Sovkino.[29] This period of relative autonomy came to an end in 1928/1929 with Stalin's "Great Turn," which signaled a radical change in the economic policies of the Soviet Union, the abandoning of the New Economic Policy, and the acceleration of collectivization and industrialization.

The years of the First Five-Year Plan (1928–1932) involved a complete restructuring and centralization of the Soviet arts, and a second "nationalization" of the film industry. To be sure, many of the conferences, meetings, congresses, and decrees passed by film workers at this time called on greater oversight by the Party. Arguments against Sovkino in particular stressed the organization's commercial interests and its reliance on the import of foreign films, as well as its failure to make movies for the masses or to bring cinema to the countryside. Everyone agreed that sound cinema had the potential to be the greatest tool of influence over the masses.[30] The First All-Union Party Conference on Cinema Affairs held in March 1928 focused its attention on the problems of the Soviet film industry and the "crisis in Soviet cinema": the failure to make movies accessible to the masses, the failure of the "*cinefication* of the countryside," the failure to become a self-sustaining industry, the failure to negotiate the needs of ideology and profit. Soviet cinema had to become an "experiment, intelligible to the masses"; and moreover, it had to become a true *industry* by manufacturing its own equipment.[31] In January 1929, following the recommendations of a special commission, the Central Committee of the Communist Party issued a decree about the reorganization and purging of current cinema cadres and the centralization of the film industry into Soiuzkino, creating a single Soviet-wide agency to oversee the film and photo industries. Thus, for the Soviet Union, the centralization and second nationalization of the film industry meant a change not only in the kinds of movies that were being made, but also in who was making them, where, with what equipment, and for what audience—from cinema as a mass art to cinema "for the masses."

The massive cultural upheaval that accompanied the First Five-Year Plan led to a complete restructuring of the Soviet arts, including the cinema. As Kepley Jr. notes, this new nationalization of the movie industry did not mean that the Soviet central government took over day-to-day film affairs; rather, the government created a new bureaucratic layer, represented by Soiuzkino, to run the industry, which would be periodically accountable to government oversight. Soiuzkino was responsible for "all matters concerning production of the movie-photo apparatus (for filming, projecting, lighting, and so on), movie-photo accessories and materials (films, records, papers, photochemicals, and so on), as well as all matters concerning motion-picture production, rental, and exhibition."[32] Beyond politics and economics, the creation of this "all-union combine" translated into the massive bureaucratization of the Soviet film industry. The two-year personnel plan was to provide cinema with more than 7,000 new administrators, over three and a half times more than the number of creative personnel slated to join the industry in the same interval.

Other major transformations that directly affected the conversion to sound included the development and refurbishing of the USSR's principal production, distribution, and exhibition facilities. In 1930 the USSR virtually stopped importing foreign movies, technology, or film stock. Slogans such as "economic independence" and "Produce from Soviet materials with Soviet tools!" dominated the discourse around cinema and the new developments in the acquisition of sound; Soviet sound cinema was to be "home-grown" and free of foreign patent obligations (although Soiuzkino contracted foreign laboratories for technical advice). Research on the Soviet-made Shorin and Tager sound systems dated back into the 1920s; indeed, Tager names November 26, 1926, as the date when he first began to work on sound-on-film technology, with Shorin's first experiments following in 1927. According to Tager, August 2, 1929, marked the date of the first Soviet recording of sound footage on the streets of Moscow, and October 26, 1929, the first Soviet radio broadcast of recorded sound footage. Tager

Figure 0.3. Pavel Tager and the "Tagefon" sound camera (RGALI)

notes specifically that the Soviet Union was only one of three countries (the others being the US and Germany) to independently develop its own sound-on-film technology.[33]

Beyond the development of the sound camera and the method of synchronous sound recording, however, the USSR also needed to build factories that could produce film stock, cameras, projectors, and other equipment, as well as theaters wired for sound. A series of meetings at ARRK shows that sound production was still in complete disarray at the end of 1930, and that Soviet sound films remained in their "experimental" phase (sometimes, sound films were shot without an actual camera). A lack of functional equipment, including cameras, microphones, photo-elements, film stock, light bulbs, etc., as well as labs for playback (only available at Sovkino) or theaters wired for sound, all plagued the Soviet film industry. Moreover, studios and individual directors fought over who had access to the sound camera (preferably, Shorin's, because the Tager camera—"the coffin" as it was affectionately called—frequently broke down, although it was used to film Ekk's *The Road to Life*) and in what order. For November 7, 1930, ARRK was supposed to have access to ten projectors, but ended up with only two (one installed in Leningrad and one in Minsk). Their one sound camera was on loan from Sovkino, which might have taken it back at any time. Belgoskino had been working with a handheld model, designed by Okhtonikov and Mashkevich (which they claimed worked as well as a Shorin or a Tager); the first Sound Factory in Moscow was shooting Raitman's *The Earth Thirsts* (Zemlia zhazhdet); Leningrad was ensounding *Alone* (Odna); Kiev had only one broken camera, which was used for *Enthusiasm: Donbass Symphony* (Entuziazm: Simfoniia Donbassa, a "ruined film" as someone from the audience noted); Vostokkino, Gruziia, and Azerbaijan studios were all standing by, waiting for their access to equipment.[34]

Moreover, the USSR also needed a new federal system of distribution/diffusion of sound films in a multilanguage environment.[35] Soiuzkino would now need to coordinate the production and distribution of sound prints in line with regional language patterns. This had not been an issue with silent films, which could rely either on multilanguage intertitles or on a *bonimenteur*, that is to say, a speaker who interpreted the film for provincial audiences during projection.[36] Sound cinema required more complex plans for dubbing and subtitling to serve the USSR's multiethnic population, which led to the question of which language Soviet cinema would speak.

As Nataša Ďurovičová has noted, as soon as the prospect of sound cinema began to be developed systematically, it "revealed the problem of language."[37] For Hollywood, this meant that making films in just one language would seriously endanger the American cinema's world market, which by 1929 generated between 35 and 40 percent of a major studio's profits. Neither of the two solutions—subtitling (preservation of the original sound track, supplemented with written text) or dubbing (substitution of the original sound track)—would prove entirely satisfactory. Subtitling returned sound film to the recently abandoned use of intertitles (i.e., reliance on the written word to supplement the image); dubbing generated the problem of the "alien speaking body"—a dissonance between body and voice, with one actor performing and another one speaking on screen.[38] Moreover, with early sound equipment, maximum intelligibility was obtained only with direct recording of dialogue, and even for American film studios, "dubbing" was not a satisfactory option for roughly a decade.

Every country solved this "problem of language" in a different way. In Italy, as early as 1929, Mussolini's government decreed that all films projected on Italian screens must have an Italian-language sound track, and dubbing immediately became a powerful state weapon in the reemergent nationalist movement. In France, the debate over dubbing took a different form, requiring not only French language to be spoken by French actors (that is to say, Hollywood studios could no longer simply produce a foreign-language version of a film and distribute it to France), but even the supplementary musical track added to silent film had to be rerecorded in France. As Ďurovičová puts it, "the organic unit(y) thus posited between language and land was established as an important guiding rule for all subsequent delineation of the national cinema's identity."[39]

In the Soviet Union, since the early 1930s, NIKFI (Nauchno-issledovatel'skii kinofotoinstitut / the Cinema-Photo Research Institute in Moscow, established in August 1929) specialized in dubbing foreign films into Russian, but very few Russian-language films were being dubbed into other "national" languages, and no national-language films were being dubbed into Russian. Despite expense and difficulties in production, dubbing technology was seen as the only option for screening Russian-language films in national republics and national-language films in Russia. Subtitles/supertitles could not be read by audiences fast enough and required a high literacy level.[40] And the idea of national studios making films only in Russian, or in multiple versions, undermined the drive for native production of the different national cinemas.[41]

In 1938 a special commission of the Bakinsk, Tashkent, and Ashkhabad national studios produced a report on dubbing, which proposed following the example of France, where all sound films were rerecorded from scratch in a different language, thereby generating a second (or third) version of the film. To do this, the commission suggested that all Soviet films be recorded onto three separate tracks—dialogue, sound effects, and music—in order to facilitate voice overdubbing and eliminate the need to rerecord the music, use a full orchestra, and the like. The most prominent Russian-language films—such as *Chapaev* (dir. Vasil'ev Brothers, 1934) and *Lenin in October* (Lenin v oktiabre, dir. Romm, 1937)—were to be dubbed into every national language. Other films—such as *The Rich Bride* (Bogataia nevesta, dir. Pyr'ev, 1937)—could be dubbed into two to three strategic languages (ones that would be understood in several national republics).[42]

Youngblood stresses the degree to which by 1930 the Soviet film industry had been completely disrupted: "The pessimism in the film industry by the end of the decade, even before the purges were in full swing, was extraordinary . . . [The Soviet film industry] had not yet mastered silent film technology, nor produced film stock or equipment, when along came a radical new development which necessitated the complete replacement of existing equipment with sophisticated and expensive devices."[43] Conversion to sound became a top priority, allowing for a more direct transmission of party slogans, platforms, and ideological directives. According to Jay Leyda, Stalin was particularly interested in sound cinema, instructing Aleksandrov and Eisenstein and their cameraman Eduard Tissé to study European and American sound technology while abroad. "Knowing about our planned trip to America," writes Aleksandrov in his op. ed., "The Great Friend of Soviet Cinema," "Josef Vissarionovich told us: 'Study the sound film in detail. This is very important to us. When our heroes discover speech, the influential power of films will increase enormously.'"[44]

Early Sound Counterpoint

In 1930 the first Soviet sound films went into production, including Room's *The Plan for Great Works*; and by 1931, the first feature sound films appeared on Soviet screens. Their appearance did not so much mark the end of silent film (an end that in any case was prolonged by the lack of sound theaters around the country, ensuring that silent films continued to play in Soviet theaters well into the 1930s, with all sound feature films released in "silent" versions), but it did bring to an end the *silent film era*, with experimentation for the most part now transferred from images to sound.[45] Jay Leyda has suggested that because of the longer period of transition, Soviet filmmakers were able to avoid many of the mistakes made by foreign film studios (such as the "all-talkie" craze), just as Tager and Shorin were able to avoid mistakes made by foreign sound engineers (such as trying to develop sound-on-disk technology).[46] I would argue further, that because of the longer period of transition, Soviet directors had a chance to experiment with sound to a degree that was unavailable to filmmakers in the US and Europe, working under the pressures of commercial cinema. As a result, they made remarkable films that reflected the chaos but also the possibilities of the new sound apparatus, and that were totally unlike those created in the West.

In their 1928 manifesto on sound, "Budushchee zvukovoi fil'my. Zaiavka," Eisenstein, Pudovkin, and Aleksandrov welcomed the coming of sound and the first period of experimentation with the textures (*faktura*) of sound, but described the second period that would quickly follow as one of a "loss of innocence" (*uviadanie devstvennosti*).[47] Dismissing "talking pictures" as those in which "sound is recorded in a natural manner, synchronizing exactly with the movement on the screen and creating a certain 'illusion' of people talking, objects making noise, etc.," this first period of "sensations" (*sensatsii*) though innocent in itself, would lead to cinema's "automatic" (*avtomaticheskogo*) uses of sound for "dramas of high culture" and other photographed presentations of a theatrical order. The mere "adhesion" (*prikleivanie*) of sound and montage fragments would increase the fragments' "inertia" and their "independent" significance, going against the idea of montage as a *juxtaposition* of film fragments. We might note the degree to which the filmmakers' statement is inflected by the notion of the materiality/texture of sound, which is juxtaposed to "automatic" uses of sound prevalent in Hollywood "talkies."[48] To avoid this "passive" approach to sound, the directors argued instead for contrapuntal uses of sound that would be in "sharp discord with the visual image." Only such an "assault" (*shturm*) of cinema by sound would produce the correct "feelings" (*oshchushcheniia*),[49] liberating avant-garde cinema from a series of "blind alleys," such as the need for intertitles and long establishing shots to explain and situate the film's action, both of which interrupt and slow down the rhythm of the film. Sound used as counterpoint and as an element of montage—in other words, as an "independent" variable combined with the visual image—would ensure that sound cinema would become an even more powerful means of persuasion and influence on the viewer.

Adrian Piotrovsky, the head of the Lenfilm script department, similarly called for a revolutionary approach to sound film in his 1929 editorial in the journal *Zhizn' iskusstva* called "Tonfil'ma" (Sound film).[50] Piotrovsky stressed in particular the ways Soviet cinema must be different from American and European sound film, whose direction in 1929 was toward dialogue and the reproduction of naturalistic sounds effects. Specifically, he mentions the unheard of and unprecedented "sensation" created by *The Jazz Singer* (which premiered in Moscow on November 4, 1929) and Al Jolson's "cabaret" songs. For Piotrovsky, this focus on sensation (singing and dancing) meant that sound cinema had abandoned the editing and optical techniques of its earlier, silent years. Like Eisenstein, Pudovkin, and Aleksandrov, Piotrovsky argues specifically for contrast; he advocates the dialectical possibilities of conflict, struggle, and disagreement instead of having the sound track "passively" following the course set by the image track. Nonparallel construction, confrontation, and disjuncture would provide the new sound film with political and social value, opposing it to the merely aesthetic/naturalistic/reactionary forms of American and European sound cinema.[51]

Yet, as Aleksandrov makes clear in his memoirs about the period (*Gody poiskov i truda* / The Years of Searching and Labor, 1975), while the

Soviet Union was certainly experimenting with sound, at the end of the 1920s, "sound film" had yet to become a reality. In *Epokha i kino* (The Epoch and the Cinema, 1976), Aleksandrov describes in detail the moment he and Eisenstein first learned about the advent of sound cinema in the West. Having read the announcement in the morning papers, and being already excited by the possibilities that this new technology opened up, Aleksandrov and Eisenstein ran into an equally excited Pudovkin, and the three of them continued to talk, argue, and debate the problem of sound film well into the night, at which point, the famous "Statement" was born.[52] While the "Statement" has been read retroactively as a stance of montage theorists *against* sound film, Aleksandrov stresses that it is the opening line of the "Statement"—"Our cherished dreams of a sound cinema are being realized"—that most accurately reflected the three filmmakers' excitement about the possibilities of sound film, even as they also voiced their anxiety about what a really "talkie" (*boltlivyi*) cinematograph would do to the art of cinema. He points out, for example, that when they wrote in the "Statement" that the "Americans, having developed the technique of sound cinema, have embarked on the first stage towards its rapid practical implementation," they had yet to see a single sound film.[53] It was not until 1929 in Berlin that Aleksandrov, Eisenstein, and Tissé would have the opportunity to see their first sound film—Al Johnson's new hit *Sonny Boy* (Archie Mayo, dir. 1929, USA)—which made a profound impression. Aleksandrov claims that after that screening, "they stayed up all night." The fact that the Great Silent had "learned to speak" altered their entire filmmaking practice.[54]

Interestingly, in his memoirs, Aleksandrov plays down the role the acquisition of new sound technology played in their going abroad, claiming instead that this was a trip meant to bolster the relationship between the USSR and the West. He does mention, however, that while in Paris, they had numerous discussions with René Clair, while he was shooting his first sound film, *Under the Rooftops of Paris* (Sous les toits de Paris, 1930), and had a chance to make their own first "experimental sound film," *The Sentimental Romance* (Sentimental'nyi romans), in which they experimented with both synchronized and contrapuntal sound, with prioritizing the sound track over the image track, or with editing the sound track independently of the image track, as a separate element of montage (*kak samostoiatel'nyi ideino-smyslovoi element*).[55] In *The Epoch and the Cinema*, he likewise mentions that while in Berlin, Eisenstein formed a close friendship with Joseph von Sternberg while he was shooting *The Blue Angel* (Der

Figure 0.4. On the set of Vsevolod Pudovkin's first sound film *Ochen' khorosho zhivetsia* (Life Is Good!), later renamed *Prostoi sluchai* (A Simple Case). Filming on the streets of Moscow, 1929. Left to right: assistant Shchipanovsky, sound engineer Leonid Obolensky, cameraman Grigory Kabalov, and the inventor Pavel Tager. (Sovetskii erkran, no. 41 [1929]).

blaue Engel, 1930). The three of them were involved with the shooting and were often "consulted." In this way, writes Aleksandrov, "The Eisenstein group stood at the cradle of the first German sound film."[56]

But perhaps the most successful practitioner of the contrapuntal theory of sound was Pudovkin, one of the authors of the "Statement," and well known in the 1920s for his breakthrough uses of montage in *Mother* (Mat', 1926) and *The End of St. Petersburg* (Konets Sankt-Peterburga, 1927), films that told a coherent narrative while employing many of the devices popularized by more "difficult" directors, like Eisenstein and Vertov. In the early 1930s, Pudovkin both wrote extensively on how sound should and should not be used, and was able to put his theories into practice with his 1933 film *Deserter* (Dezertir).[57] In an interview with American photographer Margaret Bourke-White in 1929, Pudovkin stated that sound film had a tremendous future, but that this development would only come if sound was used in a new manner: "Sounds and human speech should be used by the director not as a literal accompaniment, but to amplify and enrich the visual image on screen." Under such conditions, "sound film could become a new form of art whose future development had no predictable limits."[58]

Pudovkin originally conceived his 1930 film *Life Is Good!* (Ochen' khorosho zhivetsia) as a sound film in which the image track and the sound track would be filmed separately and then edited together for maximum effect. While he did not get the chance to sonorize the film, which was released in a reedited silent version as *A Simple Case* (1932),⁵⁹ Pudovkin left notes as to what he imagined the sound track of the film could do. In the final scene, for example, as the two main characters Mashenka and Langovoi are saying goodbye, Pudovkin imagined a complicated sound-image montage, in which the noises of a departing train would be matched to images of a train that has not yet left the station. The sound, in other words, would anticipate the movement of the train, adding tension to the scene by underscoring the couple's inevitable separation. In his 1937 biography of Pudovkin, N. Iezuitov describes this sequence in detail:

> Here is how he hoped to construct the scene in which Langovoi and Mashenka say goodbye, before the departure of the heroine to the countryside. In the frame: the motionless train, standing at the platform. Mashenka's face is visible in the carriage window. "I want to tell you something," she says to Langovoi. At this moment, there is the sound of a train moving and the accelerated chugging of its wheels, whereas the picture shows the train motionless as previously. "What, then, what?" Langovoi asks, to the accompaniment of shifting carriages. "I've forgotten," And these words of Mashenka's are barely audible in the midst of the feverish thundering of the wheels. The train on the soundtrack picks up speed and we hear the end of the sentence, " . . . you are taller than me. . ." Then the sound of the moving train breaks in. And on the screen, with the separation of the couple Mashenka and Langovoi, the actual train leaves. In this scene the sound track ran ahead of the image. For what purpose? In order to create a greater strain in the scene of departure, in order to summon up disturbance and agitation in the viewer towards the fate of the heroine. From this we may draw the chief conclusion that, in combining sensations of time, time is not necessarily just as it is actually recorded but that we may feel that it stretches to the final second, that we can pack into it the experience of months.⁶⁰

For Pudovkin, this radical audio-visual montage was meant to complicate our notion of time by putting it "out of joint." As Amy Sargeant has pointed out, *A Simple Case / Life is Good!* was a development of Pudovkin's notion of time, presented in his 1931 essay, "Close-Ups in Time," where he describes techniques for halting and speeding up time-on-screen as equivalents to long shots and close-ups in space.⁶¹ What is interesting for our purposes is the way that sound for Pudovkin is yet another device (like fast-cranking or under-cranking during recording, or rapid montage in editing) by means of which time can be expressed on film.

This radical disjuncture—what Pudovkin calls "the dual rhythm of sound and image"—is reproduced in the ending of his first sound film, *Deserter* (1933).⁶² While the two sequences could not be more different in content (a sentimental scene of a parting couple in *Life is Good!* versus a workers' demonstration that ends in bloodshed in *Deserter*), Pudovkin is doing something similar with sound in both cases, purposefully decoupling it from the visual image to anticipate a future event. In the case of *Deserter*, this event is the eventual victory of the proletariat and this is marked in the film by the triumphal march that sounds from the screen, even as the film shows us the workers' defeat in no uncertain terms. The contrapuntal/asynchronous music here works precisely against the moving image, heralding a future in which the German proletariat will emerge triumphant. As Pudovkin explained, "Marxists know that in every defeat of the workers lies hidden a further step towards victory," and claimed that, "music must in sound film *never be the accompaniment*. It must retain its own line."[63]

In his 1933 "Asynchronism as a Principle of Sound Film," Pudovkin argues that while the technical side of sound-film making may be regarded "as already relatively perfected, at least in America," there is a great difference between the technical development of sound and "its development as a means of *expression*." He asserts that, "many theoretical questions whose answers are clear to us are still provided in practice only with the most primitive solutions," and concludes that, "theoretically, we in the Soviet Union are in advance of Western Europe and U.S.A."[64]

Indeed, *Deserter* is an astonishing example of early Soviet sound experimentation and speaks to many of the themes I return to throughout this book: silence versus sound; sound technology as *acousmêtre*; the voice of power issuing from the screen; and multilingualism and the question of language. The climactic scene of *Deserter* is delivered entirely in German, with Karl Renn, the speaker, "mis-hearing" the applause of the crowd as gunshots from a firing squad. Throughout the film, silence is used as a montage element, cutting to a dead sound track precisely where we would expect synchronized sound, to underscore image and sound as two *different* and *independent* elements of montage. In this way, Pudovkin avoids what he perceives as the abuses of "naturalistic sound" that predominated in Western European and American movies during the period when the novelty of "seeing and *hearing* a door slam *per se*" fascinated the audience. "The role which sound is to play in film is much more significant than a slavish imitation of naturalism on these lines; the first function of sound is to *augment the potential expressiveness of film's content*," Pudovkin writes.[65] "I believe that sound film will approach nearer to true musical rhythm than silent film ever did, and this rhythm must derive not merely from the movement of the artists and objects on screen, but also—and this is the consideration most important for us today—from exact cutting of the sound pieces into a clear counterpoint with the film."[66]

As Kristin Thompson suggests, factors like Eisenstein's absence from Russia during this crucial time, plus the late development of sound technology, plus the imposed doctrine of Socialist Realism from 1934 onward, have shaped our understanding of the period of transition to create the impression of relative inactivity during the years 1931 to 1933.[67] Yet, if we look closely, we will find that during this period Soviet filmmakers were actively seeking solutions to the problem of sound, both theoretical and actual, and were in fact, as Thompson puts it, "largely prepared, through their deep grounding in film theory, to welcome sound as another montage element."[68] At the same time, however, they also understood the potential of sound to act as a force on the moving image, disrupting, undermining, or heightening the visual effects of cinema. Sound was not merely a supplement to the moving image, or it was a supplement in a strictly Derridean sense, "an inessential extra" that when added to something that was complete in itself revealed its originary lack.[69]

What is more, parallel to the development of sound recording equipment, a group of Soviet innovators were also experimenting with other forms of "sound-on-film" technologies, specifically, "graphic" or "drawn" sound. As Andrey Smirnov suggests, this new way of synthesizing sound from light was developed as a direct consequence of the newly invented sound-on-film technology, "which made possible access to sound as a visible graphical trace in a form that could be studied and manipulated."[70] Among the first Soviet sound films was Room's *The Plan for Great Works* shot in the Shorin's Central Laboratory of Wire Communication in Leningrad in 1929. The group working on this film included the painter, book illustrator, and animator Mikhail Tsekhanovsky, the chief of the composer's brigade Arseny Avraamov, and the inventor Evgeny Sholpo, who was already working on new techniques of so-called performerless music.[71] Drawing directly on film stock opened up possibilities not just for the image track but for the sound track as well. And although the Canadian animator Norman McLaren is the most recognized name in this field, it was the Soviet pioneers of graphic sound that made the most significant contributions to the invention and development of this technique, also known as "designed," "drawn," "paper," "animated," "synthetic," or "artificial sound."[72]

As Nikolai Izvolov shows, using the standard animation technology of the day, in the summer of 1930 Avraamov became the first person to create drawn sound, and he demonstrated the results of his experiments at a conference on sound in Moscow the following autumn.[73] An editorial in the newspaper *Kino* in 1931 describes the invention in the following way:

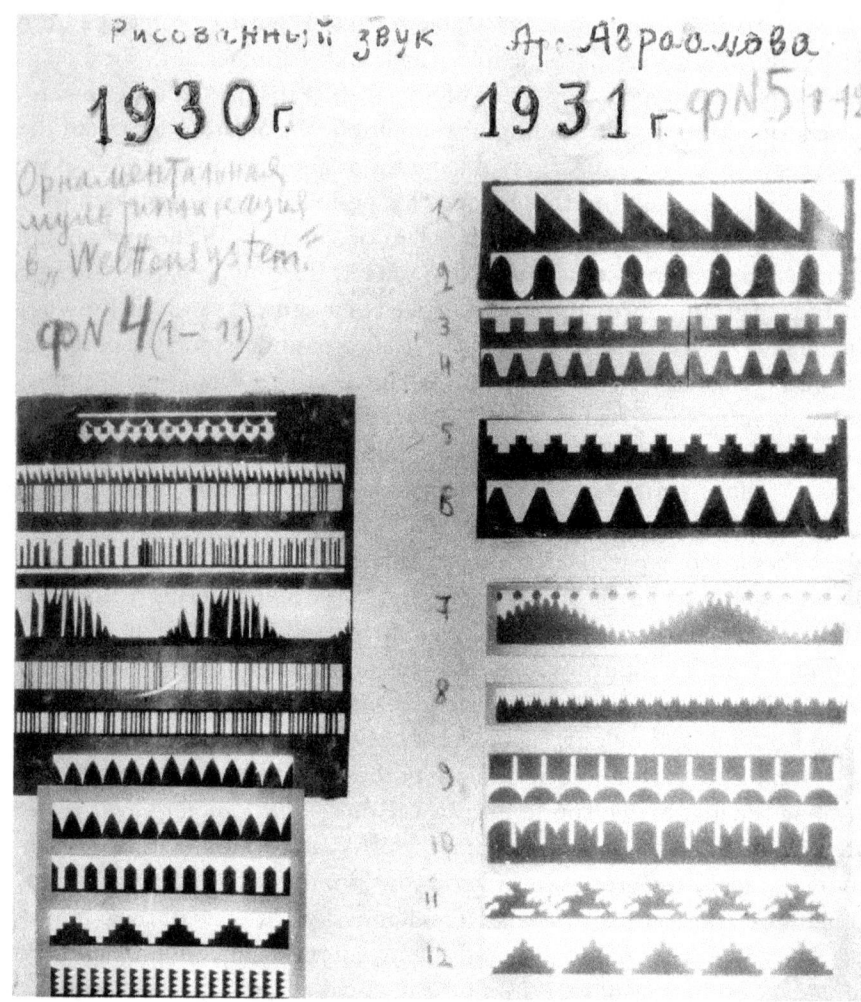

Figure 0.5. Arseny Avraamov's experiments with drawn sound
(Courtesy of Andrey Smirnov)

"Composer Arseny Avraamov at the scientific-research institute conducts interesting experiments on the creation of hand-drawn music. Instead of standard sound recording on film by means of microphone and photocell, he simply draws on paper geometrical figures, then photographs them on the sound track of the filmstrip. Afterwards this filmstrip is played as a normal movie by means of film projector. Being read by a photocell, amplified and monitored by loudspeaker, this filmstrip turns out to contain a well-known musical recording, while its timbre is impossible to relate to any existing musical instrument."[74] Each of the three remaining creators of drawn sound invented his own original device designed to facilitate the drawing of sound on film. As Smirnov notes, by 1936 there were several main, relatively comparable trends of graphical sound in Russia: "Hand-drawn Ornamental Sound," achieved by means of shooting still images of drawn sound waves on an animation stand, with final soundtracks produced in a transversal form (Arseny Avraamov, early Boris Yankovsky); "Hand-made Paper Sound" with final transversal soundtracks (Nikolai Voinov); "Automated Paper Sound" with soundtracks in both transversal and intensive form (Evgeny Sholpo, Georgy Rimsky-Korsakov); the Syntones method, based on the idea of spectral analysis, decomposition and resynthesis, developed in 1932–1935 by a pupil of Arseny Avraamov, the young painter and acoustician Boris Yankovsky.[75] At exactly the same time very similar efforts were being undertaken in Germany by Rudolf Pfenninger in Munich and, somewhat later, by the animator and filmmaker Oskar Fischinger in Berlin. Among the researchers working with graphical sound after World War II were the famous filmmaker Norman McLaren (Canada) and the composer and inventor Daphne Oram (UK). Unfortunately, as Izvolov notes, most of the works by the inventors of drawn sound have not survived to the present day.[76]

In their debates over the coming sound in the late twenties, Soviet filmmakers, theorists, and ideologues emphasized a different set of issues than the ones that concerned the American film industry. Critics were divided between seeing in sound cinema the continuation of avant-garde revolutionary filmmaking (that defined cinema as first and foremost a product of technology and montage) and an opportunity, on the other hand, to create a "cinema for the millions," a cinema that would directly address the masses. The final result—the end of the avant-garde and the advent of Socialist Realism—was marked in the early films of the period of transition by an emphasis on public address, on the technology of sound that made visible as well as audible the imposition of a voice (almost always nondiegetic, often marked as inhuman) onto the fabric of the film. Early Soviet sound films self-consciously mark the relationship between cinema and power via the new technology of sound, which is figured as an inhuman demand to answer the call of the State. Many of the sound decisions made in early Soviet film (from about 1930–1932), as Russian film historian Evgeny Margolit has argued, had to do with the fact that, in contrast to Western European and American cinema, sound came to the USSR first in nonfiction film. Thus we can point to the "laconic" (*nemnogoslovie*) nature of Soviet sound films of the first half of the thirties and the prevalence of

Figure 0.6. Loudspeakers (Vertov, *Enthusiasm: The Symphony of the Donbass* [Entuziazm: Simfoniia Donbassa], 1930, frame capture)

industrial noise over human speech. Radio is one of the "important characters" in Dziga Vertov's *Enthusiasm: Symphony of the Donbass* (Entuziazm: Simfoniia Donbassa, 1930), or in the *agitprop* documentary antiwar film *Maybe Tomorrow* (*Vozmozhno, zavtra*, 1931), by Dmitry Dalsky and Liudmila Snezhinskaya.[77]

In early Soviet sound film, there is a preponderance of loudspeakers, radios, gramophones, and other devices for reproducing sound that underscore sound cinema's ability to directly address the viewer. Unlike Hollywood cinema that strove to accurately record the human voice, it is the "voice of technology" (of industry and machines) that was first privileged for Soviet sound cinema. Piotrovsky particularly stressed that the Soviet way of making sound films should rely heavily on noise (*shumy*) and other forms of disharmony (*negarmonizovannost'*), which, as a result, would produce a sound track that was more expressive, with sounds new to the ear. In second place in terms of its importance for sound film, Piotrovsky suggests ranking music and song, and only in *third place*, human speech (although he argues that even here, we should privilege non-speech—"yelps, screams, sharp intonations"—over dialogue or any form of comprehensible speech).⁷⁸ As Sabine Hänsgen has pointed out, with reference to the futurist poet Aleksei Kruchenykh, Russian futurism had similarly imagined sound in film as noise, first and foremost, and *zaum* (transrational) as the true language of cinema.⁷⁹ For Kruchenykh, whose ideas about noise in cinema had a direct influence on Vertov, the new stars of sound film would be airplanes, trains, and other technical inventions and "tricks" (*triuki*). "And when the silent cinema speaks, its language—of the noise of machines, screeching and clanking of iron—would of course be transrational (*zaumnaia*)!"⁸⁰ Which was of course precisely what Vertov had tried to do in his first sound film, by privileging industrial noise over human speech.

Many Soviet filmmakers working for the first time with sound equipment tried to capture the sounds of Soviet industry; Vertov filmed inside the coal mines of Donbass, while Shub was commissioned to document the building of Dniepr Hydroelectric Station, producing her first documentary sound film *K.Sh.E.* (Komsomol: Patron of Electrification / Komsomol: shef elektrifikatsii). Similarly, both Aleksandr Macheret and Dovzhenko shot their first feature sound films at Dneprostroi. Macheret's 1932 *Men and Jobs* (Dela i liudi) and Dovzhenko's *Ivan* (1932) are both "production" films, focusing on the sights and sounds of heavy industry, one of the key elements of the First Five-Year Plan. In each case, the sounds of the USSR's massive construction overwhelm its human subjects, silencing human speech. In *Ivan* this happens quite literally: the sequence showing an accident at the construction site and the death of one of the workers is followed by a loss of all sound. What had previously been a cacophony of orchestral score and industrial noise (train whistles, sounds of hammers, and the like) is cut off at the moment of the accident. The human cry is cut short and replaced with the sound of a train whistle, just as there is an abrupt cut from the site of the accident to a shot of a train receding into the distance. The rest of the sequence is shot in total silence, as the body of the worker is carried out and placed in front of the factory wall, and the mother stands over the body of her son. At this point, sound returns, but now in a menacing form as pure industrial noise, as the factory comes back to life. We understand that the mother, made small and insignificant in comparison to the cranes, engines, and clam shell shovels of the construction site, has no voice—even as she attempts to speak to the head of the factory about the accident, she has no powers of speech to compete with those of heavy industry. Similarly, as Emma Widdis has pointed out, Macheret's solution to the "problem" of the voice in sound cinema was to create a central protagonist who could not speak. Instead, the film exploits the full potential of other forms of sound technology: machines rumble and click, drills grind, gravel tumbles noisily. A "synchrony" between sound and visual material is used as a means of anthropomorphizing machinery. In *Men and Jobs*, "the machines speak more eloquently" than the protagonist.[81]

But it is perhaps the role of the radio/loudspeaker in early Soviet sound films that most effectively shifts the power of speech from the human to the nonhuman subject. As Stephen Lovell has noted, when we reach the Soviet period, "the relationship between orality and literacy is further complicated by innovations in communication technology." In Russia, from the early 1920s onward, "the spoken word received new kinds of amplification, both literally (in the form of the loudspeakers that were set up in public places in urban areas) and metaphorically (in the form of broadcasting)." Radio "offered a way of projecting the voice of authority into every workplace and communal flat in the USSR and of showing Soviet people exactly how to 'speak Bolshevik.'"[82] And Margolit similarly underscores that the common assumption that early talkies should remind us of photographed theater, cannot be applied to the first Soviet sound films, because, "the nature of the word here is fundamentally different." For Margolit, the closest analogy is not theater, but radio, "and moreover, radio in its specific Soviet manifestation." On May 1, 1921, loudspeakers that "looked like gramophone pipes" were erected in the town squares of Kazan and began to deliver the contents of some newspapers articles, and this became the privileged way that the radio entered Soviet life. A megaphone at the top of a high pole (and its more intimate counterpart—the radio speaker on the wall of a room, hanging from the ceiling), delivering to the consciousness of its audience the State's directives, simply by its position "made the official word sacred." The concept of a "voice-over" was literalized, materialized in the form of an intrusive address, accessible to everyone. With the coming of sound to cinema, writes Margolit, this Word was "embodied" in the form of shadows, "speaking from the large canvass screen, and addressing the audience located beneath it."[83]

We see this most clearly in Grigori Kozintsev and Leonid Trauberg's *Alone* (*Odna*, 1931), where the invention of the new sound technology is embodied by a loudspeaker in the middle of an empty square that speaks directly to the heroine; but we also find it in Dovzhenko's *Ivan*, where a voice from the loudspeaker pursues a character all across the village, while enumerating his faults; and in Pudovkin's *Deserter*, where it issues commands and directives to the workers on their lunch break, issuing a *prizyv* (a call or call to arms) to work harder. Itself figured as technology

Figure 0.7. Alexander Rodchenko, "Press stand with Radio-speaker in 1929" [Radiofitsirovannyi gazetnyi kiosk v 1929] (Art © Estate of Alexander Rodchenko/RAO, Moscow/VAGA, New York)

(loudspeaker), the address is also made possible by means of technology—the technology of synchronized sound that allows us to *hear* as well as see and read the messages of the film.

It is useful here to evoke Michel Chion's idea of the *acousmêtre*—a disembodied voice whose "sourcelessness" suggests "the paranoid and often obsessional panoptic fantasy . . . of total mastery of space by vision"—to better understand the ubiquity of the loudspeaker (or radio, telephone, gramophone, slogans, and other forms of direct address) in these transitional films.[84] For Chion, the *acousmêtre* is not simply a commentator, but must be both included and excluded from the film. He must, Chion writes, "even if only slightly, have *one foot in the image*, in the space of the film; he must haunt the borderlands that are neither the interior of the filmic stage nor the proscenium—a place that has no name, but which the cinema forever brings into play." Its powers, Chion argues, are four—"the ability to be everywhere, to see all, to know all, and to have complete power. In other words: ubiquity, panopticism, omniscience, and omnipotence." Media such as the telephone and radio, "which send acousmatic voices traveling and which enable them to be here and there at once, often serve as vehicles of this ubiquity."[85]

It is my argument here (and elaborated in the chapters that follow) that sound technology is figured as an *acousmêtre* in early Soviet sound films, bypassing the human subject in favor of a voice that speaks both from within and from *beyond* the film. Moreover, for early Soviet sound cinema, the *acousmêtre* is not merely a disembodied voice whose sourcelessness suggests the paranoid and often obsessional panoptic fantasy of total mastery of space by "vision," but also by *hearing*. Early Soviet sound film stresses both the production and the reception of sound, underscoring the way that silent cinema was not only "mute" but also "deaf."[86] Vertov's *Enthusiasm* opens with a shot of the radio operator putting on her headphones to listen to "The Last Sunday" (Poslednee voskresen'e), "music from the film *Symphony of the Donbass*." In the first Soviet "talkie," Nikolai Ekk's 1931 *Road to Life*, we see Kolya in his room, listening to the radio through headphones. Esfir Shub's 1932 *K.Sh.E.* opens with a recording of a radio program and radio announcers repeating the same speech in numerous languages, while telephone operators connect distant parts of the country to each other through yet another form of electricity.[87] This foregrounding of the technologies of sound production and the act of listening—to the radio, the phonograph, or the loudspeaker—is part and parcel of Soviet cinema's new voice, directly addressing the viewer. The radio and loudspeaker appear in early Soviet sound films as disembodied entities speaking with the "voice of power," and in almost every case, speaking directly the State's ideological message.

From Avant-garde to Socialist Realism

For the Soviet film industry, the transition from silent to "talkie" went beyond the significance of the technological synchronization of sound and image. As film critic Ippolit Sokolov put it in his review of the Second Sound Film Program in 1930:

> Our filmmakers have spent the whole of the past year in a one-sided obsession with the technical side of sound equipment or, rather, with elementary technical aspects of electrical and radio engineering and have dreamed of becoming sound mixers (without any knowledge of amplification or electrical acoustics). Naked technology has overshadowed questions of ideology and questions of content and form of sound film . . . There is now a battle going on in sound cinema between technology and content plus form. In art the substitution of naked technology for content and form is the most extreme kind of Formalism, the narrowest form of technicisation . . . A year has passed but sound cinema has still not progressed beyond the stage of "experiment for the sake of experiment."[88]

On the one hand, sound demanded a thorough rethinking of cinematic technique, including montage with its rapid cross cutting and dialectical construction. On the other hand, for the USSR, it coincided with a profound top-down shift, as the Soviet film industry was completely reorganized and given new ideological directives, which were easier to implement because the industry as a whole was now centralized under a single authority. This shift became most visible in the rejection of "Formalism" and "experiment for the sake of experiment," as Sokolov puts it, and the elaboration of the precepts of Socialist Realism (made into the official doctrine of all Soviet art in 1934) and the films of the thirties. Because the introduction of sound coincided with the historical moment of Cultural Revolution, sound in Soviet cinema helped pave the way of the film industry toward Socialist Realism, toward an ideological program that rigidly controlled what could and could not be shown and what could and could not be heard on the screen.

By 1932, the Cultural Revolution led to centralization of the arts and the formation of monolithic artistic unions (of writers, filmmakers, artists, composers, and the like). In 1930, Sovkino—the organization that since 1924 had been responsible for film production, distribution, and importation, but whose authority had been limited to the Russian Federal Republic—was eliminated and Soiuzkino created in its place, headed by Boris

Shumyatsky, "whose primary task was to develop the Soviet film industry as an industry." As Leyda put it, "Shumyatsky's ignorance of the nature of art and the psychology of artists may have recommended him for the new job. The two most vocal defenders of the artist's place and function within a socialist film industry were somewhere else: Mayakovsky was dead and Eisenstein was in Mexico."[89] Souizkino was given greater authority over the studios of the national republics, reflecting the new goals of centralization. It became the sole body to produce and control films made in the USSR.

Reorganization and centralization of the film industry led not only to internal instability but also to the introduction of new bureaucratic administrative units in charge of censorship and review. Screenplays as well as finished films were now vetted by many different organizations, whose authority conflicted and overlapped. Depending on the year, scenarios had to be discussed by the studio's Party organization, members of the ODSK (Society of Friends of Soviet Cinema), AKKR (Association of Revolutionary Workers of Cinematography), the GUFK (Chief Directorate of the Film and Photo Industry), trade unions, and the Komsomol before they could be approved for production. From 1934 onward almost every issue of the journal *Sovetskoe kino* (Soviet Film) included scenarios, published in order to encourage public discussion. In 1937 the authorities created special commissions from the representatives of the Party and of social organizations. Sometimes workers or trade unions were invited to participate in the discussion. The Komsomol demanded the evaluation and discussion of all scripts dealing with the problems of youth. This level of censorship was largely responsible for the severe script shortages that plagued the Soviet cinema industry in the thirties. It also meant that even those films approved at the script level might not make it through production, or having been completed, would not be released. A film like Ivan Pyr'ev's *The Conveyer Belt of Death* (Konveer smerti, 1933), for example, was remade fourteen times over a period of three years. Out of 130 planned films for 1935, only 45 were completed (46 out of 165 in 1936; and 24 out of 62 in 1937).[90] Moreover, scholars estimate that about a third of the completed films were never exhibited.[91]

The *perestroika* (as it was called at the time) and centralization of the film industry was only one of the major changes that marked the transition from the twenties to the thirties. The other two were the coming of sound and the imposition of the doctrine of Socialist Realism as the single method of all Soviet art. The First Congress of Soviet Writers took place in Moscow in August 1934, in which countless delegations of kolkhoz members, workers, pioneers, soldiers, and readers' clubs surged in to make statements, read messages of friendship, state their demands, or issue orders on literary and aesthetic matters. The 1,500 members of the new Union of Soviet Writers represented the literatures of fifty-two Soviet nationalities, but the dominant figures at the Congress were unquestionably Maxim Gorky, who presided, and Andrei Zhdanov, the secretary of the Central Committee, along with Nikolai Bukharin and Karl Radek. The Congress established Socialist Realism as the official method of Soviet art, stressing specifically that artistic works should display the socialist idea (*ideinost'*), national character (*narodnost'*), and Party loyalty (*partiinost'*). As Zhdanov defined it, Socialist Realism demands of the artist "the truthful, historically concrete representation of reality in its revolutionary development"—that is to say, "not life as it is, but as it should and will be."[92] The film that perhaps came to best exemplify the spirit and the letter of Socialist Realism was *Chapaev* (1934), which was watched by millions of viewers. "The Whole Country is Watching *Chapaev*," declared the headline of the newspaper *Pravda* on November 21, 1934. Stalin watched the film repeatedly, remarking each time on its topicality. Audiences came to the theaters again and again, many hoping that this time, the Red Army commander would survive the final attack and emerge alive at the end of the film.

In 1935, the second All-Union Creative Conference on Cinema Affairs adopted the principles of Socialist Realism as set out for literature. Indeed, for the Soviet film industry, the first shift in ideology can be traced back to the 1928 All-Union Party Conference on Cinema Affairs, which decreed that Soviet cinema "must furnish a 'form that is intelligible to the millions.'"[93] From this point forward, Soviet films had to be entertaining first and foremost; unlike their avant-garde predecessors, they needed to have a simple plot and to be organized around a coherent storyline. Moreover, as the new head of the centralized film industry, Shumyatsky wrote in 1933, "We need genres that are infused with optimism, with the mobilizing emotions, with cheerfulness, *joie-de-vivre* and laughter. Genres that provide us with the maximum opportunity to demonstrate the best Bolshevik traditions: an implacable attitude to opportunism, with tenacity, initiative, skill and a Bolshevik scale of work."[94]

By 1935, Soviet cinema had produced two sound films that became instant classics of Socialist Realism: the civil war film *Chapaev* and the musical comedy *Jolly Fellows* (dir. Aleksandrov, 1934). And although the

Soviet Union continued to release silent versions of feature films well into the 1930s, the era of avant-garde experimentation, as well as the era of silent film, had come to an end. Between them, the two major cinema conferences of 1928 and 1935 marked the beginning and the end of the transitional period—both technological and ideological—aided by the publication, also in 1935, of Boris Shumyatsky's *Cinema for the Millions*, which became a blue print for Stalinist cinema. Before that happened, however, Soviet cinema produced a handful of films—in a variety of genres, styles, techniques, and languages—that fit neither the earlier models of silent era Soviet montage, nor the Socialist Realist cinema yet to come. In this way, early Soviet sound cinema imagined "an alternative future for sound film," one in which the aural was not subordinated to the visual, but was exploited to draw out the visceral effects of cinema.[95]

The following chapters examine the notion of Soviet sound cinema as a "new apparatus," to borrow language from Ian Christie, looking at the ways the technology of sound altered the relationship between the film and the viewer, by doing away with "internal speech" and substituting in its place the audible word that issued directly from the screen. While keeping in mind the historical and theoretical frameworks of the transition to sound, the body chapters concentrate on individual films or sets of films that together comprise the "canon" of early Soviet sound film. The films range from well-known works to lesser-known examples; from the documentary to new Soviet musical film; and from the avant-garde to the Socialist Realist. In each case, the focus is on the way individual films and filmmakers self-consciously mark the relationship between cinema and power via the new technology of sound.

I begin the case studies with the "first" Soviet sound film, Grigori Kozintsev and Leonid Trauberg's *Alone* (Odna). Released in movie theaters on October 10, 1931, the film contained only one line of spoken dialogue, but its sound track included both music and sound effects: Dmitry Shostakovich's musical score, the song "How Good Life Will Be!," the sound of the howling wind, and the ritual chant of a village shaman. More importantly, *Alone* relied on extradiegetic, illustrative, contrapuntal sound to communicate the possibilities of new technology: alarm clocks, radio, trams, loudspeakers, typewriters, telephones—numerous mechanical objects produce sound in *Alone*, silencing the words of the heroine. Throughout the film, we are constantly addressed by the demands of the state transmitted via the new sound technology: loudspeakers, typewriters, radio, and telephone communicate the messages of "appeals, slogans, codes, orders, and decrees." In this first chapter, I trace the ways the new technology of synchronized sound allows us, for the first time, not merely to see, but to *hear* the ideological message of the new Soviet state.

Chapter 2 explores the notion of the haptic (what Jennifer Barker has called "the tactile eye") as it relates to early Soviet documentary sound cinema and specifically to Dziga Vertov's *Enthusiasm: The Symphony of the Donbass* (Entuziazm: Simfoniia Donbassa, completed in November 1930; released on April 1, 1931) and Esfir Shub's *K.Sh.E.* (Komsomol: Patron of Electrification, 1932). Like Vertov, Shub argued for "authenticity" in nonplayed cinema, and there is a clear relationship between the 1930 *Enthusiasm* and the 1932 *K.Sh.E.*; both films attempt to capture, by means of documentary filmmaking on the one hand, and by means of the new sound technology on the other, the biggest industrial projects of Stalin's First Five-Year Plan—the coal mines of Donbass and the completion of the first Soviet hydroelectric plant on the Dniepr River. Both films also emphasize and make audible the new *sound* apparatus, in order to convey the materiality of sound and the means of its production and reproduction. In this second chapter, I trace a trajectory from Vertov's desire to record new, never-before-heard documentary sounds to Shub's experiments in bringing us sound as a form of the haptic—that is to say, an organic, *tactile* art that moves us beyond cinema's insistently visual language.

Chapter 3 examines the role of music (and musical comedy) in the emergence of Soviet sound cinema, focusing specifically on Igor Savchenko's *The Accordion* (Garmon', released in 1934 and pulled from all Soviet and foreign screens in 1936). Based on a poem by Komsomol writer Aleksandr Zharov, *The Accordion* most directly answered the call of "cinema for the millions," by providing a light musical comedy, filled with singing and dancing. In making the film, Savchenko rejected the silent film conventions of music as orchestral accompaniment, to achieve a union between the visual and the musical expression. Formally, *The Accordion* is operatic, with the plot advanced entirely through dialogue sung with accompanying music. There is a continuous music score whose rhythm permeates the story. Unlike a standard Hollywood musical or Stalinist musical comedy, in *The Accordion* we have no disjuncture between narrative and numbers. At no point in the film are we located beyond music's influence, and every sound (including dialogue) and every movement (including work) is subordinated to a particular rhythm and cadence. As the first—though by no means the most well-known—Stalinist musical comedy, *The Accordion* offers us a link between two different kinds of "utopia": the Socialist Realist "reality in its revolutionary development" and the "feeling of utopia" generated by the musical.

Chapter 4 examines Alexander Dovzhenko's first two sound films—*Ivan* (1932) and *Aerograd* (1935), along with *The Last Crusaders* (Poslednie krestonostsy, 1933, dir. S. Dolidze and V. Shvelidze) and *The Return of Nathan Bekker* (Vozvrashchenie Neitana Bekkera, 1932, dir. Boris Shpis and Mark Milman)—as a series of responses to the shifting political, ideological, and linguistic landscape of the USSR. This chapter examines the ways foreign, accented, non-Russian, and in other ways "estranged" speech plays a role in constructing the new Soviet state, by looking at the many occurrences of multilingualism in early Soviet sound films, particularly in those made outside the two dominant studios of Moscow and Leningrad. And while after 1933 Dovzhenko made all of his films in Russian and in Moscow, his first sound film, like his earlier groundbreaking silent films, was made in Ukraine, and the language of choice—Ukrainian—became one of the key elements of its reception. Indeed, because sound arrived to Soviet cinema while the USSR still promoted national languages and cultures, and before dubbing became a widely available technology, the new sound apparatus briefly offered the possibility of the creation of a multilingual cinema not available elsewhere.

In Chapter 5, I look at Dziga Vertov's synchronous and asynchronous sound practices in his 1934 *Three Songs of Lenin* (Tri pesni o Lenine; re-edited in 1938, and then again in 1970), and Vertov's resistance to the imposition of a singular, nondialogic voice. Vertov's initial desire to place all sounds on equal footing (by making all sound "documentary" and rejecting the idea of studio-recorded sound), gives way in *Three Songs of Lenin* to a fetishistic desire to reproduce Lenin's voice on film. In *Three Songs of Lenin*, audiences hear a recording of Lenin's voice projected over images of his public speaking and combined with footage from his funeral; but they also hear several instances of synchronic recording, such as interviews with shock workers presented to us without montage as "live," uninterrupted speech. In this film, "Lenin" (whose free-floating voice is unmoored from his body lying in state) acts as a pure signifier of power, his disembodied voice contrasted with the synchronized, accented, stuttering speech of the workers. Looking closely at multiple variants—both sound and silent—of *Three Songs of Lenin* helps us to see the way ideology is superimposed over the body of the film via the technology of sound.

I conclude the book with a brief history of the first 100 percent Soviet "talkie," Nikolai Ekk's *The Road to Life* (1931), and Boris Shumyatsky's overview of the first four years of Soviet sound cinema in his 1935 book *Cinema for the Millions*, to show the way sound becomes implicated in the development of the method of Socialist Realism, making the "voice of technology" synonymous with the "voice of the State." In his book, Shumyatsky calls for a unified audio-visual space with no disjunctions between sound and image, voicing a standard criticism of early/transition era sound films (both in the USSR and abroad) in which sound experimentation and sound effects overwhelmed viewers not yet accustomed to hearing films. As sound technology became more sophisticated and sound films more diffuse, integration of sound and image, coherence, and "naturalness" became prized for sound film. And while the history of the transition to sound for each national cinema is different, the final product of that transition—Hollywood-style editing, the primacy of dialogue, nondiegetic music used to "suture" the gaps in cinematic discourse, realism, and a unified audio-visual space—would begin to look and sound the same the world over.

Notes

1. For example: Peter Kenez, *Cinema and Soviet Society: From the Revolution to the Death of Stalin* (London: I. B. Tauris, 2001); Jay Leyda, *Kino: A History of Russian and Soviet Film* (Princeton: Princeton University Press, 1960); Denise Youngblood, *Soviet Cinema in the Silent Era, 1918–1935* (Ann Arbor: UMI Research Press, 1985); Neya Zorkaya, *The Illustrated History of Soviet Cinema* (New York: Hippocrene Books, 1989).

2. The First Congress of Soviet Writers (Moscow, August 1934) established Socialist Realism as the official method of all Soviet art, stressing specifically that artistic works should display the socialist idea (*ideinost'*), national character (*narodnost'*), and Party loyalty (*partiinost'*). See *Pervyi vsesoiuznyi s"ezd sovetskikh pisatelei: Stenograficheskii otchet* (Moscow: Khudozhestvennaia literatura, 1934); partially translated as: H. G. Scott, *Problems of Soviet Literature: Reports and Speeches at the First Soviet Writers' Congress* (Moscow: Cooperative Publishing Society of Foreign Workers in the U.S.S.R., 1935). On Socialist Realism see Katerina Clark, *The Soviet Novel: History as Ritual* (Chicago: Chicago University Press, 1981); Régine Robin, *Socialist Realism: An Impossible Aesthetic*, trans. Catherine Porter (Stanford: Stanford University Press, 1992); Evgeny Dobrenko, *Political Economy of Socialist Realism* (New Haven: Yale University Press, 2007); and Petre Petrov, *Automatic for the Masses: The Death of the Author and the Birth of Socialist Realism* (Toronto: University of Toronto Press, 2015).

3. Youngblood, *Soviet Cinema in the Silent Era*, 204.

4. Kenez, *Cinema and Soviet Society*, 123.

5. In 1933, 81 percent of films produced in Japan were silent, despite the fact that talkies had been made in Japan since 1931. In 1937 and 1938, roughly a third of films produced were still silent. Even in 1942, 14 percent of films exhibited in Japan were still silent. For details, see Freda Freiberg, "The Transition to Sound in Japan," in *History on/and/in Film*, ed. T. O'Regan and B. Shoesmith (Perth: History & Film Association of Australia, 1987), 76–80. Home Ministry statistics, quoted in Motion Picture Development in Japan Proper, 1939, Special Report 79 from USA Assistant Trade Commissioner in Japan, National Archives, Washington, has the following information: in 1937, 1,626 talkies and 916 silents were made; in 1938, 1,362 talkies and 701 silents were made (Freiberg, "The Transition to Sound in Japan," 80, n. 4).

6. Ian Christie, "Soviet Cinema: Making Sense of Sound," *Screen* 23, no. 2 (1982): 34–49; here: 36.

7. For this history, see, for example, Valérie Pozner, "To Catch Up and Overtake Hollywood: Early Talking Pictures in the Soviet Union," in *Sound, Speech, Music in Soviet and Post-Soviet Cinema*, ed. Lilya Kaganovsky and Masha Salazkina (Bloomington: Indiana University Press, 2014), 60–80; and Vincent Bohlinger, "The Development of Sound Technology in the Soviet Union during the First Five-Year Plan," *Studies in Russian and Soviet Cinema* 7, no. 2 (Summer 2013): 189–205.

8. Freiberg, "The Transition to Sound in Japan," 76.

9. See, for example, two editorials in the newspaper *Vecherniaia Moskva* (Evening Moscow), under the header "Soviet Cinema Must Have Sound!," which include subheadings such as "We Are Falling Behind" (*my otstaem*) and "We Must Catch Up" (*nado dognat'*). "Sovetskoe kino dolzhno zazvuchat'," *Vecherniaia Moskva* (March 26, 1930): 3; and *Vecherniaia Moskva* (April 2, 1930): 2.

10. Eisenstein, together with his cameraman Eduard Tissé and assistant director Grigori Aleksandrov, went abroad to Europe and the US in part to study and in part to make sound films. However, a series of complications, including the stock market crash of 1929, prevented Eisenstein from producing a sound version of *General Line / Old and New* (General'naia liniia / Staroe i novoe, 1929), or making a sound film for United Artists. For a detailed account, see Natalia Ryabchikova, "The Flying Fish: Sergei Eisenstein Abroad, 1929–1932," Ph.D. dissertation, 2016.

11. For example, the first, most well known, and frequently republished piece of theoretical writing on sound was Eisenstein, Pudovkin, and Aleksandrov's 1928 "Statement on Sound," first published in an authorized German translation as "Achtung! Goldgrube! Gedanken über die Zukunft des Hörfilms," in *Die Lichtbildbuehne* on July 28, 1928; and as "Tönender Film: Montage und Kontrapunkt. Gedanken über die Zukunft der Filmkunst," in *Vossische Zeitung* on July 29, 1928. The Russian original was published as "Zaiavka (Budushchee zvukovoi fil'my)," in *Zhizn' iskusstva* (Life of Art) on August 5, 1928; and in *Sovetskii ekran* (Soviet Screen) on August 7, 1928; with an English translation appearing under the title "The Sound Film. A Statement from USSR," in *Close Up* in October 1928. Jay Leyda included his own version as "A Statement" in Sergei Eisenstein, *Film Form: Essays in Film Theory*, ed. and trans. Jay Leyda (New York: Harcourt, Brace, 1949), republished in Elisabeth Weis and John Belton's seminal volume, *Film Sound: Theory and Practice* (New York: Columbia University Press, 1985), 83–85. This volume also includes Pudovkin's "Asynchronism as a Principle of Sound Film" (*Film Sound*, 86–91).

12. I am referring to the way many Soviet critics and filmmakers characterized the coming of sound as specifically "talking pictures": "Velikii nemoi zagoforil" (The Great Silent / Mute has learned to talk) was one of the common phrases used during the period of transition to speak about the acquisition of sound. For more on this, see Chapter 1.

13. Béla Balázs, in *Theory of the Film*, writes, "A few more years of film art and our scholars will discover that cinematography enables them to compile encyclopedias of facial expression, movement and gesture, such as have long existed for words in the shape of dictionaries. The public, however, need not wait for the gesture encyclopedia and grammars of future academies: it can go to the pictures and learn it there." (Béla Balázs, *Filmkultúra [a film muveszetfilozofiaja]* [Budapest: Szikra Kiadas, 1948]; translated as: *Theory of the Film (Character and Growth of a New Art)*, trans. Edith Bone [London: Denis Dobson Ltd., 1952], 42. An earlier version was published in Russian as Bela Balash, *Iskusstvo kino* [Moscow: Goskinoizdat, 1945].)

14. For two excellent studies of the technological, aesthetic, and ideological impact of Hollywood's transition to sound, see Rick Altman, *Silent Film Sound* (New York: Columbia University Press, 2004) and Donald Crafton, *The Talkies: American Cinema's Transition to Sound 1926–1931* (Berkeley: University of California Press, 1997). For the technological difficulties of the conversion and its impact on early sound film, see John Belton, "Awkward Transitions: Hitchcock's

Blackmail and the Dynamics of Early Film Sound," *The Musical Quarterly* 83, no. 2 (Summer, 1999): 227–246.

15. The "Great Turn" or the "Great Break" (*Velikii perelom*) was the radical change in economic policy in the Soviet Union in 1928/1929, which primarily consisted in abandoning the New Economic Policy (NEP) and the acceleration of collectivization and industrialization. The term was taken from the title of Joseph Stalin's article "The Year of the Great Turn" (God velikogo pereloma: k XII godovshchine Oktiabria) published on November 7, 1929, on the twelfth anniversary of the October Revolution.

16. Crafton, *The Talkies*, 21. Emphasis in the original.

17. David Bordwell, Janet Staiger, and Kristin Thompson, *The Classic Hollywood Cinema: Film Style and Mode of Production to 1960* (New York: Columbia University Press, 1985), 301. As Alan Williams notes, however, while sound recording in and of itself may have changed Hollywood filmmaking relatively little, "it nonetheless helped to change the rest of world cinema in quite a fundamental way" (Alan Williams, "Historical and Theoretical Issues in the Coming of Recorded Sound to the Cinema," in *Sound Theory / Sound Practice*, ed. Rick Altman [New York: Routledge, 1992], 126–137; here: 137).

18. Douglas Gomery, *The Coming of Sound: A History* (New York: Routledge, 2005), 3–5.

19. James Lastra, *Sound Technology and the American Cinema: Perception, Representation, Modernity* (New York: Columbia University Press, 2000), 121.

20. See, for example, Scott Eyman, *The Speed of Sound: Hollywood and the Talkie Revolution 1926–1930* (New York: Simon and Schuster, 1997). For a concise account of the critical debates around the US transition to sound, see Williams, "Historical and Theoretical Issues in the Coming of Recorded Sound to the Cinema"; and Rashna Wadia Richards, *Cinematic Flashes: Cinephilia and Classical Hollywood* (Bloomington: University of Indiana Press, 2013), 33–75.

21. The first successful European dramatic talkie was the all-British *Blackmail*. Directed by twenty-nine-year-old Alfred Hitchcock, the movie had its London debut June 21, 1929. Originally shot as a silent, *Blackmail* was restaged to include dialogue sequences, along with a score and sound effects, before its premiere. On August 23, 1929, the modest-sized Austrian film industry came out with a talkie: *G'schichten aus der Steiermark* (Stories from Styria), directed by Hans Otto Löwenstein. Sweden's first talkie, *Konstgjorda Svensson* (Artificial Svensson), premiered on October 14th. Eight days later, Aubert Franco-Film came out with *Le Collier de la reine* (The Queen's Necklace), shot at the Épinay studio near Paris. Conceived as a silent film, it was given a Tobis-recorded score and a single talking sequence—the first dialogue scene in a French feature. André Hugon's *Les Trois masques* (The Three Masks) debuted on October 31, 1929, and is generally regarded as the initial French feature talkie, though it was shot, like *Blackmail*, at the Elstree studio, just outside London. The first all-talking German feature, *Atlantik*, had premiered in Berlin on October 28, 1929; a British International Pictures production with a British scenarist and German director, it was also shot in English as *Atlantic*. In 1930, the first Polish talkies premiered, using sound-on-disc systems: *Moralność pani Dulskiej* (The Morality of Mrs. Dulska) in March and the all-talking *Niebezpieczny romans* (Dangerous Love Affair) in October. In Italy, the first talkie, *La Canzone dell'amore* (The Song of Love), also came out in October 1930. The first Czech sound film, *Tonka Šibenice* (Tonka of the Gallows), was ensounded at the Gaumont Studios in Paris in 1930. For details, see E. I. Sponable, "Historical Development of Sound Films," *Journal of the Society of Motion Picture Engineers* 48, nos. 4–5 (April/May 1947); and David Morton, *Sound Recording: The Life Story of a Technology* (Baltimore: Johns Hopkins University Press, 2006).

22. Aida Hozic, quoted in Richards, *Cinematic Flashes*, 36.

23. As Gomery notes, this was particularly surprising, since the original studios, built over a fifteen-year period, were valued at only $65 million (Gomery, *Coming of Sound*, 3).

24. In fact, as Tino Balio points out, United Artists, along with most Hollywood studios, did not feel the effects of the crash acutely at least for another year because of the success of talking

pictures (Tino Balio, *United Artists, the Company Built by the Stars* [Madison: University of Wisconsin Press, 2009], 96. Quoted in Ryabchikova, "The Flying Fish," 83).

25. Crafton, *The Talkies*, 15.

26. Gomery, *Coming of Sound*, 107.

27. In 1930, Western Electric, RCA, and Tobis-Klangfilm formed a loose cartel that divided the world into four territories. Tobis-Klangfilm secured exclusive rights for Europe and Scandinavia, while Western Electric and RCA obtained the US, Canada, New Zealand, India, and the Soviet Union. For the British market, royalties were split one-fourth for Tobis-Klangfilm, three-fourths for Western Electric and RCA. The rest of the world was open territory (see Gomery, *Coming of Sound*, 108–109).

28. Vance Kepley Jr., "The First 'Perestroika': Soviet Cinema under the First Five-Year Plan," *Cinema Journal* 35, no. 4 (1996: Summer): 31–53; here: 36.

29. Kepley Jr., "The First 'Perestroika'," 38.

30. Quoted in: Pavel Tager, "Ochen' kratko o sovetskom zvukovom kino," RGALI, f. 2690–1–91.

31. See *Puti kino. Vsesoiuznoe partiinoe soveshchanie po kinematografii*, ed. Ol'khovyi (Moscow, 1929), 429–444.

32. Kepley Jr., "The First 'Perestroika'," 42–43.

33. Tager, "Ochen' kratko o sovetskom zvukovom kino."

34. RGALI, f. 2494–1–287–302. On the history of ARRK's transition to sound, see Natalie Ryabchikova, "ARRK and the Soviet Transition to Sound," in *Sound, Speech, Music in Soviet and Post-Soviet Cinema*, 81–99.

35. Kepley Jr., "The First 'Perestroika'," 45; see also Pozner, "To Catch Up and Overtake Hollywood: Early Talking Pictures in the Soviet Union," in *Sound, Speech, Music in Soviet and Post-Soviet Cinema*, 60–80.

36. Kepley Jr., "The First 'Perestroika'," 47.

37. Nataša Ďurovičová, "Translating America: The Hollywood Multilinguals 1929–1933," in *Sound Theory / Sound Practice*, 138–153; here 139.

38. Ďurovičová, "Translating America," 148.

39. Ďurovičová, "Translating America," 150.

40. Title cards could be easily exchanged or removed to accommodate different linguistic situations; they could also (as was the case for the USSR) be read aloud, translated, and explained by qualified political workers sent to assist at film screenings throughout the Soviet Union.

41. For details, see Kepley Jr., "The First 'Perestroika'," 38.

42. See "Soveshchaniie po dubliazhu rabotnikov dubliazhnykh grupp Bakinskoi, Tashkentskoi i Ashkhabadskoi studii" and "Protokol zasedanii komissii po razrabotke norm i standartov po dubliazhu, rabotnikov dubliazhnykh grupp Bakinskoi, Tashkentskoi i Ashkhabadskoi studii," both: RGALI 2450-2-34 (September 28 and 30, 1938).

43. Youngblood, *Soviet Cinema in the Silent Era*, 221.

44. Grigorii Aleksandrov, "Velikii drug sovetskogo kino," *Iskusstvo kino* (December 1939); quoted in Leyda, *Kino*, 269. Needless to say, in his memoirs from the 1970s, Aleksandrov does not mention the conversation with Stalin about sound, writing simply, "At the end of 1928, on the recommendation and the introduction of the Commissar of Enlightenment, A. V. Lunacharskii, our 'triumvirate'—Eisenstein, our wonderful artist/cameraman Eduard Tissé, and myself—left for a long business trip abroad" (Grigorii Aleksandrov, *Gody poiskov i truda* [Moscow: Soiuz kinematografistov SSSR, 1975], 37, ellipsis in the original).

45. Youngblood makes the exact opposite point, stressing that "the conventions and aesthetics of silent cinema resisted change ... the silent era did not pass with the coming of sound" (Youngblood, *Soviet Cinema*, 225).

46. Leyda, *Kino*, 278.

47. Eizenshtein, Pudovkin, and Aleksandrov, "Zaiavka," *Zhizn' iskusstva* (August 5, 1928): 4–5. Translated as "Statement on Sound," in *The Film Factory: Russian and Soviet Cinema in Documents*, ed. Richard Taylor and Ian Christie (London and New York: Routledge, 1994), 234–235. Translation modified.

48. This notion of "automatic perception" is most likely a reference to Viktor Shklovsky's "Art as Technique" (Iskusstvo kak priem, 1917; also translated as "Art as Device"), which comprised the first chapter of his seminal *Theory of Prose* (O teorii prozy) first published in 1925. On Shklovsky and Eisenstein, see Valérie Pozner, "Shklovskii/Eizenshtein—dvadtsatye gody. Istoriia plodotvornogo neponimaniia," *Kinovedcheskie zapiski* 46 (2000). Accessed at: http://www.kinozapiski.ru/ru/article/sendvalues/586/.

49. While *oshchushcheniia* is more often translated as "sensation" than "feelings" (*chuvstva*), I am using the latter to underscore the difference from the authors' earlier usage of *sensatsiia* (sensation). For a thorough discussion of Socialist feelings during this period, see Emma Widdis, *Socialist Senses: Film, Feeling and the Soviet Subject* (Bloomington: Indiana University Press, 2017).

50. Adrian Piotrovskii, "Tonfil'ma," *Zhizn' iskusstva* 30 (1929): 4–5.

51. Piotrovskii, "Tonfil'ma," 4–5. Eisenstein et al. were reacting specifically to the "monstrous 'all-singing all-talking' films" turned out by Hollywood in the first years of the transition. As Marian Hannah Winter notes, in these early talkies "quality was sacrificed to quantity: theme songs became unbearable, but production quotas were met" (Marian Hannah Winter, "The Function of Music in Sound Film," *The Musical Quarterly* 27, no. 2 [April 1941]: 146–164; here: 151–152). John Riley similarly suggests that the "Statement" was probably inspired by Eisenstein's experiences on his two most recent films: the literalist musical arrangement for *October* (Oktiabr', 1927), and "the pot-pourri of classics" played by the Bolshoi Theater orchestra to accompany *Battleship Potemkin* (Bronenosets Potemkin, 1926). It was Eisenstein's collaboration with Austrian composer Edmund Meisel for the German releases of the two films that produced the most radical and best-known Soviet silent film scores. (See John Riley, *Dmitri Shostakovich: A Life in Film* [London: I. B. Taurus, 2005], 4–5.)

52. Grigorii Aleksandrov, *Epokha i kino* (Moscow: Izdatel'stvo politicheskoi literatury, 1976), 114–116.

53. Aleksandrov, *Epokha i kino*, 117.

54. Aleksandrov, *Epokha i kino*, 118.

55. Aleksandrov, *Gody poiskov i truda*, 43.

56. Aleksandrov, *Epokha i kino*, 119.

57. Like Eisenstein and Aleksandrov, Pudovkin was exposed to sound film technology in Europe, where he was able to experiment first hand with the new sound cinema.

58. Margaret Bourke-White, *Eyes on Russia* (New York: Simon and Schuster, 1931), 69–70.

59. *Life is Good!* was released in December 1930, but to such a hostile reception that it was withdrawn after only two days. For details, see Amy Sargeant, *Vsevolod Pudovkin: Classic Films of the Soviet Avant-Garde* (London: I. B. Tauris, 2000), 143–149.

60. N. Iezuitov, *Pudovkin* (Moscow: Iskusstvo, 1937), 174–175; English translation in Sargeant, *Vsevolod Pudovkin*, 149.

61. Sargeant, *Vsevolod Pudovkin*, 147–178.

62. See his "Dvoinoi ritm zvuka i izobrazheniia," in *Akter v filme* (Leningrad: Gos. Akademiia Iskusstvoznaniia, 1934), 60–65; translated as "Dual Rhythm of Sound and Image," in V. I. Pudovkin, *Film Technique and Film Acting*, trans. Ivor Montague (New York, Lear, 1949), *Film Acting*, 90–98.

63. Pudovkin, *Akter v filme*, 62; *Film Acting*, 93; Pudovkin, "Asinkhronnost' kak printsip zvukovogo kino," *Sobranie sochinenii*, vol. 1 (Moscow: Iskusstvo, 1974–1977); translated as: "Asynchronism as a Principle of Sound Film," *Film Technique and Film Acting*, 155–165; here:

162, emphasis in the original. Hans Eisler would do the same in *Kuhle Wampe*, also as a way of arousing the viewer; in the film, the slum district is shown to accompanying music which is "brisk, sharp," "contrasted with the loose structure of the scenes, this acts as a shock deliberately aimed at arousing resistance rather than sentimental sympathy" (Quoted in Sargeant, *Vsevolod Pudovkin*, 152).

64. Pudovkin, "Asinkhronnost' kak printsip zvukovogo kino," 158; "Asynchronism as a Principle of Sound Film," 155, emphasis in the original. This chapter, along with "Rhythmic Problems in My First Sound Film," was included in the 1933 revised edition of Pudovkin's *Film Techniques*, both written specifically for the edition and "Englished" by Marie Seton and Ivor Montague.

65. Pudovkin, "Asinkhronnost' kak printsip zvukovogo kino," 158; "Asynchronism as a Principle of Sound Film," 155–156.

66. Pudovkin, "Rhythmic Problems in My First Sound Film," 166–174; here: 171. For a thorough analysis of early Soviet sound films and their uses of contrapuntal sound, see Kristin Thompson's seminal essay, "Early Sound Counterpoint," *Yale French Studies* 60, Cinema/Sound (1980), 115–140.

67. Thompson, "Early Sound Counterpoint," 116.

68. Thompson, "Early Sound Counterpoint," 117.

69. Jacques Derrida, *Of Grammatology* (Baltimore: The Johns Hopkins University Press, 1976), 141–164.

70. Andrey Smirnov, *Sound in Z: Experiments in Sound and Electronic Music in Early 20th Century Russia* (London: Koenig Books, 2013), 175.

71. Smirnov, *Sound in Z*, 175.

72. For another excellent account of drawn/animated sound, see Richard S. James, "Avant-Garde Sound-on-Film Techniques and Their Relationship to Electro-Acoustic Music," *The Musical Quarterly* 72, no. 1 (1986): 74–89.

73. On February 20, 1930, Arseny Avraamov mentioned this new trend in his lecture for the sound-on-film group at ARRK (Avraamov 1930). In October 1930 a new technique was described in the article "Multiplikatsia zvuka" (The Animation of Sound), by E. Veisenberg (Veisenberg 1930). Arsenii Avraamov, "Sinteticheskaia muzyka," *Sovetskaia muzyka* 8 (1939): 67–75. Mikhail Tsekhanovskii, "O zvukovoi risovannoi fil'me," *Kino i zhizn* 34–35 (1930): 14. On Soviet experiments with graphic sound see Nikolai Izvolov, "From the History of Graphic Sound in the Soviet Union; or, Media without a Medium," in *Sound, Speech, Music in Soviet and Post-Soviet Cinema*, 21–37; here: 22; originally published as N. Izvolov, "Moment ozhivleniia spiashchei idei," *Kinovedcheskie zapiski* 15 (1992): 290–296; and Andrei Smirnov, "Graphical Sounds," http://asmir.info/graphical_sound.htm, and *Sound in Z*.

74. *Kino* 1931.

75. Smirnov, "Graphical Sounds," http://asmir.info/graphical_sound.htm.

76. Avraamov's experiments were kept at his house and were accidentally destroyed. Yankovsky's inventions never left the laboratory stage and may have existed only in single copies. Voinov's films were much more fortunate. Some of them were released in theaters and exist in multiple copies. Four of his films are preserved in the Russian film archives. Probably the most well preserved archive is that of Sholpo. Several dozen of his movies, along with fragments of those by other inventors, were shown for the first time at the animated film festival in Utrecht in November 2008. Izvolov, "From the History of Graphic Sound," 26.

77. Evgenii Margolit, *Zhivye i mertvoe. Zametki k istorii sovetskogo kino 1920-kh –1960-kh godov* (St. Petersburg: Seans, 2012), 131.

78. Piotrovskii, "Tonfil'ma," 4–5.

79. Sabine Hänsgen, "'Audio-Vision': o teorii i praktike rannego sovetskogo zvukovogo kino na grani 1930x godov," in *Sovetskaia vlast' i media*, ed. H. Günther and S. Hänsgen (St. Petersburg: Akademicheskii proekt, 2006), 350–364; here: 355.

80. Quoted in Hänsgen, "'Audio-Vision,'" 355.

81. Emma Widdis, "Making Sense without Speech: The Use of Silence in Early Soviet Sound Film," in *Sound, Speech, Music in Soviet and Post-Soviet Cinema*, 100–118; here: 103.

82. Stephen Lovell, "Broadcasting Bolshevik: The Radio Voice of Soviet Culture, 1920s–1950s," *Journal of Contemporary History* 48, no. 1 (2013): 78–97; here: 80.

83. Margolit, *Zhivye i mertvoe*, 86.

84. Michel Chion, *The Voice in Cinema* (New York: Columbia University Press 1999), 24.

85. Chion, *The Voice in Cinema*, 24. Emphasis in the original.

86. As Chion stresses, "could anyone rightly call this cinema silent, which was always accompanied by music from the outset—the Lumière Brothers' very first screening at the Grand Cafe in Paris—not to mention the sound effects created live in some movie houses? There were also the commentators, who freely interpreted the intertitles that the audience could not read, since many moviegoers were illiterate and most were unable to cope with subtitles in foreign languages. The movies were even less deserving of the term "mute," if by that we're supposed to understand that the characters did not speak. On the contrary, film characters were quite chatty. ... So it's not that the film's characters were mute, but rather that the film was deaf to them. This is the reason for using the term 'deaf cinema' for films that gave the moviegoer a deaf person's viewpoint on the action depicted" (Chion, *The Voice in Cinema*, 7–8).

87. As Lovell has argued, radio was a boon to the Bolsheviks on several grounds: it made possible the almost instantaneous dissemination of politicized information over huge distances; it held out huge promise as a collective organizer, reaching vastly more people than any orator could hope to do; and finally, it was the epitome of modernity: "It would accelerate progress from darkness to light, from ignorance to enlightenment." As Lovell notes, "the bearded *muzhik* in headphones was one of the iconic images of the 1920s" (Stephen Lovell, "How Russia Learned to Listen: Radio and the Making of Soviet Culture," *Kritika: Explorations in Russian and Eurasian History* 12, no. 3 [2011]: 591–615; here: 592). For a full history of Soviet radio, see his *Russia in the Microphone Age: A History of Soviet Radio, 1919–1970* (Oxford: Oxford University Press, 2015).

88. I. Sokolov, "Vtoraia programma tonfil'm," *Kino i zhizn'*, no. 27 (October 1930): 11; translated as Ippolit Sokolov, "The Second Sound Film Programme," in *The Film Factory*, 308–309.

89. Leyda, *Kino*, 278.

90. Richard Taylor, "Boris Shumyatsky and the Soviet Cinema in the 1930s: Ideology as Mass Entertainment," *Historical Journal of Film, Radio and Television* 6, no. 1 (1986): 43–64; 60.

91. For a full account, see Kenez, *Cinema and Soviet Society*, 129–130. For a detailed history of the Soviet film industry under Stalin, see: Maria Belodubrovskaya, *Not According to Plan: Filmmaking under Stalin* (Ithaca: Cornell University Press, 2017).

92. *Pervyi vsesoiuznyi s"ezd sovetskikh pisatelei: Stenograficheskii otchet* (Moscow: Khudozhestvennaia literatura, 1934); Scott, *Problems of Soviet Literature: Reports and Speeches at the First Soviet Writers' Congress*.

93. *Puti kino. Vsesoiuznoe partiinoe soveshchanie po kinematografii*, 429–444.

94. Boris Shumiatskii, "Tvorcheskie zadachi templana," *Sovetskoe kino* 12 (December 1933): 1–15; here: 1.

95. Paraphrasing Richards, *Cinematic Flashes*, 64. Richards is referring specifically to F. W. Murnau's *Sunrise* (1927) that used the new Fox Movietone sound-on-film system, making *Sunrise* one of the first feature films with a synchronized musical score and sound effects soundtrack.

chapter one

THE VOICE OF TECHNOLOGY AND THE END OF SOVIET SILENT FILM
Grigori Kozintsev and Leonid Trauberg's *Alone*

THE 1930 WORKING SCREENPLAY OF Grigori Kozintsev and Leonid Trauberg's first Soviet sound film *Odna* (Alone, 1931) contains the following crossed-out passage, addressed to the viewer:

> Look up at the airplane, with a red star on its side, flying overhead.
> Listen to the sound of the motor.
> Follow with your eyes the flying arrow.
> Feel the weight of the heavy machine, soaring into the void.
> Someday the state will grind you up inside its motor, will force you ahead, along with itself, or crush you under its merciless weight.[1]

Alone tells the story of a twenty-year-old teacher, Elena Kuzmina (played by FEKS actress Elena Kuz'mina[2]), whose assignment to run a school in Altai leads to her near death. From the frozen wasteland, Kuzmina is rescued and brought by airplane back to the city (Moscow in this initial version), where an operation that amputates four of her toes saves her life. The crossed-out address to the viewer comes at the point when the airplane, sent to Kuzmina's rescue, can be seen flying over the desolate Siberian steppe.

Kozintsev and Trauberg began work on *Alone* in June of 1929, inspired by a newspaper account of a school teacher rescued by airplane from certain death. The airplane serves as a symbol of technological progress and the advances of the Soviet State. It appears in stark contrast not only the backwardness of the Altai village, but also to the vulnerable human body which it has been sent to rescue, bringing civilization and the never halting march toward the future to the remote corner of Siberia. And yet, the inexorable march of history, progress, and technology is marked in this first screenplay by a palpable anxiety. "Watch out," the crossed-out text of the screenplay says to the viewer, the inhuman machinery of the state is coming for you.

The Alarm

Grigori Kozintsev and Leonid Trauberg's first Soviet sound film opens with a close-up of a bedside clock that begins ringing loudly as soon as the screen fades in from black. From the face of the clock we move to a close-up shot of the face of a young woman asleep, a woman who does not want to respond to the insistence of the alarm's call, and instead does her best to continue sleeping. She turns away from the alarm, she tries to silence it by throwing a pillow at it—but eventually, she must answer its call—she must get out of bed and begin the day.

This opening sequence is an allegory for the movie itself, since the plot of *Alone* centers on a young woman who, despite her initial reluctance, obeys the call of the state that sends her to a teaching post in a remote corner of Western Siberia. Filmed on location in Leningrad[3] and Altai, the film tells the story of a recent graduate from a pedagogical institute, awaiting her first teaching assignment. She is in love with a handsome *fizkul'turnik* Petya (Petr Sobolevsky) and has made plans for a beautiful life in Leningrad with her fiancé. Instead, she receives an assignment to teach in a remote village in Altai, far away from her dreams of happiness in the big city. She tries to refuse the assignment, but is ashamed and accepts it instead, bringing her alarm clock and the picture of her fiancé Petya with her to her new post.

But the opening sound of the alarm clock works as an allegory in another way as well. *Alone* was put into production in June of 1929, and by October of 1930 the directors Kozintsev and Trauberg were making use of the newly emergent sound-on-film technology, responding to the call for mass entertainment, industrialization, and the cultural revolution that accompanied the First Five-Year Plan. Conceived from the beginning as a sound film,[4] *Alone* was one of a handful of films fulfilling the new demand for "talkies" and paving the way for what Boris Shumyatsky called "cinema for the millions" and the birth of Socialist Realism.[5] The sound of the alarm clock that we hear in the beginning of the film served as a wake-up call not only for the heroine, but also for the viewer. It marked the transition from silence to sound, for the first time, bringing the new technology of sound to the Soviet screen. According to film historian Neya Zorkaya, "the close-up of a jangling alarm clock, the opening frame of the film *Alone* (1931), caused a furor in the cinema theaters. The people laughed and rejoiced."[6]

Figure 1.1. Time to Wake Up! (*Alone*, frame capture)

Kozintsev and Trauberg's *Alone* straddles the silent/sound divide.[7] The film relies on the new technology of sound to deliver its ideological message.[8] In his memoirs, Kozintsev referred to the ringing of the alarm as a *nastoichivyi prizyv*—an "insistent call" or "appeal"; a "slogan," a "military call-up" or "draft"; the call of "destiny"; and finally, *Leninskii prizyv* (Lenin's call).[9] First the alarm and then sounds from the open window, including the singing of birds, the noises of traffic, and music from a hurdy-gurdy interrupt Kuzmina's sleep, disturbing the quiet of her small private room with their very public presence. Indeed, throughout the first part of the film, Kuzmina is constantly addressed by the demands of the state transmitted via different kinds of technology: loudspeakers, typewriters, radio, and telephone communicate the messages of "appeals, slogans, codes, orders, and decrees" (*prizyvy i lozungi, svodki, prikazy, postanovleniia*),[10] interpellating the heroine into the role of Soviet citizen.[11] Moreover, this is the baring of the cinematic device; like the heroine we, the audience, are addressed by the new technology, learning to accept our new position as *auditors* as well as viewers. In the film (and working screenplays), we find the word *ty* (you, fam.) written in large letters on walls, on posters, on fliers. The film, therefore, is consciously addressing itself to the viewer—its "sound effects" are meant to produce a response in *us*.

Kozintsev and Trauberg began work on *Alone* in June of 1929, and by October 1930 *Alone* was on its way to becoming one of the first Soviet sound films, along with Dziga Vertov's *Entuziazm: Simfonia Donbassa* (Enthusiasm: The Donbass Symphony), Sergei Yutkevich's *Zlatye gory* (Golden Mountains), and Nikolai Ekk's *Putevka v zhizn'* (The Road to Life), all released in 1931. Unlike Yutkevich's *Golden Mountains* or Ekk's *The Road to Life*, *Alone* did not make use of dialogue, "naturalistic" music, or laughter. The film contained only one line of spoken dialogue and relied instead on an extradiegetic sound track that included Dmitri Shostakovich's musical score, the song "How Good Life Will Be!" (*Kakaia khoroshaia budet zhizn'*), sounds of the howling wind, and the ritual chant of the village shaman. Shostakovich—who had earlier written the score for Kozintsev and Trauberg's *New Babylon* (*Novyi Vavilon*, 1929)—completely changed his way of film scoring, producing small pieces that could be easily cut, altered, and shuffled around. John Riley refers to *Alone*, with its "kaleidoscopic soundtrack"—a clever mélange of music, sound effects, and speech—as "one of the most innovative early sound films."[12]

Indeed, in an interview in 1935, the actor Sergei Gerasimov, who played the chairman of the village Soviet (council) in the film, stressed the dual nature of *Alone*, arguing that even though his role was completely silent, and even though the sounds of his snoring were added during postproduction, he, nevertheless, perceived work on the film as a whole as having taken place on a new plane of *sound* cinematography. "My part was not a sound part," he said. "Of course, it was a purely silent part. Even the snoring was done by the 'imitator' Krzhanovsky. And yet, for me, this was work at the level of a markedly more complex and more intelligent sound cinematography."[13] Or, as Denise Youngblood has put it,

> Grigori Kozintsev and Leonid Trauberg's first "sound" film, *Alone*, has more silence than *Golden Mountains* but is less a silent film. . . . Although it has very little dialogue, visually it is much more a sound film than most others of this period. The camera work is realistic, almost documentary in style, most if it outdoors; the shots are long; the cuts are fluid. Much of the sound was added later and is unrealistic (babbling voices, clacking typewriters), but Shostakovich's music is illustrative, rather than the "naturalistic" music (like singing) which was all too common in these early films.[14]

Closer in experimental spirit to Vertov's *Enthusiasm*, *Alone* relied on extradiegetic, illustrative, almost contrapuntal sound to communicate the possibilities of new technology using alarm clocks, radio, trams,

Figure 1.2a and 1.2b. "How Good Life Will Be!" (*Alone*, frame capture)

loudspeakers, typewriters, telephones—these objects produce sound in *Alone*, interfering with or silencing the words of the heroine.[15] Like Alexander Dovzhenko's *Ivan* or Aleksandr Macheret's *Men and Jobs* (Dela i liudi, both films released in 1932), so in *Alone* the technological object is privileged over the human subject. What begins as a story about a teacher lost in the snows of central Asia is transformed into a story about the new voice of technology.

What is vital in thinking about *Alone* specifically as a *sound* film is the ways in which, starting from the initial ringing of the alarm clock, the film as a whole serves as an allegory for the transition from *Velikii nemoi* (The Great Silent or Mute) to synchronized sound, and from avant-garde experimentation to Socialist Realist convention. Most accounts of the Soviet industry's conversion to sound, while concentrating on the details of the industry's transformation (conferences, purges, reorganization, and centralization), have largely not taken into consideration the ideological impact of the transition, the ways in which the introduction of synchronized sound coincided with and in some ways, made possible, the shift in Soviet filmmaking away from avant-garde cinema of the 1920s, to Socialist Realist cinema of the 1930s and beyond.[16] The use of sound in *Alone* makes clear the larger ideological stakes of lending a "voice" to film, of being able to, for the first time, *hear* the "voice of power" issuing directly from the screen.[17]

Like that of the US or Western Europe, the Soviet film industry's transition from silence to sound was both technological and economic; but it was also, and perhaps primarily, ideological and aesthetic. The coming of sound demanded a thorough rethinking of cinematic technique (particularly evident with acting, where a highly gestural and iconic acting style gave way to a more naturalistic style), and more specifically, the elimination (or restriction) of montage with its rapid cross-cutting and dialectical construction. Moreover, for the Soviet film industry, this purely technological innovation also coincided with an ongoing cultural crisis and a profound top-down shift, as the cinema industry was completely reorganized and given new ideological directives that were easier to implement because the industry as a whole was now centralized under a single authority.

The first semiofficial conference on the shortcomings of the Sovkino film studio, a joint-stock production and distribution company, was held in October 1927. The conference—a "debate" organized by the Society of Friends of Soviet Cinema (ODSK) and the Young Communist League (Komsomol)—underscored the vital role that cinema was to play in cultural revolution of the First Five-Year Plan (1928–1932) and voiced its concerns over the failures of the current Soviet film industry. As a result, the Party promised to keep a closer eye on cinema. The First All-Union Party Conference on Cinema Affairs held in March 1928 focused its attention on the problems of the Soviet film industry, including its failure to make movies accessible to the masses, its failure to "cinefy" the countryside, its failure to become a self-sustaining industry, and its failure to negotiate the needs of ideology and profit. In January 1929, following the recommendations of the special commission, the Central Committee of the All-Union Communist Party of the Bolsheviks (TsK VKPb) issued a decree about the reorganization and purging of current cinema cadres and the centralization of the film industry. The purges of the film industry began in June, ended in August 1929, and were once again in full force by spring 1930.[18] In keeping with the secrecy of the purges, Sovkino was quietly liquidated and in its place, in February 1930, Soiuzkino was formed, following the decree of the Council of People's Commissars (SovNarKom) on the establishment of a single Soviet-wide agency to oversee the film and photo industries. In November 1930, Boris Shumyatsky was appointed as its director. Sound film was born at the same time. And while the aesthetic and ideological shift away from the heterogenous film industry of the twenties became most visible in the elaboration of the precepts of Socialist Realism (made into the official doctrine of all Soviet art in 1934) and the films of the thirties, it is already apparent in the films of the period of transition that attempt to speak with a new "voice of technology," and to use the new technology of sound to pose questions about authority, language, national identity, and the relationship between the state and the citizenry.

Perhaps in no other country was the initial response of major filmmakers and critics *against* sound technology as profound as in Soviet Russia.[19] Sound technology restricted the freedom with which film could be edited, requiring auditory and therefore visual continuity where silent film had not. Moreover, meaning would no longer be left to the assembly and comprehension of the viewer. The site for the production of meaning would shift away from what the formalist critic Boris Eikhenbaum, in the 1927 volume *Poetika kino*, called the spectator's "internal speech" (*vnutrenniaia rech'*), to the audible word addressing the spectator directly from the screen.[20] In his essay, "Problem of Cinema Stylistics," Eikhenbaum stresses the absence of the audible word as the central organizing principle of silent cinema, making the development of inner speech possible. He writes,

> The invention of the movie camera made possible the exclusion of the basic dominant of theatrical syncretism, *the audible word,* and its replacement by

another dominant, *motion seen in details*. . . . The film viewer was placed in completely new conditions of perception, the opposite of the process of reading: from the object, from visual motion, to the process of making sense of it, to the construction of internal speech. The success of film is in part related to this new type of mental work which does not arise in everyday activities. . . . Film culture, as a sign of the epoch, stands in opposition to the culture of the word, literary and theatrical, which ruled the previous century. The film viewer seeks relief from the word; he wants only to see and divine.[21]

In his memoirs, Sergei Eisenstein similarly describes the difficult mental labor involved in watching movies. He imagines watching a film as a process of mentally gathering together different fragments of a single totality [*oskolki tselogo*], specifying that understanding film requires the ability to syncretize, to bring together the various details passing before one's eyes into an impression of a single unified whole. This hard mental labor is the essence of intellectual montage—the mental assembly of disparate images into a meaningful whole, the ability to "see and divine" the language of film. And it is easy to see how the introduction of sound—of the audible word—in cinema would forever alter the relationship of spectator to film and shift the site for the production of meaning away from the viewer, back to the film itself.[22]

Kozintsev and Trauberg may or may not have conceived *Alone* from the beginning as a sound film, nevertheless, once introduced, sound came to structure the film, shifting the story away from a tale of "human sacrifice" to a tale about technology. Because the introduction of sound coincided with the historical moment of The Great Turn, sound in Soviet cinema helped pave the way of the film industry toward Socialist Realism, toward an ideological program that rigidly controlled what could and could not be shown and what could and could not be spoken on the screen. It is no wonder, then, that Ian Christie stresses the nature of Soviet sound cinema as a "new apparatus."[23] The technology of sound altered the relationship between the film and the viewer, doing away with "internal speech" and substituting in its place the audible word that issued directly from the screen. Sound cinema made it possible to hear the voice of the Other, addressing itself to the spectator. No longer would the film viewer simply "see and divine" a multiplicity of meanings from the language of film—meaning would lose its plurality, imposing the singularity of the spoken word onto the multiplicity of the moving image. Cinema's new voice "hailed" the viewer from the screen, casting the Soviet subject in the role of its addressee.

The Loudspeaker

Kuzmina begins the film as a naïve and slightly silly woman, whose dreams of the happy life that awaits her are represented by an outmoded and ideologically dangerous love for things: together with her fiancé Petya, she admires the beautiful store displays with tea sets and modern furniture, dreaming of a future life in the great city, full of objects of desire (with Petya, one object among them). As with the sound of the alarm, she is then (re)called to herself when she receives her teaching assignment; from Leningrad and a happy future of well-behaved pupils, marriage, and material comforts, she must go to teach in a desolate Altai village, in the *glush'* (backcountry) of the Siberian steppe.[24] Kuzmina receives this call in two ways. The first comes in the form of a letter—her teaching assignment that she collects along with her diploma; the second comes in the form of a loudspeaker in the middle of an empty square addressing itself to passersby: "Comrades! Today we are deciding the fate not of one, not of hundreds, but of millions of people. At this moment, we are facing the question: what have you done? What are you doing? What are you going to do?" Responding to the demand of the loudspeaker, Kuzmina answers with her only line of spoken dialogue in the film: "I'm going to complain!" (*Ia budu zhalovat'sia!*), she says.[25]

We might read this scene not only for its comic or dramatic effect (Kuzmina, in all of her innocence, answering a piece of technology *as if* it were speaking directly to her; or, the tragedy of the modern subject in a technocratic world), but also for what it teaches us about the relationship of "internal speech" to the word of the Other as it is made manifest by the new sound-on-film technology. As Avital Ronnel has argued in her writings about the telephone, in picking up the receiver and choosing to answer the call, "you're saying yes, almost automatically, suddenly, sometimes irreversibly. Your picking up means the call has come through. It means more: you are its beneficiary, rising to meet its demand, to pay a debt.... It is a question of answerability. Who answers the call of the telephone, the call of duty, and accounts for the taxes it appears to impose?"[26]

Like Ronnel's telephone, the *nastoichivyi prizyv* of the loudspeaker is more than simply an insistent "call" or "appeal" to Soviet citizens at large. Located in the middle of an empty square, bellowing its message out whether or not there is anyone there to listen, this call neither demands nor forces anyone to respond, "to take the call," or answer its appeal. Yet once answered—even if in the negative, even if to say, "I'm going to complain!" the call becomes a call of duty, it levies a tax, it asks to be repaid a debt. It is precisely at the point of answering the call that the *nastoichivyi*

Figure 1.3a. Narkompros (*Alone*, frame capture)

Figure 1.3b. The loudspeaker (*Alone*, frame capture)

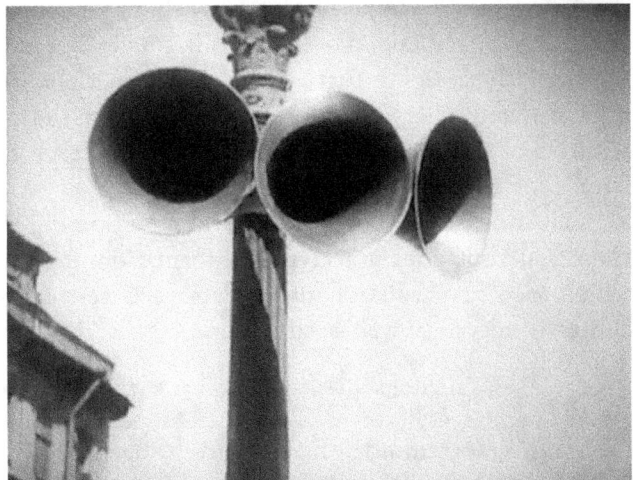

Figure 1.3c. Direct address (*Alone*, frame capture)

prizyv shifts from its milder sense of "appeal" to the much more militant "draft," "conscription," and finally—"the call of destiny."²⁷ All citizens are called, but only those who answer the call find themselves forever in debt, always paying for the charges. As Ronnel writes, "No matter how you cut it, on either side of the line, there is no such thing as a free call. Hence the interrogative inflection of a yes that finds itself accepting charges."²⁸

The call of the loudspeaker is an obvious example of an ideological "hail," articulated by Louis Althusser as the process by which ideology "constitutes concrete individuals as subjects."²⁹ Considering the production and reproduction of subjects of power in his 1970 essay, "Ideology and Ideological State Apparatuses," Althusser isolates two functions of ideology: "recognition" and "misrecognition" (or *méconnaissance*). The function of recognition allows subjects recognize "the *obviousness* of the fact that they are subjects: free, ethical, etc. [with the] inevitable and natural reaction of crying out (aloud or in the 'still, small voice of conscience'): 'That's obvious! That's right! That's true!'" This function allows us to recognize ourselves and others as subjects, and to perform the necessary rituals constitutive of subjectivity (we shake hands, call each other by name, have names that are "unique" and individual, etc.).³⁰

As Althusser argues, however, the function of recognition "performs the ritual" but does not give us information about the mechanisms by which ideology "hails or interpellates concrete individuals as concrete subjects." Ideology, writes Althusser,

> "acts" or "functions" in such a way that it "recruits" subjects among the individuals (it recruits them all), or "transforms" the individuals into subjects (it transforms them all) by that very precise operation which I have called *interpellation* or hailing, and which can be imagined along the lines of the most commonplace everyday police (or other) hailing, "Hey, you there!"
>
> Assuming that the theoretical scene I have imagined takes place in the street, the hailed individual will turn around. By this mere 180-degree physical conversion, he becomes a *subject*. Why? Because he has recognized that the hail was "really" addressed to him, and that "it was *really him* who was hailed" (and not someone else). Experience shows that the practical telecommunication of hailings is such that they hardly ever miss their man; verbal call or whistle, the one hailed always recognizes that it is really him who is being hailed.³¹

A "hail"—a military call of recruitment—produces subjects out of mere individuals. To fail to answer the hail would mean remaining an individual outside of subjective construction, not subject to ideological recruitment or the call of the big Other.

In *Alone* the heroine hears and, perhaps more importantly, answers the "voice of ideology" addressing her directly from a loudspeaker in the city square. Itself figured as technology (loudspeaker), the address is also made possible by means of technology—the technology of synchronized sound allows us to *hear* as well as see/read the messages of the film. The disembodied male voice issuing from the loudspeaker relies on sound cinema's ability to produce the effect of "truth" through the disengagement of voice from body. Similar to the function of the voice-over in documentary films, the free-floating male voice, unanchored to a specific body, takes on the attributes of omniscience and omnipotence.[32] The voice's "radical otherness with respect to the diegesis," the fact that it is not produced by a body that we can *see*, allows it to assume superhuman or extrahuman status—the status of a pure signifier of power.[33] Yet, unlike the voice-over in documentary films, while maintaining the separation of voice from body (the voice is a recording, a mechanical reproduction, a moment of cinematic ventriloquism), the bellowing loudspeaker in *Alone* nevertheless invites us to ask, "Who is speaking?" "Where?" "In what time?" and "For whom?"[34]

To begin to answer these questions we need to consider that this free-floating voice of ideology may in itself be a kind of *Leninskii prizyv* (Lenin's call to arms), in that it marks the absent presence of the Leader, now "more alive than anyone" (*Lenin i teper' zhivee vsekh zhivyh*), issuing directives from beyond the grave. The specter of Lenin haunts not only Vladimir Mayakovsky's 1924 poem "Vladimir Ilych Lenin," in which he is unable to come to terms either with Lenin's death nor with his own continued existence, it also haunts *Alone*, echoing in the demands the state places on its citizens—or, more specifically, the demands by which the state produces its citizens.[35] Like Mayakovsky's voice in the poem that asks, "But I'm not the only one / Am I better than others?" (*Da ne ia odin!/ Da chto ia luchshe, chto li?*), Kuzmina asks the fateful question, "Am I alone [the only one]?" (*Chto ia, odna?*). And whereas we naturally inflect Mayakovsky's question with positive meaning—not only Mayakovsky, but thousands and thousands would give their lives (or their very small deaths) to keep Lenin alive—we nonetheless hear its echo in Kuzmina's plea. Like Paul de Man's understanding of the figure of *apostrophe*, the disembodied voice (*Leninskii prizyv*) issuing from the screen alters the relation between the dead and the living. The effort to maintain Lenin as the "liveliest of all" requires that Mayakovsky stage his own death (and he is not alone). To answer his call means to "join the dead."[36]

Hoping to make a "call" of her own, Kuzmina enters the Narkompros[37] building to file her complaint and to telephone Petya. First unable

Figure 1.4a and 1.4b. The telephone (*Alone*, frame capture)

to get into the phone booth because of a man discussing dinner with his wife, she then seems unable to get out. The telephone booth is yet another *apparat* (apparatus, technological device) that subordinates the desires of the heroine to its own technological demands. Though we see her making the phone call, we cannot hear what she says; clacking typewriters and dictating voices projected over the film drown out Kuzmina's speech, so that while we see her desperate gestures, we cannot hear her voice.[38] Finally, in a last act of mute desperation, Kuzmina presses her hands and face against the glass of the phone booth, as if unable to escape. She is, in this instance, the human subject trapped by technology, incapable of making herself heard, unable to extract herself from the apparatus demanding payment. Like the crossed-out passage from the screenplay ("Someday the state will grind you up inside its motor, will force you ahead, along with itself, or crush you under its merciless weight"), this sequence demonstrates the ways in which (Soviet) subjects are, alternately, disciplined and coerced. The power of the state, "embodied" in the technological apparatuses that proliferate in this film, does not merely produce subjects, it produces docile, disciplined subjects whose noncompliance may be read as a direct threat against the state.

This threat becomes explicit in the following scene between the heroine and the head administrator of the department of people's education (*otdel narodnogo obrazovaniia*), whose face we never see but whose grey hair pulled back into a bun is meant to remind us of Lenin's wife, Nadezhda Krupskaya.[39] The working screenplay for the film imagines this moment as a direct confrontation between the heroine and the state. In Kuzmina's embattled consciousness she understands that everyone is against her, that she is "alone": "The government is against her. Phones ring, circulars are written, motorcycles drive in and out—and all of them, against her" (*vse protiv nee*). The woman (Krupskaya) represents a possible way out, some kind of human understanding. As the screenplay concludes, "A calm woman with gray hair and, perhaps, a bandaged throat, sits at the table. Why should [Kuzmina] address her? The young woman doesn't know. Maybe, because her name is—Nadezhda [Hope] ... maybe because her face is infinitely kind ... the woman with the gray hair will understand, she will feel sorry for her, comfort her."[40]

Having listened to Kuzmina's complaint (again, given to us without words or intertitles, but communicated only via gestures), Krupskaya allows the heroine a way out, and we hear her off-screen voice giving dictation overlaid on the sound of a typewriter, as Kuzmina walks down the corridor holding her new teaching assignment. Like the voice of the loudspeaker,

Krupskaya's disembodied voice is now turned into the voice of pure ideological demand and even, of reprimand. Answering Kuzmina's dream of the "happy life" (*kakaia khoroshaia budet zhizn'!*), Krupskaya formulates the reply in the following way: "Enemies of the power of the Soviets are not needed in these places," she says, "and therefore, if it is possible to allow the teacher Kuzmina, who does not want to go to Siberia, to remain here."

This response clearly demonstrates the way that the "hail" of ideology is not a neutral act but, as Judith Butler has put it, "a power and force of the law to compel fear at the same time that it offers recognition at an expense." Butler writes that the "one"—the individual hailed by ideology—does not appear "to be in a condition of trespass prior to the call," it is the call itself that establishes a given practice as a trespass. Before the call, the individual is not "fully a social subject, is not fully subjectivated, for he or she is not yet reprimanded."[41] Following Butler, we might say that the reprimand of the administrator ("enemies of the power of the Soviets are not needed in these places . . . and therefore . . .") is part and parcel of the demand of the loudspeaker ("What have you done? What are you doing? What are going to do?"). Together they form the ideological hail that turns the individual, not yet in trespass of any law, into a Soviet citizen, always in fear of breaking the law by which s/he is constituted. Kuzmina must accept the assignment lest she become an "enemy" of Soviet power and receive a different reprimand from the state. And again here it is useful to underscore that the administrator who delivers the reprimand is meant to remind us of Lenin's widow. Like her very presence (surviving after Lenin's death as a kind of painful reminder/remainder), her appearance in this film, together with Lenin's portrait on the wall before her, points us to Lenin as the unnamed source of disembodied authority, addressing us with the voice of the (un)dead.[42]

It is this voice—the disembodied voice of the big Other, the voice of ideology, the voice of recorded, mechanically reproduced, ventriloquized speech—that the sound camera makes audible in *Alone*. As the heroine stands for the second time in front of the loudspeaker "idiotically" (that is, automatically and inhumanly) repeating its slogans, we too find ourselves addressed by its persistent hail (*nastoichivyi prizyv*). The repetition reminds us that *we* have not yet answered, that we are still "in demand," still hoping that Kuzmina *alone* might pay for the charges. The voice of the loudspeaker addresses anyone who will listen and respond—as a voice issuing from the screen, it addresses *us*, with its impossible to meet demand.[43] But the disembodied voice of power does more than transform the heroine from individual to subject; it also transforms her from a creature of desire (dreaming of a happy future) to a creature of what in psychoanalysis is called "drive"—mechanical, maniacal, a pure insatiable demand directed at the world.[44] From a woman who wants *things*—attentive pupils, tea sets, modern furniture, a husband—she becomes an instrument for the production of Soviet citizens.

THE HOSTILE WHITE SILENCE

From the sunny streets of Leningrad, shot white-on-white to remove all contrast, Kuzmina arrives in the desolate steppe of Altai, also white, but now inhumanly, uncannily so. At the entrance to the village she is greeted by the skin of a recently flayed horse, complete with head and exposed teeth, hung on a post above the village gate. Meant to ward off evil spirits, the horse symbolizes the backward, ancient power of the village, with its roots in shamanistic rituals and pretechnological civilization. Kuzmina arrives in Altai with certain baggage; out of her travel bag comes the photograph of Petya, an alarm clock, a globe, and the dream of teaching children about the wonders of technology. As her work in the village becomes more and more fraught with difficulty—the local bey (*bai* or chieftain) forces the children to tend to the sheep instead of attending school and then sells the sheep for slaughter, depriving the village of its only source of livelihood, while the head of the local Soviet (Gerasimov) refuses to help bring the children back or to help save the sheep from slaughter—we watch Kuzmina transform from an individual addressed by the voice of ideology *into* the voice of the ideology. Not only through her teaching, but also through her meddling in the affairs of the village—affairs, that according to both the bey and Gerasimov need not concern her—Kuzmina becomes the voice of the Soviet state, speaking its ideological messages.

Sound plays a vital role here: the song "How Good Life Will Be!" accompanies Kuzmina while she watches the sleeping Gerasimov and his helpless wife, an ironic sonic gesture to underscore her previously naïve (and dangerously anti-Soviet) state. In fact, Gerasimov himself gets a musical gesture—"trombone *glissandi* signifying his sloppiness and rejection of Soviet thought."[45] Tired of listening to him snore, Kuzmina tries to rouse the sleeping Gerasimov, and the sound of her voice is replaced by the now familiar ringing of the alarm clock. Kuzmina has become the technology she earlier tried to ignore. At another moment, as she daydreams of teaching the village children about the wonders of technology, her upbeat fantasy (set to energetic music) is interrupted by the uncanny singing of the village shaman, while the film cuts again to a close up of the dead horse. The horse's "singing" is a reminder that the dead horse is a symbol

Figure 1.5a and 1.5b. The dead horse (*Alone*, frame capture)

of entrenched anti-Soviet power. Disturbingly animate and inanimate at the same time, recognizable yet unfamiliar because of its radically altered shape, the horse is part of the larger hostile environment (that includes the people, but also the snow-covered landscape of Altai) from which Kuzmina will need to be rescued at the end of the film.

While the new technology of sound is used in *Alone* to deliver the ideological messages of the film (including, but not limited to the voice of power issuing directly from the screen), the visual field of *Alone*, famously shot "white on white" by the cinematographer Andrei Moskvin, speaks to similar concerns over the technologies of the state. In his previous films made in collaboration with Kozintsev and Trauberg, Moskvin relied on shade and shadow, projector lights and nighttime filming to convey a sense of irreality, instability, confusion, and deception.[46] Starting with his work on *The Overcoat* (*Shinel'*, 1926), Moskvin also introduced the "subjective camera," that is, a camera that recorded events not from an impassive position of a disinterested spectator, but from the position of the character, conveying their mood, registering not only *what* they see, but also *how* they see it.[47] This was particularly important for a film like *The Overcoat*, in which Akaky Akakievich's "reality" acquires a phantasmagoric, grotesque, *subjective* dimension, in which he is pursued by objects, threatened by shadows, and overwhelmed by visions. Here, the order of Imperial Russia mercilessly crushes the "little man" (*malen'kii chelovek*), and this sense of overwhelming power is, in Yury Tynyanov's screenplay for *The Overcoat*, coupled with the image of the "corpse of Russian reality" (*trup rossiiskoi deistvitel'nosti*).

In *Alone* Moskvin also employs a reduced color scheme to underscore the denaturalized world of the modern Soviet city. In this case, however, he is not filming a world of darkness but instead, a world of light. Early shots of the sunny streets of Leningrad—with white clothes, white trams, white flowers, white steps, white objects behind glass—eliminate contrast, creating a desaturated screen in order to show a joyful, conflict-free existence. Moskvin's Soviet biographer F. G. Gukasian notes that Moskvin built his compositions in *Alone* "*belym po belomu*" (white on white) at a time when most cinematographers tried to exclude anything white from their shots (because of the nature of film stock, white appeared overwhelmingly bright on the screen), and instead, used yellow to produce the effect of white. Moskvin, on the contrary, used many shades of white and a special treatment of film stock in order to produce the richness of the all-white screen.[48] It is easy to see that this reduced color palette serves a particular ideological purpose. The effect of the white-on-white shots in

Figure 1.6. The hostile while silence (*Alone*, frame capture)

this early part of the film is two-fold. First, it underscores the joyous nature of the new Soviet world—airy, bright, light, filled with spring, with flowers, with love. Second (and perhaps, conversely) it underscores the "light-mindedness" of the heroine, seduced by the joys of taking part in this "happy life," and is accompanied by the musical refrain, "*Kakaia khoroshaia budet zhizn'!*" that we cannot but hear ironically.

What I want to suggest, however, is that the sense of the overwhelming and crushing power of the state made possible by the mobile, subjective camera, that the Soviet critic Gukasian easily identifies in *The Overcoat*, is not lost or abandoned three years later in Moskvin's work on *Alone*. Despite their diametrically opposed color schemes and their historically (and therefore, ideologically) opposed settings, we might productively read *The Overcoat* as a subtext for *Alone*, as yet another film about one small individual ruthlessly crushed by the merciless power of the state. Note, for example, the shot of Kuzmina standing on the diagonal border between darkness and light, with the shadow of the unseen Narkompros building covering half of the screen and blocking out the light as she receives her *raspredelenie* (teaching assignment). We can read this shadow as the product of subjective camerawork, reflecting Kuzmina's interior state, all of her hopes suddenly dashed by the order sending her to Altai. But we can also read this as a broader message about the workings of Soviet power. When Kuzmina receives her teaching assignment, the screen is divided into two: a great looming shadow cast by a building (presumably the government building which she has just exited) covers half of the screen on a diagonal, reducing the white space and leaving Kuzmina on the border between darkness and light. This play between shadow and light, between an all-white landscape covered over by temporary darkness, prefigures the landscape of Altai, again mostly white, but now uncannily, menacingly so.

Indeed, the initial reduced color scheme of the Leningrad sequence appears in stark contrast to the second location of the film: Altai, Western Siberia.[49] Here, the desaturated palette (stark white snow against stark white sky) works to create a sense of terror, particularly once the stark white is compromised by black shadow. In Altai, Kuzmina is greeted by the sounds of the howling wind and the incomprehensible song of the village shaman. All around her, we can hear the uncanny sounds of this *othered* landscape—the howl of the Siberian wind, the wail of the village shaman performing a death ritual, the mechanical sounds of village life.[50] What seems clear from this set-up, in its direct contrast with the earlier scenes of Leningrad, filled with fast moving trams and fast moving people, is that Altai represents civilization's "beyond," the landscape of the "real." Moreover, it is the place of death. The plot of this second half revolves around the conflict between Kuzmina and the local authorities (the bey who owns the land and the sheep and, therefore, the children Kuzmina has set out to teach, and the representative of the village Soviet whose famous initial act of slowly polishing his boots signals his laziness and corruption) and her near death in the snow-covered steppe. The film ends when an airplane dispatched by the People's Commissariat (Narkomat) arrives in the village, rescuing Kuzmina from certain death. Immobile, with arms bandaged up to the elbows, she is loaded onto the airplane (called a "dead bird" by the villagers) and the final shot captures the plane as it flies over the skin of the flayed horse, carrying the dying teacher away from Altai.

The lost sixth reel of the film, destroyed in the fire at the Lenfilm studio during the Leningrad blockade, contained the sequence of Kuzmina's near death in the frozen Siberian steppe. The missing sequence of Kuzmina abandoned in the middle of the snow-covered plain, "surrounded by a hostile white silence"[51] speaks (or would have spoken) to the unmitigated horror of the all-white landscape, now revealed in its most inhuman. "The landscape surrounding the death (*gibel'*) of the teacher," writes Kozintsev in his memoirs, "needed to reflect the tragedy. We were shooting on the ice-covered Lake Baikal. Day after day we waited for hours for the sun to emerge and then hide again behind the clouds—[the cameraman] Moskvin would shoot in those brief moments (normally in such weather conditions the shooting would be called off because of the instability of the light); we were amassing shots—giant shadows, like black wings, would rush across the lake, pursuing the girl."⁵² This account may be contrasted with Kozintsev's later observations about the general shooting conditions in Altai: "Many years ago Moskvin and I were shooting the frozen, empty Baikal—the enormous plane of ice—for the film *Alone*. We needed a severe, ancient silence. But what we kept getting instead, was cheerful, powdery snow—a vacation spot! We were forced to keep changing shooting angles, color filters, types of film stock, in order to get the right mood."⁵³ The frozen shores of Lake Baikal (where the missing sixth reel was shot) and the heroine buried in the snow, completely consumed by the whiteness that surrounds her, speaks to nature in its most "natural"—that is to say, inhuman—form.

The setting of this scene is key for reading the film as an allegory of the workings of Soviet power. Kuzmina's near death is the final result of answering the ideological hail, her final attempt to repay the state with her life for having offered her recognition at her own expense. Indeed, the economic metaphor (debt and payment) suggested above continues to operate in the second, Altai part of *Alone*. Once she answers the call of the state, Kuzmina continues to pay for the charges and both the early screenplays and the film mark Kuzmina's progress in specifically economic terms. In the 1930 screenplay, Kuzmina collects a salary (17 rubles and 34 kopeks) as soon as she arrives in the village. This salary is issued to her even before her arrival, and she feels it in her pocket "not only as money" but as a "symbol" (*Ne tol'ko kak den'gi. Kak simvol*). The symbolic status of this salary underscores the notion that this is a payment "in advance," a debt to be repaid, money that will eventually be recuperated by the state. Contemplating the inevitability of Kuzmina's death from exposure, Gerasimov calculates that she will be buried with money from the "collective account" (*za obshchestvennyi schet*). The screenplay makes these mechanisms of payment and debt even more explicit: "It will be difficult to save her. She will die. All the better for the government. In the ledger, under the salary owed for this half-month, across from the state teacher Elena Kuzmina's name will be a blank space. The money will go to benefit the state" (*den'gi poidut v dokhod gosudarstva*).⁵⁴ More vitally, her eventual recovery (included in the screenplay, but not in the film) is also marked as payment, but now

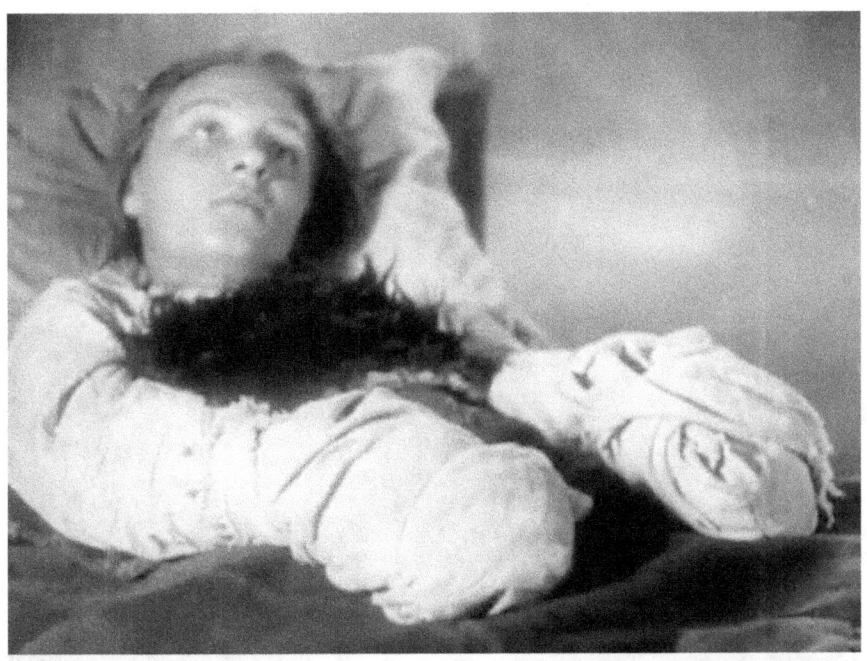

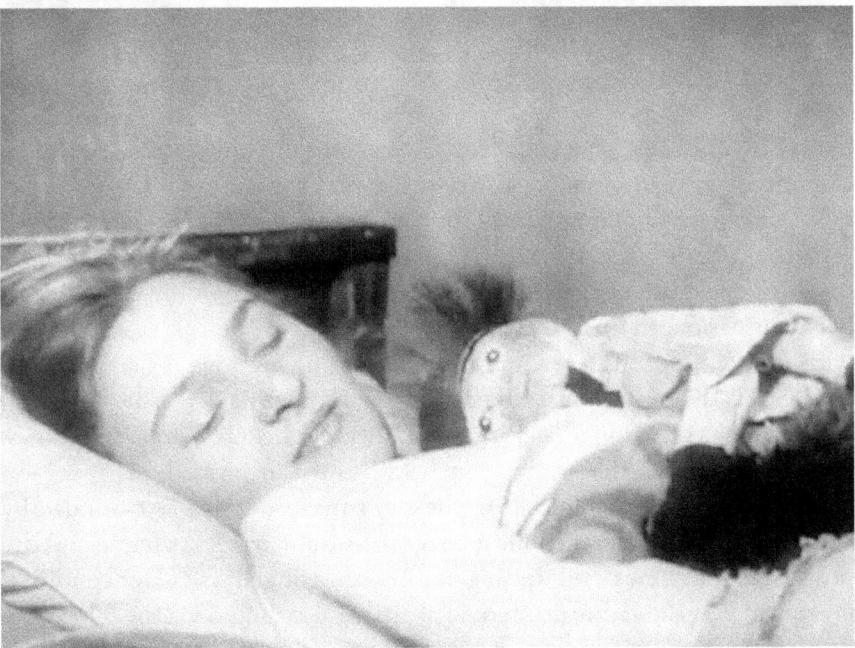

Figure 1.7a and 1.7b. "The teacher Kuzmina is dying in Altai" (*Alone*, frame capture)

Figure 1.8. "I'll be back!" (*Alone*, frame capture)

in bodily terms. To save her life, the surgeons amputate four of her toes, but since "ten minus four is six," the screenplay suggests that Kuzmina has given only a small part of herself for her chance to rejoin the collective, to return, as another Socialist Realist hero puts it, "to ranks and to life."⁵⁵

Moreover, the image of the mutilated and dying heroine (in bed with her arms bandaged up to the elbows, clutching a rag doll) is synchronized with the sound of the telegraph communicating messages to all points in the USSR. The same loudspeaker that asked Kuzmina what she was going to do is now reporting on her imminent death; "Listen, listen," it bellows, "the teacher Kuzmina is dying in Altai! Only an immediate operation could save her!" In the middle of the city square, but now surrounded by a multitude of people, the loudspeaker calls out Kuzmina's name and the progress of her illness, reminding us of Lenin's final days.⁵⁶ Her condition is reported on the radio, printed up as fliers, distributed via the telegraph. She has become part of the mechanized reproduction of power made audible in this film by the new technology of sound.⁵⁷

In his memoirs, Kozintsev notes that the juxtaposition of image and sound in *Alone*, created "a dialogue between the main character (the image) and some kind of soulless power (the sound)."[58] This "soulless power" is, first and foremost, the sound of the frozen steppe beyond the enclosures of the heroine's home, the yurt in which she lives and teaches, and as such, is once again the manifestation of that incomprehensible and inhuman "real" that confronts Kuzmina when she first enters the village in the guise of a dead horse. But it is also the voice of power—denatured and dehumanized (*bezdushnaia sila*)—hailing her as a subject and demanding a response. Dying, her arms requiring amputation, Kuzmina continues to teach the village children from her deathbed, and her final words, "I'll be back soon," given to us as an intertitle, speak to the fact that once engaged, the commitment to the Soviet cause can never be exhausted, but must be reproduced, again and again, even by ailing, mutilated, and otherwise suffering bodies. Pressed against the window of the airplane, Kuzmina is a kind of "apparition"—another manifestation of the Stalinist "living dead"—and her declaration that she will return soon, like Arnold Schwarzenegger's famous "I'll be back!" in his *Terminator* movies, is less of a promise than a threat. It is the final word of a creature devoid of desire or subjectivity that continues to answer the call of Soviet ideology.[59]

The Airplane

Kozintsev and Trauberg's *Alone*, which opens with the ringing of the alarm clock and sounds that invade the heroine's bedroom, disturbing her sleep, ends with her rescue by yet one more technological device: the airplane sent by Narkomat at the request of the villagers. In his writings, Kozintsev complained that "the last part of the film didn't work out at all." The theme of the government's help was "too abstract [*otvlechennyi*], schematic. . . . Slogans, reported on the radio; inscriptions-appeals [*nadpisi-prizyvy*] calling to aid the teacher freezing in the steppe; the airplane, symbolically flying over the skin of the horse; the light reflected off the propeller and the songs about the good life—all of these were lifeless [*beszhiznennye*]. Without human eyes the screen appeared flat, and the visual images [*zrelishchnye kadry*]—unworthy."[60] The ending of the film is a series of shots of the departing airplane (mostly, its rapidly spinning propeller) and close-up shots of the faces of Altai villagers, waving their hats in the air in imitation of the propeller. As such, it signals the transformation of the human into the mechanical, the power of the state to create lifeless, mechanized subjects.

As Kristin Thompson has noted, *Alone* takes Pudovkin's perceptual device of blank film leader inserts—in this case white—and uses it in combination with sound for an emotional effect. As the villagers cheer

Kuzmina's promise to return, the image cutting gradually accelerates. Triumphant Shostakovich music plays as the scene builds up to an emotional climax, finally "single frames of a low-angle shot of the plane alternate with single frames of white leader for about 30 shots, ending as the plane pulls away to take off."[61] For Thompson, the cutting and the music combine to create an extreme moment of triumph as the film ends (making up for the bleakness of its portrayal of contemporary life), but I would argue that something else is also at stake.

Kozintsev may be right that the final effect of the ending is precisely *lifeless*, closing with shots of the black metallic airplane and its violently spinning propeller. The final shots of the film deliver the message about Soviet subjectivity and Soviet technology precisely through their *otvlechennost'*—lifelessness and dehumanization. As the crossed-out passage from the screenplay suggests, if we follow with our eyes the flying arrow, feeling the weight of the heavy machine, we too can sense that someday, the state will crush us under its merciless weight. Held within yet another *apparat* (an "apparatus" or "mechanical device," but also, the "machinery of state"), Kuzmina is herself an "apparition"—a ghostly manifestation of the Stalinist system, trying to communicate with the villagers below. Her final posture, with her face pressed against the window, echoes the earlier shot of her inside the telephone booth, trapped and dehumanized by the "alienating armor" of technology.

The crossed-out warning of the 1930 screenplay leaves its trace on the film in the form of an anxiety over technology and the operations of the state. At first glance, *Alone* appears well on its way to Socialist Realism: light, bright, filmed entirely during daytime, filmed white on white to reduce contrast, as opposed to the play of shadows, of darkness and light so common for the earlier films of Kozintsev, Trauberg, and Moskvin. And yet, the limited color palette here too speaks not only to its own impossibility (that "white on white which is impossible to film"[62]), but also, perhaps, to a certain resistance on the part of the filmmakers to the new ideological directives of the state. Bridging the silent/sound divide, *Alone* makes audible for the first time the introduction of alien speech, of the word of the Other issuing directly from the screen. In *Alone* sound technology gives voice to the power that produces the heroine as a Soviet subject, while at the same time, registering the anxiety over technology and the operations of the state that underpins Kozintsev and Trauberg's last silent avant-garde, first Soviet sound film.[63]

Notes

1. «Когда-нибудь государство переработает вас в своем моторе, устремит вперед вместе с собой или задавит неумолимою тяжестью.» RGALI f. 966-2-347, l. 41, crossed out.

2. Together with Sergei Yutkevich and Leonid Kryzhitsky, Kozintsev and Trauberg organized and led the Factory of the Eccentric Actor (FEKS, 1921–1929). The FEKS group collaborated with Yury Tynyanov (writer), Andrei Moskvin (cinematographer), Elena Kuz'mina (actress), Sergei Gerasimov (actor-director), Igor Vuskovich (artist), and Dmitri Shostakovich (composer), among others. Initially FEKS was the main platform for experimental actors, directors, and artists, and was strongly influenced by theater director Vsevolod Meyerhold and the poet Vladimir Mayakovsky.

3. The original screenplays set the first half of the film in Moscow. See RGALI f. 966-2-347; RGALI f. 3016-1-2; and RGALI f. 2639-1-59.

4. Neya Zorkaya and Yakov Butovsky both argue that the film was *from the beginning* conceived as a sound film. See Neia Zorkaia, "'Odna' na perekrestkakh," *Kinovedcheskie zapiski* 74 (2005): 143–158; Iakov Butovskii, "'Odna' na perekrestkakh obshchikh problem rossiiskogo kinovedeniia," *Kinovedcheskie zapiski* 77 (2006): 310–319. *Letopis' rossiiskogo kino 1930–1945* lists October 3, 1930, as the date that Kozintsev and Trauberg began work on the sound version of *Alone* (*Letopis' rossiiskogo kino 1930–1945*, ed. Aleksandr Deriabin [Moscow: Materik, 2007], 53).

5. The resolution of the December 1928 Conference of Soiuzkino workers stated that an essential part of any experimental work was to be "artistic expression that is intelligible to the millions." In 1935, Boris Shumyatsky used the phrase "cinema for the millions" to describe the main goal of Soviet cinematography. See Boris Shumiatskii, *Kinematografiia millionov: Opyt analiza*, (Moscow: Kinofotoizdat, 1935).

6. Neya Zorkaya, *The Illustrated History of the Soviet Cinema* (New York: Hippocrene Books, 1989), 107.

7. Writing about early Hollywood sound films, Rashna Wadia Richards notes the ways conversion-era films switch between silent cinema's "background" music and sound cinema's "complete synchronization." As John Belton has pointed out, "part-talkie films tend to unravel before the audience's eyes and ears, repeatedly reverting to silence and then back into synchronized sound." See Rashna Wadia Richards, *Cinematic Flashes: Cinephilia and Classical Hollywood* (Bloomington: Indiana University Press, 2013), 59; John Belton, "Awkward Transitions: Hitchcock's *Blackmail* and the Dynamics of Early Film Sound," *Musical Quarterly* 83, no. 2 (1999), 227–246; here: 228.

8. B. Leaming, *Grigori Kozintsev* (Boston: Twayne Publishers, 1980), 130.

9. Definitions of *prizyv* from Kenneth Katzner, *English-Russian Dictionary*, revised ed. (New York: John Wiley & Sons, Inc., 1994); and S. I. Ozhegov, *Slovar' russkogo iazyka* (Moscow: Russkii iazyk, 1988). *Leninskii prizyv* was the recruitment of the best and brightest members of the working class into the party in the year of Lenin's death.

10. Grigorii Kozintsev, *Sobranie sochinenii v piati tomakh* (Leningrad: Iskusstvo 1984), 1: 195.

11. As defined by Louis Althusser in his *Lenin and Philosophy and Other essays*, trans. Ben Brewster (New York: Monthly Review Press, 1971).

12. John Riley, *Dmitri Shostakovich: A Life in Film* (London: I. B. Taurus, 2005), 13–14.

13. "Litso sovetskogo kinoaktera: E. Kuz'mina i S. Gerasimov," Kinofotoizdat, 1935. RGALI f. 2639-1-59, l. 34 (reverse).

14. Denise J. Youngblood, *Soviet Cinema in the Silent Era, 1918–1935* (Ann Arbor: UMI Research Press, 1985), 226–227.

15. Karl Radek attacks both *Enthusiasm* and *Alone* in his April 23, 1931, review, "Two Films." Karl Radek, "Dve fil'my," *Izvestiia* (April 23, 1931). On contrapuntal sound in early Soviet sound film, including *Alone*, see Kristen Thompson, "Early Sound Counterpoint," *Yale French Studies*, no. 60, Cinema/Sound (1980), 115–140.

16. See, for example, Peter Kenez, *Cinema & Soviet Society 1917–1953* (Cambridge, England: Cambridge University Press, 1992); Youngblood, *Soviet Cinema in the Silent Era, 1918–1935*; Zorkaya, *The Illustrated History of the Soviet Cinema*.

17. Several articles on *Alone* have touched on this topic. See N. Nusinova, "'Odna', SSSR (1931)," *Iskusstvo kino* 12 (1991): 162–164; Zorkaia, "'Odna' na perekrestkakh"; Sabine Hänsgen, "'Audio-Vision': o teorii i praktike rannego sovetskogo zvukovogo kino na grani 1930-x godov," in *Sovetskaia vlast' i media*, ed. Hans Günther and Sabine Hänsgen (St. Peterburg: Akademicheskii Proekt, 2006), 350–364. In particular, Elena Stishova has argued that in *Alone* we can see the work of an apparatus that suppresses (*rabotu apparata podavleniia*) (in Zorkaia, "'Odna' na perekrestkakh"). I am particularly grateful to Elena Mikhailovna for bringing this film to my attention.

18. Youngblood, *Soviet Cinema*, 189.

19. Sergei Eisenstein, Vsevolod Pudovkin, and Grigori Alexandrov's 1928 "Statement on Sound" has often been read as an antagonistic response to the coming of sound. (Originally published as "Zaiavka," *Zhizn' iskusstva* [August 5, 1928]: 4–5; translated in *The Film Factory*, ed. Richard Taylor and Ian Christie [London and New York: Routledge, 1994], 234–235). Thus, for example, John Riley notes in his monograph on Dmitri Shostakovich's film music: "In their *Statement on Sound*, Eisenstein, Pudovkin and Alexandrov opposed realistic sound, proposing a 'counterpoint' between it and the image.... Musical counterpoint comprises two or more *independent* voices, but here the image was the primary element, with the soundtrack either reflecting or setting up a 'sharp contrast' to it" (Riley, *Dmitri Shostakovich*, 4; emphasis in the original).

20. Boris Eikhenbaum, "Problemy kino-stilistiki," in *Poetika kino*, ed. B. Eikhenbaum (Moscow: Kinopechat', 1927), 13–52; translated as B. Ejxenbaum, "Problems of Cinema Stylistics," in *Russian Formalist Film Theory*, ed. Herbert Eagle (Ann Arbor: Michigan Slavic Publications, 1981), 55–80.

21. Eikhenbaum, "Problemy kino-stilistiki," 24–25; "Problems of Cinema Stylistics," 61; emphasis in the original; translation modified. See also Béla Balázs on the talkie as an "unnatural form of art—rather as though a painter were to prefer painting pictures without colors" (Béla Balázs, *Theory of the Film* [New York: Dover Thrift, 1970], 71–72). As Youngblood points out, Eikhenbaum and Tynyanov (whose essay "On The Foundations of Cinema" also appeared in the 1927 *Poetika kino*) were some of the most outspoken critics of the new sound technology (Youngblood, *Soviet Cinema in the Silent Era*, 223).

22. Sergei Eizenshtein, *Memuary* (Moscow: Redaktsiia gazety "Trud," 1997), 2: 36.

23. See Ian Christie, "Soviet Cinema: Making Sense of Sound," *Screen* 23, no. 2 (1982): 34–49; here: 36; republished as Christie, "Making Sense of Soviet Sound," in *Inside the Film Factory: New Approaches to Russian and Soviet Cinema*, ed. Richard Taylor and Ian Christie (London: Routledge, 1991), 176–192.

24. «Ее одолевает легкий кошмар. Неужели—нет спасенья? И государство, пославшее ее в эту глушь, в эти леса, на этот мороз, не спасет ее?» (She is overcome by a vague terror. Is it possible that there's no rescue? That the government sending her to this backcountry, to these forests, to this cold, won't save her?) RGALI f. 966–2–347, l. 37.

25. Zorkaya points out that other lines of dialogue were recorded but did not make it into the final cut of the film—such as the line "I will go!" (*Ia poedu!*), looped and later replaced by intertitles, and the awkward "He is killing your sheep for meat!" (*on rezhet na miaso vashikh baranov*) that Kozintsev made Kuzmina practice over and over. According to Zorkaya, Kuzmina's voice in the film is dubbed by Maria Babanova (Zorkaya, "'Odna' na perekrestkakh," 148).

26. Avital Ronnel, *The Telephone Book: Technology, Schizophrenia, Electric Speech* (Lincoln: University of Nebraska Press, 1989), 2.

27. This also reflects the common use of *prizyv* in the twenties. Some examples are: Nikolai Svishchov-Paola's photograph *"Prizyv"* (1920s); Yakov Protazanov's 1925 film *Ego prizyv / His Call*. Another use of the loudspeaker to deliver the *Leninskii prizyv* can be seen in Gustav Klucis's

"Maquette for Radio-Announcer" (1922), a design for a street-based loudspeaker to be placed at city intersections where it was to broadcast a speech by Lenin on the fifth anniversary of the Russian Revolution.

28. Ronnel, *Telephone Book*, 5.
29. Althusser, *Lenin and Philosophy*, 116.
30. Althusser, *Lenin and Philosophy*, 116, 117; emphasis in the original.
31. Althusser, *Lenin and Philosophy*, 118; emphasis in the original.
32. This, of course, goes against the use of strictly realistic sound in Soviet cinema, in which, as Youngblood points out, "the viewer should always be able to tell [the sound's] source" (Youngblood, *Soviet Cinema*, 224). On the notion of *la voix acousmatique* see Michel Chion, *La voix au cinéma* (Paris: Editions de l'Etoile, 1982); translated as *The Voice in Cinema* (New York: Columbia University Press, 1999); on its use in *Alone* see Hänsgen, "Audio-Vision," 358–362; on *la voix acousmatique* and totalitarianism see Slavoj Zizek, *Looking Awry: An Introduction to Jacques Lacan through Popular Culture* (Cambridge, MA: The MIT Press, 1992), 126–130.
33. Mary Ann Doane, "The Voice in the Cinema: The Articulation of Body and Space," *Yale French Studies* 60, Cinema/Sound (1980): 33–50; here: 42.
34. On the ideological implications of the voice-over, see Pascal Bonitzer, "Les Silences de la voix," *Cahiers du Cinéma* 256 (February–March 1975): 22–33. Quoted in Mary Ann Doane, "The Voice in Cinema," 42.
35. Vladimir Maiakovskii, "Vladimir Il'ich Lenin," *Polnoe sobranie sochinenii v trinadtsati tomakh* (Moscow: Gos. izadt. khud. lit., 1957), 231–309.
36. Maiakovskii, "Vladimir Il'ich Lenin." For a discussion of the way Lenin's absent presence in the poem disturbs the standard binary opposition of life and death, marking the place of slippage between the two states, see Dragan Kujundzic, *The Returns of History: Russian Nietzscheans After Modernity* (Albany: SUNY Press, 1997), 113–114. On the figure of the apostrophe, see Paul de Man, "Autobiography as De-Facement," in *The Rhetoric of Romanticism* (New York: Columbia University Press, 1956): 67–81.
37. The building is either Narkompros (The People's Commissariat of Enlightenment) or Narobraz (The Department of People's Education).
38. This sequence is a precursor to Charles Chaplin's *Modern Times* (1936) in which everything *but* the human beings make noise. Chaplin's suggestion is that every advance in technology (and sound film being yet another leap in the technological rather than aesthetic development of cinema) extends our capabilities while chipping away at our humanity. Kuzmina's brief imprisonment in the telephone booth that prevents *her* voice from reaching the viewer suggests a similar take on the powers of technology.
39. In the original screenplay the woman in the administrator's office answers to "Nadezhda Konstantinovna" (RGALI f. 966–2–347, l. 16). In the film, Krupskaya is never mentioned by name, but we still see her grey bun and a picture of Lenin over her desk.
40. RGALI f. 966–2–347, ll. 14–16.
41. Judith Butler, *Bodies That Matter: On the Discursive Limitations of "Sex"* (London: Routledge, 1993), 121.
42. As with the earlier scene of the loudspeaker, this sequence is about partial disembodiment, voice-over that is and is not anchored to a body we can see. For Lenin as Soviet culture's "undead" also see Zizek, *The Sublime Object of Ideology* (London: Verso, 1989).
43. The 1930 screenplay draft of *Alone* ends with the following address to the audience: "[Kuzmina] disappears into the crowd. Along with the crowd she walks toward the camera [*apparat*]. And toward the camera, toward the audience, come the simple words: we've won—one! . . . What will *you* do?" («Она смешалась—с толпой. Вместе с толпой—она идет—на аппарат. И на аппарат, на зрительный зал идут простые слова: мы победили—раз! . . . Что же делаешь ты?»). RGALI f. 966–2–347, l. 44. The apparatus continues to reproduce the insistent call of the state.

44. That is to say, not acting out a wish or desire but a compulsion—what Freud termed "instinct" or "drive" (Ger: *Trieb*) that operates beyond the subject's agency. See Sigmund Freud, *Beyond the Pleasure Principle*, in *The Standard Edition of the Complete Psychological Works of Sigmund Freud*, trans. James Strachey (London: The Hogarth Press, 1986), 18: 3–64.

45. Riley, *Dmitri Shostakovich*, 14. In his otherwise excellent analysis, Riley substitutes the bey for Gerasimov in this scene.

46. See, for example, *The Devil's Wheel* (Chertogo koleso, 1926) and *The Overcoat* (Shinel', 1926).

47. Despite the invention of the dolly (around 1914), in most Soviet films made in the early-to-mid-twenties, the camera remained stationary, as a kind of passive observer or recorder of events—what F. G. Gukasian in his introduction to the volume *Kinooperator Andrei Moskvin* calls "the indifference of the film camera" (*besstrastie kinokamery*). F. G. Gukasian, *Kinooperator Andrei Moskvin: ocherk zhizni i tvorchestva; vospominaniia tovarishchei* (Leningrad: Iskusstvo, 1971).

48. Gukasian, *Kinooperator Andrei Moskvin*, 65.

49. The Republic of Altai is situated in the center of Asia at the junction of the Siberian taiga, the steppes of Kazakhstan, and the semideserts of Mongolia. However, Kozintsev, Trauberg, and Moskvin shot the climactic death sequence on Lake Baikal, because it provided a better location for the scene.

50. Part of the uncanny sounds of *Alone* were produced by Shostakovich's inclusion of the theremin in the sound track. See Albert Glinsky, *Theremin: Ether Music and Espionage* (Urbana: University of Illinois Press, 2000), 253. For more on the uses of the theremin in early Soviet sound film, see Chapter 2.

51. In Russian: "*kholodnoe i vrazhdebnoe beloe bezmolvie.*" E. Misalandi, *Odna*, VHS cassette, Russian Screen Classics, 2002.

52. Kozinstev, *Sobranie sochinenii*, 1: 196.

53. Kozinstev, *Sobranie sochinenii*, 4: 89.

54. RGALI f. 966–2–347, l. 38.

55. The ending of Nikolai Ostrovsky's *How the Steel Was Tempered* (Kak zakalialas' stal', 1932–1934) reads, "His heart beat fast. His cherished dream was realized! The steel bonds had burst, and once again, armed with a new weapon, he was returning to the fighting ranks and to life" (Nikolai Ostrovsky, *How the Steel Was Tempered*, trans. R. Prokofieva [Moscow, 1959], 2: 383).

56. I am referring to Lenin's *nekrolog* (obituary)—the chart that was set up on the building outside his home that reported on his condition: his temperature, his blood pressure, his mood. We see an animated version in Dziga Vertov's *Lenin Kino-Pravda* (Leninskaia kino-pravda / Kino-pravda #21, 1925).

57. As Riley notes, while the film avoids synchronized speech, there are intelligible voices, which the makers considered an "important element." He writes, "they often appear off-screen, but this can give them a God-like quality: cutting between Leningrad street tannoys [loudspeakers / public-address systems] and the Altai fills the entire country with news of Kuzmina's rescue" (Riley, *Dmitri Shostakovich*, 14).

58. In Russian: "*bezdushnaia sila*" (Kozintsev, *Sobranie sochinenii*, 1: 197).

59. This is precisely the difference in psychoanalysis between "desire" and "drive"; as Zizek puts it, "The horror of [the terminator] consists precisely in the fact that it functions as a programmed automaton who, even when all that remains of him is a metallic, legless skeleton, persists in his demand and pursues his victim with no trace of compromise or hesitation. The terminator is the embodiment of the drive, devoid of desire" (Zizek, *Looking Awry*, 22).

60. Kozinstev, *Sobranie sochinenii*, 1: 198. We might note in particular Kozintsev's last point about human eyes as well as about spectatorship/specularity (*zrelishche*): besides being a cinematographer of "lighting" Moskvin was also known for his shots of blazing eyes (this becomes

evident in *Ivan Groznyi* [Ivan the Terrible, dir. S. Eisenstein, 1944, 1958]), and their absence here can again be read as evidence of dehumanization.

61. Kristen Thompson, "Early Sound Counterpoint," 132.

62. Referring to Claude Ollier and the films of Michelangelo Antonioni, Gilles Deleuze refers to the "zone of emptiness," the "white on white which is impossible to film," as the "truly invisible" (Gilles Deleuze, *Cinema 1: The Movement-Image* [Minneapolis: University of Minnesota Press, 1986], 18).

63. As Kozintsev puts it in a letter to the actor Boris Chirkov in 1933, once the question of production of *The Bolshevik* had been resolved, "Trauberg and I left for Leningrad in order to join the battle for Socialist Realism" (Grigorii Kozintsev, "Iz pisem kinematografistam," *Iskusstvo kino* 7 [1995]: 112–121; here: 113).

chapter two

THE MATERIALITY OF SOUND
Dziga Vertov's *Enthusiasm* and
Esfir Shub's *K.Sh.E.*

IN THE MIDDLE OF DZIGA Vertov's *Stride, Soviet!* (Shagai, Sovet!, 1926), we find this remarkable sequence: an election is being broadcast over radio and loudspeaker, but the participants are all machines. We watch as buses assemble in front of the city Soviet, where "instead of an orator" there is a loudspeaker; "instead of applause" there are horns honking; where cars and buses, car horns and speakers "greet us" "in the name" of the Moscow Soviet. As Yuri Tsivian notes,

> What began as a commission by the sitting Moscow Soviet for a promotional movie, one which would show all the good things the Soviet had done for its city, was transformed by Vertov into something else entirely: a film experiment, an emotional film—anything but a picture that would help the Mossovet be reelected. In the end, the Mossovet refused to recognize *Stride, Soviet!*, and it was largely boycotted by film theaters. One can imagine the distress authorities must have felt when they saw what had been made of their election rally. No people are seen, just buses, cars, and various other vehicles gathered in the square to listen to the loudspeaker: one mechanical device talking to other mechanical devices about weapons and tools.[1]

While still a silent film, *Stride, Soviet!* relies on the visual image and rhythmic editing to communicate the idea of *sound*; machines speak to machines, "which listen (cone motif), watch (circular motif), and applaud (horns and pulsing)."[2] But what is perhaps most notable here is that sound—and more importantly, voice—is given over entirely to machines.

Documentary scholar Bill Nichols has stipulated that "nowhere in the world does the coming of sound to documentary film correspond exactly to the coming of sound to the feature fiction film," although we might argue that for Soviet cinema, the two transitions occurred more or less simultaneously, with documentary cinema leading the way in the introduction and uses of sound.[3] As Evgeny Margolit has pointed out, the production of sound films in the USSR was tied directly to the production of the *agitka* (that is, nonfiction propaganda) films, rather than to fiction films, as it was for the US or Western Europe.[4] Film historians, concludes Margolit, have up to now paid "little attention to the unprecedented fact that, unlike other cinemas, Soviet sound film begins with the production not of art, but of nonfiction films."[5] This meant that techniques and concerns of documentary (nonacted) films carried over into fiction films, including an emphasis on hearing and listening to technology.

In this chapter I am interested in how two of the most prominent Soviet documentary filmmakers—Dziga Vertov and Esfir Shub—alternately struggle with and showcase the new sound technology, attempting at the same time to remain true to their respective ideas about documentary, nonfiction, or "nonplayed" film. Moreover, I argue that in foregrounding sound and sound technology in their first sound films, Vertov and Shub are also highlighting film's *materiality* and the ability of sound to reach beyond the screen to physically (and not simply metaphorically) move the viewer. In both cases, this movement is ideologically driven—the production of Soviet subjects, directly addressed by the new sound technology—but it is also more than that. Vertov and Shub are interested in the *haptic* possibilities of a new sound cinema, in what we cannot see, but can sense via hearing and touch.

In the preface to her 2000 book, *The Skin of the Film*, Laura Marks notes that her title offers a metaphor to emphasize the way film "signifies through its materiality, through a contact between perceiver and object represented."[6] Early cinema, intercultural cinema, avant-garde, and experimental cinema—any cinema produced on the margins of dominant cinematic institutions—tends to foreground film's material nature, while "classic" narrative cinema eschews the baring of the cinematic device. Thus, the title credits that appear over the opening shot of Michael Haneke's 2005 *Caché* block the image we are ostensibly there to see, forcing us to pay attention to the surface, the skin of the film. But perhaps it is the opening sequence from Kira Muratova's *Melodiia dlia charmanki* (Melody for a Street Organ, 2009) that really communicates what film theory has been calling "the haptic": as the screen fades in from black, we see the frosted glass of a window pane, and then, a hand pressed on the glass, melting the ice, a hand print that slowly disappears. Here the emphasis is clearly on the *surface* of the image. The hand leaving an impermanent print on the frosted glass speaks to the nature of the cinematic trace, its materiality on the one hand (here as touch, surface, recognition/awareness of the textural [*faktura*]), and its *immateriality* on the other (the impermanence of the image, its lack of a true, honest relationship to the profilmic world). In other words, what Muratova gives us here is the simultaneous production and erasure of materiality.

As digital technology brings on the convergence of sound and image, voice and text, by erasing the difference between the different kinds of cinematic materiality, it is useful to go back to one of the moments when the material nature of cinema could still be perceived as a "contact between perceiver and object represented"—to the moment of the advent of sound, the moment when, as Friedrich Kittler puts it, "ears and eyes [first] become autonomous."[7] This chapter will explore the notion of the haptic as it relates to early Soviet documentary sound cinema and specifically to Vertov's 1930 *Enthusiasm: The Symphony of the Donbass* (Entuziazm: Simfoniia Donbassa) and Shub's 1932 *K.Sh.E.* (Komsomol: Patron of Electrification / Komsomol: shef elektrifikatsii) and the way sound gives film a material form, interacting directly with the viewer in a completely new way.

ENTHUSIASM: SYMPHONY OF THE DONBASS

Although in terms of their notions of documentary filmmaking Vertov and Shub occupied different ideological positions (Vertov's "life caught unawares" was perceived by critics in the twenties to be an exercise in subjective filmmaking, while Shub was praised for her completely objective "compilation documentaries," that assembled new films from preexisting archival footage), there is a fairly clear relationship between Vertov's 1930 *Enthusiasm* and Shub's 1932 *K.Sh.E.* Both films attempt to capture, by means of documentary filmmaking on the one hand and by means of the new sound technology on the other, the big industrial projects of Stalin's First Five-Year Plan—the coal mining industry of the Don Basin, and the completion of the first Soviet hydroelectric plant on the Dniepr River. Both films also emphasize and make audible the new *sound* apparatus by attempting to convey the materiality of sound and the means of its production and reproduction. We might, therefore, trace a kind of trajectory starting with Vertov's attempts to record new, never-before-heard documentary sounds to Shub's experiments in bringing us sound as a form of the haptic, where both attempt to use the new sound technology to "organize" hearing, to make sound in documentary film an organic part of the film's composition.

Dziga Vertov began his career in the cinema by experimenting with sound. According to Aleksandr Lemberg, the first time he met Vertov at the "poet's café" in Moscow, Vertov told him about his experiments with the recording of sound. Using a Pathéphone, he had attempted to record and edit street and factory noises. Talking to Lemberg at the café, Vertov discovered that his ambition of capturing reality could be better achieved through cinema. Lemberg, a newsreel cameraman, agreed to teach Vertov the basis of the medium.[8]

But Vertov's interest in sound predates even this early conversation with Lemberg. As far back as his school years, Vertov had already come up with a "Laboratory of Hearing," an attempt to translate sounds—and specifically, *industrial* sounds—into verbal language:

> On vacation, near Lake Ilmen. There was a lumber-mill which belonged to a landowner called Slavjaninov. At this lumber-mill I arranged a rendezvous with my girlfriend.... I had to wait hours for her. These hours were devoted to listening to the lumber-mill. I tried to describe the audio impression of the lumber-mill in the way a blind person would perceive it. In the beginning I wrote down words, but then I attempted to write down all of these noises with letters.
>
> Firstly, the weakness of this system was that the existing alphabet was not sufficient to be able to write down all of the sounds that you hear in a lumber-mill. Secondly, except for sounding vowels and consonants, different melodies, motifs, could still be heard. They needed to be written down as musical signs. But corresponding musical signs did not exist. I came to the conviction that by existing means I could only achieve onomatopoeia, but I couldn't really analyze the heard factory or a waterfall.... The inconvenience was in the absence of a device by means of which I could record and analyze these sounds. Therefore I temporarily left aside these attempts and switched back to work on the organization of words.
>
> Working on the organization of words, I managed to destroy that contrast which in our understanding and perception exists between prose and poetry.... Some of these works, which seemed to me more or less accessible to a wide audience, I tried to read aloud. More complex works, which required a long and careful reading, I wrote down on big yellow posters. I hung out these posters in the city. I attached them myself.
>
> My work and the room where I worked were called the "Laboratory of Hearing."[9]

Thus for Vertov, there was, in a sense, no time when image was privileged for its own sake but rather that sound-on-film technology had not yet caught up to what he had always imagined cinema to be. In 1925, he proposed the notions of *kinopravda* and *radiopravda*, suggesting that, "we must now talk about recording audible facts."[10] "Technology is moving swiftly ahead," he wrote, "A method for broadcasting images by radio has already

Figure 2.1. Vertov and Svilova at the editing table (SPUTNIK / Alamy Stock Photo)

been invented. In addition, a method for recording auditory phenomena on film tape has been discovered. In the near future man will be able to broadcast to the entire world the visual and auditory phenomena recorded by the radio-movie camera."[11] "Radio-ear," wrote Vertov in 1931, is the link between science and radio technology with the same goal—the organization of the workers' hearing, a transcript of the audible world. "Radio-eye" ("film-eye" plus "radio-ear")—is an opportunity to order the sights and sounds of the entire world.[12]

Even more than other Soviet montage directors, Vertov frequently relied on rhythmic editing and musical structure to communicate the idea of sound in silent cinema. "In their first statements concerning the future of the not-yet-invented sound cinema," wrote Vertov in 1929, "the kinoks (now the radioks) defined their course as leading from kino-eye to radio-eye, that is, to an *audible kino-eye, transmitted by radio*." He claimed that the kino-eye workers did not restrict themselves to the struggle for nonacted cinema; they also "prepared to meet the transition [to sound] fully armed, anticipating work within the radio-eye plan, the plan for nonacted sound cinema." He wrote that in *A Sixth Part of the World*, the titles were already replaced by a "word-radio-theme in contrapuntal construction." And his *The Eleventh Year*, he said, "was constructed as a film-object of sight and sound, edited to be heard as well as seen." He concluded that "the kinoks' theoretical and practical work (in contrast to acted cinematography,

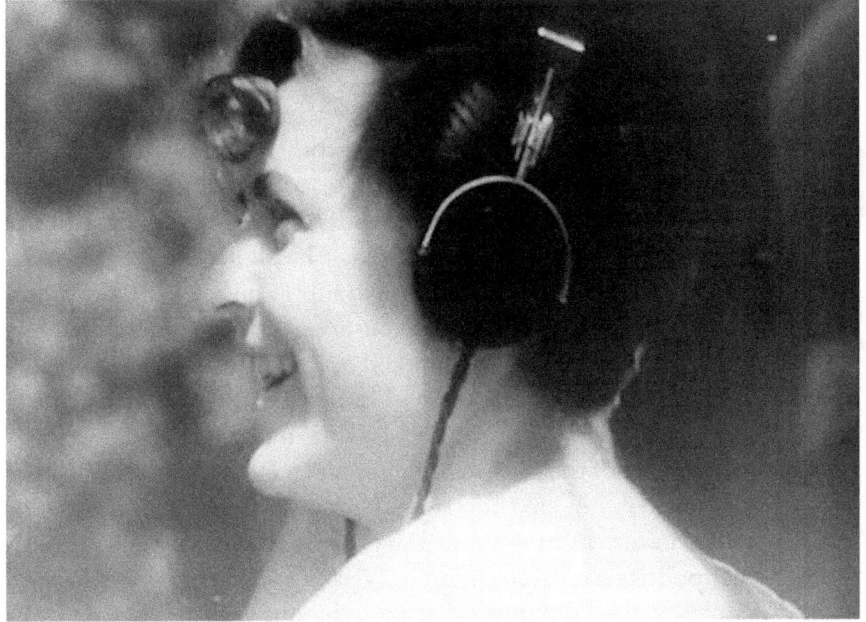

Figure 2.2. Radio operator (*Enthusiasm*, frame capture)

caught off guard) was in advance of our technical possibilities; they have long awaited the *overdue* (in relation to kino-eye) technical base for sound film and television."[13]

Vertov wanted direct, "live" sound to go with his "live" images, and this is what we see in his *Enthusiasm: Symphony of the Donbass* (completed in November 1930; released in April 1931[14]): the production of live recorded sound—not necessarily sync-sound, but sound recorded directly at the source rather than recreated in the studio—of sound and image as two equal elements of cinema. Importantly, Vertov was *not* one of the signatories to Sergei Eisenstein, Vsevolod Pudovkin, and Grigori Alexandrov's "Statement on Sound" (1928),[15] insisting that the real distinction to be made was not between synchronized and asynchronous/contrapuntal sound (or whether or not the source of the sound is visible on-screen), but between "authentic" and "natural" sound recordings and "fake" sounds produced in the studio. As he put it in a letter to the editors of the journal *Kinofront* (Cinema Front) in 1930, "Neither synchronization nor asynchronization of the visible with the audible is at all obligatory, either for documentary or for acted films. Sound and silent shots are both edited according to the same principles and can coincide, not coincide, or blend with one another in various, essential combinations. We should also completely reject the absurd confusion involved in dividing films according to the categories of talking, noise, or sound."[16]

In *Enthusiasm*, Vertov experimented with every different kind of sound and every possible kind of sound recording (with the exception of imitative sounds produced in a studio). Unlike his fellow avant-garde filmmakers, Vertov was never tentative about working with sound or with the new sound equipment, and he threw himself headlong into the project. His correspondence with the All-Ukrainian Film Studio (VUFKU), concerning the film that was to become *Enthusiasm*, dates from September 3, 1929. By the end of the year, he had worked out detailed production plans, instructions, and schedules, as well as ideas for the film's musical score.[17] As Vertov's Soviet biographer Lev Roshal wrote in 1982, "Enthusiasm" was not merely the name of the film and did not just refer to the enthusiasm of the Donbass workers—it also described Vertov's attitude toward his film and the new experiment in documentary sound cinema.[18] Indeed, if internal Soviet politics had been different, Vertov's *Enthusiasm* would have been the first Soviet sound film. As it was, the one and only Soviet-built sound camera designed by Aleksandr Shorin was given first to Abram Room at the Soiuzkino film studio to film *Plan for Great Works* (Piatiletka. Plan velikikh rabot, 1930) and Vertov had to wait for several months before he was finally able to get his turn with the new equipment.[19]

Because of this delay, the kinoks shot first without sound in the Donbass region from September to November 1929, and then in Leningrad in January 1930 (at St. Isaac's Cathedral, at the first sound theater and other locales around the city), while at the same time engaging in an intensive study of sound technology in Shorin's laboratory. After a crash course in Shorin's system of sound recording (involving experiments conducted both at the laboratory and in the open-air), the Vertov group shot documentary sounds and images in and around Leningrad until May 1930. A special "screening" of just the film's sound track took place in the Leningrad "Dom kino" (House of Cinema), previewing the capabilities of the sound camera and the possibilities of documentary sound recording.[20]

In June, the kinoks were in Kharkov for the Eleventh Ukrainian Party Congress (June 5–15, 1930), and soon after that went to the Donbass, where they remained until the end of July 1930.[21] The enforced delay in Leningrad allowed Vertov to work closely with Shorin on the new sound equipment and led to the production of a "lightweight" sound camera that the kinoks were able to take back inside the coal mines of Donbass. As Vertov's cameraman Boris Tseitlin wrote in the journal *Kino i zhizn'* (Cinema and Life)

Figure 2.3. Bodies and Machines (*Enthusiasm*, frame capture)

in May 1930, "The group's Leningrad work is coming to an end and the group is moving to Donbass, where the filming will be done exclusively synchronically, using the portable sound camera especially designed in Shorin's laboratory. The new camera 'Mikst' constructed by comrade Timartsev will be so compact and light that it will allow us to film in the most uncomfortable and difficult to reach places."[22]

The portable sound-on-film equipment allowed the kinoks to record authentic urban sounds: industrial noises in the harbor; sounds of the railroad and the railway station, streets, and trams; and snippets of conversations, marching bands, crowds at a May Day parade, and the like. In *Enthusiasm* sound is both "live" (produced by people and machines and recorded on the spot), and postproduced (manipulated and postsynchronized, which is to say, added to the image or used along with the image as part of the elements of montage). Vertov structured the film as a programmatic four-movement symphony in which leitmotifs and refrains develop a musical narration.[23] Instead of using imitative instruments to recreate

Figure 2.4. The din of machinery (*Enthusiasm*, frame capture)

sounds, the techniques that Vertov developed in his film were based on montage and relied on varying the speed of recorded sounds in postproduction. In this way, Vertov could edit the sound track by "cutting sounds, putting them in loops and combining them according to principles of musical composition."[24] For this, in late November 1929 together with the composer Nikolai Timofeev, Vertov developed a musical score that integrated noises and their transformation, distortion, and variation—anticipating the aesthetics of *musique concrète* by nearly two decades.[25]

In his 1931 text, "Let's Discuss Ukrainfilm's First Sound Film: *Symphony of the Donbass*," Vertov argued against the assertions by sound technicians and film workers (both in the USSR and abroad) that one can only record sound under the special conditions of a soundproofed, isolated studio; that one should only record artificially produced sounds on film; and that it is impossible to shoot documentary—and in particular, outdoor—sound. As Vertov put it, in shooting *Enthusiasm*, not only did the kinoks move the sound equipment outside, but they also made both the camera and the microphone "walk" and even "run," serving as the "lead icebreaker" for documentary film everywhere: "The final, decisive month of our sound shooting took place in a setting of din and clanging, amidst fire and iron, among factory workshops vibrating from the sound. Penetrating into the mines deep beneath the earth and shooting from the roofs of speeding trains, we abolished, once and for all, the fixity of sound equipment and *for the first time in history* recorded, in documentary fashion, the basic sounds of an industrial region (the sound of mines, factories, trains, etc.)."[26] More vitally, even though the sound recording in Donbass was done with portable equipment and recorded on a single track with the image (and while part of the original footage was lost due to technical factors), Vertov nevertheless strove to produce a film that was maximally complex in its interactions of sound and image, creating a nuanced interplay between the two tracks, while at the same time, both foregrounding and commenting on the new sound technology. Sound dominated the visual image, which was edited to fit the audio track, not the other way around.

As Lucy Fisher and Jeremy Hicks both note, Vertov's complex use of sound in *Enthusiasm* is an attempt to reveal the film's constructed nature—that is to say, that Vertov "disrupts naturalistic expectations of sound, manipulating or detaching it from source to remind the spectator that this is a film."[27] Sync-sound is only one of the ways that sound is used in this film; Fisher lists at least fifteen different sound techniques used by Vertov in the first part of the film alone, from disembodied sound to superimposition to distortion to sound collage.[28] Marching bands are recorded in synchronous sound, as well as numerous industrial machines, including hooters, pit-head lifts, coal trucks, drills, trains, whistles, and hammers, all recorded on location and combined synchronously with the image. There is also the pioneering use of sound in synchronized speeches, predating Soviet film's first interviews. Yet, as Hicks notes, by far the most interesting use of sound in this film is in the repetition and the detachment of industrial sound from its source and its use as a motif; over and over, we hear the sound of a steam hooter or whistle, whose sound is nothing if not uncanny.[29]

In his literary scenario for *Enthusiasm*, Vertov describes the use of sound in his film in terms of physical movement, an "invasion" (*vnedrenie*) of industrial sounds that penetrate deep into the factories, the streets, and the town squares. He writes,

> And finally, the most important observation.
> When, in *Enthusiasm*, the industrial sounds of the All-Union Stokehold arrive at the square, filling the streets with their machine music to accompany the gigantic festive parades;
> when on the other hand, the sounds of military bands, of parades, the challenge-banners, the red stars, the shouts of greeting, the battle slogans,

the orators' speeches, etc., fuse with the sounds of the machines, the sounds of competing factory shops;

when the work of bridging the gap in the Donbass passes before us as an endless "Communist Sabbath," as "the days of industrialization," as a red star, red banner campaign[;]

we must view this not as a shortcoming, but as a *serious, long-range experiment*.[30]

There is a material, physical force to the sound track of *Enthusiasm*, with sounds aggressively pushing against each other, and out to the consciousness of the audience. Fisher notes that "what one is most struck by in the first section of *Enthusiasm* is the sense of incredible tension that exists between the sound and visuals. The sound physically pushes itself away from the screen; and the two seem related in the manner of magnets with like poles aligned—physically separate, but interacting through lines of force." She notes that by breaking the unity of the film—by having the sound and the image to some degree "repel each other"—Vertov forever leaves the viewer within the space of the theater, "continually made aware of the sound track and visual track as separate entities."[31] This aggressivity was particularly on display in London, during the screening of *Enthusiasm* for the Film Society of London on November 15, 1931, when Vertov insisted on controlling the sound projection and "raising the volume at climaxes to an ear-splitting level," until he ended up being forcibly removed from the projection booth.[32] Despite this incident—which caused Thorold Dickinson to label Vertov "the most obstinate film personality of all time"—it was that London performance of his film that, according to Vertov, allowed him to hear his film properly for the first time and earned him his most cherished accolade, a note from Charles Chaplin, who called the film "one of the most exhilarating symphonies I have ever heard" and suggested that the "professors should learn from [Vertov], not quarrel with him."[33]

Yet, Vertov's choice of verbs of motion—*vkhodit'*, *vnedriat'sia* (to enter, to penetrate/invade)—also gives a bodily quality to the film and its sound track that echoes other references in his notes to the "living" and "breathing" power plants and factories, and the "voices of machines" which can be heard on the sound track. The 1929 sound scenario for *Enthusiasm* describes the sound of the ticking clock in the film's opening as a "heartbeat," and the "breathing" of the factory in the distance, with its "beating heart" and "electric pulse."[34] Not only the factory and the power plants, but also the film itself becomes a body with a pulse and a heart, and (later on) flesh and bone—sound that gives it a material form, pushing out beyond the two-dimensional surface into the movie theater and toward the consciousness of the spectator.

Writing about the haptic in *The Tactile Eye: Touch and the Cinematic Experience*, Jennifer Barker has noted that "as a lived-body in and for the world," the cinema uses *"modes of embodied existence* (seeing, hearing, physical and reflective movement) as the vehicle, the 'stuff,' the substance of its language." Thus, both film and viewer might engage in the act of looking closely, exhibiting doubt, or becoming enthralled, dizzy, or agitated, but each would enact those behaviors in a different way, because the "technologies" that enable those behaviors (e.g., the camera and the cornea, the zoom lens and the inner ear) are different, biological in the case of the viewer and mechanical in the case of the film. Viewer and film share certain ways of "being in, seeing, and grasping the world," despite their vast differences as "human and machine, one blood and tissue, the other light and celluloid."[35]

Particularly central to an understanding of Vertov's anthropomorphic bodily language is Barker's description of the film's "viscera" that consists of those "organs" or structures that "enable its conscious activities but are not, except in extraordinary circumstances, under its direct control." She notes that the power source, light source, sprocket holes, projector's gate, and other parts of the mechanism keep light and celluloid moving through the camera and projector "the same way that our viscera keep blood and other vital fluids moving through our bodies." And just as we cannot ordinarily control the rhythm of our heartbeat or circulation, the film doesn't have access to these things except in a few cases (film projection speed, for example) and special circumstances, as when experimental filmmakers turn their attention inward, meditating on the inner mechanisms of cinema. "Like lungs expanding and collapsing, the heart filling and emptying," she writes, "sprocket holes and optical sound-tracks are parts of the apparatus that usually escape the film's notice and our own, and that very rarely come into play in the telling of a story."[36] In *Enthusiasm*, both the actual body of the film (the film stock, optical sound track, sprocket holes, etc.) and the metaphorical body (the heartbeat, lungs, and pulse of the factories) are brought to our awareness; they penetrate into our consciousness, and physically interact with our own bodies, sitting in the theater. This is a form of embodied spectatorship that places particular emphasis on the interaction between spectator and film, with sound as the main mechanism of embodied perception.[37]

Contemporary critics referred to *Enthusiasm* as a "cacophony" (a charge that Vertov greatly resented). "Vertov fetishizes the machine and its sounds," wrote Petr Sazhin in *Kino-front* (March 1930), "Vertov has not given us a socialist Donbass Symphony. He has given us a cacophony of machines, he has given us crashing noise, din, hell."[38] Another article in

Figure 2.5. Biomechanics (*Enthusiasm*, frame capture)

the same paper claimed that they received a letter signed by eighteen cinematography students, describing *Enthusiasm* as a chaos of sounds and formalist nonsense: "From the sides of the screen comes nonstop nasal whistling and wheezing of the loudspeakers. A chaos of sounds made of metal structures and machine parts, wildly spinning frames, formalist nonsense. And all this is called, 'The Symphony of Donbass.'"[39] And Karl Radek, writing an editorial in the newspaper *Izvestiia*, quipped, "It is my deep conviction ... that we should call it 'Cacophony of Donbass' and never show it again."[40]

In his defense, Vertov complained that he was dealing with "deaf" critics (*glukhaia kritika*), while noting that while his film had been "wounded in battle," torn, with missing limbs and a hoarse voice, it was nevertheless victorious in what it had tried to do: "A champion, who has lost in battle three toes on the left and three toes on the right foot; torn, hoarse, covered in scars."[41] This "bodily" language appears not only in Vertov's own writings, but repeatedly, also in those of his critics. We see it, for example, in the discussion following the third preview of *Enthusiasm* in Moscow on February 8, 1931: "The Gastev approach noticeably lords over the entire film: the human being is but an appendage of the machine. Because the film has no 'backbone,' it completely falls to pieces and we can't see where it's leading."⁴² Like the observations of the (most likely imaginary) cinematography students and Vertov himself, these descriptions underscore the *materiality* of the film: its whistling and wheezing; its hoarse voice and torn skin; its wounded and invalided body.

Vertov's failure (at least for his contemporary Soviet critics) lay in part in his underestimation of what Michel Chion would later refer to as cinematic "vococentrism"—the prioritizing of the human voice-over and above all other sounds in cinema. "In actual movies, for real spectators," writes Chion, "there are not *all the sounds including the human voice. There are voices, and then everything else.* In other words, in every audio mix, the presence of a human voice instantly sets up a hierarchy of perception."⁴³ Chion's vococentrism helps to clarify the way in which Vertov's *Enthusiasm* failed to produce the right kind of effects on an audience first learning to "hear" films. Like many of the major Soviet filmmakers of the twenties, Vertov thought of the human voice as only one element of sound cinema among many. Vertov wanted sound to remain material and, to some degree, separated from the moving image. The woman listening to the radio through headphones in the beginning of the film foregrounds sound's physical presence. It seems vital, as Oksana Bulgakowa suggests, that later in the film she translates the sounds she hears not into images, but into sculpture, into a form that is tactile and tangible.⁴⁴ Detached from its source for much of the film, the industrial whistle we hear in *Enthusiasm* reminds us that we are, for the first time, "hearing" film.

Vertov imagined that of the different kinds of sounds recorded for the film, ideological speeches and slogans would assume a primary, active role, over the general din of the factories and machines. (As he wrote in his 1930 author statement, this is "the first film written with the voices of machines."⁴⁵) However, because of the numerous difficulties involved with initially obtaining and working with brand new, Soviet sound equipment, as well as with screening the film in Soviet theaters with inadequate sound projection, the stratification of the sound levels of the film did not come through.⁴⁶ In a diary entry from 1934/1935, Vertov mourned that he "had made a mistake when [he] gave in, submitted to management's demands and began to edit *Enthusiasm* even though [he] knew full well that all the recorded human material was ruined due to technical reasons [*ves' zasniatyi chelovecheskii material po tekhnicheskim prichinam pogib*]."⁴⁷ Contemporary Soviet critics attacked *Enthusiasm* in part because in this film the distinction between the different kinds of recorded sounds was not given any clear hierarchy; radio, speeches, music, church bells, factories—all

Figure 2.6. Loudspeaker (*Enthusiasm*, frame capture)

spoke with the same urgency, failing to prioritize human and nonhuman "voices." It was a mistake Vertov would try to rectify in his next film, *Three Songs of Lenin* (Tri pesni o Lenine, 1934).

K.Sh.E. (Komsomol—Patron of Electrification)

This of course was not the first time Vertov's films came under severe criticism.[48] After the release of *The Eleventh Year* (Odinnadstatyi, 1928), *Lef* critics Viktor Shklovsky, Osip Brik, and Sergei Tretyakov criticized Vertov's fast-moving, "metrical" montage editing of short takes and artistic cinematography of "life caught unawares" as distorting material reality and as incomprehensible to the masses. By contrast, fellow documentary filmmaker (and close friend of Vertov) Esfir Shub's reliance on found archived footage and her use of long takes were seen as restoring authenticity to the film document and connected with the masses. This was particularly true of the reception of her *Fall of the Romanov Dynasty* (Padenie dinastii Romanovykh), assembled and released in 1927, and commonly thought of as the first compilation documentary ever produced. Following Shub's lead, *Lef* critics argued in favor of documentary films composed largely of long takes, which would allow for contemplation and examination of the

Figure 2.7. "A constructivist evening" [Vecherinka konstruktivistov], with Esfir Shub (bottom right) and Rodchenko's poster for Vertov's Kino-Eye (Art © Estate of Alexander Rodchenko/RAO, Moscow/VAGA, New York)

material. They claimed that this method and form would help film become less a product of an individual vision, literally and figuratively, and thus less likely a distortion of reality. Using many different people to film raw material would make the images more relevant to a variety of viewers. And the long take would restore authenticity to the document by imbuing particular images with more authority.

Like many early Soviet filmmakers, Shub began her career in the theater, as one of the officers in the Theater Department of the People's Commissariat of Education (Narkompros). Prior to 1917, Shub had studied literature in Moscow, with much of her time spent with the family of Aleksandr Ertel, a writer with close connections to such prominent avant-garde poets, writers, and artists as Vladimir Mayakovsky, Velimir Khlebnikov, Andrei Bely, and David Burliuk. After the Revolution, Shub dropped her study of comparative literature to attend the seminar of the Institute for Women's Higher Education given by progressive scholars and social activists in Moscow. As part of her theater work for Narkompros, Shub collaborated with Vsevolod Meyerhold and Mayakovsky, continuing her close ties to the Russian avant-garde.

Figure 2.8. Esfir Shub at flatbed with celluloid-strip
(From the Holdings of the RGAKFD, Krasnogorsk)

Her career in the cinema, however, began as a film editor for Goskino (State Cinema), in 1922, where she was put in charge of reediting foreign films imported for Soviet distribution, and where she produced her own compilation documentary films, of which the best known are *The Fall of the Romanov Dynasty* (1927), *The Great Road* (Velikii put', 1927), and *The Russia of Nicholas II and Lev Tolstoy* (Rossiia Nikolaia II i Lev Tolstoy, 1928). At Goskino, Shub reedited over 200 foreign films and ten domestic feature films. Because of the nature of her work, Shub became an expert at montage, experimenting with composition and rearrangement, and creating new montage units on the editing table. Together with Sergei Eisenstein, for example, Shub reedited Fritz Lang's *Dr. Mabuse* (1922), in which, according to Shub, they "changed the narrative structure of the film as well as the intertitles. Even the film's title was changed; it became *Gilded Mold* (Pozolochennaia gnil')."[49] Friends with Vertov and married to avant-garde artist Aleksei Gan,[50] Shub thought of cinema as a constructivist enterprise, in which the method of montage allowed her to assemble archival footage in order to tell a new story with previously existing material. To make successful compilation films she needed to edit not just for artistic and ideological consistency, but also for differences in style, quality, format of film stock, and speed—all this was necessary to achieve visual consistency.[51]

Shub thought of her work as similar to that of an engineer who would construct a new building or machine from already existing parts. Mikhail Yampolsky calls Shub's films "reality at second hand," a kind of "ready-made" cinema, in which raw material remained "simply material until it could be carefully examined."[52] The length of an edited sequence became one of Shub's main formal achievements. For fellow filmmakers and critics, like Lev Kuleshov, Shub's success lay in the slower pacing of her editing, particularly when compared to that of Mikhail Kaufman (Vertov's brother and main cameraman in the late 1920s), who, according to Kuleshov, "had not grown out of his inclination towards rapid montage." In 1929 Shub formulated the basic aim of her montage practice, writing, "emphasis on the fact is an emphasis not only to show the fact, but to enable it to be examined and, having examined it, to be kept in mind."[53] For Yampolsky, Shub presents the raw material of newsreels as something alienated from the viewer and director, "as some kind of unknown, alien and inert object, at which one must look askance."[54] While this may be true for the compilation documentaries of the twenties, I want to argue here that in *K.Sh.E.* we see something else. Shub's first sound film is not about distancing objects, but about bringing them closer. In *K.Sh.E.*, the objects "speak" for themselves, through a mode of narration that goes beyond the visual.

Like many of her fellow filmmakers, Shub initially understood the coming of sound and its first implementations in the West as a major step backward for the Soviet montage school. She described her first experiences watching German and American sound films (including Al Jolson's *The Singing Fool*, 1928) in Berlin in 1929 as a moment of profound disappointment, but also of optimism. Commenting on the American film *Submarine*, in which sound was added in postproduction, she writes, "The musical accompaniment, the din of the sailors' voices, the pounding and the noise—none of these were organically linked with the work as a whole. The sound was metallic, deafening, unclean."[55] This is not defeat, however, she notes, but simply the wrong approach. Sound film is the future: "We know that the sound film and the radio screen will give the non-played film a real opportunity to become the most perfect instrument of international communication." Like Vertov, Shub argues that in nonplayed cinema, "the most important thing is to learn to record sound, tone, voice, noise, etc., authentically, with the same utmost expressiveness with which we have learned to record authentic, unstaged, real nature." "We want to direct all our efforts," she writes, "towards mastering the invention, forcing it to serve us without surrendering the positions we have won in silent cinema." We are, says Shub, "the future organizers of sound."[56]

The 1932 sound documentary *K.Sh.E.* was Shub's first attempt to "organize sound." Shub was commissioned by the Central Committee of the Komsomol (TsK VLKSM) to make the film; however, as she notes, she had also asked for permission to make a film about Magnitogorsk (a commission that went to a different director who promised to make the film half documentary half "played"—the film was never completed); and another about the construction of the White Sea-Baltic Canal, which she could not undertake because she was busy with *K.Sh.E.*[57] In her memoirs she described the sound work on the film in the following way:

> The film *K.Sh.E.*—along with the movies *Counterplan, Men and Jobs*, etc.—is one of the first sound films. It was supposed to reflect the struggle of the Komsomol for the electrification of the countryside. I made not only synchronous recordings, but also simply recorded documentary noises, sounds of machinery in factories, the noise of construction sites, water, crowds, echo, singing birds, the sounds of the gramophone merging with the noise of water during the scene of Americans bathing on the bank of the Dnieper, and more. When the film was ready, I edited these sounds and synchronous recordings together with the images.[58]

In *K.Sh.E.* there is genuine location sound, as well as other forms of audio recordings. Rather than sound working as a separate, independent

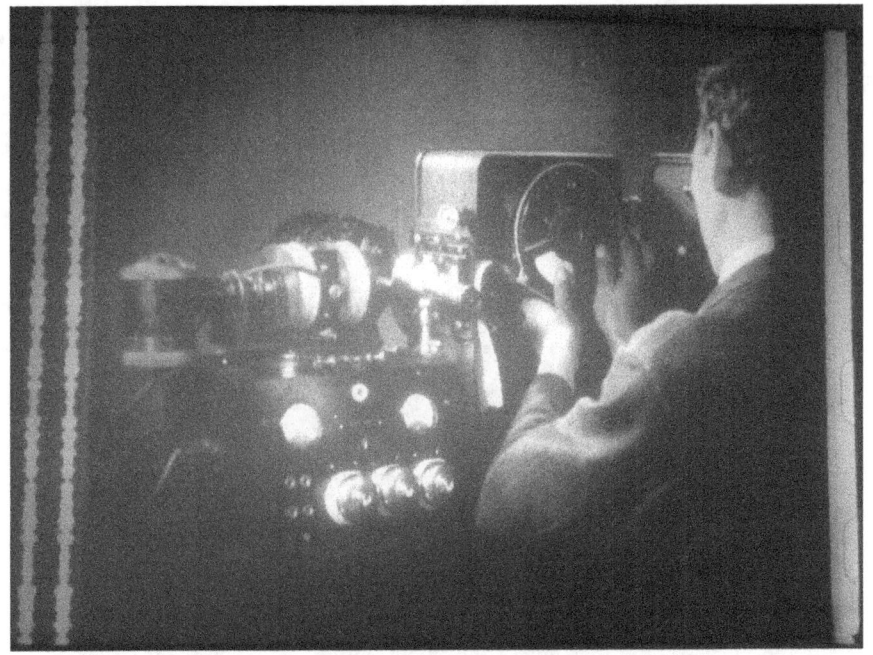

Figure 2.9. Threading the film camera (*KShE*, frame capture with visible soundtrack)

element in contrast to the image (as was advocated by Eisenstein et. al. in their "Statement on Sound"), Shub, as Hicks puts it, "respects the integrity of each sound, its real length and relation to the event," and consequently synchronizes much more than Vertov did in *Enthusiasm*.[59] (But much less, for example, than fellow documentary filmmaker Vladimir Erofeev, whose *The Olympics of the Arts* [Olimpiada iskusstv, 1930], famously recorded sound and image on the same piece of film, therefore eliminating—or at least, greatly reducing—the possibility of montage.)

Moreover, in *K.Sh.E.*, direct sound recording and dubbed sound are combined with the symphonic music Gavriil Popov scored for the film. The opening sequence—an "overture" that corresponds to the first movement of Popov's Suite from 1933[60]—takes place in a studio where a musical performance is shown being recorded, featuring a theremin, whose unusual sound is offset with human voices of soprano and tenor. After seeing *K.Sh.E.*, Eisenstein fired off a telegram to Popov, congratulating him on the "marvelous sound-sight victory."[61] The film's opening shows us preparations for sound recording, an orchestra tuning up, a hand playing the theremin, and sound being recorded onto the sound track, shots all meant to underscore the materiality of the new sound recording equipment, as

Figure 2.10. Orchestra and Theremin (*KShE*, frame capture with visible sound track)

well as to capture what cannot be seen—what both John MacKay and Joshua Malitsky have called the "movement of energy" or the "movement of power"—electricity flowing between objects and making possible cinema itself.[62] Indeed, while Vertov emphasized hearing and listening (the "radio-ear") in *Enthusiasm*, he did not particularly focus on the recording and production aspects of the new sound cinema, the way he had emphasized the "kino-eye" and the entire filmmaking process, from shooting to editing to screening in his 1929 *Man with a Movie Camera*. Shub, on the other hand, does precisely this in *K.Sh.E.*; she opens the film with a "working moment"—the recording of Popov's overture at the Moscow Sound Factory, placing sound recording and reproduction at the forefront of her experiment.[63]

Indeed, it is worth looking closer at this opening sequence. *K.Sh.E.* opens with a series of title cards, followed by a close-up of a filmstrip being threaded through a projector. In the background, we hear voices talking and an orchestra tuning up. We see the cameraman moving his unit into place (tracking left to right across the screen), one of the sound engineers adjusting the potentiometer, and Shub's assistant Nato Vachnadze waiting to turn on the sound recording equipment.[64] A tight close-up of a hand vibrating in space is synchronized with eerie musical sounds and a male

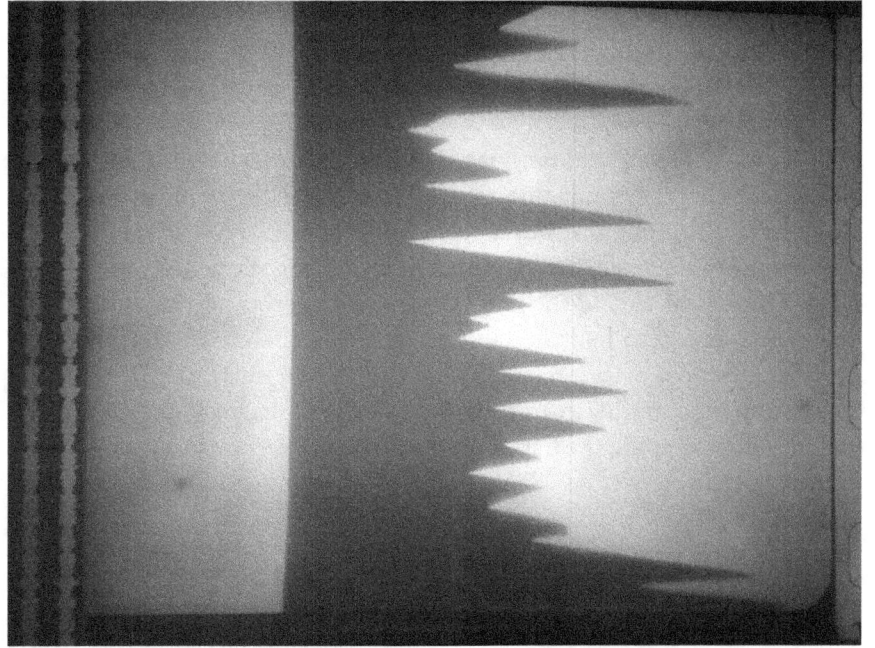

Figure 2.11. Visualizing the sound track (*KShE*, frame capture with visible sound track)

singing voice, while the next several shots clarify what we are seeing and hearing. A cut to a medium shot reveals the soloist Konstantin Kovalsky playing the theremin, with the rest of the orchestra behind him, and then the camera tracks back to show us the cone of the sound recording apparatus. A crane shot completes this sequence by giving us an overhead shot of the studio where Popov's overture is being performed, followed by medium shots of the cameraman looking through the viewfinder but seeing the optical sound track on which the music is being recorded.

From here, we return to shots of the technology (projector, film, potentiometer) with which we started, but now presented in reverse order: the cameraman tracks right to left across the screen, moving into his original position; the film strip rushes through the gates of the projector and comes to a stop; and Vachnadze turns off the sound recording apparatus. The camera, returning once more to the overhead shot of the studio orchestra, captures the final, exuberant notes of the overture. A slow tilt up into the black space above the studio stage brings this prologue to a close, and in the next shot we see Lenin's Mausoleum in Red Square and hear the toiling of the bells of Spasskaya Tower. Before that happens, however, we have this curious sequence. As the music reaches a crescendo, we cut to a close-up of the conductor's profile and animated movements, his beak nose and enthusiastic conducting graphically matching the optical sound track in the next shot. A cut back to Vachnadze shows her laughing, as if she is in on the joke.

The joke here, as Malitsky has suggested, may very well be the resemblance between the conductor's pointed nose and the pointed lines of the variable area sound track, but it speaks also to the larger issue at stake in this opening sequence.[65] Not only is the opening sequence to *K.Sh.E.* a clear moment of baring the device—the uncovering of the work of the cinematic apparatus and the labor involved in the production of sound film—the prologue, and this series of shots in particular, are also drawing a direct connection between the film and the body, between energy and sound, foregrounding the haptic, embodied relationship of the new sound cinema and the spectator. "Seeing" the animated lines of the sound track, Vachnadze laughs, marking the degree to which the film's body and the spectator's body might be said to "exist in a relationship of analogy and reciprocity."[66] As Barker notes in *The Tactile Eye*, though neither identical nor completely divergent, the film's body and the viewer's body are irrevocably related to one another: "They are counterparts, their muscular behaviors inspired, imitated, and sometimes resisted by one another."[67]

We see a clear indication of this reciprocity in Shub's opening sequence, in the way the film body "models itself on human styles of bodily comportment" (in this case, the exuberant physical performance and looks of the conductor), and in the way the viewer's body in turn "mirrors the muscular behaviors of the film body" (Vachnadze's laughter as a bodily response to the sound track's imitation of another human body).[68] Just as the earlier shots revealed the invisible movement of energy between the body of the performer (Kovalsky) and the theremin—a reciprocity between the human body and the instrument—so too the final shots of the prologue underscore the analogy of the film body and the body of the viewer. The choice of the theremin is not incidental here, but again underscores the relationship of reciprocity between the human body and another "body"— this time, not the film body, but the body of the instrument.[69] The theremin produces sound by means of an electro-magnetic disturbance. The metal antennae sense the position of the player's hands, specifically, the electrical capacity between the instrument and the performer's entire body. Indeed, the theremin, though it is played without direct bodily contact, "is very sensitive to the performer's bodily movement and even to his/her emotional state."[70]

Lev Theremin called his invention a "singing-vocal instrument"; Lydia Kavina, herself a thereminist (performer) calls it a "sinaesthetic instrument." The melody, she writes, "becomes visualization in the gesture. The fingers of a player draw listeners to look to them, like a magnet. The observer seems to see the music in the performer's hands."[71] Shub's choice of the theremin reminds us that this musical instrument was a Soviet invention, while also underscoring the fact that this is an instrument played by means of electricity—while we see the hand in motion, we are also aware of the lack of physical contact between the hand and the instrument. As Malitsky underscores, "the suspended hand wasn't a hand anticipating action. It was always already acting, always already producing music. It was a site of energy production not of potential energy."[72] In *K.Sh.E.*, music and sound are produced by means of an electrical current whose presence we can sense but not see.

From the opening "overture" of *K.Sh.E.*, we move to shots of telephone operators, people speaking about the First Five-Year Plan on the radio (in a variety of languages other than Russian), a singer being recorded, and repeated shots of a gramophone speaker. Shub is clearly in dialogue with Vertov here, in some sense, doing what *Enthusiasm* did not do—foregrounding the arrival "of the instrument in 'flesh and blood.'"[73] While Vertov's opening shots emphasize listening and hearing, he does not show us the technological aspects of sound recording. Instead, *Enthusiasm* is about capturing the sounds of socialist construction, providing an aural and visual document of industrial labor. While this is true for Shub as well, she goes further. In *K.Sh.E.* everything is meant to give us the tools of sound production and reproduction, stressing specifically the role of electricity in the generation of sound. Microphones, telephones, gramophone, radio—Shub's first sound film emphasizes again and again the materiality of the cinematic apparatus.

Unlike *Enthusiasm*, whose most memorable sound (besides the ringing of the church bells) might be the uncanny industrial noise produced by some kind of steam-powered whistle, Shub emphasizes human speech and music. She is credited with using the first ever sync-sound recording in the Soviet Union,[74] pointing to the fact that what we hear over and over in this film are speeches—frequently in languages other than Russian, including Armenian, English, French, and German—directly recorded by the camera. The DzoraGES segment of the film includes a direct sound recording of the well-known Soviet-Armenian writer Marietta Shaginian, the author of *Hydrocentral* (Gidrotsentral', 1930–1931), a novel based on her time spent at the construction of the Hydroelectric Power Station on the Dzoraget River in Armenia four years earlier. In general, there is a privileging of sync-sound recording throughout, the same way that Shub had earlier privileged the long take; sequences are allowed to unfold at their own pace, speeches are given in full, and dance numbers—of which there are several in this film—are shown at length.

Yet, Shub is doing still more. She is also emphasizing something ephemeral—what Jane Bennett in her work on new materialism has called "vibrant matter."[75] In *K.Sh.E.*, Shub is trying to show us, via sight and sound, but going beyond both, the nature of electricity as a force, as an organic link that ties together all the elements of the film on the one hand, and the film itself to the world it represents, on the other. This organic link is established by different kinds of visual rhymes that tie together elements we might not consider as related. Moreover, the film's very topic—electricity, and its association with Lenin—creates the invisible force by which all the filmic elements are united. Not only does a quote from Lenin ("The country must know its heroes") appear as a title card before the film begins, but separating the prologue from the sequence showing us the many different kinds of sound technologies is a shot of the Red Square and Lenin's Mausoleum. Like Vertov's 1934 *Three Songs of Lenin*, Lenin's absence and his directives haunt this project—like electricity, his "absent presence" is one of the many invisible forces that operate beneath the surface of this film.

Staying with this cut away for a minute, we might note the way Lenin's Mausoleum also visually echoes the patterns of the physical sound track we saw earlier reproduced on the screen. The jagged curves of Shorin's "variable area" optical recording are visually echoed by the sharp constructivist lines of Aleksei Shchusev's design for the mausoleum, and again, by the flags carried by demonstrators in Red Square. Another set of visual rhymes is set up between the film crew and the work crew, by means of a graphic match: the turbine for the Dneporstroi Power Plant visually reproduces the film camera's external features, linking the generation of electrical power to the device that will capture it on film. Shub is not satisfied, in other words, with merely foregrounding sound and its uses. She is interested instead in "organicity"—an organic link between image and sound, between film body and human body, between film and world.

Shub's writing about *K.Sh.E.* returns over and over to this notion of the "organic": she argues for an "organic link" (*organicheskaia sviaz'*) between the different montage elements and episodes of the film but also for the organic link between the film crew (*brigada*) and the construction crews of the Dneprostroi. She writes, "At Dneprostroi, our brigade was at first met with resistance. It was necessary to overcome this resistance, because it was impossible to work without an organic link to the Komsomol brigade and committee."⁷⁶ She stresses what she perceives to be her "organic participation" in the "grand epoch" (*moe organicheskoe uchastie v etoi [grandioznoi] epokhe*), but admits in a later statement that while the individual episodes of both *Today* (Segodnia, 1930) and *K.Sh.E.* were brilliant, the films lacked organicity, a narrative coherence to tie the episodes into an "organic, emotionally moving whole" (*otsutstvie organicheskoi, volnuiushchei sviazi v tselom*).⁷⁷ The whole thinking here is what Bennett and others have called "organicist": a model of coexistence in which each member obediently serves the whole.⁷⁸

In *Vibrant Matter*, Bennett contrasts an organicist model to that of *assemblage*, "ad hoc groupings of diverse elements, of vibrant materials of all sorts." Assemblages, she writes, are "living, throbbing confederations that are able to function despite the persistent presence of energies that confound them from within." An electrical power grid offers a good example of an assemblage: "It is a material cluster of charged parts that have indeed affiliated, remaining in sufficient proximity and coordination to produce distinctive effects." Vitally, the elements of such an assemblage, "while they include humans and their (social, legal, linguistic) constructions, also include some very active and powerful nonhumans: electrons, trees, wind, fire, electromagnetic fields."⁷⁹

Bennett's goal in her work is to expand our notion of agency beyond the human or even the biological, to "dislodge agency from its exclusive mooring in the individual," pushing it beyond human bodies and intersubjective fields "to vital materialities and the human-nonhuman assemblages they form."⁸⁰ In a chapter called, "A Life of Metal," she poses the following question: "It is no longer so controversial," she says, "to say that animals have a biosocial, communicative, or even conceptual life. But can nonorganic bodies also have a life? Can materiality itself be vital?" "Does life only make sense as one side of a life-matter binary or is there such a thing as a mineral or metallic life, or a life of the it in 'it rains'?"⁸¹ Quoting from Gilles Deleuze and Félix Guattari, Bennett formulates the notion of "life" as a "restless activeness, a destructive-creative force-presence that does not coincide fully with any specific body," what Deleuze, in *A Thousand Plateaus*, names "matter-*movement*" or "matter-*energy.*"⁸²

Just such a notion of the movement of energy was at stake in Vertov's films dedicated to the Donbass region.⁸³ John MacKay traces precisely this element of Vertov's cinematic construction in his second film on the

Donbass, *The Eleventh Year*.⁸⁴ He argues that in *The Eleventh Year*, Vertov finds a way to show that all existent phenomena are "manifestations of a single, continually mobile energy that leaves traces of its effects while not being itself directly representable." For Vertov, the task of documentary moving photography is to register "as vividly as possible the traces of energy"; the job of montage, on the other hand, "is to narrate the trajectory of energy, the conversions it undergoes, including the forms that still-latent energy might adopt." *The Eleventh Year* is thus "a film about energy, the harnessing of energy, and the forms that energy takes, as registered across changing material surfaces," in which an "energeticist" model, or myth, of cinematic signification finds its fullest expression.⁸⁵

The introduction of sound in *Enthusiasm*, however, does not heighten this notion of energy as a force that moves and organizes the world. Instead, sound in Vertov's film often works against the image, reminding us that what we see on the screen is a construct, a film-work that insistently showcases its difference from the world outside. I would argue, however, that Vertov's "movement of energy" is picked up by Shub in *K.Sh.E.*, which is in direct dialogue with *Enthusiasm*, as well as with Vertov's other films and his polemical statements about documentary cinema as a whole.⁸⁶ In her earlier work, Shub was a master of pure montage. Her compilation films assembled out of disparate pieces a visually and ideologically coherent narrative that went beyond (or even, often, against) the images' own intended content. But in *K.Sh.E.* something entirely different is at stake, produced as the effect of the introduction of sound. The power grid may be an excellent example of *assemblage*, but in Shub's film, it becomes part of the organicist view of the world: each member obediently serving the whole. Shub is no longer assembling preexisting pieces of film. Instead, "matter-*movement*" and "matter-*energy*" are at the heart of Shub's "organic link" between the different montage elements of her film, between the film crew and the construction crew, between the individual and the collective, between documentary film and the physical reality it tries to capture.

This notion is vital to Shub's representation of electricity, the central subject of the film. Electricity and electrification are part of the stakes of this film, which set out to document one of the Soviet Union's greatest construction projects—in this case, the building of Dniepr Hydroelectric Station on the Dniepr River in Ukraine to provide electrical power to a large portion of the country. The Dneprostroi Dam was built on deserted land in the countryside to stimulate Soviet industrialization. The design of the dam dated back to the GOELRO (the State Electrification Commission) electrification plan for the USSR, adopted in early 1920s. The

Figure 2.12. GOELRO Plan poster (author's collection)

dam and its buildings were designed by the constructivist architects Viktor Vesnin and Nikolai Kolli. Construction began in 1927, and the plant started to produce electricity in October 1932. Generating some 650 MW, the station became the largest Soviet power plant at the time and one of the largest in the world.

The massive electrification campaign, of which the building of the Dneprostroi and Dzoraget power plants were a part, was meant to transform everyday life in all corners of the Soviet Union at once, integrating center and periphery. Developed in conjunction with *radiofikatsiia*, electrification was envisaged as part of a communicative infrastructure, uniting vast distances both physically and symbolically, creating what Gleb Krzhizhanovsky called an "electrical skeleton" of power lines.[87] The image of an electrical grid covering all of the Soviet Union became an important symbol of the new spatial perception of the country as a single, unified whole, "forged into a single whole by a powerful network of national electronic transmissions, that grow from year to year."[88]

Yet, as Emma Widdis argues, the actual organization of the electrical grid was almost secondary to its metaphorical weight: "As a unifying network, the power grid was to carry ideological as well as electrical energy."

Lenin's little light bulbs (*lampochki Il'icha*) would "illuminate the darkest corners of the Soviet Union," lighting the way toward knowledge and the acceptance of Soviet power. Lenin's famous pronouncement in 1920 that "communism is Soviet power plus the electrification of the whole country" (*Kommunizm—eto est' Sovetskaia vlast' plius elektrifikatsiia vsei strany*), made clear the link between Soviet ideology and electric light: both brought "enlightenment" to the nation and both were meant to penetrate into every corner of the Soviet territories, no matter how distant or remote.[89]

This is again why the episode with the theremin is vital to an understanding of Shub's project in *K.Sh.E.* Lev Theremin began the research that led to the development of his musical instrument by using the human body as an electrical conductor—its ability to store up charges, or the property known as "capacitance." Theremin was intrigued by the notion that a person's natural body capacitance, when standing near an electrical circuit, could interfere with the capacity of the circuit, cause a change in its parameters, and set off a signaling device—a kind of simple, invisible burglar alarm.[90] As he developed his invention (not yet musical), he also became aware that the movements of his hand near the circuitry were interpreted as fluctuations in density, this time registering as changes in pitch. There was, as Theremin's biographer Albert Glinsky has put it, "some sort of music in this capacitometer, a new way of producing tones—maybe even an instrument."[91]

Theremin initially called his invention the "Etherphone," a reference to "ether waves" and the new era of radio broadcasting, unveiling the new device in October 1920. His first public concert and lecture was delivered the following month before the students of the Mechanical Engineers' Group at the Physico-Technical Institute, where he worked. In 1921, Theremin filed a Russian patent on the Etherphone, and in the fall of the same year he made his public debut with the instrument at the Eighth All-Union Electro-Technical Congress in Moscow, and—more importantly—at the national conference of the GOELRO. The conference was a forum for new applications of electricity, and Theremin "proudly piped the voice of his instrument through the new technology of the loudspeaker, just then available in Russia."[92] Moreover, the GOELRO debut won Theremin a meeting with Lenin, who understood the instrument as an ideal propaganda tool for electricity. Within weeks of the Kremlin audience, *Pravda* published Lenin's preface to Ivan Skvortsov-Stepanov's *Electrification of the Russian Socialist Federated Soviet Republic in Connection With the Transition Phase of World Economy*, a book that outlined Lenin's electrification plan, promoted the theremin, and summarized Lenin's famous pronouncement in

1920 that "communism is Soviet power plus the electrification of the whole country."[93]

Tactility, reciprocity, analogy—the movement of energy between bodies and machines—these are the operative terms of Shub's project in *K.Sh.E.*, an "organic" link between the new sound apparatus, driven by electricity, and the production of electrical power it is there to witness and to record. As Malitsky puts it, "Electrical energy—its production and circulation both inside and outside human bodies" is the central topic of Shub's first sync-sound feature-length documentary. For Malitsky, Shub turns to sound to make the invisible transfer of energy and the location of latent energy *sensible*: "What we see in this opening scene is both her primary theme and her method. The theme is that of energy (that which is normally invisible) and its sensibility, here as sound. Her method is that of registration (sound on film stock) and amplification (to the rest of the Union)."[94]

Still, in *K.Sh.E.*, we have a different vision of electricity and electrification than the typical images found in Soviet films of the 1920s, different even from Shub's own earlier representation of electrification in her 1927 *The Great Road*, in the episode titled "Let's Electrify the Soviet Village!" In *The Great Road*, as Widdis notes, the process of electrification was charted in a representative succession of images: "From a panorama of the village (illuminated at night, as in many images of the period), the camera moved successively closer, to street lamps, and then followed a cable running into an individual home and moved through a lighted window into the home itself."[95] In Vertov's 1926 *Stride, Soviet!* we see a similar visual metaphor at work; the electrical grid spreads out from the center to periphery, from Moscow to small towns to country villages, and finally inside the peasant hut, illuminating a portrait of Lenin, the "father of electrification," hanging on the wall. Soviet films promoting new electric (and by extension, Bolshevik) power typically showed electrical wires connecting an electrical tower to a house in a village, on the one hand, and a peasant family inside their home, working by electric light, on the other.[96]

In *K.Sh.E.*, Shub, instead, gives us electricity as music, and the production of "Lenin's little light bulbs" as a waltz. Defending her film against polemical attacks about incoherence and formalist uses of montage, she writes,

> Now, about light bulbs. Komsomol member Paramonova, from the light bulb plant, is a wonderful person. Paramonova tells me that we have surpassed the U.S. in light bulb production, that we have mastered the technology. And she has even written a book about how to make light bulbs. And now, she says, just look at us working . . . That's precisely what I wanted to

Figure 2.13a and 2.13b. Dancing lightbulbs (*KShE*, frame capture with visible sound track)

show: the absolutely magnificent rhythm of work—the rapid movement of hands. She is smiling, she doesn't even have time to talk. She makes it look easy and fun [*radostno, prosto i legko*]. And at the same time, this is purposeful work because they are free, because they don't have clocks or supervisors, because they know they are responsible for fulfilling the plan. And all this lightness and ease unwittingly [*nevol'no*] leads to a kind of waltz. Popov saw this, and he wrote a waltz that absolutely synchronized [*smontirovalsia*; came together, fit] with these segments.[97]

The sequence begins with a direct, sync-sound interview with Paramonova, but quickly changes to something else. From women's hands handling nearly transparent light bulbs we move to the light bulbs themselves, spinning and twirling, as if performing a dance. We see the glass of the light bulb melting into a drop, reminding us that glass is never completely solid, but remains partially liquid for its entire existence.[98] Finally, as Shub's camera moves closer and closer to the light bulbs, the glass surrounding the filigree elements melts away completely, and we see only the elements themselves, and eventually just an abstract play of lights, as the camera goes out of focus, blurring our vision. This moment of making light and energy *material* (visible, tangible as a light bulb, as glass) is equally a moment of the dematerialization of cinema. There is an insistence here on both the opaque and the transparent, on glass as something that is never completely solid but always in a state of change, always moving. Like Muratova's image of the hand leaving its print on the train window, what we have here is glass (the lens, the camera) looking at glass (the light bulb), which is itself produced from something liquid and melting that then takes on solid form. But Shub does something else here as well—in the last shots of the sequence she "melts" the image—everything becomes simply a play of light, cinema reduced to its most basic form: the traces of energy left on the filmstrip.

The absolute fit or perfect synchronization between the dancing light bulbs and Popov's waltz points us to the way Shub conceived of her film as a unified thing. For her first sound film, Shub was not interested in the contrapuntal or disjunctive uses of sound and image but in the creation of an *organic* whole. There is much more synchronous sound in *K.Sh.E.*— speeches, musical performances, radio programs, phonographs, sounds of industry recorded on site—and even when not using direct recording, Shub still synchronizes sound and image, creating a unified audio-visual field. In the Dneprostroi sequence, for example, images of the rushing water freed by the dam are accompanied by Popov's musical score, where the notes of the orchestra imitate the sounds of the water.

Thus, when the light bulbs begin to "waltz," there is a sense of the music emanating *from* the screen, rather than superimposed over it. There is no guiding narrative voice here, no disjunction between sound and image. Instead, we have an organic composition, in which objects and people speak "naturally" and "directly" from the screen. It is worth noting, for example, that even though we see both Stalin and Mikhail Kalinin at the Dneprostroi Dam on October 10, 1932, their commemorative speeches are not included in this film. Shub focuses instead on the speeches of workers, Komsomol leaders, industry experts—and, of course, Marietta Shaginian—delivered in a variety of languages, untranslated, and without pomp. Even in the famous sequence of the American civil engineer Hugh Cooper who has a dream he can speak Russian, Shub focuses on his humorous introductory remarks, underscoring the problem of translation. As Cooper notes, because he does not speak Russian, he will never know if his translator has communicated his message correctly, but he hopes the audience will enjoy it anyway. *K.Sh.E.*, in other words, lacks a standard documentary "voice" in the sense described by Bill Nichols in his *Speaking Truths with Film*; its address to the viewer is neither didactic nor imperative, but in fact is closer to the "overseen" and "overheard" quality of most fiction film.[99] There is no ideological "hail" here, no "Hey, you!" of interpellation that is the hallmark of documentary film. There is not even the "soft-spoken 'Consider this' of a poetic documentary."[100] Instead, we have engagement on an entirely different—sensorial and bodily—level, created through a play of music and light. Moreover, the emphasis on the hands and the rhythm of the work returns us to the opening prologue and the theremin. Indeed, a brief shot of Kovalsky's hand playing the theremin precedes the sequence of the dancing light bulbs. Going beyond optics, Shub is interested in the haptic modes of perception and communication, in rhythm, tactility, and the body as it interacts with the world via movement and touch.

In *K.Sh.E.*, Shub tries to represent the invisible by means of the visible and the audible, to give a sensory perception to that which we cannot see but can only feel (as light, as warmth, as energy). To a certain extent this accounts for the musical presence in the film, not only the opening concert, or the "waltz" of the light bulbs, but also the sounds of the marching band, the sailors' dance to an accordion, the phonograph on the beach (playing a jazz tune to which the Americans dance). All of these are attempts to show "by other means" the presence of energy—to generate a haptic sensory perception that moves us beyond silent cinema's insistently visual language. The closing sequence of the film takes place in a high voltage research lab with a demonstration of high voltage transmission. The abstract shapes of the electrical power transmitters are edited in fairly rapid montage and synchronized to an equally "rapidly" edited sound montage of electrical feedback and Popov's orchestral score. We hear the sonic booms of crossed electrical wires and the descending chromatic scales of stringed instruments—the movement of energy made visible and audible on the screen.

NOTES

1. [Tsivian, Yuri] 2008. *Dziga Vertov and the Soviet Avant-Garde*, program notes for a film series at Harvard Film Archive (March–April), adapted from Le Giornate Del Cinema Muto's catalogue, accessed January 31, 2015, http://hcl.harvard.edu/hfa/films/2008marchapril/soviet.html.

2. Joshua Malitsky, *Post-Revolution Nonfiction Film: Building the Soviet and Cuban Nations* (Bloomington: Indiana University Press, 2013), 155–156.

3. Bill Nichols, *Speaking Truths with Film: Evidence, Ethics, Politics in Documentary* (Berkeley: University of California Press, 2016), 74.

4. Evgenii Margolit, *Zhivye i mertvoe. Zametki k istorii sovetskogo kino 1920-kh–1960-kh godov* (St. Petersburg: Seans, 2012), 131.

5. Margolit, *Zhivye i mertvoe*, 84.

6. Laura U. Marks, *The Skin of the Film: Intercultural Cinema, Embodiment, and the Senses* (Durham: Duke University Press, 2000), xi.

7. Friedrich A. Kittler, *Gramophone, Film, Typewriter*, trans. Geoffrey Winhrop-Young and Michael Wutz (Stanford: Stanford University Press, 1999), 3.

8. Aleksandr G. Lemberg, "Dziga Vertov prikhodit v kino," in *Iz istorii kino: materialy i dokumenty*, ed. S. Ginzburg et al. (Moscow: Akademiia nauk SSSR, 1958–1962), 13: 39–49. See also Seth Feldman, "'Cinema Weekly' and 'Cinema Truth': Dziga Vertov and the Leninist Proportion," in *Show Us Life! Toward a History and Aesthetics of the Committed Documentary*, ed. Thomas Waugh (London: The Scarecrow Press, Inc., 1984), 3–20.

9. Quoted in: Andrey Smirnov, "The Laboratory of Hearing," in *Sound in Z: Experiments in Sound and Electronic Music in Early 20th-century Russia* (London: Koenig Books & Sound and Music, 2013), 25–28.

10. Dziga Vertov, "Radio-glaz," in *Iz naslediia* (Moscow: Eisenstein Center, 2008), 2: 99. Translated as Dziga Vertov, "Kinopravda & Radiopravda" (1925), in *Kino-Eye: The Writings of Dziga Vertov*, ed. Annette Michelson (Berkeley: University of California Press, 1985), 56.

11. Vertov, "Radio-glaz," in *Iz naslediia*, 2: 100.

12. Dziga Vertov, "Kino-Glaz, Radio-Glaz i tak nazyvaemyi 'dokumentalizm'," RGALI, f. 2091-1-91 (Vertov, articles, notes 1931–1933).

13. Vertov, "Ot 'kino-glaza' k 'radio'glazu. Iz azbuki kinokov," in *Iz naslediia*, 2: 408–412; Vertov, "From Kino-Eye to Radio-Eye" (1929), in *Kino-Eye*, 91. Emphasis in the original.

14. According to Feldman, "The production of *Enthusiasm* took approximately six months. There were considerable difficulties with the Ukrainfil'm (the name adopted by VUFKU in 1930) labs. This, along with problems in postproduction, delayed the preview of *Enthusiasm* until November 1, 1930. The official premiere of the film was delayed even further, until April 2, 1931. Even so, the film was released to the public some two months before Nikolai Ekk's *Road to Life*, the work often regarded as the first Soviet talkie" (Seth R. Feldman, *Dziga Vertov: A Guide to References and Sources* [Boston: G. K. Hall & Co., 1979], 13–14).

15. Sergei Eizenshtein, Vsevolod Pudovkin, and Grigorii Aleksandrov, "Zaiavka," *Zhizn' iskusstva* (August 5, 1928): 4–5. Translated as "Statement on Sound," in *The Film Factory: Russian*

and Soviet Cinema in Documents, 1896–1939, ed. Richard Taylor and Ian Christie (London: Routledge, 1988), 234–235.

16. Vertov, "Otvety na voprosy" (Leningrad, April 25, 1930), in *Iz naslediia*, 2: 192–195; "Replies to Questions," in *Kino-Eye*, 102–106; here: 106.

17. Feldman, *Dziga Vertov*, 13.

18. Lev Roshal', *Dziga Vertov* (Moscow: Iskusstvo, 1982), 224.

19. This first Soviet sound film did not survive. In his "March of the Radio-eye" (1930), Vertov accused Room of plagiarism, claiming that much of the *Plan for Great Works* was based on materials from his silent *The Eleventh Year* (1928), and that Room "had squeezed a rattling mass of the documentary 11th inside the prison of an acoustically isolated studio, dismembered the film in part and tattooed it with artificial toy-sounds." See "Mart Radio-glaza" (March of the Radio-eye), *Kino i zhizn'* 20 (1930): 14; and Smirnov, *Sound in Z*, 167.

20. For details, see N. P. Abramov, *Dziga Vertov* (Moscow: Izdat. Akademii nauk SSSR, 1962), 118.

21. For details, see John MacKay, "Disorganized Noise: Enthusiasm and the Ear of the Collective," *KinoKultura* 7 (January 2005), accessed at: http://www.kinokultura.com/articles/jan05-mackay.html.

22. Boris Tseitlin, "Simfoniia Donbassa," *Kino i zhizn'* 14 (May 11, 1930): 19. The camera was not precisely "lightweight": as John MacKay notes, "it turned out that their heavy and cumbersome sound equipment, in addition to their other gear, had to be pulled around most of the time by hand. At the film's first preview on 1 November 1930 in Kiev, Vertov said that the recording apparatus, which he had at his disposal for 1 month and 10 days in the Donbass, weighed 78 *poods* (approximately 2,808 pounds), that they had no transportation for it, and that 80 percent of the group's work consisted in 'sheer physical labor'" (MacKay, "Disorganized Noise").

23. Oksana Bulgakowa, "The Ear against the Eye: Vertov's Symphony," *Kieler Beiträge zur Filmmusikforschung* 2 (2008): 142–158; here: 143; Smirnov, *Sound in Z*, 167.

24. Smirnov, *Sound in Z*, 167.

25. MacKay, "Disorganized Noise." Smirnov makes a similar argument in his *Sound in Z* (see p. 167, for example), tracing the full history of early Russian/Soviet avant-garde experiments with sound.

26. Vertov, "Obsuzhdaem pervuiu zvukovuiu fil'mu 'Ukrainfil'm'—'Simfoniia Donbassa' (Avtor o svoem fil'me)," in *Iz naslediia*, 125–127; "Let's Discuss Ukrainfilm's First Sound Film: *Symphony of the Donbas* (the author on his film)" (1931), in *Kino-Eye*, 109.

27. Jeremy Hicks, *Dziga Vertov: Defining Documentary Film* (London: I. B. Taurus, 2007), 76; Lucy Fisher, "*Enthusiasm*: From Kino-Eye to Radio-Eye," *Film Quarterly* 31, n. 2 (Winter 1977–78): 25–34; here: 30.

28. Fisher, "*Enthusiasm*: From Kino-Eye to Radio-Eye," 30–31.

29. Hicks, *Dziga Vertov*, 76.

30. Vertov, "Entuziazm." Literaturnyi stsenarii. 1929. RGALI, f. 2091–1–35; originally published in *Sovetskoe Iskusstvo* (February 27, 1931); here, in the translation of "Let's Discuss Ukrainfilm's First Sound Film," in *Kino-Eye*, 111–112. Emphasis and punctuation in the original. Hicks makes a similar point about Vertov's use of the verb "to go" (Hicks, *Dziga Vertov*, 75).

31. Fisher, "*Enthusiasm*: From Kino-Eye to Radio-Eye," 33, 27.

32. Jay Leyda, *Kino: A History of the Russian and Soviet Film* (Princeton: Princeton University Press, 1983), 282; Feldman, *Dziga Vertov*, 14.

33. Facsimile in Abramov, *Dziga Vertov*, 123.

34. Vertov, "Zvukovoi stsenarii i skhema ozvuchivaniia fil'ma "Entuziazm" (Simfoniia Donbassa)" (December 31, 1929), RGALI 2091–1–36.

35. Jennifer M. Barker, *The Tactile Eye: Touch and the Cinematic Experience* (Berkeley: University of California Press, 2009), 8.

36. Barker, *The Tactile Eye*, 127.

37. For cinema and embodied affect, particularly as it applies to Sergei Eisenstein, see Anne Rutherford, "Cinema and Embodied Affect," *Senses of Cinema*, issue 25 (March 2003), accessed at http://sensesofcinema.com/2003/feature-articles/embodied_affect/. On the concepts of sensation, feeling, and touch, see Emma Widdis, *Socialist Senses: Film, Feeling and the Soviet Subject* (Bloomington: Indiana University Press, 2017).

38. Petr Sazhin, *Kino-front* (March 1930), RGALI, f. 2091–1–91, l. 99.

39. *Kino-front* (March 1930), RGALI, f. 2091–1–91, l. 99.

40. Karl Radek, "Dve fil'my." *Izvestiia* (23/IV/1931).

41. Vertov, "Pochemu molchit zvukovoe kino? Pervye shagi," *Kino* n. 21, RGALI, f. 2091–1–91; "Pervye shagi" (10/IV/1931), RGALI, f. 2091–2–174.

42. Quoted in MacKay, "Disorganized Noise" (see his n. 7 for details).

43. Michel Chion, *The Voice in Cinema* (New York: Columbia University Press 1999), 5. Emphasis in the original.

44. Oksana Bulgakova, *Sovetskii slukhoglaz: kino i ego organy chuvstv* (Moscow: NLO, 2010), 76.

45. Vertov, "Zaiavlenie avtora" (February 12, 1930), RGALI f. 2019, op. 1, d. 42.

46. According to A. Amasovich, Vertov's film was originally 3,100 meters in length. Soiuzkino "did not release the film in theaters in time for the October celebrations," but they did preview the film: twice in Moscow and once in Leningrad (on November 1, 1930), before Vertov reedited the film. The new version was 1,800 meters, released April 2, 1931. A. Amasovich, "Protiv bestolkovshchiny—chto proizoshlo s 'Entuziazmom'," RGALI f. 2091–1–91 (2). According to *Repertuarnyi ukazatel'*. Kinorepertuar (1936) the original film was 2,600 meters in length. See Feldman, *Dziga Vertov*, 115.

47. Dziga Vertov, *Stat'i, dnevniki, zamysly*, ed. S. Dobrashenko (Moscow: Izd. Iskusstvo, 1966), 187.

48. See Feldman, *Dziga Vertov*, 11.

49. Esfir' Shub, *Zhizn' moia—kinematograf* (Moscow: Iskusstvo, 1972), 75. See also Vlada Petric, "Esther Shub: Film as a Historical Discourse," in *Show Us Life! Toward a History and Aesthetics of the Committed Documentary*, ed. Thomas Waugh (London: The Scarecrow Press, Inc., 1984), 21–46.

50. Aleksei Gan was a Russian anarchist avant-garde artist, art theorist, graphic designer, and a key figure in the development of Constructivism after the Russian Revolution. Gan collaborated with Aleksandr Rodchenko and Varvara Stepanova on a Constructivist manifesto in 1922 and published his own pamphlet *Konstruktivism* in the same year. In 1922, he also founded the first Soviet film journal, *Kino-Fot* (or Kinofot).

51. On this, see Graham Roberts, "Esfir Shub: A Suitable Case for Treatment," *Historical Journal of Film, Radio and Television* 11, no. 2 (1991): 149–159.

52. Mikhail Yampolsky, "Reality at Second Hand," trans. Derek Spring, *Historical Journal of Film, Radio and Television* 11, no. 2 (1991): 161–171; here: 162–163.

53. Both quotes in Yampolsky, "Reality at Second Hand," 162–163.

54. Yampolsky, "Reality at Second Hand," 163.

55. Shub, "Pervye vpechatleniia," in *Zhizn' moia—kinematograf*, 271.

56. Shub, "K prikhodu zvuka v kinematograf," *Kino* (1929), reprinted in Shub, *Zhizn' moia—kinematograf*, 269–270; Shub, "The Advent of Sound in Cinema," *The Film Factory*, 271.

57. See Shub, "Khochu rabotat'," in *Zhizn' moia—kinematograf*, 288.

58. Shub, "Krupnym planom," in *Zhizn' moia—kinematograf*, 225.

59. Hicks, *Dziga Vertov*, 78–79.

60. Like Dmitry Shostakovich, his friend and fellow graduate of the Leningrad Conservatory, Gavriil Popov was an early and eager recruit to the task of composing for Soviet sound film. *K.Sh.E.* was Popov's first completed film score, and he would go on to work with many of the Soviet Union's most distinguished directors, and to score some forty films during his career,

including, most famously, the score for *Chapaev* (dir. Vasil'ev Brothers, 1934). For details see David Hass, *Leningrad's Modernists: Studies in Composition and Musical Thought, 1917–1932* (New York: Peter Lang, 1998).

61. Shub, "Krupnym planom," in *Zhizn' moia—kinematograf*, 227.

62. John MacKay, "Film Energy: Process and Metanarrative in Dziga Vertov's *The Eleventh Year* (1928)," *October* 121 (Summer 2007): 47–78; Joshua Malitsky, "The Movement of Energy," unpublished ms. On Shub's earlier work, see Malitsky, *Post-Revolution Nonfiction Film*, 156–188.

63. Located on Lesnaya St., in March 1931, the Moscow Sound Factory was amalgamated with two of the Souizkino factories to form the new "Moscow Amalgamated Factory 'Soiuzkino' after the Tenth Anniversary of October" (Moskovskaia ob"edinennaia fabrika 'Soiuzkino' im. Desiatiletiia Oktriabria). In 1934 the film studio was renamed Moskinokombinat, and in 1936—Mosfilm.

64. Nato Vachnadze was a well-known Georgian actress who was recommended to Shub as an assistant director by Grigori Kozintsev. Vachnadze started her career in the silent film era, and continued to work as an actress during the sound era until her death in a plane crash in 1953. After working as an assistant director for Shub, she returned to Georgia, restarting her career in some of the earliest Georgian sound films, such as 1933's *The Last Crusaders* (Poslednie krestonostsy, dir. S. Dolidze and V. Shvelidze) and Mikheil Chiaureli's *The Last Masquerade* (Poslednii maskarad, 1934). She was one of the first film stars of the Soviet Union to receive numerous honors, including the title of People's Artist of the Georgian Soviet Socialist Republic and the Stalin prize. See Shub, "Krupnym planom," in *Zhizn' moia—kinematograf*, 223–227.

65. Malitsky, "The Movement of Energy," unpublished ms. A "transversal variable area optical recording on film" (such as the one invented by Aleksandr Shorin and used in *K.Sh.E.*) is divided longitudinally into two components, one opaque and one transparent—in contrast with an "intensive variable density optical recording on film" (such as the one invented by Pavel Tager), which uses variable striations at right angles to the film edge.

66. Barker, *The Tactile Eye*, 77.

67. Barker, *The Tactile Eye*, 77.

68. Barker, *The Tactile Eye*, 77.

69. The theremin, one of the first electronic instruments, was invented by Lev Theremin (known in the West as Léon Theremin), a Russian physicist and mathematician, in 1919, and patented in the US in 1928. The instrument was dubbed "Thereminvox" (*termenvoks* or Theremin's voice) by the Russian press because, unlike many other electronic instruments, this one sounds like a human voice. See Lydia Kavina, "Therminvox," in *Electrified Voices: Medical, Socio-Historical and Cultural Aspects of Voice Transfer*, ed. Dmitri Zakharine and Nils Meise (Göttingen: Vandenhoeck & Ruprecht, 2012), 187–200; here: 187. See also Albert Glinsky, *Theremin: Ether Music and Espionage* (Urbana: University of Illinois Press, 2000), 26.

70. Kavina, "Therminvox," 187.

71. Kavina, "Therminvox," 189, 196.

72. Malitsky, "The Movement of Energy," unpublished ms.

73. Jean-Louis Baudry, "Ideological Effects of the Basic Cinematographic Apparatus," *Film Quarterly* 28, no. 2 (Winter 1974–75): 39–47.

74. See, for example, *Elektronnaia evreiskaia entsiklopediia*, "Esfir' Shub," accessed at http://www.eleven.co.il/article/14953.

75. Jane Bennett, *Vibrant Matter: A Political Ecology of Things* (Durham: Duke University Press, 2010).

76. Shub, "Tema moei rechi," in *Zhizn' moia—kinematograf*, 283.

77. Shub, "Tema moei rechi" and "Khochu delat' fil'mu o zhenshchine" (both written in 1933), in *Zhizn' moia—kinematograf*, 284, 285.

78. Bennett, *Vibrant Matter*, 23. But see also Gilles Deleuze and Félix Guattari, *A Thousand Plateaus: Capitalism and Schizophrenia* (Minneapolis: University of Minnesota Press, 1987), and

Brian Massumi, *Parables for the Virtual: Movement, Affect, Sensation* (Durham: Duke University Press, 2002).

79. Bennett, *Vibrant Matter*, 23–24.
80. Bennett, *Vibrant Matter*, 30.
81. Bennett, *Vibrant Matter*, 53.
82. Bennett, *Vibrant Matter*, 54.
83. This project culminated in 1934 in Vertov's *Three Songs of Lenin* with the opening of the great Dniepr Hydroelectric Station, the very first stages of whose construction he depicted in the first reel of *The Eleventh Year* in 1928.
84. MacKay, "Film Energy," 49.
85. MacKay, "Film Energy," 50.
86. Liudmila Dzhulai sees Shub's film as a direct response to Vertov's work with sound documentary in *Enthusiasm*. See Liudmila Dzhulai, *Dokumental'nyi illiuzion* (Moscow: Materik, 2005), 25.
87. In Emma Widdis, *Visions of a New Land* (New Haven: Yale University Press, 2003), 22.
88. Gleb Krzhizhanovskii, *10 let GOELRO* (Moscow: Ogiz, 1931), 13.
89. V. I. Lenin, "Otchet o rabote Tsentral'nogo ispolnitel'nogo komiteta" (February 2, 1920), in V. I. Lenin, *Polnoe sobranie sochinenii v 55 tomakh* (Moscow: Politizdat, 1958), 40: 159. For details, see Widdis, *Visions of a New Land*, 23–27.
90. Glinsky, *Theremin*, 23.
91. Glinsky, *Theremin*, 24.
92. Glinsky, *Theremin*, 27.
93. Ivan Skvortsov-Stepanov, *Elektrifikatsiia RSFSR v sviazi s perekhodnoi fazoi mirovogo khoziaistva* (Moscow: Gosizdat, 1922). Prefaces by V. I. Lenin and G. Krzhizhanovskii.
94. Malitsky, "The Movement of Energy," unpublished ms.
95. Widdis, *Visions of a New Land*, 27.
96. Widdis, *Visions of a New Land*, 27.
97. Shub, "Tema moei rechi," in *Zhizn' moia—kinematograf*, 284.
98. Glass is neither a liquid nor a solid, but an "amorphous solid"—a state somewhere between those two states of matter. On the ideological uses of glass in Soviet culture, see Julia Bekman Chadaga, *Optical Play: Glass, Vision, and Spectacle in Russian Culture* (Evanston: Northwestern University Press, 2014).
99. Bill Nichols, *Speaking Truths with Film*, 74. As Nichols puts it, "With the coming of sound at the end of the 1920s, voice takes firm root in 'Voice of God' commentary (unseen but heard narrators who guided us through a situation of issue from the film's perspective)." In particular, see his chapter, "Documentary Film and the Coming of Sound," 61–73; and "To See the World Anew: Revisiting the Voice of Documentary," 74–89.
100. Nichols is directly referencing Louis Althusser's theory of ideology. See Louis Althusser, *Lenin and Philosophy and Other essays*, trans. Ben Brewster (New York: Monthly Review Press, 1971). For Althusser and early Soviet sound film, see chapter 1.

chapter three

THE HOMOGENEOUS THINKING SUBJECT, OR SOVIET CINEMA LEARNS TO SING
Igor Savchenko's *The Accordion*

"As the one genre not possible in silent film, musicals were inevitable."
—Richard Barrios, *A Song in the Dark: The Birth of the Musical Film*

ONE OF THE DEBATES SURROUNDING the coming of sound to cinema focused on the question of how music was to work in sound film. In 1931, writing for the French journal *Plans*, the composer Arthur Honegger noted: "Sound cinema is inarticulate. At the moment, music and sound do no more than add *emphasis*, though somewhat more successfully than orchestral accompaniment. The sound cinema will only come into its own when it achieves *a union between the visual and the musical expression of the same thing so tight that they explain and complement each other as equals*. The synthesis will be the birth of a curious art addressed simultaneously and equally to the two senses."[1] As Julie Hubbert has pointed out in an essay on Sergei Eisenstein's theory of film music, during the silent period, film music theory centered to a certain extent on the idea of music as illustration of the images. The goal was to contribute to the "mood" of the picture on the screen through the use of musical stereotypes, "the conventions of happy or sad music, for instance, or to realize the sound for specific sonic events pictured on the screen, such as the musical approximation of thunderstorms, trains, animal noises, and so on." Additionally, "the practice of assigning themes to identify specific characters, emotions, or events in the film, and repeating those themes in a Wagnerian or leitmotivic fashion to generate thematic coherence, also occupied a significant portion of the early film music discussion."[2] Sound film, on the other hand, which required that speech and gesture be "at one another's service," would accept neither conventional stage performing nor silent-film acting; it was, in the words of director René Clair, "neither theater nor cinema, but something altogether new."³

We can see some of this discussion on the pages of the prominent Soviet film journal *Zhizn' iskusstva* (The Life of Art) in 1929, about the "cinefication of music" (*kinofikatsiia muzyki*). The discussion was started by Adrian Piotrovsky, the head of the Lenfilm script department, in an attempt to articulate the relationship of music to the new "sound" film (*tonfil'ma*). Piotrovsky suggests that for music to become a truly contemporary art (which in his case means a "revolutionary art" as opposed to bourgeois art), it needs to transform itself along the lines of avant-garde cinema. Cinema, according to Piotrovsky, is an industrial art based on two principles: "on industrial technology, as a method of registration of raw material, and on montage, as a method of its organization." Similarly, music must become the "capturing of the world's sounds, regardless of their material source." "The reconstruction of music along the principles of cinema—that is to say, the principles of *montage* and the registration on tape of disorganized naturalized fragments of the world's sounds," would lead to a new form of art: the sound film as "pure music."⁴

Music, in other words, could learn something from the cinema. For Piotrovsky, contemporary music was in crisis: its standard form was nonindustrialized and therefore backward (Piotrovsky refers to this as *kustarnoe proizvodstvo*, meaning something "handmade," rustic, primitive), and this crisis was not to be resolved in the long term by turning to "global" music and incorporating the music of "native peoples," including African American music. Instead, he proposes that music become "industrialized"—a photographic recording of the sounds of the world, organized by means of montage.⁵ (In essence, this is what Dziga Vertov will go on to do with *Enthusiasm: Symphony of the Donbass* [Entuziazm: Simfoniia Donbassa, 1930].)

In a follow-up article, S. Gres, who dismisses Piotrovsky's argument regarding the "cinefication of music" and the need to move music in the direction of the recording of "natural sounds" and arranging them by means of montage, nevertheless agrees that part of the problem with nonindustrialized music is its unique and singular performance: its "onceness" (*razovost'*) and nonrepeatability (*nepovtorimost'*). Even on the radio, Gres says, which is an "advanced industrialized apparatus," each performance of a musical piece happens only once; what is lacking are the means of "mechanical reproduction" (*mekhanizirovannoe povtorenie*). Arguing against the gramophone as a petty-bourgeois invention intended for the drawing room and, as such, of little value to Soviet mass culture or society, Gres underscores its limit also in terms of volume and duration—by the limitations of the record on which the music is recorded. The gramophone needle has done its duty, Gres suggests, but the next step is sound photography (*zvukovaia fotografiia*).[6]

Anticipating Walter Benjamin, Gres notes that mechanical reproduction will bring music, in its recorded form, to the masses. The same recording will be placed in a box and sent to everyone (*vsem-vsem-vsem*), to cities and villages, where it will sound a countless number of times without any loss to the quality of the recording and in all possible gradations of volume—from the living room, to the concert hall, to the open air—anywhere you might set up the basic attributes of the radio: the amplifier and the loudspeaker (*gromkogovoritel'*). For Gres, sound film represents precisely this moment of the industrialization (mechanical reproduction) of music, which relies on the simultaneous recording and reproduction of the sound and image tracks. He notes silent film's dedication to the acquisition of speech ("The persistent aspiration of the 'Great Mute' to acquire the gift of speech"[7]), as well as the general need for an apparatus that will allow for the synchronic (simultaneous) recording and the simultaneous reproduction of the elements of "movement and sound." Here the goal is both "talking" and "sound" cinema (*govoriashchee i zvuchashchee kino*).

The problem of film and music is also picked up in the same issues of *Zhizn' iskusstva* by V. Bogdanov-Berezovsky as part of the discussion of the release of *New Babylon* (Novyi Vavilon, dir. Kozintsev and Trauberg, 1929).[8] Bogdanov-Berezovsky notes that this is the first time that music has been composed specifically for film: Dmitry Shostakovich has written an original musical score to accompany this latest FEKS film. However, lacking the necessary technology to produce synchronized sound, either in recording or reproduction, means that the music, though composed for the film, remains separate from it. "Can we really call this film music?," asks the critic. If, he suggests, "the demonstration of the film is mechanized, then the accompanying music should also be subjected to mechanization. Only this would ensure the non-separation [*nerazryv*] of the film from its musical illustration."[9]

Dissatisfaction with early film music could be partially blamed on the lack of synchronized and mechanized sound technology, which meant that (in the case of *New Babylon*) Shostakovich's careful scoring could not be adequately reproduced in the theater. As Joan Titus has noted, contemporaneous critics claimed that Shostakovich's music was the source of the film's failure, whether through copying errors, lack of rehearsal and eventual alignment with the film, or the musical complexity of the score. Soviet musicologist Yulian Vainkop wrote that the music was "played horribly everywhere, although to be fair we should say that M[ikhail] V[ladimirovich] Vladimirov (conductor at the Picadilly cinema) treated it with more care than the rest, achieving the most piquancy and expressiveness and the fewest mistakes and [least] tempo confusion."[10] Other critics similarly related that the performances at theaters in Leningrad and Moscow were unsuccessful. Lev Arnshtam noted how badly Shostakovich's music was performed in theaters, claiming that the composer ran from venue to venue only to find that orchestras were nearly destroying his score.[11] Since the music was given to theater orchestras only days before the premiere, there was no time for rehearsal, and film orchestras were unaccustomed to performing specially tailored scores of this level of difficulty.

Yet, as Titus shows, Shostakovich's music was not necessarily to blame, and mechanical factors were not the only reasons for the film's presumed failure. New arguments about the appropriate "Soviet" quality and intelligibility of cinema were being applied for the first time to *New Babylon*. Following the directives set by 1928 All-Union Conference on Cinema Affairs, *New Babylon* was intended to be "intelligible," and its perceived stylistic modernism generated conflicted and often negative reactions. As Titus notes, "reviewers complained that the film was too 'formalist' or 'aesthetic,' using language that foreshadowed the criticism of the following decades." This often meant that the film editing was "too quick and fragmented, and the shooting and lighting too dark and impressionistic" for reviewers who were looking toward a new era of intelligibility and, inevitably, Socialist Realism.[12]

Indeed, by 1929, the pages of *Zhizn' iskusstva* as well as other Soviet film journals and newspapers were filled with the language of the "crisis in Soviet cinema" and Soviet films' apparent inability to be "intelligible to the masses." "We call our cinema Soviet," writes Leningrad director Pavel Petrov-Bytov, in another editorial in the same journal, "Do we have the right to call it that at present? In my view, we do not." "*We have no workers' and peasants' cinema,*" he laments, "no cinema that speaks to the everyday life [*byt*] of the masses, which the masses answer by leaving the theater." These masses—the workers and the peasants—are the real audience of Soviet cinema, the audience missed almost entirely by radical avant-garde filmmakers. "For peasants we have to make straightforward realistic films with a simple story and plot," continues Petrov-Bytov. "We must talk in his own sincere language about the cow that is sick with tuberculosis, about the dirty cowshed that must be transformed into one that is clean and bright, about the child that is stirring in the peasant woman's womb, about crèches for the child, about rural hooligans, the kolkhoz, and so on." "*Every film must be useful, intelligible and familiar to the millions,*" he stresses. "We are surrounded by such obscenity, such dirt, poverty, coarseness, and thickheadedness," Soviet cinema must sift through this "vile filth" on the "dung hill of everyday life" to uncover the "beautiful life" hidden deep within.[13]

Thus, already in 1929, as Richard Taylor and Ian Christie point out, we can "detect the kernel of the later doctrine of Socialist Realism," that informs this way of thinking.[14] In his 1933 "Creative Goals of Thematic Planning" (Tvorcheskie zadachi templana), the new head of the Soviet film industry Boris Shumyatsky argued for the need for films "infused with optimism, with the mobilizing emotions, with cheerfulness, *joie-de-vivre* and laughter."[15] He urged a concentration on three genres: drama, comedy, and fairy tales. "The victorious class wants to laugh with joy," he stressed, "That is its right and Soviet cinema must provide its audiences with this joyful Soviet laughter."[16] Of the 308 films produced in the 1930s, fifty-four were made for children, and of the musical comedies, twelve were set in factories, and seventeen took place on collective farms; one strongly got the impression, as Taylor noted, "that the countryside was a round of never-ending dancing and singing."[17]

In his diary entries from Kremlin film screenings in 1934, Shumyatsky recorded that Stalin was particularly interested in "light" films, noting specifically that, "the viewer needs joy, cheerfulness, laughter. He wants to see himself on screen." Shumyatsky spends a long time accounting for the lack of humor in current Soviet cinema, before assuring Stalin that the next films coming up—*Jolly Fellows* (Veselye rebiata), *The Enthusiasts* (Entuziasty), and *The Accordion* (Garmon')—will be refreshingly comical: "cheerful" and "happy." But the screening of Igor Savchenko's *The Accordion* on the night from June 9–10, 1934, does not go well. While the first half of the film is watched with general approval and good humor, the second half is found to be tedious and "false." As Stalin puts it a few screenings later, "Are you still making crap, like *The Accordion*?" ("A driani podobno 'Garmo'' bol'she ne stavite?"). Part of the falseness, according to Shumyatsky's Kremlin notes, lies in the fact of repetition: the film has a circular structure that Stalin found objectionable and unnecessary.[18] For us, looking at this film eighty years later, the structure is part of what turns this film from light, comic entertainment into an example of the "ISA," an "Ideological State Apparatus," as Louis Althusser called it. The fully mechanized

Figure 3.1. Timosha and his trusty accordion (*Accordion*, Muzei kino)

synchronization of sound and image produces the effect of entrapment, whereby every bodily movement is tightly synchronized to the musical score. A closer look at *The Accordion* suggests some of the ways sound in Soviet cinema comes to organize the visual field and discipline the body, both of the characters *on screen* and of the audience *off screen*.

ENTERTAINMENT AND UTOPIA

In many ways, Igor (Ihor) Savchenko (1906–1950) is a pivotal figure in the history of Soviet cinema, yet his work is very little known in the West. Born in what is now Ukraine (Vinnitsa) but educated in Leningrad, Savchenko made films in Moscow, Kiev, and Ashkhabad. He returned throughout his career to Ukrainian topics, most notably and often controversially in the films *Horsemen* (Vsadniki, 1939), *Bogdan Khmelnitsky* (1941), *Partisans in the Ukrainian Steppes* (Partizany v stepiakh Ukrainy, 1942), and *Taras Shevchenko* (released posthumously in 1951). In this chapter, I am interested in Savchenko's role in the emergence of Soviet sound cinema, most notably as the director of the first Soviet musical, *The Accordion*, released the same year as its better-known counterpart, Grigori Aleksandrov's *Jolly*

Figure 3.2. Marusya (*Accordion*, frame capture)

Fellows, but pulled from all Soviet and foreign screens in 1936.[19] *The Accordion* was based on a poem by communist youth poet Aleksandr Zharov, written "to defend the old village ways of music and dancing and passing the time from the changes brought on by collectivization"—specifically, to ensure that the accordion, associated with traditional (and therefore, backward) village life, would become instead an instrument cherished by communist youth.[20] The plot of the film is basic in the extreme: the short lyrical poem transferred to the screen tells the story of a young communist leader, Timosha, who rejects his accordion in favor of his new role in the Party, only to discover that he is much more useful to the collective as an accordion player than he is as the secretary of the village Soviet. Or, as Soviet critic Mark Zak put it in his synopsis, "It's a story of Timosha and his two girlfriends: the girl Marusya and . . . his trusty accordion."[21]

Yet, while celebrating the pleasures of accordion music, the film stages the new "enjoyment" of singing and dancing not in terms of pure unfettered pleasure, but in terms of self-control; the youthful Soviet body is disciplined and rigid, its movements stiff and controlled, while the "old" kulak body is represented as loose, dissipated, and disorderly.[22] This body

Figure 3.3a and 3.3b. The kulaks (*Accordion*, frame capture)

must be eliminated from the Soviet ranks (validating the project of collectivization, which "liquidated the kulaks as a class"), and this is done in Savchenko's film via the introduction of music: sound-on-film technology subordinates the bodily movements of the characters, acting as an external force and subjecting the new disciplined Soviet bodies to a rhythm whose source is located elsewhere, both inside (diegetic) and outside (extradiegetic) to the image track.

There are two different ideological mechanisms at work in *The Accordion*. The first has to do with the way this film was received by Soviet audiences, and this ideology can be reduced to an "us" versus "them." The kulaks are bad because they drink vodka, sing anti-Soviet songs, and are lazy. The young communists are good because they don't drink vodka, and they enjoy themselves within limits and only after a solid day of *Stakhanovite*-type work. This is the "literal," so to speak, ideology of the film—the one that was remarked on by all Soviet critics, both at the time and up until the fall of the Soviet Union. The second type of ideology at work here, however, is the one we do not necessarily see (which, according to Antonio Gramsci, is what makes it ideology in the first place). It is the operation of cinema itself—and in this case, *sound* cinema specifically—as an Althusserian ISA: an ideological tool for disciplining the Soviet subject. This second type of ideology is about the production of subjects and the reproduction of power not through coercion but through education, discipline, and, if we add in Michel Foucault, pleasure. As Althusser notes, the Repressive State Apparatus functions predominantly by repression, while functioning secondarily by ideology. ISAs function massively and predominantly by ideology, but they also function secondarily by repression, even if ultimately, but only ultimately, this is very attenuated and concealed, even symbolic.[23] Film music, rhythm, and tight synchronization of sound and image are some of the tools by means of which this film participates in the ideological production of disciplined Soviet subjects.

Generally considered an "escapist" genre, the Hollywood musical gets this reputation from the musicals produced in the early 1930s—the image of tuxedoed Fred Astaire and high-heeled Ginger Rogers dancing their way through the Great Depression. But the 1930s musical was also a tool for the reaffirmation of the American dream that, after the stock market crash of 1929, seemed to have been lost or sacrificed. In his article, "Some Warners' Musicals and the Spirit of the New Deal," Mark Roth has suggested that the musical is not so much an opiate or drug that puts the spectators to sleep, inducing them to ignore the problems of the real world (as most critics who wrote about musicals as escapist contended), but that the musical instead disarms the spectator, lowering his resistance, and thereby permits ideologically laden messages to sneak through. For Roth, the spirit of the New Deal for example, found its expression in the Warner musicals of the period. Films like *42nd Street* (1933) and *Footlight Parade* (1933) demonstrated a spirit of unity, optimism, and pride that was being fostered by the rhetoric of the FDR administration, hoping to repair the shattered American dream.[24]

In the 1930s, Hollywood had two favorite genres—the musical and the gangster film—and their popularity had to do with the crisis of the American dream and the viability of American capitalism. But if in the gangster film the hero had to "go it alone," in Warner musicals each person was shown to be part of an interdependent group. The musicals focused on the production of a show-within-the-film (standard musical gimmick) and involved, among other things, famously elaborate chorus-line style musical numbers, choreographed by Busby Berkeley, where scantily clad rows of girls kicked together or formed pyramids on enormously spectacular sets. (We see a similar conceit in Grigori Aleksandrov's 1936 *Circus* [Tsirk], which borrows from these earlier American musicals.) The dance numbers in particular symbolized the importance of social cohesion and harmony. The Hollywood musical reaffirmed the American dream of unity and social cohesion at a time of strife and social unrest. In particular, as Roth suggests, the Warner musical placed the director of the show in a new position of mastery and control; the message was that cooperation, planning, and the guidance of a single leader were now necessary for success.

Similarly, for Soviet cinema and its new search for a "cinema for the millions," *The Accordion* represented the possibility of the new genre of musical comedy. Some of the reviews celebrated *The Accordion* as "the first attempt at creating a musical film comedy," "cheerful and happy," and "not an imitation of foreign productions of cine-operas, so popular abroad."[25] Others, such as the critic Khrisanf Khersonsky, objected to Savchenko's use of the term "musical comedy," noting that the film is closer to a lyrical poem and has not yet established a new genre.[26] The Soviets rejected the term "the musical" because of its association with bourgeois culture (Shumyatsky called *The Accordion* the "first attempt at musical operetta"), but embraced the notion of the musical comedy, which depicted the joys of collective enterprise—at first, singing and dancing as in *The Accordion*, *Jolly Fellows*, and *Circus* and, eventually, the joys of collective labor as exemplified by the Stalinist tractor musical.[27] *The Accordion* captured what Soviet critics Nina Luchina and Tatiana Derevianko described as "the poetic atmosphere of the Russian village," noting that the film is "masterfully and rhythmically edited to the music (*v lad*) of Sergei Pototsky and his broad use of Russian sing-song, dance, and folk musical intonations."²⁸

We begin the film with a female chorus, and while we may not at first distinguish the lyrics, we understand that what we are hearing is a folk (*narodnaia*) melody, which calls forth the title of the film (we hear the chorus sing the word *garmon'* as the film title appears on our screen). A second voice—this time, solo and male, but also not so much singing as reciting in a singsong voice—gives us Zharov's poem, "The dear accordion, the poetry of the Soviet village," which the female chorus immediately picks up and repeats, now as song. As Richard Dyer has noted in his seminal work on entertainment and utopia, the chorus is a standard device of the musical used to generate the *feeling* of collective utopia that musicals (both Hollywood and Soviet) strive to produce:

> Two of the taken-for-granted descriptions of entertainment, as "escape" and as "wish-fulfillment," point to its central thrust, namely, utopianism. Entertainment offers the image of "something better" to escape into, or something we want deeply that our day-to-day lives don't provide. Alternatives, hopes, wishes—these are the stuff of utopia, the sense that things could be better, that something other than what is can be imagined and maybe realized.
>
> Entertainment does not, however, present models of utopian worlds, as in the classic utopias of Thomas More, William Morris, et al. Rather the utopianism is contained in the feelings it embodies. It presents, head-on as it were, *what utopia would feel like* rather than how it would be organized. It thus works at the level of sensibility, by which I mean an affective code that is characteristic of, and largely specific to, a given mode of cultural production.²⁹

Or, as Evgeny Margolit puts it writing about Savchenko's film, "On screen, we see a frankly utopian reality, an image of the harmony-to-come."³⁰

The chorus picks up the individual poem, transforming it into a collective sentiment; but we might note also that there is a gender distinction that is already made here in the opening lines: the female voices sing together, the male voice stands alone. This is the point of the film: collectivity versus individualism and the production of a *correctly* disciplined (male) Soviet subject. The second point is also audible here in these first opening lines: that of speech versus song. The poem is read but, as I already mentioned, in such a way as to make it almost musical (what is called in opera, "recitative/ *recitativo*"). It is then turned into music by the chorus, signifying the primacy of the musical over the verbal in this film. Indeed, as I hope to go on to show, the soundscape—specifically music and rhythm—dominates the visual image in this film, subordinating the image track to the sound track.

Figure 3.4a. Kulak "Tosklivyi" (*Accordion*, frame capture)

(Savchenko himself called the film an "operetta," signifying the primacy of song and music over speech and dialogue.[31]) As Margolit notes, "The picture overwhelms us with its beauty, with the elegance of each frame, with the inexhaustible imagination of its editing, and with the ingenuity of its sound decisions, in which everything—the word and the image—is subject to a musical rhythm."[32]

This is true as well of the next sequence, in which the young women call out to each other; as Natascha Drubek-Meyer shows, already their "speech" is sung in the key of C (*Maru-us'! A-u! Idesh'? Idu!*), giving the dialogue a rhythmic structure.[33] The melody is then picked up and repeated by the chorus we hear in the background (*A-u-u*). And again, in the next sequence, when the now complete group of young peasant women encounters the kulak Tosklivyi[34] (played by Savchenko himself), conversation with him is quickly turned into a musical number. Indeed, in *The Accordion* we have no disjuncture between narrative and numbers, typical of the musical. At no point in the film are we located beyond music's influence and every sound (including dialogue) and every movement (including work) is subordinated to a particular rhythm and cadence. Thus, characters do not

Figure 3.4b. The girls (*Accordion*, frame capture)

so much break into song as they cannot seem to break out of it. As Khersonsky noted in his 1934 review of the film, *The Accordion* was taking a real risk with its sound composition by having the characters "sing rather than speak," while surrounded by a realistic environment, with birch trees, village huts, and the like.³⁵ The cadence of the *chastushki* in this first exchange with Tosklivyi, with their "plaintive misery," similarly points away from realistic dialogue and toward poetry/song.

The Right to Sing

This insistence on the predominance of the audible and specifically the musical is one of the ways this film marks itself as a *sound* film, and it is worth thinking about how this film fits into our notions of the "musical" as a genre—both in its Soviet and Hollywood manifestations.³⁶ Richard Barrios calls the musical an inevitable consequence of the introduction of synchronized sound, and indeed, if we look at the first years following the coming of sound to Hollywood, we will find an astonishing number of musicals: about sixty musical films released in 1929 and another sixty in 1930.

As Hubbert argues, the purpose of music as an accompaniment to film in the silent period was primarily to reinforce mood, characters, or geographic locations—little thought was given to how music might structure the visual image. If we take what is generally acknowledged as the first sound film, Alan Crosland's 1927 *The Jazz Singer*, we can see the way that music becomes primary for the film's diegesis. The film is a story of a Jewish boy trained as a cantor who wants to sing American Jazz, and the film's strength lies in the musical performances of its star, Al Jolson, a Russian-born Jew who often performed in blackface, underscoring both his difference from and his integration into American culture.

In total, the movie contains barely two minutes of synchronized talking, much or all of it improvised. The rest of the dialogue is presented through caption cards, or intertitles, as was standard for silent film. Jolson's first vocal performance, about fifteen minutes into the picture, is of "Dirty Hands, Dirty Face," and the first synchronized speech, uttered by Jolson to a cabaret crowd and to the piano player in the band that accompanies him, occurs directly after that performance. His first spoken words: "Wait a minute, wait a minute, you ain't heard nothin' yet!" had developed as something of an in-joke. The words were part of a well-established stage patter of Jolson's. But here they clearly also refer to the film's new use of sync-sound recording, marking the coming of sound. *Life* magazine's reporter Robert E. Sherwood described the spoken dialogue scene between Jolson and Besserer as "fraught with tremendous significance." He wrote, "I for one suddenly realized that the end of the silent drama is in sight."[37]

Similarly, a film like René Clair's 1930 *Sous les toits de Paris* was already playing with the notion of music as the structuring element of the film. Thus the film as a whole is based around the repeated performance of the title song, heard rehearsed in the street, played on the gramophone, etc. Here already we see music/sound not simply used to reinforce mood, characters, or geographic locations (although it does all that), but also as a means by which the narrative itself is organized. By the time we get to Friz Lang's 1931 *M*, we have music/voice/sound as the primary force that dominates the screen: the film opens on a group of children playing a game in the courtyard of a Berlin apartment building and singing a song about a child murderer. This foreshadows the appearance of Hans Beckert (Peter Lorre), a serial killer who preys on children. Vitally, the audience does not see Beckert until the second half of the movie; rather, his presence is marked in the film by his shadow, partial shots of his body, and—most importantly for our purposes—the sound of his whistling the tune "In

Figure 3.5a. "Khorovod" (*Accordion*, frame capture)

the Hall of the Mountain King" from Edvard Grieg's *Peer Gynt Suite No. 1*. (Ironically, Peter Lorre himself could not whistle—it is actually Lang who is heard whistling the tune.) This use of a leitmotif—an association of a musical theme with a particular character or situation—was a technique borrowed from opera that has since become a film staple, and Lang's *M* was one of the first to make use of it, associating "In the Hall of the Mountain King" with the murderer. Throughout the film, the sound of the song lets the audience know that Beckert is nearby, hidden in that off-screen space just beyond the frame that "cinema always both denies and brings into play."[38]

In the first Soviet sound films, such as Grigori Kozintsev and Leonid Trauberg's *Alone* (Odna) or Nikolai Ekk's *The Road to Life* (Putevka v zhizn', both from 1931), music still plays an illustrative rather than structural purpose. In *Alone* we hear Dmitry Shostakovich's wonderful "Kakaia khoroshaia budet zhizn'" (How Good Life Will Be!), which does precisely what Hubbert describes for silent cinema: it sets the mood and gives us a sense of the character. Even more illustrative, however, is the first song we hear while Kuzmina is waking up: "Konchen, konchen tekhnikum..."

Figure 3.5b. Non-mechanized collective labor (*Accordion*, frame capture)

(loosely translated as "Graduated from university"), with lyrics written by Ilya Trauberg, the director's younger brother. Here the lyrics literally describe Kuzmina's life and list activities as she does them, noting that she lives on top of a five-story "sky scraper" (*ia zhivu na verkhu bol'shogo neboskreba*), how many exams she has left to finish (two), and her movements as she brushes her teeth and hair (*poroshkom chichshu zuby*, etc.).[39] In Savchenko's *The Accordion*, on the other hand, music is meant to do something else; it is not illustrative, but structural. It does not serve as an accompaniment to the visual image but rather to organize the visual field.

In Savchenko's film, music is *the* primary structuring element of the film. In fact, we could even go so far as to argue that *The Accordion* is not a musical at all, in its strictest definition: a true musical negotiates between realistic narrative and fantastical musical numbers, and the transition from the one to the other (often quite forced) is part of what makes the musical, at least in its Hollywood form, recognizable as such.[40] In classic Hollywood cinema, musical numbers interrupt—or provide a break from—narrative flow. Laura Mulvey, in her seminal essay on "Visual Pleasure in Narrative Cinema" compares the iconic representation of women on screen to the ways in which musical numbers halt narrative: both come as a break—the sudden close-ups of the female body or the song-and-dance number disturbing narrative flow in favor of pure cinematic spectacle and visual pleasure. She writes, "Mainstream film neatly combines spectacle and narrative. (Note, however, how in the musical song-and-dance numbers interrupt the flow of the diegesis)."[41] Like Al Jolson's blackface in *The Jazz Singer*, musical numbers in films are an artifice and a disjunction—they are marked as something *other*, an interruption in story telling in favor of pure entertainment.

Dyer similarly notes the "deeply contradictory nature of entertainment forms." He writes,

> In Variety, the essential contradiction is between comedy and music turns; in musicals, it is between the narrative and the numbers. Both these contradictions can be rendered as one between the heavily representational and verisimilitudinous (pointing to the way the world is, drawing on the audience's concrete experience of the world) and the heavily nonrepresentational and "unreal" (pointing to how things could be better). In musicals, contradiction is also to be found at two other levels—within numbers, between the representational and the nonrepresentational, and within the nonrepresentational, due to the differing sources of production inscribed in the signs.[42]

The three broad tendencies of musicals, Dyer suggests, are those that keep narrative and number clearly separated (most typically, the backstage musical); those that retain the division between narrative as problems and numbers as escape, but try to "integrate" the numbers by a whole set of papering-over-the-cracks devices (e.g., the well-known "cue for a song"); and those which try to dissolve the distinction between narrative and numbers, thus implying that the world of the narrative is "also (already) utopian."[43]

In *The Accordion* we have no disjuncture between narrative and numbers, and thus are squarely in the world of utopia. This is more than simply an "integrated musical," but a film in which musical rhythm and cadence dominates and structures what we see on screen.[44] Savchenko himself commented on the problem of musical numbers that are barely motivated by plot: in his short article, "The Right to Sing" (Pravo zapet', 1934), he writes: "Music in film is usually introduced in some pedestrian way, and its presence is modestly concealed by the 'fig leaf' of a hurdy-gurdy that happened just at that moment to have entered the yard, or by a musical neighbor playing a heartbreaking waltz. At best, music serves as an accompaniment to some episode—that is to say, it works in exactly the same way as in the earlier case, but without the justification of [a visible] sound source."⁴⁵ The need to find a "justification" (*opravdanie*) for the source of the sound for the most part reflected the first Soviet experiments in sound cinema. Unlike their Western colleagues, Soviet filmmakers were interested in precisely making visible the source of cinematic sound, by repeatedly emphasizing sound-making apparatuses such as the radio, the phonograph, and the loudspeaker in their films (for example, Dziga Vertov's famous "radio-ear" from the opening shots of *Enthusiasm*). Savchenko wants the opposite; he wants the music/sound to be integrated into the very fabric of the film, making it an indivisible part of the visual image. Thus, even the moments of silence are part of the film's soundscape: the sudden cuts in sound "shock" the characters (as if sound is cut off for them as well), while the sequence of Timosha tap-dancing the *chechotka* in the closing moments of the film is given to us without a musical accompaniment as pure unadulterated rhythm.

In *The Accordion* the soundtrack structures the visual field. As Drubek-Meyer notes, this was something that was pointed out by all Soviet critics writing after Khersonsky: the form of the film's visual montage was said to be determined by the autonomous sound track, with music and poetry dominating over the images.⁴⁶ Like the voice, the body in this film is also subject to a particular kind of disciplinary control; it moves rigidly in time to the music. The entire world of the film is structured by rhythm and sound, whether musical or not. There is a beat, there is a cadence, there is a structure into which all the different sound elements fit in and, more vitally for my purposes, which regulate movement, subordinating it to sound. We might note how rigidly Marusya—Timosha's girl—moves her body, in comparison, for example, with the male dancers. Her circumscribed movements speak to an imposition of a certain form of bodily discipline (which has to do with gender, among other things). The girls walk arm in arm, forming an unbreakable chain. Although distinguished to a certain degree by voice and facial expression, the girls all tend to walk, speak, and move as one, while the men remain isolated and individualized.

The nature of the circle is vital here and goes again beyond the simple fact that we are watching a folk dance around a maypole. The film itself, as I mentioned earlier, has a circular structure—it concludes with the same poem and the same images with which it had started. Moreover, there is an insistence on circularity throughout: among other things, we watch Marusya and Timosha pick petals off daisies, reciting obsessively, "He

Figure 3.6a, 3.6b, and 3.6c. The female collective (*Accordion*, frame capture)

loves me, he loves me not," in a way that begins to resemble nothing so much as a compulsion to repeat. The circularity is folkloric and "natural" on the one hand—that is to say, pointing to the cyclical life of the village, of their work that is closely tied to the seasons—but it also suggests entrapment. In his 1934 review of the film, cameraman K. Strod wrote that in Savchenko's film, form and content were at odds with each other to such a degree that it must have been done on purpose. He notes that the filters used for shooting outdoor scenes give them a dark and brooding tint, a "depressing tone" that is in direct opposition to the content of the frame: the happy singing and dancing Soviet youth. Strod goes so far as to call the color of the sky in the opening sequence "sinister" and "ominous" (*zloveshchii*).[47] Similarly, breaking out of the circle has significant consequences for all the characters in the film, and reveals the presence of both disciplinary and repressive forces at work in this imaginary utopian space. Thus, for example, the opening sequence—*Maru-us' 'A-u!'*—is repeated half way through the film, only this time, Marusya refuses to go with the girls because she is secretly meeting Timosha. But the meeting ends badly for the two lovers, who end up isolated and unhappy, in part because they have broken away from the collective. (And the collective also suffers; without Timosha's accordion to unite them, the girls grow bored and restless, vulnerable to Tosklivyi's seduction.)

The central conflict of the film is precisely about isolation and integration. When Timosha, who has been daily entertaining the Soviet village with his accordion, is elected Communist Party secretary, he "liquidates his accordion as a class," and isolates himself in the *izba* (the hut serving as Party headquarters) to write meaningless slogans about the dangers of alcohol. As a result, the accordion falls into the hands of the kulaks, who, drunk with vodka and sexual desire, begin to sing sentimental anti-Soviet songs and molest the girls. This happens precisely at the moment when Timosha and Marusya are off by themselves having their lovers' quarrel, and when they run back to the village, they find that it has been taken over by the kulaks. Nearly undone by Tosklivyi's plaintive melody, Timosha comes out of his house brandishing a gun, ready to shoot, with Marusya urging him to "shoot them all." But Timosha does not fire. Instead, he throws away his gun and takes out his accordion. "We won't get them with a gun, but with its opposite" (*ikh nuzhno ne naganom, a sovsem naoborot!*) he says. I am specifically interested in this reversal (*sovsem naoborot*), because it marks precisely the difference between a (Repressive) State Apparatus and an ideological one (ISA). With either mechanism at work, the result is the same: the expulsion of Tosklivyi from the village and his (implied) arrest

Figure 3.7. Timofei Dudin with a gun (*Accordion*, frame capture)

at the end of the film. But here, the mechanism is not one of coercive brute power (the gun) but rather of a "natural" force (the song).

The climax of the film is a sing-off between the different rivals (*kulaki* vs. *komsomol'tsy*, unreformed kulaks vs. good Soviet youth), in which the two radically different melodies (one in a major key, the other in a minor) resolve into a kind of polyphony, and the main bad guy, kulak Tosklivyi, is expelled as if by the very force of Timosha's song. While Timosha returns to playing his accordion tightly surrounded by good-natured Soviet youth, Tosklivyi finds himself on the edge of the village, in the middle of carefully arranged stacks of wheat, which he begins to tear apart, even going so far as to bite the stocks with his teeth. In his book on Savchenko, Zak describes Tosklivyi's act as a "paroxysm of spiteful feelings" that overtakes him in the wheat field: "In a frenzy he tears and tramples the collective farm's bread . . . the sounds of his hoarse half-song, half-cry turn into a wild animal wail that is carried over the fields like a dull echo."[48] While Timosha sings about the righteousness of the Soviet village, surrounded on all sides by straightlaced Soviet youth, Tosklivyi rages alone in the field. His scream reaches the *ear* of what we can only assume to be a manifestation of the superego; on the screen, we see a close-up of a man's ear, followed shortly by shots of a man on a horse, and another one with a gun.

Figure 3.8a.
Kulak rage (*Accordion*, frame capture)

Figure 3.8b.
The Bolshevik ear (*Accordion*, frame capture)

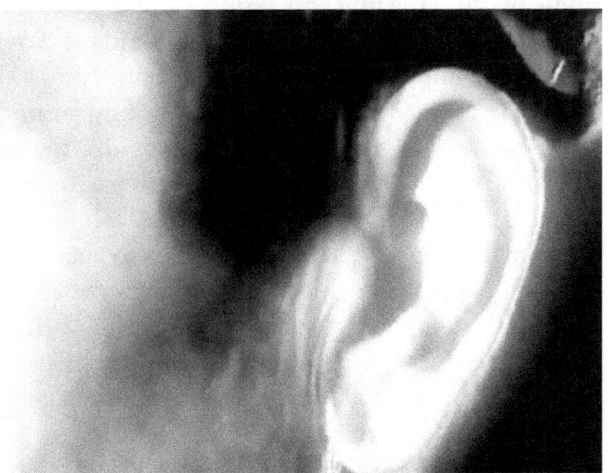

Figure 3.8c.
The man with the gun (*Accordion*, frame capture)

The Homogenous Thinking Subject

Two theoretical notions might help us read this image. As Freud writes in one of the more curious passages in *The Ego and the Id*, the ego "wears a cap of hearing" on one side only ("it might be said to wear it awry," he notes), a position he later assigns to the superego.[49] This substitution of the superego for the cap of hearing has been interpreted by a number of scholars to suggest that the superego is determined primarily by the activity of listening, which is precisely what is being demonstrated in this sequence.[50] The second theoretical concept at work here is Michel Chion's notion of the *acousmêtre* and its four powers, "the ability to be everywhere, to see all, to know all, and to have complete power. In other words: ubiquity, panopticism, omniscience, and omnipotence."[51] Who is this man, this Bolshevik, who can hear Tosklivyi's scream from so far away? Where does he come from? Because the film's diegesis is unable to provide us with an answer to this, we can only postulate that he stands in for "Soviet power" that can see and—most importantly in this early sound film—*hear* all.

In fact, we can actually organize the film around Freud's three psychic agencies: the ego, the superego, and the id. Timosha's crisis in the film is about self-control: giving in to desire (entertainment, sexual attraction) versus labor (both physical and political). In order not to err on the side of too much pleasure, Timosha chooses to abandon his accordion in favor of rigid self-control, which limits him to the confines of his hut, and to making slogans about the dangers of alcohol. When the village girls come looking for him at home, he announces that from now on he will be known by his name and patronymic, as "Timofei Vasil'evich," a name appropriate for a village "elder." But like a typical socialist realist hero, Timosha cannot actually move from the place of the "son" to the place of the "father"; he cannot, in fact, transcend "Timosha" to become "Timofei Vasil'evich," as he now thinks he should be addressed.[52] The place of real power is reserved for the representation of the Party/Leader/Bolshevik, and in this film, it takes the form of a man on a horse.[53] Timosha does not need to and cannot shoot the kulaks, not only because, in terms of genre, he is in a musical comedy and not in a tragedy (although for a brief moment while brandishing a gun, he does look the part), but also because that action is reserved for the real representative of the Party. Timosha has to recognize his proper place in the system.

In the sequence where Tosklivyi, in a moment of complete self-abandonment, drunk with vodka and rage, destroys the carefully arranged stacks of wheat, we can see all three of Freud's psychic mechanisms at

Figure 3.9a.
A member of the village Soviet (*Accordion*, frame capture)

Figure 3.9b. and 3.9c.
Timofei Vasil'evich Dudin (*Accordion*, frame capture)

Figure 3.10. Timosha, back in the collective (*Accordion*, frame capture)

work: while Timosha sings about the righteousness of the new Soviet village, Tosklivyi, as a manifestation of the film's id, rages alone in the field (the unconscious, Freud wrote, does not know "no"). His scream reaches the "ear" of the superego that, as Freud reminds us, has a direct link to the id, bypassing the ego. Thus, while Timosha remains safely cocooned within the collective, the danger to that collective is eliminated and utopia is restored.

So what is the nature of this utopia? One way to get at it is to think about how in this film the body is subject to a particular kind of disciplinary control: it moves rigidly in time to the music. Drubek-Meyer suggests that in Savchenko's film, melody is incompatible with rhythm. She notes specifically the absence of music in the *chechotka* (tap dance) sequence at the end of the film, arguing that while rhythm is linked to instrumental music, it is never the starting point for a musical theme. The "primary element of sound production is not rhythm, but music," she writes.[54] For my purposes, I would contend that while rhythm and music might in fact be used for different purposes in the film, they are both part of the film's soundscape, whose primary role is to organize the film's visual field. There is a beat, a cadence, and a structure to which all the different sound elements belong and, more vitally, which regulate movement, subordinating it to sound. If cinema is first and foremost an art of movement (*moving* pictures, but not in the same way as dance), then the question of the relationship between sound and movement becomes primary for the new sound cinema in general and for the first musical film in particular.

Before he can be fully reintegrated into the collective, Timosha has to be taught a lesson in bodily discipline through movement. To prove his belonging, Timosha has to do something besides playing the accordion: he has to enter the circle and dance (an act he initially refuses by claiming that the accordion won't let him). The *chechotka* that he performs without music is strictly an exercise of bodily discipline. Timosha must beat out a rhythm dictated by an unheard/imaginary source; he must demonstrate that his body is ready to fall in line. We might note again how very rigid his movements are in this sequence. This is not about "letting yourself go" but rather about self-control. The female bodies—cheeks, lips, hands—in this sequence become musical instruments, again underscoring the subordination of the body to rhythm.

This disciplining of the subject is at work both on the level of the characters but also on the level of the audience. Just as early film audiences had to be trained in watching films, audiences in the early 1930s had to be trained in listening to sound films. In particular, as a number of early sound films demonstrate, with the advent of sound, audiences were exposed for the first time to the "voice of power/ideology" issuing directly from the screen. Indeed, Soviet film reviewer Nikolai Aduev noted in 1934 that by themselves Timosha's limericks and cheerful melody are no match for Tosklivyi's melancholy song and therefore cannot possibly be used to destroy the class enemy. What you need is the thunderous force of the "Bolshevik word."[55]

The disciplinary structures evidenced in this film are directly related to what Stephen Heath has identified as sound film's process of "homogenization"—the moment when "every actor begins to speak the same thing"—that comes with the advent of sound or sound's new regime of cinema. For Heath, sound cinema is the development of a powerful standard of the body, of the voice as "a hold of the body in image, literarily ordered and delimited as speech for an intelligibility of the body, of people—agents and characters—fixed in the order of the narrative and its meanings, its unities and resolutions." In the silent cinema, Heath argues, the body is always pulling toward an emphasis, an exaggeration, a burlesque; in the sound cinema, the body is "smoothed out," with the voice as the medium, "the expression, of a homogenous thinking subject—actor and spectator—of film."[56]

In the Soviet Union the introduction of sync-sound technology coincided with cultural, political, and ideological shifts produced by the implementation of the First Five-Year Plan, industrialization, collectivization, and the full centralization of the film industry and other arts. The coming of sound also coincided with a massive shift in ideology from avant-garde practices to the implementation of Socialist Realism as the single method for all Soviet arts.[57] Soviet films made during the period of the transition to sound and the transition to Socialist Realism all mark this ideological shift: each film stages its relationship to the technology of sound as a relationship to power. For Soviet cinema, sound will come to play a major role in the dissemination of Socialist Realism on the screen and the creation, as Heath puts it, of "a homogenous thinking subject," *both* actor and spectator of film. While *all* sound cinema is fundamentally about this process of homogenization, early Soviet sound cinema makes the process explicit.

The stakes are the simultaneous production of two different kinds of utopia—Socialist Realist *and* cinematic—and Stalinist musical comedies become a way to link the notion of "reality in its revolutionary development" to the "feeling of utopia" generated by the musical. As Anna Nisnevich suggests, in the musical comedies of Grigori Aleksandrov and Ivan Pyr'ev that would quickly follow Savchenko's foray into the genre, music—and in particular, song—was much more than a mere accompaniment; rather, it performed several ideological functions: "It stood for the solidity of the Soviet community, portended the profusion of a specifically Soviet talent, and articulated the joyous symbiosis of the singing individual and the sung-about realm." Isaak Dunaevsky's music and lyrics written for these films celebrated the Soviet nation as an essentially "fertile, resilient and vast social force." Above any one particular musical style, "variously extemporized upon in the course of their films, eminently paraphraseable" (that is, always ready to be sung along to), these songs transmitted and reproduced something beyond their concrete musical mold, "the numinous, transubstantiating awe of Soviet togetherness."[58] Savchenko's *Accordion* makes this process of utopian homogenization explicit by subordinating all movement in the film to a single unifying rhythm.

Notes

1. Arthur Honegger, "Du cinema sonore à la musique réelle," *Plans* (January 1931): 77. Quoted in Lea Jacobs, *Film Rhythm After Sound: Technology, Music, and Performance* (Berkeley: University of California Press, 2015), 21.

2. Julie Hubbert, "Eisenstein's Theory of Film Music Revisited: Silent and Early Sound Antecedents," in *Composing for the Screen in Germany and the USSR*, ed. Robynn J. Stilwell and Phil Powrie (Bloomington: Indiana University Press, 2008), 127.

3. See Richard Barrios, *A Song in the Dark: The Birth of the Musical Film* (Oxford: Oxford University Press, 2010), 44; René Clair, quoted in Barrios, *A Song in the Dark*, 67.

4. Adrian Piotrovskii, "Kinofikatsiia muzyki," *Zhizn' iskusstva* 9 (1929); part of a series of articles in *Zhizn' iskusstva*, starting with Piotrovskii, followed by P. Vul'fius, V. Beliaev, and S. Gres.

5. Piotrovskii, "Kinofikatsiia muzyki."

6. S. Gres, "Industrializatsiia muzyki," *Zhizn' iskusstva* 13 (1929).

7. «Настойчивое стремление «Великого немого» обрести, наконец, дар речи»

8. V. Bogdanov-Berezovskii, "Novyi Vavilon," *Zhizn' iskusstva* 11 (1929).

9. Bogdanov-Berezovskii, "Novyi Vavilon."

10. Iulii Vainkop, "Muzyka k 'NovomuVavilonu'," *Rabochii i teatr* (April 1, 1929), 9. Quoted in Joan Titus, "Silents, Sound, and Modernism in *The New Babylon*," in *Sound, Speech, Music in Russian and Soviet Cinema*, 52. Translation modified from Yakubov, "Muzyka D. D. Shostakovicha," 545.

11. L. Arnshtam, "Bessmertie," in *D. Shostakovich. Stat'i i materialy*, ed. G. M. Schneerson (Moscow: Sovetskii kompozitor, 1976), 115–116. Quoted in Titus, "Silents, Sound, and Modernism in *The New Babylon*," in *Sound, Speech, Music in Russian and Soviet Cinema*, 52.

12. Titus, "Silents, Sound, and Modernism in *The New Babylon*," 53. For a full account of Shostakovich's early film work, see Joan Titus, *The Early Film Music of Dmitry Shostakovich* (Oxford: Oxford University Press, 2016).

13. Pavel Petrov-Bytov, "U nas net sovetskoi kinematografii," *Zhizn' iskusstva* (April 21, 1929), 8; translated as "We Have No Soviet Cinema," in *The Film Factory*, 259–262; emphasis in the original.

14. Taylor and Christie, *The Film Factory*, 247.

15. Boris Shumiatskii, "Tvorcheskie zadachi templana," *Sovetskoe kino* 12 (December 1933): 1–15; here: 1.

16. Boris Shumiatskii, *Kinematografiia millionov. Opyt analiza* (Moscow: Kinofotoizdat, 1935), 249.

17. For a full account see Richard Taylor, "Boris Shumyatsky and the Soviet Cinema in the 1930s: Ideology as Mass Entertainment," *Historical Journal of Film, Radio and Television* 6, no. 1 (1986): 43–64.

18. The film also showed work in the field done exclusively by hand, without the use of tractors, therefore, failing to highlight the new mechanization of the countryside. For the full transcript, see: "'A driani podobno 'Garmon'' bol'she ne stavite? . . . 'zapiski besed B. Z. Shumiatskogo s I. V. Stalinym posle kinoprosmotrov. 1934 g.," in *Kinovedcheskie zapiski* 61 (2002): 281–346.

19. In response to a request from V. Molotov (the Chairman of the Council of People's Commissars from 1930 to 1941), Shumyatsky issued the order to pull the film from all Soviet screens, to withdraw all foreign copies, and to forbid the sale of the film for international release. See "Dokladnaia zapiska B. Z. Shumiatskogo V. M. Molotovu o sniatii s prokata kinokartiny 'Garmon'' 27 avgusta 1936 g," in *Kremlevskii kinoteatr. 1928–1953: Dokumenty* (Moscow, 2005).

20. Zharov was a member of the Komsomol, the All-Union Leninist Young Communist League, the youth division of the Communist Party of the Soviet Union (CPSU). The Komsomol in its earliest form was established in urban centers in 1918, and in 1922, with the unification of the USSR, it became the youth division of the All-Union Communist Party. The poem and the film are addressed not simply to Soviet youth, but specifically to this youth division of the Communist Party.

21. Mark Zak, L. Parfenov, and O. Iakubovich-Iasnyi, *Igor' Savchenko* (Moscow: Iskusstvo, 1959), 21.

22. This body is "old" not because of its chronological age, but because it belongs to the old world. In Soviet newspapers of the period, the kulaks were often referred to as "former people." The use of dancing in this film is similar to the opening shots of Dziga Vertov's *Kino-Eye* (Kinoglaz, 1924), which showed the "effects of homemade vodka on the village women."

23. Louis Althusser, "Ideology and Ideological State Apparatus (Notes towards an Investigation)," in *Lenin and Philosophy and Other Essays*, trans. Ben Brewster (New York: Monthly Review Press, 1971), 85–126: here: 97–98.

24. Mark Roth, "Some Warners' Musicals and the Spirit of the New Deal," *The Velvet Light Trap* 77 (Winter 1977): 1–7.

25. Anon., *Krasnaia gazeta* (June 10, 1934).

26. Khrisanf Khersonskii, "Garmon'," *Iskusstvo* 138 (June 15, 1934). For reviews of the film in the year of its release, 1934, see: RGALI 1992–1–59; for early versions of the script, see RGALI 1992–1–56 and 1992–1–57.

27. On Soviet musicals in the 1930s, see in particular Richard Taylor, "Singing on the Steppes for Stalin: Ivan Pyr'ev and the Kolkhoz Musical in Soviet Cinema," in *Slavic Review* 58, no. 1 (Spring, 1999): 143–159; Richard Taylor, "K topografii utopii v stalinskom miuzikle," and Katerina Clark, "'Chtoby tak pet', dvadtsat' let uchit'sia nuzhno': Sluchai *Volgi-Volgi*," both in *Sovetskoe bogatstvo. Stat'i o kul'ture, literature i kino*, ed. Marina Balina, Evgeny Dobrenko, and Yury Murashov (St. Petersburg: Akademicheskii proekt, 2002), 358–370 and 371–390, respectively; David C. Gillespie, "The Sounds of Music: Soundtrack and Song in Soviet Film," in *Slavic Review* 62, no. 3 (Autumn, 2003): 473–490; and Rimgaila Salys, *The Musical Comedy Films of Grigorii Aleksandrov: Laughing Matters* (Bristol: Intellect Press, 2010).

28. Nina Luchina and Tat'iana Derevianko, *Igor' Savchenko. Sbornik statei i vospominanii* (Kiev: Mistetstvo, 1980), 6, 7.

29. Richard Dyer, "Entertainment and Utopia," in *Only Entertainment* (London: Routledge, 1992; 2002, 2nd ed.), 19–35.

30. Evgenii Margolit, "Zaklinanie eposom. *Garmon'* Igoria Savchenko i genezis sovetskoi muzykal'noi komedii," *Kinovedcheskie zapiski* 13 (19921): 120–133. Here, Margolit is underscoring the acoustic similarity between *garmon'* (the accordion) and *garmoniia* (harmony/accord) that structures the film. There are a number of musical puns in the film, including Timosha's last name, "Dudin," that connects him to another musical instrument: *dudka* (a flute or penny whistle).

31. Igor' Savchenko, "Pravo zapet'," *Sovetskoe kino* 5 (1934): 57–61; and Savchenko, *Kak ia stal rezhisserom* (Moscow, 1946).

32. Margolit, "Zaklinanie eposom," 121. On the problem of rhythm for early sound film, see Jacobs, *Film Rhythm after Sound*.

33. Natascha Drubek-Meyer, "Zvukomontazh v fil'me 'Garmon'' (1934) Igoria Savchenko," in *Welt der Slaven, Schwerpunkt: "Stumm oder vertont. Krisen und Neuanfänge in der Filmkunst um 1930,"* ed. D. Zakharine, vol. 54 (2009), 2: 309–325; here: 313. See also, Drubek-Meyer, "Zvuki muzyki. (Anti-)medium v sovetskikh muzykal'nykh komediiakh," in *Sovetskaia vlast' i media*, ed. Hans Günther and Sabine Hänsgen (St. Petersburg: Akademicheskii proekt, 2006), 578–592.

34. The Russian *toska* may be translated as "longing," "yearning," or "ennui," and this is what Tosklivyi's name, as well as his melancholy songs, evoke.

35. Khersonskii, "Garmon'," *Iskusstvo* 138 (June 15, 1934).

36. For literature on the musical (that goes well beyond 1930s Hollywood), see Jane Feuer, *The Hollywood Musical* (Bloomington: Indiana University Press, 1982); Rick Altman, *The American Film Musical* (Bloomington: Indiana University Press, 1988); *Hollywood Musical: The Film Reader*, ed. Steven Cohan (New York: Routledge, 2001); *Movie Music, the Film Reader*, ed. Kay Dickinson (New York: Routledge, 2003); Steven Cohan, *Incongruous Entertainment: Camp, Cultural Value, and the MGM Musical* (Durham, NC: Duke University Press, 2005); *The Hollywood Film Musical Reader*, ed. Mervyn Cooke (Oxford: Oxford University Press, 2010).

37. Scott Eyman, *The Speed of Sound: Hollywood and the Talkie Revolution, 1926–1930* (New York: Simon and Schuster, 1997), 141.

38. Gilles Deleuze, *Cinema 2: The Time Image*, trans. Hugh Tomlinson and Robert Galeta (Minneapolis: University of Minnesota Press, 1989), 235.

39. See Artem Sopin, "Ob avtore pesni k fil'mu 'Odna'," *Kinovedcheskie zapiski* 84 (2007): 371–372. Sopin notes specifically the Obeirut influence on both the lyrical content and the visual layout of Trauberg's poem.

40. Jacques Demy's *The Umbrellas of Cherbourg* (Les Parapluies de Cherbourg, 1964) is not considered a musical, for example, because the film's dialogue is all sung as recitative. Formally, *The Umbrellas of Cherbourg* is an operetta in that songs as well as dialogue advance the action.

41. Laura Mulvey, "Visual Pleasure and Narrative Cinema," in *Visual and Other Pleasures* (Bloomington: Indiana University Press, 1989), 19.

42. Dyer, "Entertainment and Utopia," 27.

43. Dyer, "Entertainment and Utopia," 28.

44. As Taylor notes, "Although the term musical was not used at the time, because it was deemed to be redolent of 'bourgeois' Hollywood, and the terms *comedy* or *musical comedy* prevailed, it can safely be applied to a number of key films of the period, even if we confine it to those films that would have been designated 'integrated musicals' in the west" (as defined by Rick Altman in his *Genre, The Musical: A Reader* [London: Routledge, 1981] and *The American Film Musical* [Bloomington: Indiana University Press, 1989]). Taylor, "Singing on the Steppes for Stalin," 146.

45. Savchenko, "Pravo zapet'," 59.

46. Drubek-Meyer, "Zvukomontazh," 321–322.

47. K. Strod, "Iskusstvo ili remeslo?" (1934), RGALI 1992-1-59/10.

48. Zak, *Igor' Savchenko*, 26.

49. Freud, "The Ego and the Id," *The Standard Edition of the Complete Psychological Works of Sigmund Freud*, ed. James Strachey (London: Hogarth Press, 1986), 19: 25.

50. See Kaja Silverman, *The Acoustic Mirror: The Female Voice in Psychoanalysis and Cinema* (Bloomington: Indiana University Press, 1988), 98.

51. Michel Chion, *The Voice in Cinema* (New York: Columbia University Press, 1999), 24.

52. For the Stalinist myth of the "Great Family," see: Katerina Clark, *The Soviet Novel: History As Ritual* (Chicago: Chicago University Press, 1981), 114–135.

53. In the literary scenario, the man on the horse and the one with the gun are both simply called *ob"ezdchik* ("overseer" or "surveyor"), and no explanation is given for who they are or where they come from. RGALI f. 1992-1-57/78.

54. Drubek-Meyer, "Zvukomontazh," 314, 315.

55. Nikolai Aduev, "Muzykal'naia ili liricheskaia epokha," *Kino* 5 (1934). RGALI f. 1992-1-59/16.

56. Stephen Heath, "Body, Voice," in *Questions of Cinema* (Bloomington: Indiana University Press, 1985), 191.

57. The First All-Union Congress of Soviet Writers (August 1934) marked the official implementation of the term "Socialist Realism" for all Soviet art. See *Pervyi vsesoiuznyi s"ezd sovetskikh pisatelei: Stenograficheskii otchet* (Moscow: Khudozhestvennaia literatura, 1934). In 1935, the All-Union Creative Conference on Cinema Affairs adopted the principles of Socialist Realism as set out for literature.

58. Anna Nisnevich, "Ear of the Beholder: Listening in *Muzykal'naia Istoriia* (1940)," in *Sound, Speech, Music in Soviet and Post-Soviet Cinema*, ed. Lilya Kaganovsky and Masha Salzkina (Bloomington: Indiana University Press, 2014), 193–211; here: 194.

chapter four

MULTILINGUALISM AND HETEROGLOSSIA IN ALEXANDER DOVZHENKO'S *IVAN* AND *AEROGRAD*

IN THE HISTORY OF EARLY Soviet cinema, Alexander (Oleksandr) Dovzhenko stands out as perhaps its most unusual director. Dovzhenko came from a poor, peasant background (at the time when most Russian film directors were educated, middle class, and urban); and he had had no formal training in film (before the Revolution and Civil War, Dovzhenko was a school teacher, after, he was a political cartoonist), when he suddenly decided to become a film director at the age of thirty-two. In 1928 he helped found the Kiev Film Studio, where he planted an orchard, and from which he was forced out four years later (and which was posthumously named after him). He spent the rest of his life in Moscow making films for Mosfilm (where he also planted an orchard), never allowed to move back to his native Ukraine. In the beginning of his filmmaking career, Dovzhenko made gorgeous silent films that gave us sweeping views of the Ukrainian countryside, its rivers and fields, people and animals. In the middle, he made classics of Socialist Realism, under a direct mandate from Stalin, receiving the Order of Lenin in 1935. Toward the end of his life, he was attacked by Stalin when he tried to speak about Ukrainian suffering during WWII in *Ukraine in Flames* (Ukraina v ogne, 1943).[1] His last film, *A Poem of the Sea* (Poema o more, 1955–1959) remained unfinished before his death in 1956, and was completed by his wife, the actress Yulia Solntseva.

Some of the facts about Dovzhenko's life are quite well known, while others remain unclear. Dovzhenko was born in 1894 in Sosnytsa, a village about one hundred kilometers north of Kiev. His parents were relatively poor peasants, but proud descendants of Don Cossacks, and he was one of fourteen children, only two of whom survived into adulthood, and of whom only Alexander received a full education. At the age of sixteen he went to train as a teacher, graduating in 1914, and after, taught at a secondary mixed elementary school in Zhytomyr. He managed to avoid military conscription during WWI on medical grounds, enrolling in Kiev's Commercial Institute in economics in 1917—the start of the Revolution and Ukraine's three-year Civil War.

It is at this point that narratives of Dovzhenko's life diverge. According to his own biography and the work done by Vance Keply Jr., Dovzhenko, like countless other Ukrainians, flirted with different nationalist and socialist factions, but as the civil war ran its course, he moved steadily to the left, eventually making a full commitment to Bolshevism and to political unity with Russia. He enlisted in one of several Ukrainian regiments of the Red Army and fought in the Civil War in 1919 and 1920, serving under the Red Army hero Nikolai Shchors (the subject of Dovzhenko's most well-received film from 1939).[2]

George Liber, however, writes this narrative in quite a different way. During the very complex period 1917–1919, when many different groups were vying for power in Ukraine, Dovzhenko's nationalist sympathies brought him in direct conflict with the Bolshevik movement. At this time, he was a member of the Ukrainian Socialist-Revolutionary Party, which was agitating for an autonomous republic within a wider federal system. According to Liber, Dovzhenko fought against the Red Army, joining the Communist Party only in April 1920 after his capture, arrest, and incarceration.[3] After his second meeting with Stalin (May 22, 1935) in the Kremlin office, Stalin sent Dovzhenko a record player and Ukrainian music, which Dovzhenko took to be a sign that Stalin knew about his pro independent Ukraine Petliura service during the Civil War, about his arrest and conviction in 1919. This was a "warning shot," a direct reminder that Dovzhenko could not escape his nationalist past.[4]

In the early 1920s, Dovzhenko was a diplomatic representative for the Soviet Ukrainian Government, first in Warsaw, and then in Berlin, where he formally studied art and moved among artists associated with the German Expressionist movement.[5] After he was recalled to Ukraine in 1923, he worked as a political cartoonist and illustrator in Kharkiv for three years (1923–1926), as a member of Ukraine's most important literary organization, VAPLITE (Free Academy of Proletarian Literature). Then, in 1926, after a sleepless night, he left Kharkiv for Odessa and joined the All-Ukrainian Photo-Cinema Administration (VUFKU) to become a film director. As he famously wrote in his autobiography, "In June 1926 I sat up all night in my studio, assessed my thirty-two unsuccessful years of life, and in the morning I picked up my cane and suitcase, leaving behind my canvasses and painting supplies, and departed, never to return. I went to Odessa to get a job in the film studio as a director. You could say that I stood a naked man on the Black Sea coast."[6]

Contradictory narratives of Dovzhenko's revolutionary activities from 1917–1919 in part reflect the history of the period (many would rewrite their biographies in order to bring them into line with official Soviet ideology), but in part speak to the conflicting forces at work in Dovzhenko's films. His films, at least up until the 1939 *Shchors*, are not straightforward translations of ideology—even to the extent that such a thing may be possible in the first place—but rather nuanced and complex attempts to capture with visual language the ambiguity of Soviet reality and its political projects. His films cover subjects like the Revolution and Civil War, collectivization, and the conquest of the Far East. Yet, they also transcend these historical events to speak instead about life and death, about tradition and technological progress, freely mixing folklore and realism, myth and propaganda.

Despite the loss of the negative for *Earth* (Zemlia, 1930) during the German bombing of Kiev during WWII, the film remains one of the iconoclastic works associated with the Soviet cinematic avant-garde, while Dovzhenko is regarded as a pioneer of cinematic modernism, and, as Philip Cavandish writes, "a poetic visionary who eschewed conventional narrative forms and genres, and sought radically to reshape cinema as a means of expressive communication."[7] At VUFKU in Ukraine, Dovzhenko worked closely with cameraman Danylo Demutsky (Demuts'kyi, 1893–1954), who was instrumental in bringing to the screen the "poetic" visual sensibility for which Dovzhenko is so famous—history combined with folklore, combined with sweeping shots of the Ukrainian landscape. Dovzhenko's films about his native Ukraine are considered to be among the most lyrical works of Soviet cinema, and they derive much of their beauty from a Ukrainian pastoral tradition and from an abiding faith in peasant custom. As Viktor Shklovsky once noted, speaking of Dovzhenko's cinema, "The trees audibly 'rustled' in his silent films."[8]

But Dovzhenko was also a revolutionary filmmaker and a filmmaker of the revolution. Simultaneous with the lyrical visuals, his films also insisted on modernity, calling for the abandonment of old Slavic traditions in favor of the revolutionary transformation of Soviet society. This is already true of *Earth* but, in particular, is also true of the two films at the center of this chapter: the 1932 *Ivan* and the 1935 *Aerograd*. Western reception of Dovzhenko has largely focused on the former—his role as a sensitive lyric poet whose art reflected an individual sensibility; and attempted to downplay the latter—his political awareness and acumen, his relationship with Stalin and the Soviet state.

In the thirties, fearing arrest, for example, Dovzhenko appealed to Stalin, and his rapturous description of his two meetings with the Great Leader reads like a page out of a Socialist Realist novel: "It is obvious that the world is so constructed," wrote Dovzhenko in the journal *Iskusstvo kino* (The Art of Cinema, 1937),

> that an ordinary person, even a brave and decisive one who is acutely conscious of his sincerity and disposition, is prone to experience a feeling of profound excitement when he approaches for the first time a great and remarkable man. It was precisely this feeling that I experienced on my way to see the man who for the whole of the best and most progressive part of mankind is the greatest and most dearly beloved—Comrade Stalin.
>
> A whole series of circumstances that arose before I started filming *Aerograd* made me go straight to Comrade Stalin. Things were very difficult for me. I reflected that I had already turned to Comrade Stalin in writing on one occasion at a difficult moment in my life as an artist and he had saved my artistic life and assured my further creativity. There was no doubt that he would help me now as well. I was not mistaken. Comrade Stalin received me exactly twenty-two hours after the letter had been posted.
>
> Comrade Stalin introduced me to Comrades Molotov, Voroshilov and Kirov so well and warmly and in such a fatherly fashion that is seemed as if he had known me well for a long time. So I felt more at ease.
>
> Comrades Stalin, Voroshilov, Molotov and Kirov listed attentively to the script of *Aerograd*. Comrade Stalin offered a number of observations and elucidations. From his remarks I realized that he was not only interested in the professional side of our work. Questioning me about the Far East, Comrade Stalin asked if I could indicate on the map where I would build a city if I were a builder rather than a film director....
>
> I left Comrade Stalin with a clear head, with his wishes for success and his promise of help.

Everyone who wanted to remain in favor made sure to speak the language of the Great Family and this is what we find in Dovzhenko's account, producing an idealized image of Stalin as "Father of the People."[9] But if we read between the lines of the offered text, we might note something else at work in Dovzhenko's description. Of his second visit to Stalin, in which he is asked explicitly about getting to work on *Shchors*, Dovzhenko writes,

> In the midst of his work on matters of enormous state importance, Comrade Stalin found time to remember an artist, to check up on his state of mind and to relieve him of any feeling, however imaginary, that he lacked freedom, and to present him with complete freedom of choice.

I told Comrade Stalin that I was ready to make *Shchors*. I thanked him for the idea and consciously reproached myself on more than one occasion because I, a Ukrainian artist, had not thought of it myself. . . .

I wanted to shout . . . but I left quietly and at the door I once more bowed to him and Voroshilov, Molotov and Kirov. In the Kremlin courtyard the sun was shining, Moscow was roaring around the hill, and the visibility was stunningly clear to all four corners of the earth.¹⁰

What seems "clear" from this passage is that Dovzhenko is perfectly well aware of his incredibly precarious position vis-à-vis state power. While Stalin assures him that he is under no "obligation" to make *Shchors*, that he is a "free man," Dovzhenko understands correctly that the nonobligation to do as he is told is literally a matter of life and death. Dovzhenko's lyrical description of the sun, of Moscow, and of his new found "visibility," while on the surface suggesting a kind of transformation Socialist Realist heroes have upon meeting Stalin, speaks instead to his clear understanding of the consequences of disobedience. As he puts it earlier in the article, "I want to write in greater detail about my second visit to Comrade Stalin. I want my comrades in art to be happy and proud and our enemies to have cause for reflection."¹¹

In this chapter, I offer a way of reading Dovzhenko's cinema not only as a highly personal aesthetic project (which is how his films are generally read), but also as a series of responses to the shifting political, ideological, and technological landscape in which he worked. Specifically, I consider the uses of sound in his first sound films, *Ivan* and *Aerograd*, as a way of seeing how the new technology of sound made possible a different kind of cinematic voice, one that was explicitly tied to the demands of Socialist Realism being formulated at the time. I am interested here in all of the different implications of the notions of "voice"—in Dovzhenko's own authorial voice, in his reliance on direct address to speak the messages of his films, in his choice of language, in his uses of silence, and finally, in the voice of power issuing from the screen. And while after 1933 Dovzhenko made his films in Russian and at Mosfilm,¹² his first sound film, like his groundbreaking silent films, was made in Ukraine, and the language of choice—Ukrainian—became one of the key elements of its reception. Indeed, because sound arrived to Soviet cinema while the USSR still promoted national languages and cultures, and before dubbing became a widely available technology, the new sound technology briefly offered the possibility of the creation of a multilingual cinema not available elsewhere.¹³

Before cinema became "silent" and "mute," it was characterized by its internationalist language—"image, devoid of text, speaking to all viewers, regardless of language."¹⁴ Thus, for example, the manifesto preceding Dziga Vertov's 1929 *Man with a Movie Camera* (Chelovek s kinoapparatom), stresses the "creation of an authentically international absolute language of cinema." Or, similarly, Osip Beskin, the editor of the journal *Sovetskoe kino* (Soviet Cinema), the official organ of the Association of Workers in Revolutionary Cinematography (ARRK), wrote in 1928 that "only film gives us the opportunity to effectively strengthen the social cohesion in our multilingual country."¹⁵ Of course, even silent film was accompanied by words: films consisted of moving pictures but also of title cards with text reproducing dialogue or specifying various elements of the scenario. These title cards could be easily exchanged or removed to accommodate different linguistic situations; they could also (as was the case for the USSR) be read aloud, translated, and explained by qualified political workers sent to assist at film screenings throughout the Soviet Union. As Gabrielle Chomentowski has pointed out, however, with the arrival of sound, film studios and directors had to make the choice of a language that was not necessarily understood by everyone beyond geographical and ethnic boundaries. Very quickly, the hopes of political leaders for the production of "cinema as an international language," were undermined by problems that were at once organizational, political, economic, and technical.¹⁶

By 1927 the Soviet film industry included some thirteen production organizations, which represented an array of regional and national interests. These included Sovkino (Russia), by far the largest of the Soviet film studios, formed in 1924 from a consolidation of smaller production companies; VUFKU (Ukraine); Mezhrabpom-Rus' (German-owned, private film production company); Gosinprom Gruzii (Georgia); and Belgoskino (Belarus), to name the five largest.¹⁷ Of these, the Ukrainian VUFKU grew into the USSR's second largest film organization. Its "native" market represented almost 22 percent of the total Soviet film market, with a series of films, including those of Dovzhenko, emphasizing Ukrainian cultural heritage. Because of its position as the second largest film organization in the USSR, in the 1930s VUFKU faced particular scrutiny and threat. Soviet cinema was supposed to be "national in form but socialist in content," and VUFKU frequently came under the charge of "nationalist deviation," followed by purges and arrests.¹⁸

Under the New Economic Policy (NEP, 1921–1928), each national republic maintained considerable autonomy for its national film market, in part to prevent colonization by larger distributors, like Sovkino. Bilateral trade agreements between different republics were developed based on size and numbers of films produced: Vance Kepley Jr. gives the example of a

10:3 exchange rate between the two largest markets, Sovkino and VUFKU (with Ukraine accepting ten Russian films for every three Ukrainian films playing in the Russian republic), while the exchange rate between VUFKU and Georgia's Gosinprom Gruzii was 9:5.[19] The March 1928 First All-Union Conference on Cinema Affairs was the first move toward the centralization of the film industry, which brought the different national film studios under more direct control of the State. Anatoly Lunacharsky's resignation as the Commissar of Education (from Narkompros, the official body in charge of film organizations) in 1929, and a shift in the policies on nationalism and national languages during the First Five-Year Plan, undermined the autonomy of the different republics.[20] Purges and arrests followed, including allegations of excessive "nationalism" that could be employed against national studios. In 1930, Sovkino was eliminated and a new agency was given sweeping authority over all movie and photo production; Soiuzkino (the All-Union Combine of the Movie-Photo Industry) was put in charge of "all matters concerning production of movie-photo apparatus (for filming, projecting, lighting, and so on) and also all matter concerning motion picture production, rental, and exhibition."[21] This significantly curtailed the autonomy of the national film studios, which now answered directly to one centralized institution, located in Moscow.

Among other things, Soiuzkino was meant to oversee the transition from silent to sound filmmaking, to develop plans to refurbish the USSR's principle production facilities, and to continue the process of creating new exhibition installations. But it also needed a new federal system of distribution/diffusion of sound films in a multilinguistic environment.[22] Souizkino would now need to coordinate the production and distribution of sound prints in line with regional language patterns. This had not been an issue with silent films, which could rely either on multilanguage intertitles or on a *bonimenteur*—a speaker who interpreted the film for provincial audiences during projection.[23] Sound cinema required more complex plans for dubbing and subtitling to serve the USSR's multiethnic population, which led to the question: Which language would Soviet cinema speak?

Ivan

Like Esfir Shub, Dovzhenko took a positive but still somewhat attenuated stance toward the coming of sound, writing in 1928, in a typically metaphorical and physiological language:

> I believe that the Great Silent will speak. I see in this a new era in world culture and the most powerful tool in raising the cultural level of the masses.

It's true that when they first graft on the Mute's tongue [*prish'iut Nemomu iazyk*], he will lisp and stammer to the joy and laughter of the high-priests and the petty-bourgeoisie of the cinema. But in time, his speaking voice will improve, and we will witness a new, unheard of achievement. I will be happy the day when I come face to face with the talkie. But I can't tell you yet how I'm going to apply its principles to my work, since I don't yet understand how it works.[24]

In June of 1930 Dovzhenko traveled abroad, in part to study sound film, in which he saw unlimited possibilities.[25] And one year later, in June 1931, he began work on his first sound film, *Ivan*. Dovzhenko claimed that *Ivan* would be a "simple film" ("ia delaiu fil'mu prostuiu i iasnuiu," he wrote in 1932); with an unheroic hero, who doesn't lead, but is instead "led by the proletariat."[26] The focus of the film is on the transformation of the Ukrainian peasant into the Ukrainian worker, and the plot centers on the title character, Ivan, who leaves his village in order to join the Dneprostroi construction project. During construction, an unskilled worker is killed, the dam is threatened, and Ivan learns that in order to be a better worker, he must not only have physical strength, but also education. The final shot of the film is Ivan at school. The film also contains two brilliant sequences tangentially related to the story of Ivan's transformation from peasant to worker: the story of the "shirker" (*porkhun-progul'shchik*) who fishes instead of working and yet still tries to collect his pay, and the story of the mother who mourns her son's death.

According to Dovzhenko, there would be simplicity to the formal composition, an absence of long shots with their busy screens, and the liquidation of rapid montage.[27] Indeed, the opening shots of *Ivan*, filmed from the river and lasting an incredible ten minutes, are some of the greatest shots in cinematic history. These are not simply establishing shots; the camera is mobile, lyrical, capturing first the tranquility and then the raw power of the Dnieper River. Sergei Eisenstein praised these shots as some of the best examples of sight and sound in cinematography.[28] "I am experimenting with overcoming the static nature of the landscape," wrote Dovzhenko in 1932. "In this, I was helped by sound. I made the landscape sonorous [*ia zastavil peizazh zvuchat'*]."[29]

The sonorous landscape is particularly noticeable in the second set of shots of the opening sequence, filmed from a rowboat situated low on the water, with the accompanying chorus of women's voices singing a traditional Ukrainian song. Moving from wide shots of the peaceful Dnieper River accompanied by sounds of the orchestra of the Kiev Broadcasting Center (and what would come to be a fairly standard audio-visual montage for a film opening, with wide panoramic establishing shots coupled

Figure 4.1. Ukrainian SSR. Alexander Dovzhenko on the set of "Ivan" 1932 (ITAR-TASS Photo Agency / Alamy Stock Photo)

with extradiegetic music), the second series of shots produces something remarkable: because the women are never shown on screen, their song appears to be emanating *from* the landscape itself, as if the trees and hills of the Ukrainian countryside have a voice of their own. As Soviet critic Ramil Sobolev describes it (writing in 1980), Dovzhenko "rejected the use of professional singers and replaced them with milkmaids and milk sellers from the local market, to get a more authentic and traditional sound."[30] Their chorus is used again in a later sequence, when their song is intercut with the noises of heavy industry and rushing water at Dneprostroi in a complicated audio-montage, where pieces of traditional folk song are mixed with the "symphony of sirens" of industrial production to introduce the giant power station under construction.[31] This montage of song, industrial noise, and the screeching of machines—not precisely in the style of Vertov, because there is no real love of the machine here, nor an emphasis on true recorded sound—is an attempt to combine the earlier "sonorous landscape" with the sounds of heavy industry, a way of signaling at the level of the sound track the transformation or absorption of the peasant into the working class.

Moreover, in making his first sound film, Dovzhenko claimed to be equally interested in sound and silence, writing in 1932 before the release of *Ivan*: "I am also working on the problem of silence [*tishina*] in cinema. I think one can only reach silence through sound cinema. The silent screen,

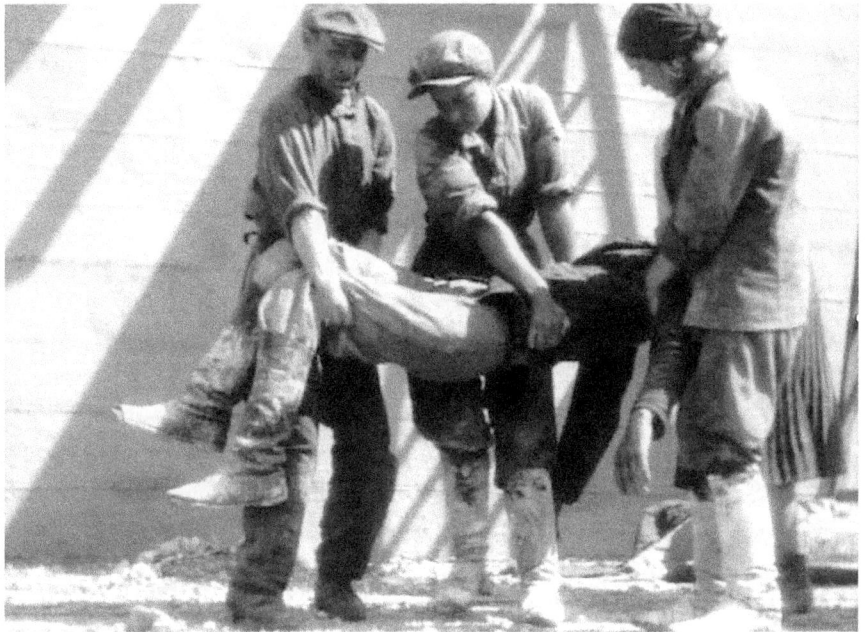

Figure 4.2. Moment of silence (*Ivan*, frame capture)

because of its conventions, was never silent, even without musical accompaniment. Silence on the sound screen doesn't always correspond to sound on the sound track."[32] Indeed, *Ivan* has a long silent sequence in the middle that radically breaks the conventions of sound use, both in early and in classic sound film. The sequence showing an accident at the construction site and the death of one of the workers is accompanied by total silence. What had previously been a cacophony of orchestral score and industrial noises (train whistles, sounds of hammers, and the like) is cut off at the moment of the accident. The human cry is cut short and replaced with the sound of a train whistle, just as there is an abrupt shift from the scene of the accident to a shot of a train receding into the distance, no longer audible on the sound track. The rest of the sequence is shot with a "dead" sound track, in total silence, as the body of the worker is carried out and placed in front of the factory wall, and as the mother stands over the body of her son.

Here, the sound comes back, but now in a menacing form as pure industrial noise, as the factory returns to life. We understand that this is the mother's perception—both aural and visual—of the construction site, no longer made safe for human beings. Her figure appears small and insignificant in comparison to the cranes, engines, and clamshell shovels of the

Figure 4.3. Mother's grief (*Ivan*, frame capture)

construction zone. In the midst of clanging machinery, she has no voice—even as she attempts to speak to the head of the factory about the accident, she has no powers of speech to compete with those of heavy industry. We are meant to understand that the head of the factory is already giving orders to prevent future accidents, but the sequence, in which the mother runs through numerous doors (again, shot silent) only to be stopped in her tracks by the sound of a gruff male voice yelling into the phone, suggests that she has no place here. In answer to the question, "What do you want, comrade?," the mother replies, "Nothing."

This is an unusual and very purposeful use of a "dead" sound track, as Kristin Thompson has described it.[33] Thompson notes that extended silence is a relatively rare device for early Soviet sound film, where silence would normally be limited to the usual pauses between distinct sounds, but instead here points to stretches of dead track without ambient noise. One exception to always filling the sound track with sounds comes from Vsevolod Pudovkin's *Deserter* (Dezertir, 1933), with whole sequences played mostly or entirely with a dead track. While Pudovkin's use of the dead track appears "arbitrary," the switch to complete silence "heightens and renews our perception of events."[34] Thompson contrasts this usage

Figure 4.4a. Construction of Dneprostroi (*Ivan*, frame capture)

with Grigori Kozintsev and Leonid Trauberg's *Alone* (*Odna*, 1931), where a brief silent scene (Kuzmina receiving her teaching assignment) is used for an emotional function, stressing Kuzmina's shock and disappointment.[35]

As in *Alone*, Dovzhenko uses the dead sound track in *Ivan* to underscore the emotional function—in this case, the worker's death and the mother's grief—but he does still more. Dovzhenko described *Ivan* as first and foremost a sound film, with a set of technical problems and opportunities created by sound technology that needed to be resolved by new methods and formal techniques.[36] For Dovzhenko, Dneprostroi appeared too vast and monotonous (*odnoobraznyi*) to be filmed well, with most films providing identical sweeping areal views of the construction site, and relying mostly on long shots to convey its power and size. Instead, he uses close ups and pans to show the enormous construction site from a new angle or different perspectives. Like the opening sequence filmed from a steamboat gently gliding on the Dnieper River, Dovzhenko's cameraman Danylo Demutsky filmed Dneprostroi by mounting a camera on a moving cement train, a tracking shot taking the viewer around the construction site as if one were there—showing us Dneprostroi from a human rather than a "cine-eye" vantage point.[37] The initial long shots of the industrial site are

Figure 4.4b. Construction site ballet (*Ivan*, frame capture)

soon replaced with close ups of construction workers, men and women, directing and controlling the machinery. Unlike Vertov, Dovzhenko does not turn the human body into an extension of the machine; rather, the human body appears in the middle of this vast industrial maze as a guide, directing operations, but never itself becoming machine-like (indeed, graphic matches are established between the different bodies, producing almost ballet-like movements). The lack of rapid montage is one of the elements that prevents this film from slipping into a celebration of the mechanical or technological. Demutsky's camera and Dovzhenko's editing remain for the most part measured and slow, mixing fluid motion with static shots of people, often filmed from below, to emphasize scale.[38] Likewise, the emphasis on the naked backs and glistening skin of the workers underscores the haptic, tactile element of this sequence—the workers' bodies are not abstracted but rather are brought closer to the viewer and placed almost within our "grasp."

There is no love of technology for technology's sake here, no "fetishism of the machine."[39] This is why the crashing, hooting, and clanking noises of heavy industry are all cut off when the worker dies. Dovzhenko is

Figure 4.5. Stepan Shkurat on the set of "Ivan" (SPUTNIK / Alamy Stock Photo)

prioritizing the human voice over the voice of technology, creating a literal moment of silence to mark the death of the worker and his mother's grief. As the mother says at the end of the film, "When my son fell, the whole world became silent." Maxim Gorky, commenting on *Ivan*, noted that in this film "man was not in charge, but was crushed by the heavy weight of the substance of matter [*razdavlen tiazhestiami veshchestva materii*]."[40] Yet, while the visuals show us the heaviness of matter, the sound track works contrapuntally, its silence drawing our attention to and making us identify with the small, vulnerable human body and the mother's silent grief.

Similarly, the role of the radio/loudspeaker in *Ivan* challenges the hierarchy produced by early Soviet sound films between the human and the nonhuman voice in such films as *Alone*, *Deserter*, and others. As, Stephen Lovell has noted, in the USSR, from the early 1920s onward, the spoken word "received new kinds of amplification, both literally (in the form of the loudspeakers that were set up in public places in urban areas) and metaphorically (in the form of broadcasting)." Radio offered a way of projecting the voice of authority into every workplace and communal flat in the USSR and of showing Soviet people exactly how to "speak Bolshevik."[41] In early Soviet sound cinema, radio—in the form of the loudspeaker, but also, telephone, gramophone, slogans, and other forms of direct address—often acts as an *acousmêtre*, bypassing the human body in favor of a voice that speaks both from within and from *beyond* the film.[42] We see this most clearly in Kozintsev and Trauberg's *Alone*, where the invention of the new sound technology is embodied by a loudspeaker in the middle of an empty square addressing itself to passersby, but we find a similar sequence in *Ivan*, as the "shirker" Huba (played by the amazing Stepan Shkurat) attempts to collect pay for work he hasn't done from a *chorna kasa*—an illegal depository for company cash.[43]

The scene opens on a ramshackle hut, pitched at a precarious angle, with a loudspeaker on top and the words *chorna kasa* on the front. In a comical sequence, aided by a duple/cut time musical score often used in musical theater, the completely stationary camera remains focused on the hut as Huba walks in and out of the frame, sometimes reappearing in unexpected locations, made possible through a series of unmarked jump cuts. Finally, after circling the hut a few times, Huba tentatively approaches the window and knocks. A close up shows us Huba as he counts his money, and then proceeds to shake the hand extended from the open window—only to find that the person inside has grabbed hold of him and won't let go. As he struggles to get away, Huba falls flat on the ground, a high-angle shot foreshadowing the position we are about to assume in relation to this "shirker," that of the all-knowing voice issuing from the loudspeaker on the roof of the hut. Over the next few minutes of film, Huba is "chased" all over the village by a voice from a loudspeaker that seems to know everything about him and from which he cannot escape. The voice from the loudspeaker addresses him by name, enumerating his failures and shortcomings, including how much he eats—two pounds of bread and pig fat (*salo*) per day, and the like. While the opening shots of this sequence were all limited to a single location, we now see Huba running all over the village, pursued by the voice from above. In particular, the voice stresses the fact that Huba is healthy and able-bodied, introducing a biopolitical element into this mix of ideology and satire.

The loudspeaker is a clear example of what Michel Chion has termed the "all-seeing voice": a disembodied voice whose "sourcelessness" suggests "the paranoid and often obsessional panoptic fantasy . . . of total mastery of space by vision," an "*acousmêtre*."[44] But whereas in *Alone*, the loudspeaker addresses itself to everyone and no one at once—we first see it positioned in the middle of an empty square, speaking its demands whether anyone is there to hear them or not—the loudspeaker in *Ivan* is speaking directly to and about Huba. This direct address marks a shift from the general to

Figure 4.6a.
Huba and the
loudspeaker (*Ivan*,
frame capture)

Figure 4.6b.
Huba and the
loudspeaker (*Ivan*,
frame capture)

the specific (and I would argue, Foucauldian) form of knowledge.[45] The voice issuing from the loudspeaker addresses Huba personally, singling him out by name and patronymic (Stepan Yosypovych) and taking note of his proclivities (how much bread and *salo* he eats), where he comes from (Yaresky village, the district of Myrhorod), his age (46 years old), his health (*zdorovyi*). Disciplinary power, like Jeremy Bentham's *Panopticon*, divides and separates individuals, making them visible and inducing a "state of consciousness and permanent visibility that assures the automatic functioning of power."[46] This is the function of the loudspeaker in *Ivan*, a clear example of the *acousmêtre* as the "all-seeing voice," from which "no creature can hide."[47]

Moreover, the loudspeaker is not the only acousmatic device that appears in Dovzhenko's film. Both the telephone and the radio are used in *Ivan* to signal a direct transmission of the voice-of-power, a direct link to the State. Thus, when Huba returns home from fishing, his son telephones the Komsomol to report him, promising to disown him at the next meeting. At the end of the film, we hear the son's voice over the radio, denouncing his worthless father. Huba's revenge is to break the radio receiver and to appear in person at the Komsomol meeting to disown his son in turn. He tries to speak with the voice of authority, laying claim to paternity as the reason why he should have his son's respect, but in the end, can only repeat a line from earlier in the film: "I am an inimitable individuality" (*Ia nepovtorimaia individual'nost'*), before falling silent. At this point, Dovhzenko, once again, cuts to a dead sound track to underscore the profound voicelessness of this scene. In a film where all the workers look alike and most are named Ivan, Stepan Yosypovych Huba is indeed an inimitable personality, constantly trying to counteract the power of the Soviets to turn everyone into a shock worker (*udarnik*). Dovzhenko's first use of direct address in *Ivan* (a technique he will return to in his 1935 *Aerograd*), was to show us a series of static portraits of real shock workers filmed looking straight into the camera, interrupted by Huba's characterization of himself as a shirker. In a comical visual riff on a performance by George Bernard Shaw,[48] Huba shows off his profile, back of the head, and walk to the camera, before announcing to the audience in the theater, "Enough already! I declare the Five-Year Plan in one year!" His inimitable individuality saves the film from the Socialist Realist style, which the ending in particular—with its Komsomol speeches, its bust of Stalin, and the arrival of Soviet power in the form of troops, cars, tanks, and airplanes—anticipates.[49] Huba's presence and his final speech to the whole workers' community underscore the degree to which Dovzhenko is aware of the function of voice in the new sound cinema, of the multiple competing voices (the voice of the landscape, of industry, the voice of the State, and the voice of the individual) that are in turn made audible or silenced by the new sound apparatus.

Multilingualism, Heteroglossia, Aphasia

Despite its very innovative uses of both image and sound and a seemingly topical plot, Dovzhenko's film was not well received. By the time of its release in 1932, Dovzhenko had a nervous break down, complaining bitterly about the building of the Brest-Litovsk highway that he could see out of his window, which was destroying the old town and its environs. *Ivan*, he felt, had come out "raw and shapeless."[50] Béla Balázs, who liked the film, wrote that, unlike *Counterplan* (Vstrechnyi, dir. Ermler & Yutkevich, 1932), and despite Dovzhenko's own formulation, this film was neither "light" nor "simple" (*kartina uzhe sovsem ne legka i ne prosta*).⁵¹

Ivan was completed on October 30, 1932, with its first public screenings held on November 2nd in Kiev and November 3rd in Kharkiv; and with an official premiere on November 6, 1932. Even before its official release, the film was accused of "Ukrainian nationalism," though no one could say precisely in what way the film was "nationalist." On November 5th cuts were made by a "special commission," while Ukrainfilm administrators ordered Dovzhenko, his wife Yulia Solntseva, and the film's editor, Hryhory Zeldovych to Moscow, to wait for the official decision, which came six weeks later as approval from Stalin and the Politburo.

Yet, despite the Politburo's approval, the film was perceived as a failure and part of that failure lay with the sound track—or, more precisely, with the choice of language that issued from the screen. Dovzhenko made his first Ukrainian sound film in Ukrainian, claiming, at the time, that Kiev had a dearth of actors, and the best ones spoke no Russian, and that no one could dub them. The choice may have been aesthetic or ideological— the film was about the transformation of the Ukrainian peasantry into a Ukrainian working class—but it was perceived as nationalist because the use of Ukrainian was said to unsettle the Russian-speaking audience of the film.⁵² As many critics have written both at the time and after, *Ivan* had "no clear message" and was filled with visual and thematic ambiguities (for one, the project of building the dam remains incomplete and, therefore, the human toll and loss of life at the heart of the film remain unjustified). After its release, Dovzhenko admitted that the use of Ukrainian, because of its closeness to Russian, undermined the film's accessibility for Russian-speaking audiences. The Russian viewers, Dovzhenko suggested, assumed incorrectly that they could understand it: "The viewer's semi-knowledge of the language is the problem. This half-knowledge introduces to the viewer's consciousness inhibitory elements that irritate the viewer. This lowers the quality of the film."⁵³

The film's "unclear" ideological message, therefore, stemmed in part from the choice of language, a language that was almost but not exactly the same as that of its audience. The audience, according to Dovzhenko, could not "abstract" itself from the language, and ended up frustrated by its proximity. As George Liber suggests in his biography of Dovzhenko, "the language of the film also became a message."⁵⁴ Indeed, one can argue that the ideological message of the film was actually quite clear; it was simply not the message that the State wanted to receive. The heavy Ukrainianization campaigns of the 1920s had proved at once ineffectual and divisive. On the one hand, Stalinist policies of *korenizatsiia* ("indigenization") aimed at converting Ukrainian from its status as the language of the peasants to a cultural force, with books, magazines, and films all translated into Ukrainian. At the same time, in order not to lose the support of the Ukrainian working class—mostly Russian speaking and located in Donbass and other major industrial regions—the Soviets did not enforce the new language policies in urban centers, or at higher educational levels. By 1930, eighty percent of all books published and ninety percent of all newspapers were written in Ukrainian, and by 1932–1933, 88 percent of elementary and secondary students in Ukraine received instruction in Ukrainian. But as the policies of *korenizatsiia* were replaced by the cultural revolution, collectivization, and industrialization, the idea of Ukrainianization became suspect. It was no longer linked to Soviet ideology of "national in form but socialist in content," but instead to Ukrainian nationalism and resistance to collectivization. Thus, Dovzhenko wasn't exactly lying when he claimed that he could find no actors who spoke Russian; rather, he was making sure that the new sound technology aided in the "Ukrainianization" of Ukrainian cinema, which by 1932, turned out to be a dangerous move.[55]

Dovzhenko's choice of language for *Ivan* may be tied to what Evgeny Margolit has termed early Soviet sound cinema's heteroglossia or multilingualism—*raznoiazychie*.[56] As Margolit argues, the first years of sound cinema saw the release of about a dozen films (Soviet film studios produced about twenty sound films a year on average in the first half of the 1930s) showcasing a broad range of heteroglossic strategies; thus, for example, we find Mustafa the thief singing in his native Mari tongue in the finale of Nikolai Ekk's *The Road to Life* (Putevka v zhizn', 1931; the first 100 percent Soviet "talkie"). Characteristically, throughout the film Mustafa speaks Russian with a comical accent, but on the eve of his death he sings in his native tongue, as though returning to his origins. Similarly, in *My Native Land* (Moia rodina, dirs. Iosif Kheifits and Aleksandr Zarkhi, 1933), the mortally wounded hero-soldier Katz abruptly switches to Yiddish in his delirium. The young soldier Vaska from *My Native Land* never masters the Chinese phrase for "The Red Army is a friend of the poor," but the Chinese youth Wan (played by Bori Khaidarov, a Central Asian actor who did not speak Chinese) can nevertheless understand him through his inflections and facial expressions. The same tactic is echoed in *The Outskirts* (Okraina, dir. Boris Barnet, 1933) released a month later; in this case, all communication between the young German soldier Müller and various Russian villagers takes place outside of spoken language. "Foreign speech," argues

Margolit, "compels the viewer to concentrate on the speaker's face, thus emphasizing their individuality and humanity, their triumph over the tyranny of the Word."[57]

Indeed, a surprising number of early Soviet sound films, beyond those mentioned by Margolit, made use of foreign and untranslated speech. In Shub's 1932 *K.Sh.E.* we hear a radio program being recorded in English, German, and French, as well as a scene of an American specialist visiting the job site with his Russian translator. The emphasis on multilingualism and translation is coupled with a reliance on American specialists to provide instruction to the Soviet labor force. On the one hand, we hear the phrase "Workers of the World Unite!" (spoken in English by the radio announcer), followed by the same speech in German and French, whose recognizable words include "Stalin," "Lenin," "Komsomol," "Five-Year Plan," and "enthusiasm." On the other hand, we see the American specialist instruct the Soviet worker in the use of the correct tool, with the translator concluding, in English, "Alright, they'll do as you say."

The emphasis on translation is particularly evident in a film like Aleksandr Macheret's *Men and Jobs* (Dela i liudi, 1932), which relies on the impossibility of translating the terms *sotsialisticheskoe sorevnovanie* (socialist competition) and *udarnik* (shock worker) into English. The miscommunication between the American engineer Cline and his translator leads to exactly the opposite of the intended effect; instead of understanding *sotsialisticheskoe sorevnovanie* as a superior form of "competition" unknown in the West, the American engineer misunderstands the translator's difficulties in putting the terms into English as evidence of the Soviet workers' lack of know-how. "Yes, my good friend, I quite understand," he tells her in English, "You mean these people don't know how to work. I saw this at once." This is of course a failure of *cultural* understanding that is marked as linguistic; while the Russian *sorevnovanie* easily translates as "competition," its true meaning is elided. Indeed, the key to understanding *Soviet* competition turns out not to be skill, but "enthusiasm." Cline's final moment of cultural comprehension anticipates a similar moment of revelation for Marion Dixon at the end of Grigori Aleksandrov's *Circus* (Tsirk, 1936). Like Marion, Cline turns to Russian to express his newfound appreciation for the Soviet state and to mark his integration into the Soviet community. Also like Marion, Cline's Russian is spoken with a pronounced accent, which ensures that in this newfound community, he is forever marked as *other*.[58] "Udarnichestvo. Kompetishon. Sorevnovanie. Gip-gip, ura!" (Shock-work. Kompetition. Competition. Hip, hip, hurray!), he concludes, reducing his final speech to pat slogans and "enthusiasm."[59]

On the one hand, multilingualism (or, more precisely, what linguists call "glossodiversity"—that is, the same words translated into different languages[60]) speaks to the universal nature of Soviet ideology: all workers can understand each other no matter what language they speak. On the other hand, the question of multilingualism in early Soviet sound films is also one of hierarchy. Which language deserves translation, and which is allowed to remain incomprehensible to the viewer? In the first sound film released by the Georgian film studio Gruziiafilm—*The Last Crusaders* (Poslednie krestonostsy, 1933, dir. S. Dolidze and V. Shvelidze)—for example, we find that the Chechens speak Russian, while the Khevsurs speak a local dialect of Georgian. The film opens with gunshots and the death of one of the Chechen shepherds, but once we move to the Khevsur side, we hear a melodious female voice singing, as the camera pans across a waterfall and mountains—showing us the natural beauty of the Georgian landscape. It is clear already from the opening sequence that the Khevsurs are tied to their land and their traditional ways of life more than the Chechens, who carry the red Soviet flag and offer the Khevsurs a cream separator as a way of ending their blood feud. (This is most likely a reference to Sergei Eisenstein's *General Line / Old and New* [*General'naia liniia / Staroe i novoe*, 1929].) The Khevsurs are too backward to see the point of this new technology that they perceive as some kind of a trick of the Soviet state—and the separator becomes the way to separate out not only cream from milk (making butter that is significantly better than that made by traditional methods), but also to divide those who embrace Soviet power from those who stand in its way. When Tsitsia's younger brother Mgelia returns to the village (wearing his city clothes in stark contrast to the traditional outfits of the Khevsur shepherds), he denounces the village's feudal system in favor of forming a *kolkhoz* (collective farm), laughs at his older brother and his "horned tractors" (the two bulls he uses to plow the land), and discovers the still untried separator beneath a cover of blankets and rocks. His first colloquy with the Chechens involves playing the "International" on his shepherd's pipe, and exchanging the word *Komsomol!* by way of greeting. The plot of *The Last Crusaders* turns on Tsitsia's mishearing Mgelia's dying word, *klass* (class), as a name of a person, rather than understanding that Mgelia was killed by the "enemies of the working class." Once again, this is a cultural rather than a linguistic misunderstanding. Throughout the film, the Khevsurs are marked as backward not only by their blood feuds, feudal structure, and their lack of technical knowledge, but also by their speech. Their use of a Georgian dialect that is itself closer to the literary Georgian

Figure 4.7. Neitan at the construction site (*Return of Nathan Bekker*, frame capture)

of the Middle Ages than to contemporary speech stands in stark contrast to the pure Russian of the Chechens.

But it is perhaps in *The Return of Nathan Bekker* (Vozvrashchenie Neitana Bekkera 1932, dir. Boris Shpis and Mark Milman), the world's first "Jewish" sound film released simultaneously in two versions, Russian and Yiddish (or, "russkii i evreiskii" as the review in the newspaper *Vecherniaia Moksva* [Evening Moscow] put it), that we see this language dynamic spelled out most clearly. Like Mustafa's singing in his native Mari, or the German soldier Katz's sudden turn to Yiddish in *My Native Land*, the Yiddish in the Russian version of *The Return of Nathan Bekker* is reduced to the language of inarticulate sounds, whose meaning lies entirely outside of comprehensible speech. Set in Belorussia during the First Five-Year Plan, the film centers on Nathan Bekker's return to the *shtetl* (still recognizable as a Jewish settlement, little transformed by Soviet power) after twenty-eight years as a bricklayer in New York. Like Macheret's Cline, Nathan is another American expert who must learn to understand that Soviet labor requires not only skill or effort, but also "head and heart"—in the USSR

Figure 4.8. Tsale teaches Jim to sing the *nigunim* (*Return of Nathan Bekker*, frame capture)

back-breaking labor is made joyful, with movements coordinated like a dance, and with friendly socialist competition taking place on a circus stage. In the Russian version—which is the only one that has been preserved, and even that, in incomplete form, without the first and the last reel—most of the other characters in the film speak perfect, unmarked Russian, with the exception of Nathan's father Tsale, played by the remarkable Solomon Mikhoels.[61] Mikhoels created his character by means of repetition (of certain movements and phrases), but his most notable sound is his constant singing of the *nigunim*, wordless Jewish melodies. Thus, for example, the first sounds we hear in the film are of Mikhoels singing, followed by his stuttered utterance, "N-n-n-Nosn!," the Yiddish form of the name "Nathan." Toward the end of the film, Nathan and Tsale conduct an entire conversation by changing the intonation of the words "well," "yes," and "no," with the longest exchange accomplished by the single word *nu*, a syllable that both in Russian and Yiddish expresses a full range of meanings, from approval to doubt to impatience and everything in between.[62]

The film closes with Nathan's friend and fellow bricklayer Jim (an African American worker who has come with Nathan from America to help build socialism) learning the *nigunim* from Tsale. Seated high above the construction site, Nathan looks down on the massive Soviet construction project with pride, while Tsale teaches Jim to sing. It is a remarkable conflation of Yiddish and African American culture, with Tsale clearly adopting Jim as a fellow Jew. Indeed, upon meeting him for the first time, Tsale asks if Jim is also Jewish, to which Nathan tells him that "he is a *bricklayer*," the profession standing in for an identity that was once determined by race, ethnicity, or religion. Yet, the ending of the film seems to belie this, keeping Nathan, the new *Soviet* worker to one side of the screen, while Tsale and Jim communicate in the "old tongue."

This conflation of black with Jewish has some implications for how we might read the film's language usage as a whole. In his famous essay "White," Richard Dyer considers the "Manicheism delirium" identified by Frantz Fanon as characteristic of colonialist sensibility, which takes an absolutist view of black and white cultures, and organizes its narrative around the rigid binarism that seemingly cannot be overcome. Here, "white" stands in for modernity, reason, order, stability, and "black" stands in for backwardness, irrationality, chaos, and violence. Dyer is particularly careful to pay attention to the way this binarism reproduces itself on the level of mise-en-scène. In a film like *Simba* (the first film Dyer examines), the whites' meeting takes place in early evening, in a fully lit room; characters that speak are shot with standard high key lighting, so that they are fully visible; everyone sits in rows; and although there is disagreement, some of it hot-tempered and emotional, it is expressed in grammatical discourse in a language the (British) viewer can understand. Moreover, the meeting consists of nothing but speech. The black meeting, on the other hand, takes place in the dead of night, out of doors, with all characters in shadow; even the MauMau leader is lit with extreme sub-Expressionist lighting that dramatizes and distorts his face. Grouping is in the form of a broken, uneven circle, and what speech there is, is ritualized not reasoned, and remains untranslated (and, as Dyer notes, is probably in no authentic language anyway), and most vocal sounds are whooping, gabbling, and shrieking.[63]

Early Soviet sound film similarly often marks non-Russian speech as incoherent or incomprehensible (song, delirium, wordless melody) and, more importantly, as "traditional" and premodern. This perhaps explains the negative reception of Dovzhenko's *Ivan*, whose thematic content—Dneprostroi, Soviet construction, worker education—should have fit brilliantly into the production films of the First Five-Year Plan, but whose choice of language placed it instead on the side of the traditional and potentially, anti-Soviet. If we compare the use of Ukrainian in *Ivan* with *The Last Crusaders*, or with *The Return of Nathan Bekker*, we can see that the use of "national" languages was tied to notions of backward and traditional cultures that needed to be reformed by the Soviet project. Thus, while with *Ivan*, Dovzhenko was participating in the broader heteroglossic, multilingual (and clearly utopian) tendencies of early Soviet sound cinema, his film tried to speak about the Soviet present with a language of the past. By giving his Russian audience a film entirely in Ukrainian, Dovzhenko was in a way declaring Ukraine's "independence" from the dominant language of Soviet cinema. Instead of a brief scene in a foreign language whose meaning could be understood through other means, the use of Ukrainian throughout the film meant the "medium *was* the message."

By 1932, Dovzhenko began to fear arrest. Demutsky, his cameraman, had already been arrested, as had a number of his colleagues and friends; and his father and mother had been expelled from their collective farm.[64] By the beginning of 1933, Dovzhenko fled to Moscow and, according to his 1939 autobiography, wrote a letter to Stalin asking for his protection. Stalin made it possible for Dovzhenko to join Mosfilm, and to begin work on his next film. *Aerograd* was set in the Far East with all the actors speaking Russian.

Aerograd

Aerograd (Air City or Frontier) is a film about a city of the future, a city that has not yet been built—nor will it have been built by the time the film concludes—about the dream of the Soviet Union's expansion into the Far East, all the way to the Pacific Ocean. Dovzhenko announced plans for a new film set in the Far East on July 25, 1933, and began an initial collaboration with the writer Aleksandr Fadeev on the screenplay.[65] *Aerograd* premiered to great acclaim in Moscow on November 6, 1935, and in Kiev on November 9, 1935. The film was made during a very tense political time. The assassination of Politburo member and head of the Leningrad party organization Sergei Kirov on December 1, 1934, opened the way for mass xenophobia, paranoia, and arrests.[66] By the mid-1930s, the Soviet Union was on the hunt for "internal enemies," but it also perceived a rising threat from the outside—from Fascist Italy, Nazi Germany, and Imperial Japan—and *Aerograd* in part reflects this paranoid state. The film is about inclusion and exclusion; foreign intervention and capitalist encirclement; the paths by which enemies can enter the Soviet Union and the paths by which friends can become enemies. The fear, specifically, is of the *chuzhie* (the other, the foreign), the "non-Russians" who threaten the Soviet Union both from within and without.

More vitally, in *Aerograd* we find the elimination of the individual voice and its replacement by the voice of the state. Everything is now marked toward the production of a particular kind of speech, made clearly audible by a reliance on direct address to communicate meaning. In *Aerograd*, Dovzhenko constructs the new technology of sound as a "voice of power" that issues directly from the screen. The question is precisely of address: Dovzhenko uses sound in his film to make the notion of "direct address" audible on the screen. Sound is not naturalized, but instead the viewer is made aware that the characters are speaking to *us* directly from the screen. The film as a whole is organized around the right to speak, and its unusual formal choices of direct address implicate the viewer in this speech act.

As one of Dovzhenko's Soviet biographers, A. Mariamov, puts it, the film is structured entirely by good and bad, black and white, with no shadows or shades.[67] The opening credits name not only the film's participants but also state their ideological positions, which include the "partisans of the Far East" (*kolkhoz* workers, taiga hunters, pilots, Red army soldiers); the old tiger-hunter partisan, Stepan Hlushak "Tiger's Death" (*tigrinaia smert'*) and his son, the pilot Vladimir; Hlushak's friend and "traitor of the Motherland" (*izmennik rodiny*), the fur farmer (*zverovod*) Vasil Khudiakov; the Chinese partisan Van Lin; a young Chukcha; and the "Old Believers, sectarians, and kulaks, who ran from us into the Siberian wilderness." Already in these opening credits, we note the direct address to the viewer: the Old Believers, sectarians, and kulaks "who ran *from us*" into the Siberian wilderness. The next title card further underscores the address and implication of the viewer: "Long live the city of Aerograd that we, Bolsheviks, must build on the shores of the Great Ocean."

The film opens with the sound of an airplane and the chorus of two male voices singing about the call of the Pacific Ocean. An aerial sweep of the taiga provides a bird's-eye view of the land below, the forests, the streams, and finally, of the ocean itself. As in his earlier films, Dovzhenko is able to show us the beauty of the natural world, though this time, it is not the "politically suspect" Ukraine, but the Soviet Far East that fills the screen. As in *Ivan*, wide shots of tranquil water are replaced with close ups of crashing waves, while the increasing tempo of the music introduces a note of alarm into this otherwise calm scene. Moreover, title cards interrupt this sequence, orienting our perception and guiding our understanding of the images, no longer satisfied to simply allow the beautiful shots

Figure 4.9a. The New Soviet Man (*Aerograd*, frame capture)

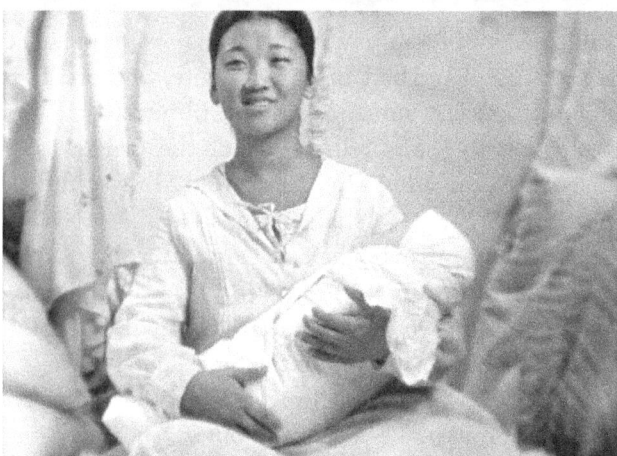

Figure 4.9b. Madonna and Child (*Aerograd*, frame capture)

of land and water to "speak" for themselves. "To the East, over the river Amur / on the shores of the Japanese sea named after Karl Marx / the Old World grows smaller and the Great Ocean becomes narrower," announce three of the cards.

Just as the male voices singing about the call of the Pacific Ocean as the "call of the Motherland" (*on menia kak rodina zovet*) contrasts directly with *Ivan*'s all-female chorus singing a traditional Ukrainian melody, so too the images of the natural world are quickly replaced by images of Soviet power. We see in the next shot that this land is neither empty nor unguarded; airplanes fly overhead and boats speed across the waters, bringing the technology of the state to the wilderness. As Emma Widdis notes, while the taiga is known to those who can "read" it, the aerial view, by

Figure 4.9c.
The "Samuri"
(*Aerograd*, frame capture)

Figure 4.9d.
The Old Believer
(*Aerograd*, frame capture)

contrast, "is that of the center and that of *osvoenie*. It seeks to convert the taiga from a land of trial and conquest into habitable and inhabited state territory."[68] Orchestral music echoes first the majestic view of the land below and then its heroic conquest, as the score returns to the melody of the song we had heard earlier, only this time, in faster tempo. And then we get our first narrative intertitle: "Across the Amur border, foreign people are carrying dynamite: six Russians and two non-Russians." "Attention," reads the second card, "we will now kill them."[69]

The second person plural here includes us, the viewer, in the narrative of the film and places us on the correct side of the ideological divide. Presumably, *we* are not the foreign, the other, *chuzhie*; presumably, we are "Russian" (in a sense that is clearly larger than basic ethnicity, but that has to do with dividing up the world between enemies and friends). And yet, the shots of the taiga, once we descend to the ground below, are almost too dense for us to see our way clearly. There is something incoherent about this wilderness, we cannot find our way through the thicket, the shots try to take in too much at once, and we feel overwhelmed by the scope that the camera is trying to capture. (In other words, Dovzhenko is no longer avoiding the business of the long shot here; he also has a different cameraman, Eisenstein's Eduard Tissé[70]). Indeed, the film immediately addresses the idea of who can "read" the taiga, noting that what is illegible to the foreigner is easy to read for the hunter who knows his way around.

Like much of the dialogue in this film, this assertion seems pointed. We are at once included and excluded from this picture. We are not the hunter with privileged knowledge, but more like the "other" whom the hunter is hunting. And what we witness in the opening scene is the elimination of these "others"—the six Russians and the two non-Russians that Hlushak, our Siberian guide, is hunting.

As Hlushak pursues the two "non-Russians" into the taiga, we hear two different sound recordings. First is the extradiegetic musical score; second is the panting and small, incomprehensible noises of the two Japanese men. Coming to a clearing, the two men decide to part ways, and their farewell is given as body language rather than proper speech. The men part, come back together, and then, craning their necks like animals in pain, run off in different directions. To return briefly to Dyer's reading of *Simba*, we are in the presence of a "Manicheism delirium." The two Japanese spies have no language—or at the very least, no *human* language—they instead communicate in gestures and signs, as if their own native tongue were unavailable to them. Caught by Hlushak, our first Japanese spy produces a notebook and reads from it in broken Russian (as do also the Koreans, the Chinese, and the Chukcha in this film). Russian appears to be the *only* possible language of this film. All other languages—foreign languages, *chuzhie iazyki*—are mute; they cannot be reproduced by Russian/Soviet film technology. In other words, in his second sound film, Dovzhenko hypercorrects for the mistakes of his earlier insistence on Ukrainian dialogue. This time, the message will not be garbled through interference, through the proximity of languages to each other, but rather will be delivered in a loud and clear voice.

Indeed, this voice is so loud and so clear that it completely breaks the "sound barrier" of the film, shattering the fourth wall to address itself directly to the viewer. There are several moments of direct address in this film when the actors face the camera and recite their lines as if they are delivering a stage monologue, as if reading poetry, as if "natural" speech had no place in cinema. "Now we will go in and kill him" (*Seichas voidem i ub'em*), says Hlushak in his first direct address to the viewer. Speaking always in the second person plural, Hlushak is the voice of the state delivering its verdict in a calm and rational manner, never discolored by emotion. In every case, he is both jury and executioner, and his direct address implicates us in his actions.

Critics have commented extensively on the ways in which this film seems to justify Stalinist repressions, arrests, and murders. As in the show trials, the Japanese saboteur, when "arrested" by Hlushak in midflight, reads out a long list of reasons for his hatred of the Soviet Union, of the land that has so much (but from which he is excluded), of its natural resources, its people and animals, its calm belief in "the bright future." He confesses to planting dynamite in the forest and thereby gives Hlushak a legitimate right to kill him: "You made no mistakes in signing your own death warrant" (*v svoei gibeli ty raspisalsia bez oshibok*), Glushak tells him.

Yet, as in all of Dovzhenko's films, there is more ambiguity here than we might see at first glance. *Aerograd* complicates the rigid binary of "Manicheism delirium" by giving us a world where it is much more difficult—indeed, nearly impossible—to tell the difference between *svoi* and *chuzhoi*, "same" and "other." Indeed, we might argue, while the film is ostensibly concerned with the *chuzhie* who live outside its borders, it is much more nervous about those who live inside—not with the two "non-Russians," in other words, but with the six *Russians*. In this film, the enemy is not limited to the Japanese (or Italian or German) fascists, or even to the "Old Believers, sectarians, and kulaks, who ran from us into the Siberian wilderness." Fundamentally, the film is concerned with the *svoi* who is really *chuzhoi*. As Peter Kenez has noted, in the seven years between 1933–1939, Soviet directors made eighty-five films that dealt with contemporary life. In more than half of these (fifty-two), the hero unmasks hidden enemies who have committed criminal acts. The hero can never be too vigilant: "In Dovzhenko's *Aerograd*, the enemy turns out to be his best friend, in Eisenstein's *Bezhin Meadow* it is the protagonist's father, and in Pyr'ev's *The Party Card* it is the heroine's husband."[71]

Hlushak's execution of his childhood friend Khudiakov (again played by Dovzhenko's favorite actor, Stepan Shkurat)—the old hunter who refuses to give up his small farm and join the collective—is presented to us as a "natural" consequence of Khudiakov's treason, and similarly echoes the purges and arrests, show trials and executions of the mid-thirties. Nearly shot by mistake in the beginning of the film, Khudiakov proves guilty of

Figure 4.10a. Khudiakov looks at the camera (*Aerograd*, frame capture)

Figure 4.10b. Khudiakov hides his face (*Aerograd*, frame capture)

Figure 4.10c. Hlushak, direct address (*Aerograd*, frame capture)

harboring the second Japanese saboteur, of killing the Chinese partisan Van Lin, and of fighting against Soviet power by joining the group of sectarians. Khudiakov is not a kulak in the proper sense, and the motivation for his treason appears to have nothing to do with Old Belief, or a hatred for Bolsheviks, or even a fear of progress, but rather with a true understanding of the workings of Soviet power. In a brief pause before the culminating fight sequence, Khudiakov stands looking at a few wild reindeer gathered on the farm. "Just like these, seventy-five of them, they rounded up and tagged," he says by way of explanation. Khudiakov's betrayal seems to come from an almost Foucauldian sense of knowledge as power. By tagging the reindeer, the Soviet government is exercising a form of bio power that extends to the land, the sea, the animals, and the people.

Dovzhenko insists on the proximity and likeness of Hlushak and Khudiakov. In a sequence that completely breaks the narrative flow of the film, Hlushak and Khudiakov face the camera, speaking the same lines in unison: "The fifty years our friendship has lasted here in the taiga seem to have rushed by like a single day. Each day I look around and ask myself, is there any place in the world that is more beautiful and abundant? No place in the world is so beautiful and abundant!" This address to the viewer, filmed as an aside—an insert into the fabric of the film[72]—is delivered in one voice to underscore the impossibility of Khudiakov's treason. The two friends speak and, therefore, think and act as one. This makes the eventual betrayal that much more devastating and that much more personal; Khudiakov not only betrays the Motherland, but he also betrays his best friend, who is then forced to kill him.

As he walks to his place of execution, Khudiakov glances at the camera and—in an amazing moment of metacinematic commentary—shields his face, hiding it from the viewer.[73] There is a constant awareness of the presence of the camera and the audience, as if Dovzhenko never once lets his characters forget that they are being watched. While the musical score underscores the emotional pathos of this scene in ways that we come to expect from sound film, the choice of dialogue—both what is said and how it is delivered—is completely at odds with what would otherwise be a perfectly conventional Socialist Realist film. As Hlushak gets ready to execute his friend, he looks straight into the camera and delivers his verdict, "I am killing a traitor and enemy of the people, my friend, Vasil Petrovich Khudiakov, sixty years old. Be a witness to my sorrow" (*Bud'te svideteliami moei pechali*), once again implicating us directly in the event. In response, Khudiakov lets out a cry—not a plea for help or surrender, but a kind of "call of the wild," as if communicating with the forest around him. He yells out, "Oh-ho-ho!," turning to all sides and in this way also calling on the taiga to bear witness to the execution, delivered through pure sound, bypassing normal speech. Of all the death scenes in this film, this is the only one where the screen does not go black and the camera does not pan away. Instead, we see Hlushak take aim, we hear the sound of the gun shot, and we watch as Khudiakov's body crumples to the ground, emitting one final sound. "Mama," he says in a small voice, which has previously echoed loudly through the forest. At this point, the film cuts back to the dead body of the Chinese partisan Van Lin, killed by Khudiakov, to remind us that Khudiakov's execution was just and fair.

The ending of *Aerograd* circles back to the opening sequence of the arrival of Soviet power to the Far East. First airplanes, then parachutists, then ships, then entire armies are shown arriving at the Pacific Ocean, to the place where the future city of Aerograd will be built. While the taiga is known only to those who can read it, to Soviet power all is revealed in other ways—they don't need to trek through the wilderness, they come by sea and over air. This sequence, so similar to the one at the end of *Ivan*, makes much better sense here: the arrival of Soviet power "in flesh and blood,"[74] the technologies of the State ensuring that this land is protected from within and without.

"Standing on the shore of the Pacific Ocean and looking west," wrote Dovzhenko in his 1939 autobiography, "I thought of Ukraine." This statement might seem strange at first, since nothing about the Pacific Ocean or the Siberian taiga should have reminded Dovzhenko of the Ukrainian steppe, yet I think at stake here are precisely the kinds of issues that Dovzhenko tried to raise in his film—questions about the right to speak, the proper time for speaking, the question of address. In the mid-1930s, Ukraine was geopolitically suspect, a major part of the Soviet Union that was always pulling away toward independence, a republic whose back had been broken by collectivization, but which nevertheless continued to be accused of nationalism, of Ukrainianism, a portion of the country that needed to be subdued over and over again. In some ways for the Soviet Union, Ukraine was an "internal enemy," the "other" (*chuzhoi*) located at the center of the *svoi*. Repeatedly, characters in *Aerograd* claim that they will not speak now, they will only speak later. "And when we finish building [the new city], then I will speak," says the young Chukcha to the camera. The different "silences" that Dovzhenko claimed were only possible in sound cinema are audible here. In order not to "garble" the Party's message (as happened earlier with both *Earth* and *Ivan*), Dovzhenko's film doesn't want to speak at all.

Figure 4.11a. Airplanes (*Aerograd*, frame capture)

Figure 4.11b. Soviet power (*Aerograd*, frame capture)

Accounting for his unusual uses of language in *Aerograd*, Dovzhenko claims that he tried to use normal everyday speech but inflect it with all the literariness and technical terminology of the present, forcing the peasant characters to speak "in their own tongue" (*ia zastavil govorit' krest'ian ikh iazykom*), not to imitate their speech.[75] As Dovzhenko went on to make sound films, and to write screenplays, short stories, journalism, and other works, his own use of language remained quite odd. In the 1994 tribute to the director (and in particular to his cinematic masterpiece, *Earth*), in the cinema journal *Kinovedcheskie zapiski* (Notes on Cinema), several critics noted Dovzhenko's strange uses of language, his hybrid Ukrainian-Russian constructions and general neologisms. One critic described these as "aphasia," while another called it a "language that could not communicate"; speech that keeps multiplying and veering away, to the side, that cannot seem to keep to a single path, "incorrect, uncontrolled speech, that allows for slips and typos" (*nepravil'naia, nekontroliruemaia rech', dopuskaiushchaia ogovorki, opiski*).[76] Ukrainian literary critic Hryhory Kostiuk (who watched *Aerograd* in the Vorkyta concentration camp, where he was incarcerated from 1935–1940) wrote in his memoirs,

> I left the screening hall in a disturbed state. The film contained everything: a talented depiction of the beauty and immensity of the open spaces of the Soviet Far East, the iron columns of the frontier troops, their commanders' menacing features, the superhuman docility of the soldiers, the diligence of the NKVD informers, the power of aerodromes, and the fearlessness of the Soviet squadrons that patrol the Pacific Ocean under the clouds and that secure the USSR's borders. In a word, the film contained everything which government propaganda needed, but it did not show the creator of *Earth* and *Ivan*. There was no great artist, there were no living, psychologically complex, but always moving Dovzhenko heroes. I left the theater in a sad state. I had the feeling that I had attended the funeral of our great "poet of the cinema."[77]

The critic Mikhail Bleiman commented, "Both *Ivan* and *Aerograd* were for Dovzhenko a period of a type of creative tragedy, a period when the artist loses his scale of work [*masshtab*], loses his subject matter, and doesn't just stop speaking sharply, but, what is still more frightening, stops speaking clearly."[78] And the scriptwriter Vsevold Vishnevsky wrote in 1935, "When I looked closely at Glushak, I kept seeing Dovzhenko. And I wondered: who is he talking to? I think he is talking to his own past: his old friendships, nurtured in Ukraine, to his childhood. And Dovzhenko fires at this friendship. He fires at the people who used to be with him. He shoots them and then he turns away."[79]

For the first time in Dovzhenko's career, his film opened without controversy.

Notes

1. On January 30, 1944, Dovzhenko, together with four Ukrainian leaders and three other prominent writers, was invited to a Politburo meeting in Moscow to discuss his novel and movie script for *Ukraine in Flames*, during which Stalin made a lengthy speech accusing the writer of "revising Leninism"; for details, see George O. Liber, *Alexander Dovzhenko: A Life in Soviet Film* (London: British Film Institute, 2002), 196–206. See also: Serhy Yekelchuk, *Stalin's Empire of Memory: Russian Ukrainian Relations in the Soviet Imagination* (Toronto: University of Toronto Press, 2004). Stalin's speech was republished in *Iskusstvo kino* no. 4 (1990).

2. See Vance Kepley Jr., *In the Service of the State: The Cinema of Alexander Dovzhenko* (Madison: The University of Wisconsin Press, 1986), 11–18.

3. See Liber, *Alexander Dovzhenko*, 31–44.
4. Liber, *Alexander Dovzhenko*, 158.
5. Kepley Jr. suggests that this was "in reward for Red Army and party service" (Kepley Jr., *In the Service of the State*, 18).
6. "1939 Autobiography," in *Alexander Dovzhenko: The Poet as Filmmaker*, ed. and trans. Marco Carynnyk (Cambridge, MA: MIT Press, 1973), 11–12.
7. Philip Cavandish, "*Zemlia/Earth*," in *The Cinema of Russia and the Former Soviet Union*, ed. Birgit Beumers (London: Wallflower Press, 2007), 57.
8. Viktor Shklovsky, *Za sorok let* (Moscow: Iskusstvo, 1965), 393. Cited in Kepley Jr., *In the Service of the State*, 3.
9. Katerina Clark, *The Soviet Novel: History as Ritual* (Chicago: Chicago University Press, 1981), 114. As Clark has noted, at the heart of Stalinist culture lay the metaphor of the Great Family: The relationships of citizens to each other and to their leaders were fictionalized and subsumed under the kinship structure by which the new Soviet State sought to define itself. Like Germany and several other countries in this period, the Soviets focused on the primordial attachments of kinship and "projected them as the dominant symbol for social allegiance." Soviet society's leaders became "fathers" (with Stalin as the patriarch); the national heroes, model "sons"; the state, a "family" or "tribe." This new root metaphor for society, Clark argues, provided the state with a single set of symbols for enhancing its increasingly hierarchical structure by endowing it with a spurious organicity.
10. Both excerpts: Alexandr Dovzhenko, "The Artist's Teacher and Friend," *Iskusstvo kino* 10 (October 1937): 15–16, in *The Film Factory*, ed. Richard Taylor and Ian Christie (London: Routledge, 1994), 383–385.
11. Dovzhenko, "The Artist's Teacher and Friend," 384.
12. Soiuzkino was renamed Moskinokombinat in 1934 and Mosfil'm in 1936.
13. Since the early 1930s, NIKFI (Nauchno-issledovatel'skii kinofotoinstitut / the Cinema-Photo Research Institute in Moscow) specialized in dubbing foreign, and later "national" films into Russian. See "Soveshchaniie po dubliazhu rabotnikov dubliazhnykh grupp Bakinskoi, Tashkentskoi i Ashkhabadskoi studii" and "Protokol zasedanii komissii po razrabotke norm i standartov po dubliazhu, rabotnikov dubliazhnykh grupp Bakinskoi, Tashkentskoi i Ashkhabadskoi studii," both: RGALI, 2450–2–34 (September 28 and 30, 1938).
14. Gabrielle Chomentowski, "Du cinéma muet au cinéma parlant. La politique des langues dans les films soviétiques," *Cahiers du monde russe* 55, no. 3 (2014): 295–320.
15. Osip Beskin, "Editorial," *Sovetskoe kino* 1 (1928): 1.
16. Chomentowski, "Du cinéma muet au cinéma parlant," 296.
17. The others were, in order of size: Gosvoenkino (Red Army); Armenkino (Armenia); Vostokkino (Far East); Uzbekkino (Uzbek Republic); Azgoskino (Azerbaijan); Turkmenkino (Turkmen Republic); Chuvashkino (Chuvash Region); and Kinosibir' (Siberia). In Vance Kepley Jr., "The First 'Perestroika': Soviet Cinema under the First Five-Year Plan," *Cinema Journal* 35, no. 4 (Summer 1996): 36. Many of these were too small initially to have their own physical plants, and often rented facilities from Sovkino.
18. Kepley Jr., "The First 'Perestroika'," 32–37. As Michael G. Smith puts it, Stalin's concise formula of 1925, "national in form but socialist in content," summarized both the liberality and the severity of Bolshevik language policy. "National in form," implied compromises on the native language front in education and culture. "Socialist in content" meant party control in politics and economics, whose language was Russian. "This logic meant that the native language, although a necessary course of study, was inherently inferior or substandard to Russian. In Stalin's pointed terms, Russian was that great 'zonal language' of the USSR driving the historical dialectic 'from multiplicity to uniformity'" (Michael G. Smith, *Language and Power in the Creation of the USSR, 1917–1953* [Berlin & New York: Mouton de Gruyter, 1998], 54).
19. Kepley Jr., "The First 'Perestroika'," 38.

20. Nationality policy in the Soviet Union, from the early 1920s to the mid-1930s, was guided by the policy of *korenizatsiia* ("indigenization"), as a way to establish Soviet rule by reversing the long-term effects of Russification on the non-Russian populations. This involved the creation of regional administrative units, recruitment of non-Russians into leadership positions, and the promotion of non-Russian languages in government administration, the courts, the schools, and the mass media (what Terry Martin has called "affirmative action"). By the late 1930s, however, there was a notable policy shift. Purges in some of the national regions such as Ukraine or the Crimean ASSR for "national deviation" led to the Russianization of government, education, and the media. In 1938, Russian became a required subject of study in every Soviet school, including those in which a non-Russian language was the principal medium of instruction for other subjects (e.g., mathematics, science, and social studies). In 1939, non-Russian languages that had been given Latin-based scripts in the late 1920s were given new scripts based on the Cyrillic script. On Stalin's policies of nationalism and national languages, see Lev Yakubinsky, "Russkii iazyk v epokhu diktatury proletariata" [Part 1], *Literaturnaia ucheba* 9 (1931): 66–76. On ethnic pluralism, see Yuri Slezkine, "The USSR as a Communal Apartment, or How a Socialist State Promoted Ethnic Particularism," *Slavic Review* 53, no. 2 (Summer 1994): 414–452. On the changing roles of Russian and non-Russian languages in Soviet education over time see Barbara A. Anderson and Brian D. Silver, "Equality, Efficiency, and Politics in Soviet Bilingual Education Policy: 1934–1980," *American Political Science Review* 78 (December, 1984): 1019–1039. On national policies, see Terry Martin, *Affirmative Action Empire: Nations and Nationalism in the Soviet Union, 1923–1939* (Ithaca: Cornell University Press, 2001).

21. In Kepley Jr., "The First 'Perestroika'," 42.

22. Kepley Jr., "The First 'Perestroika'," 45; see also Valérie Pozner, "To Catch Up and Overtake Hollywood: Early Talking Pictures in the Soviet Union," in *Sound, Speech, Music in Soviet and Post-Soviet Cinema*, ed. Lilya Kaganovsky and Masha Salazkina (Bloomington: Indiana University Press, 2014), 60–80.

23. For details, see Chomentowski, "Du cinéma muet au cinéma parlant."

24. «Верю, что заговорит Великий немой. Усматриваю в этом новую эру в мировой культуре и самое могучее орудие в деле повышения культурного уровня масс. Правда, когда пришьют Немому язык, он будет шепелявить и заикаться на радость и смех жрецов и мещан от киноэстетики. Но придет время, когда выровняется тон у Немого, и мы станем свидетелями новых, неслыханных достижений.» Aleksandr Dovzhenko, "Zagovorit velikii nemoi," in *Aleksandr Dovzhenko. Sobranie sochinenii v chetyrekh tomakh* (Moscow: Iskusstvo, 1969), 4:33.

25. Liber, *Alexander Dovzhenko*, 120.

26. Dovzhenko, "Ob Ivane," *Sobranie sochinenii v chetyrekh tomakh*, 1: 276; originally published in *Kino*, no. 5, 6 (1932); trans. from Ukrainian by Gleb Zatvornitskii.

27. Dovzhenko, "Ob Ivane," *Sobranie sochinenii v chetyrekh tomakh*, 1: 277.

28. *Iskusstvo kino* 4 (1955), 86.

29. Dovzhenko, "Ob Ivane," *Sobranie sochinenii v chetyrekh tomakh*, 1: 278. According to Leonid Kokhno's recollections, it was the cameraman Danylo Demuts'kyi who took the "all-important step of switching from a conventional to a wide-angle lens, which had the effect of dramatically opening out the scene and stretching the expanse of water that stood before them" (Philip Cavendish, *The Men with the Movie Camera: The Poetics of Visual Style in Soviet Avant-Garde Cinema of the 1920s* [Oxford: Berghahn Books, 2013], 278).

30. R. Sobolev, *Aleksandr Dovzhenko* (Moscow: Iskusstvo, 1980), 125–126.

31. Arsenii Avraamov's *Simfoniia gudkov* (Symphony of Sirens, 1923). This piece involved navy ship sirens and whistles, bus and car horns, factory sirens, cannons, the foghorns of the entire Soviet flotilla in the Caspian Sea, artillery guns, machine guns, hydro-airplanes, a specially designed "whistle main," and renderings of *Internationale* and *Marseillaise* by a mass band and choir. The piece was conducted by a team of conductors using flags and pistols. It was performed

in the city of Baku in 1923, celebrating the fifth anniversary of the 1917 October Revolution, and less successfully in Moscow, a year later.

32. Dovzhenko, "Ob Ivane," *Sobranie sochinenii v chetyrekh tomakh*, 1: 278.

33. Kristin Thompson, "Early Sound Counterpoint," *Yale French Studies* 60, Cinema/Sound (1980), 115–140.

34. Thompson, "Early Sound Counterpoint," 122.

35. Thompson, "Early Sound Counterpoint," 122.

36. Dovzhenko, "Ob Ivane," *Sobranie sochinenii v chetyrekh tomakh*, 1: 278.

37. Dovzhenko, "Ob Ivane," *Sobranie sochinenii v chetyrekh tomakh*, 1: 277. Dovzhenko explicitly contrasts his film to Vertov's, saying that in our cinema "the machine oppresses the human being" (A. Dovzhenko, "Lektsiia prochitannaia v institute kinematografistov v Moskve o fil'me 'Ivan'," December 17, 1932, RGALI 2081–1–354).

38. Demutsky filmed the outdoor shots, including the shots of the Ukrainian landscape and Dneprostroi, while Mykhailo Hlider filmed the interior shots. According to Kokhno, while both Dovzhenko and Demutsky spent several days studying the site at Dneprostroi, it was Demutsky who chose to shoot the industrial landscape in the early morning light, "*contre-jour*, with a long-distance Dallmeyer-Ross lens and colored filter" (see Leonid Kokhno, "Poeziia truda," in *Dovzhenko v vospominaniiakh sovremennikov*, ed. Liudmila Pazhitnova and Iulia Solntseva (Moscow: Iskusstvo, 1982), 79–85; here: 79–80; quoted in Cavendish, *The Men with the Movie Camera*, 278). Meanwhile, in his 1932 address to cinematography students at GIK, Dovzhenko claimed that he was primarily responsible for the placement of the camera, while "the camera operator has a purely technical function" (A. Dovzhenko, "Lektsiia prochitannaia v institute kinematografistov v Moskve o fil'me 'Ivan'," December 17, 1932, RGALI 2081–1–354); see also A. Dovzhenko, "Lektsiia prochitannaia v institute kinematografistov v Moskve," December 18, 1932, RGALI 2081–1–355). For a contextualized reading of this statement, see Cavendish, *The Men with the Movie Camera*, 276–278.

39. See Petr Sazhin's review of Vertov's *Enthusiasm* in *Kino-front* (March 1930); Sobolev notes specifically that in this way, Dovzhenko anticipates the future conflicted relationship to technology, by refusing to "love" the beauty of the machine (Sobolev, *Aleksandr Dovzhenko*, 128–129).

40. Quoted in Sobolev, *Aleksandr Dovzhenko*, 123.

41. Stephen Lovell, "Broadcasting Bolshevik: The Radio Voice of Soviet Culture, 1920s–1950s," *Journal of Contemporary History* 48, no. 1 (January 2013): 78–97.

42. Michel Chion, *The Voice in Cinema*, trans. Claudia Gorbman (New York: Columbia University Press, 1999); see in particular, chapter 1: "The Acousmêtre," 17–29. The "acousmatic" as Chion notes, is said "of a sound that is heard without its cause or source being seen," and is specifically adopted by Pierre Schaeffer to designate "a mode of listening that is common place today, systematized in the use of radio, telephones, and phonograph records" (Chion, *The Voice in Cinema*, 18).

43. *Chernaia kassa*: an illegal, unreported, and undeclared to tax authorities storage of funds for a company.

44. For Chion, the *acousmêtre* is not simply a *voice-over*, but must be both included and excluded from the film. He must, Chion writes, "even if only slightly, have *one foot in the image*, in the space of the film; he must haunt the borderlands that are neither the interior of the filmic stage nor the proscenium—a place that has no name, but which the cinema forever brings into play" (Chion, *The Voice in Cinema*, 24).

45. In *Discipline and Punish*, Michel Foucault argues that the chief function of disciplinary power is "correct training," and that instead of bending all its subjects into a single uniform mass, disciplinary power "separates, analyses, differentiates, carries its procedures of decomposition to the point of necessary and sufficient single units." Discipline "makes" individuals, writes Foucault, "it is the specific technique of a power that regards individuals both as objects and as

instruments of its exercise" (Michel Foucault, *Discipline and Punish: The Birth of the Prison*, trans. Alan Sheridan [New York: Random House, 1977], 170).

46. Foucault, *Discipline and Punish*, 201.
47. Chion, *The Voice in Cinema*, 24.
48. Dovzhenko mentions Shaw as an inspiration for this scene. He is perhaps referring to the appearance of George Bernard Shaw (or "The World's Outstanding Literary Genius," as the title card says) in a Fox Movietone Newsreel, filmed on August 26, 1928.
49. This ending makes little sense in *Ivan* (either narratively or visually), but it is repeated almost exactly in Dovzhenko's next film, *Aerograd*.
50. "1939 Autobiography," 23; cited in Liber, *Alexander Dovzhenko*, 123.
51. Béla Balázs, "Novye fil'my—novoe zhizneoshchushchenie," *Sovetskoe kino* 3–4 (1933).
52. Actually, the majority of Kiev residents at the time spoke Russian, which was a typical division in Ukraine between the urban (Russian-speaking) and the rural (Ukrainian-speaking) populations. See Liber, *Alexander Dovzhenko*, 127–128.
53. Aleksandr Dovzhenko, "Pochemu *Ivan*?" *Kino* (M) (November 24, 1932): 2; see also his "Lektsiia prochitannaia v institute kinematografistov v Moskve o fil'me 'Ivan'," December 17, 1932 (RGALI 2081–1–354).
54. Liber, *Alexander Dovzhenko*, 128.
55. For details on the shifting policies of nationalization, see Martin, *Affirmative Action Empire*.
56. Evgeny Margolit, "The Problem of Heteroglossia in Early Soviet Sound Film," in *Sound, Speech, Music in Soviet and Post-Soviet Cinema*, 119–128; originally published as, "Problema mnogoiazychiia v rannem sovetskom zvukovom kino (1930–1935)," in *Sovetskaia vlast' i media*, ed. Hans Günther and Sabine Hänsgen (St. Petersburg: Akademicheskii proekt, 2006), 378–386.
57. Evgenii Margolit, *Zhivye i mertvoe. Zametki k istorii sovetskogo kino 1920-kh—1960-kh godov* (St. Petersburg: Seans, 2012), 122.
58. The famous exchange at the end of *Circus* in which Raechka, for the fourth time in the film, asks Marion if *now* she understands—"Teper' ponimaesh'?"—is finally answered with an enthusiastic, "Teper' ponimaesh'!" (I understands!), suggesting that in the end, Americans can only parrot, but can never truly understand.
59. For an excellent reading of Macheret's film, see Emma Widdis, "Making Sense without Speech: The Use of Silence in Early Soviet Sound Film," in *Sound, Speech, Music in Soviet and Post-Soviet Cinema*, 100–116.
60. "Semiodiversity" (the diversity of meanings) is opposed to "glossodiversity" (the diversity of languages).
61. The film was made in Leningrad by the Belgoskino studio. Unfortunately, there is no surviving Yiddish version of the film, so we cannot know for sure how Solomon Mikhoel's Yiddish would have sounded in the context of everyone speaking the same language. The original (Russian-language) release was in nine parts and 2,600 meters, but has survived without parts 1 and 9. The Yiddish screenplay for the film is preserved at Gosfil'mofond.
62. On *The Return of Nathan Becker / Vozvrashchenie Neitana Bekkera*, see Harriet Murav, *Music from a Speeding Train: Jewish Literature in Post-Revolution Russia* (Stanford: Stanford University Press, 2011), 98–102. See also Claire Le Foll, "A la recherche de l'introuvable film juif-biélorusse? Politique des nationalités et cinéma en BSSR dans les années 1920 et 1930," in *Kinojudaica: Les représentations des Juifs dans le cinéma de Russie et d'Union soviétique des années 1910 aux années 1980*, ed. Valérie Pozner and Natacha Laurent (La Cinémathèque de Toulouse / Nouveau Monde Editions, 2012), 79–109.
63. Richard Dyer, "White," *Screen*, 29, no. 4 (October 1, 1988): 44–65; here 51–52.
64. West Ukrainian intellectuals became the primary target of the 1933 Ukrainian terror, starting with arrests in December 1932. Between 1934–1938 nearly 150,000 Ukrainian Party members had been arrested (a third of the total membership). For details, see Martin, *Affirmative Action Empire*, 344–372.

65. Aleksandr Fadeev was one of the cofounders of the Union of Soviet Writers and its chairman from 1946 to 1954. He is the author of such Socialist Realist classics as *Razgrom* (The Rout, 1927), *Poslednii iz Udege* (The Last of the Udege, 1930–1941); and *Molodaia gvardiia* (The Young Guard, 1946).

66. In Stalin's "Zakrytoe pis'mo TsK VKP(b): Uroki sobytii, sviazannykh so zlodeiskim ubiistvom tov. Kirova," addressed to all the organs of the party, he wrote that members of the Zinoviev group had been hanging on to their party cards in order to appear faithful to the Bolshevik party and to the Soviet Union. Kirov's murderer, L. Nikolaev, was apprehended by the Cheka three weeks prior to the murder, but because he was carrying a party card, he was not even searched. "Is it so hard for a Chekist to understand," wrote Stalin, "that a party card could be counterfeited or stolen from its owner, that by itself, without a check of its authenticity or a check of the person carrying it, a party card cannot serve as a guarantee? Where has vigilance gone?" (January 18, 1935), published in *Izvestiia* PK KPSS 8 (1989). In his address to the plenum of the TsK VKP(b) on March 3, 1937, titled, "O nedostatkakh partiinoi raboty i merakh likvidatsii trotskistskikh i inykh dvurushnikov," Stalin quoted from the 1935 letter, suggesting that the measures taken in party card exchange and verification had failed to prevent Troskyite elements from penetrating into the party (*Pravda* [March 29, 1937]).

67. «Тьма и свет, добро и зло. К этим прямым—без светотеней—противопоставлениям Довженко прибегает в «Аэрограде».» A. Mar'iamov, *Dovzhenko. Zhizn' zamechatel'nykh liudei* (Moscow: Izd. TsK VLKSM "Molodaia gvardiia," 1968), 240.

68. Emma Widdis, *Visions of a New Land: Soviet Film from the Revolution to the Second World War* (New Haven: Yale University Press, 2003), 153–154.

69. «Через Амурскую границу несут чужие люди динамит—шестеро русских и двое нерусских. Внимание. Сейчас мы их убьем.»

70. Tissé was one of three cinematographers on *Aerograd*, which also included Mikhail Gindin and N. Smirnov (who filmed the aerial sequences). Sobolev comments that Tissé's work was not well received by critics, who found his shots of the taiga "stifling" (*nedostaet "vozdukha"*) (Sobolev, *Aleksandr Dovzhenko*, 144–145).

71. Peter Kenez, *Cinema and Soviet Society from the Revolution to the Death of Stalin* (London: I. B. Tauris, 2001), 149.

72. Dovzhenko refers to this scene as a "dissolve" (*naplyv*) and claims that he filmed it thirty-eight times, wasting about 1,800 meters of film, and that the inserted scene still did not work. Dovzhenko, "Dva vystupleniia v Soiuze pisatelei" (November 13, 1935), *Sobranie sochinenii v chetyrekh tomakh*, 1: 299.

73. Kepley Jr. connects the direct address to the viewer with the notions of guilt or innocence, writing, "The ability to look an opponent in the eye is made a sign of power; the ability to look directly into the camera becomes a sign of integrity." Kepley Jr., *In the Service of the State*, 116.

74. Jean-Louis Baudry, "Ideological Effects of the Basic Cinematographic Apparatus," *Film Quarterly* 28, no. 2 (Winter 1974–1975): 39–47.

75. Dovzhenko, "Osvoenie Dal'nego Vostoka," *Sobranie sochinenii v chetyrekh tomakh*, 1: 306.

76. See A. S. Deriabin, "Poteria i obretenie nemoty," *Kinovedcheskie zapiski* 23 (1994): 181–185, here: 185, n. 7; and S. L. Gurko, "Fonogramma fil'ma *Zemlia*," *Kinovedcheskie zapiski* 23 (1994): 188.

77. Hryhorii Kostiuk, *Okaianni roky: Vid Luk'ianivs'koi tiurmy do Vorkuts'koi trahedii (1935–1940 rr.)* (Toronto: Diialoh, 1978), 114. Cited in Liber, *Alexander Dovzhenko*, 146.

78. In Sobolev, *Aleksandr Dovzhenko*, 142.

79. In Sobolev, *Aleksandr Dovzhenko*, 152. (Sobolev, writing in 1980, understands this response to mean that Vishnevky approves of Khudiakov's killing. I read it quite the opposite.)

chapter five

"LES SILENCES DE LA VOIX"
Dziga Vertov's *Three Songs of Lenin*

> The essential characteristic of orthographic (called phono-logic) writing is the exactitude of the *recording* of the voice rather than the exactitude of the recording of the *voice*: it is a matter of recording rather than voice.
>
> —Bernard Stiegler, *Technics and Time: Disorientation*

WHAT DIFFERENCE DOES SOUND MAKE to *Three Songs of Lenin*? What do we lose or gain with the removal of the sound track? In 1932, after making his last three feature films in Ukraine for the VUFKU film studio, Dziga Vertov was commissioned by Mezhrabpom-fil'm to make a jubilee film about Lenin to commemorate the ten-year anniversary of Lenin's death. The resulting film—*Three Songs of Lenin* (Tri pesni o Lenine, 1934)—has a complex history of both production and release. During production, Vertov and his film crew ran into every kind of obstacle, including persecution from RAPP (Russian Association of Proletarian Writers), lack of resources and finances, and extreme physical deprivations, including hunger, typhus, and the like.[1] Originally scheduled to premiere at the Bolshoi Theater on the anniversary of Lenin's death on January 21, 1934, *Three Songs of Lenin* was not released in Soviet theaters until November 1935 (almost a full year after it was completed), and pulled from the screens after only one week. At the same time, a silent version edited by Vertov and prepared for Soviet cinemas without sound projection, was shown widely across the USSR, while the sound version was "shelved." In 1938, bending to political pressure, Vertov reedited both the sound and the silent versions of *Three Songs of Lenin*, recutting the original negatives.[2] Thus, as far as we know, no copy of the original 1934/1935 versions survive and we can only speculate from Vertov's own writings, the film's critical reception, metrics, censorship notes, and montage lists what the film may have looked like before it was recut and new footage added in the late 1930s.[3]

In 1970, *Three Songs of Lenin* was reedited again—this time, by Vertov's assistants Elizaveta Svilova, Ilya Kopalin, and Semiramida Pumpianskaia—for a posthumous release to mark the hundredth anniversary of Lenin's birth. The three editors called this version a "restoration" because it removed some of the extra footage added in 1938, but they could not put back the shots or sequences that had been cut by Vertov to make the 1938 variants. Thus, the new reedit/restoration produced yet a third sound version of the film (and a fifth version all together), and this is the film most of us know as *Three Songs of Lenin*. This was the version used for releases on VHS and DVD in the West and in Russia, assumed to be closest to the original 1934 film compared to the "Stalinist" edit of 1938. Produced during three quite different political moments—the inauguration of Stalin's "personality cult" and the consequent waning of Lenin's during the first part of the 1930s; the height of the Stalin cult in the purge years of 1937–1938; and the ongoing anti-Stalinist revisionism of the early "stagnation" period (1969–1970)—each version of *Three Songs of Lenin* marks in some way its historical moment, not only political, but also technological and artistic.[4] Vertov's ideas about documentary filmmaking and about the relationship between image and sound continued to evolve even at the point when he was no longer allowed to make films independently, when his career was reduced to the editing of news reels. In particular, in his diaries and notes, Vertov returned time and again to *Three Songs of Lenin* as the film that fulfilled for him the requirements of the new *sound* documentary, the organic link of sound and image on screen.

Up to now, the 1970 variant has served as the definitive text of *Three Songs of Lenin*, both because of its availability, and because it removed many of the shots of Stalin assumed to have been introduced in the 1938 edit.[5] Yet, at the same time, the restoration kept some of the other sequence added after 1934—such as shots of the manned drifting ice station (North Pole-1), first opened in May 1937, images of the Spanish Communist Dolores Ibarruri, and the female combatants from the Spanish Civil War—creating a hybrid text.[6] Thus, the history of *Three Songs* is the history of "the transition into (and out of) 'Stalinist culture'," as John MacKay has argued, and the presence or absence of "Stalin" and "Stalinism" must figure centrally in any interpretation of the film.[7] Yet, because of the instability of the filmic text, those presences and absences are hard to trace with any certainty. The film, as it is available to us, is not one thing, but many, its multiple iterations producing a kaleidoscopic or palimpsestic effect. Because we do not have access to the original 1934/1935 films, and because in 1970 there was no longer any need to produce a silent version of *Three Songs*

Figure 5.1. "We are going to hear *Three Songs of Lenin*" (Pravda, 1934, Muzei kino)

of Lenin, it is worth paying closer attention to the discredited 1938 "Stalinist" variants to see how Vertov handled a different kind of problem—not the problem of the cult of personality (of either Lenin or Stalin), but the problem of sound, and more specifically, of voice.[8] Using the 1938 sound and silent releases of *Three Songs of Lenin* (as well as the restored viewing copy held at the Russian State Film Archive, Gosfil'mofond), this chapter focuses on Dziga Vertov's synchronous and asynchronous sound practices in his second sound film, *Three Songs of Lenin*, and Vertov's resistance to the imposition of a singular, nondialogic voice that after 1934 comes to dominate sound cinema. The multiple versions of *Three Songs of Lenin*—specifically, the two *silent* releases of 1935 and 1938—challenge the expected relationship of sound to the visual image, forcing us to ask in what ways sound functioned in the original composition and how its absence colors our reception of the film.

LE SON

In retrospect, already in 1934 *Three Songs of Lenin* signaled a turning point in Vertov's career.[9] This is the last film that could still be included in the canon of his work from the twenties, a work that still bears signs of avant-garde documentary filmmaking and a desire to capture "truth" on film, although it is a very different film even compared to the 1930 *Enthusiasm: Symphony of the Donbass* (Entuziazm. Simfoniia Donbassa). As Yuri Tsivian notes, while Vertov's sound films were groundbreaking, "these were not films made by a *kinok*, in the old sense."[10] Despite some initial success—*Three Songs* premiered to great acclaim at the 2nd Venice Film Festival in August 1934, and in 1935 Vertov was awarded the Order of the Red Star—and despite the dissolution of RAPP, which was openly hostile to Vertov, after 1935, Vertov found himself increasingly isolated from filmmaking; his requests for a film laboratory, for equipment and materials, for the opportunity to shoot events as they happen were consistently denied by administrators. As is clear from Vertov's diaries, despite the positive reception, *Three Songs* did not help Vertov's career or mitigate the charges of "formalism" and "documentalism" levied against him during the next decade, as he strove to combine his faith in documentary practice with the exigencies of Stalinist Socialist Realism. His consistent marginalization and exclusion from the Soviet cinema industry finally culminated in the "Open Party Session of the Central Studio of Documentary Films" on March 14–15, 1949, with 200 people attending, where, as part of the antisemitic campaign of the late 1940s–1950s, Vertov was charged with "cosmopolitanism" and accused of continuing to undermine Soviet documentary cinematography with his formalist tricks and his "love" of the machine.[11]

Nevertheless, as Martin Stollery points out, *Three Songs of Lenin* can be seen and listened to as "one of the last examples of early European film modernism."[12] Vertov conceived *Three Songs of Lenin* as a sound film first and foremost, and this meant to him much more than simply the addition of music, dialogue, or sound effects to the image track. His experiment with the sound camera in *Enthusiasm* had already taught him the possibilities and limitations of sound recording and editing, producing a film that while remarkable for its breakthrough uses of sound, remained to some degree an experiment, an exercise in exploring the possibilities of the new sound technology. *Three Songs*—while it contains no dialogue and very little diegetic sound—was envisioned by Vertov *from the beginning* as a sound film, that is to say, a film in which sound and image would be "organically" linked, so as to make it impossible to remove the one without sacrificing the other. Sound informs every part of the film, starting from the title; the three "songs" that make up *Three Songs of Lenin* place the emphasis on melody as the primary organizing principle of the film. And while a number of scholars have noted the irony of a film dedicated to an oral tradition giving us writing in place of speech (Bulgakowa[13]), or have reconceived the film's structure in a visual form, such as the triptych (Michelson[14]), it is nonetheless notable that for Vertov, the film was a "song of songs," a musical composition in which sound (voice, music, song) was the structuring force by which the other visual elements of the film were organized and constrained.[15] As Elizabeth Papazian notes, the reference to "songs" in the title extends Vertov's play throughout his career with generic designations. Both *Man with a Movie Camera* (Chelovek s kinoapparatom, 1929) and *Enthusiasm* were referred to, grandly, as "symphonies," while the later, more doctrinaire Stalinist film *Lullaby* (Kolybel'naia, 1937) bears a simpler, folksier designation. The Russian title *Tri pesni o Lenine* is also a reference to the oral epic poetic tradition, such as, for example, Pushkin's *Pesn' o veshchem Olege* (The Song of Wise Oleg, 1822).[16]

Yet, at the same time—or perhaps because of all these overlapping and overdetermined generic conventions—*Three Songs of Lenin* is not a sound film or a sound documentary in any standard sense. It has no voice-over, no dialogue, and almost no spoken text. The songs of the Far East are performed in various Turkic languages, with translations provided on screen through Russian intertitles.[17] The musical track brings together Eastern folk songs and melodies with Western classical music (including Richard Wagner's funeral music from *The Ring of the Nibelungs* cycle and Frédéric Chopin's *Marche funèbre*), Soviet patriotic marches, the "Internationale," and Yuri Shaporin's "March of the Shock Workers," written for the film. Noises, such as the bell toll of the Kremlin clock, gunshots, cannons, factory sirens, ships' horns, explosions, and the like, compete with the different kinds of music, shifting between diegetic and nondiegetic sounds. Like the image track that reuses sequences from Vertov's own films in combination with archival newsreels and new footage shot in distant geographical locations across the Soviet Far East, *Three Songs* is both a compilation film and an original composition, freely mixing the different elements to produce a new cinematic work. As Vertov himself put it, despite the incredible difficulties in bringing all the disparate audio and visual materials together into a single unified whole, they managed to achieve the impossible, "a dialectical unity of form and content."[18] And while the soundtrack of the film is mostly musical and mostly nondiegetic, there are several examples of sync-sound voice recordings that further complicate Vertov's audio-visual montage, including a recording of Lenin's voice reproduced along with revolving titles in the Second Song and four sync-sound interviews (with a shock-worker, an engineer, a collective farmer, and a collective farm president) in the Third Song. In the 1938 sound variant, the film continues for an additional 250 meters, concluding with Stalin's Electoral Speech at the

Figure 5.2a. Stalin's Electoral Speech at the Bolshoi Theatre, 1938
(*Three Songs of Lenin*, 1938 sound variant, frame capture)

Bolshoi Theatre to a meeting of voters of the Stalin Electoral Area, Moscow, December 11, 1938, filmed in sync-sound.[19]

In other words, *sound* is a fundamental component of this film, but not in any conventional sense, neither "classic" Hollywood, Socialist Realist, nor Soviet avant-garde. Vertov goes out of his way to avoid the usual clichéd uses of sound (such as voice-over and dialogue) or direct sound recording (except in the cases of interviews), and in general strives to unsync the soundtrack from the visual image. Sound here becomes truly contrapuntal—not in the sense meant by Eisenstein, Alexandrov, and Pudovkin as an element of montage that always works *against* the visual image—but in the sense that the two tracks are combined in absolutely new ways, independent of their origins.[20] If in *Enthusiasm*, Vertov strove to bring us "real" sounds recorded on location (while the question of synchronization remained unimportant), in *Three Songs* the goal is something else: a calculated attempt to treat sound and image as equal elements of montage, as two different kinds of *recording*, which could be arranged and rearranged to highlight themes, leitmotifs, and narrative lines.

Figure 5.2b. Stalin's Electoral Speech at the Bolshoi Theatre, 1938
(*Three Songs of Lenin*, 1938 sound variant, frame capture)

As had been true for his polemical stances of the twenties about non-played film and the *kino-eye*, Vertov continued to evolve his theories of the organic synthesis of sound and image as he proceeded to work (with less and less success) on his films during the thirties and forties. Writing about his film *To You, Front!* (Tebe, front!) in his diary in 1942, Vertov stresses the need for an "organic unity" (*organicheskoe sliianie*) of sound and image, the need to make a true *sound* film, as opposed to a silent version that has had sound added to it. "A synthetic film, not sound plus picture," this film cannot be shown one-sidedly, with only the visual or only the audio track. The visual is only one part of "a complex multifaceted composition":

> It is clear to everyone that the radio-film must be heard, while the silent film must be seen. But not everyone understands that the audio-visual film (*zvuko-zritel'nyi fil'm*) is not made simply by mechanically combining the radio-film with a silent film, but by bringing the two together in such a way that it excludes the possibility of an independent existence of the image track and the sound track. A third composition is born, one that cannot be found on either the image or the sound track, but exists only through the constant interaction [*vzaimodeistvie*] of the phonogram and the visual image.[21]

As composer and filmmaker Robert Robertson notes, analyzing Vertov's montage of music and sounds in the funeral sequence of *Three Songs of Lenin*, Vertov achieves "complete integration" between visual image, music and sound, creating a "virtually uninterrupted interaction of music with image," using sound in a specifically musical way.[22] In the funeral scene, Wagner's music segues "seamlessly" into the tolling bell, which is matched by the sharp bursts of cannon and rifles. The long tones of the horns and sirens that we hear during the five minutes of motionlessness provide a "release of tension." At the same time, he notes, the visual images move from indoors, where Lenin's body is on display, to outside and onto the crowded streets, then to the big empty spaces where the cannons are fired, to the empty wilderness of all Russia.[23]

Sound in the film is edited in blocks, with the same themes and leitmotifs played over similar kinds of visual sequences. Shaporin's march, for example, sounds whenever we are shown images of progress (production, construction). The same musical score swells to a pitch anticipating Lenin's speech, both the actual voice recording we hear in the Second Song, and as intertitles (without voice) in the Third. At the end of the Second Song, we hear Chopin's funeral march again, just as we did in the beginning, while visually, we return to the mourning women in the hall, as the camera pans from left to right, reversing its original direction. Thus, both visually and aurally, the Second Song comes full circle, just as the First Song had, opening and closing with shots of Gorki, and the same musical refrain. In this way, *Three Songs* develops a complex relationship to sound, underscoring the fact that sound is not one thing, but consists of separate, interrelated elements: music, noises, voice.

While nearly all Soviet sound films made in the 1930s were released in both sound and silent variants to accommodate rural theaters across the USSR not yet equipped for sound, most of these silent versions were edited by assistants, with title cards inserted to make up for the absence of sound. *Three Songs of Lenin* was different. Vertov personally edited the film (in 1935 and again in 1938) to create the silent variant(s), introducing new filmic material, new compositions and combinations, and adding new title cards that helped to orient the viewer in relation to the images (providing names, dates, places, and the like). The elimination of the musical score means that we are no longer emotionally guided by its melodramatic effects (not by the plaintive voices of the Turkic women, nor the slow funeral music, nor Shaporin's upbeat marches), while the addition of numerous intertitles (containing the words of speeches, song lyrics, names, dates, and locations), shifts the film back entirely into the visual register.

In her review of the 1938 silent version, screened at the Locarno Film Festival (Soviet retro) on August 4, 2000, Deborah Young notes that this version was eleven minutes shorter than the "usual running time" and that "sans sound, the cinematic effects are extremely powerful and Lenin's apparitions on historic newsreels almost dreamlike." She goes on to write,

> Vertov is about the only director who personally re-edited the silent versions of his films, instead of handing the task over to an assistant. This refit has an added prologue showing the worker who caught Lenin's assassin in 1918. In addition, some episodes have been switched around, some new shots added, and the meticulously synchronized sound sequence with worker Mariya Belik axed. Both this silent version and the familiar sound one are in fact later retouchings done in 1938 (again by Vertov), following Stalin's demand that all images of his victims be removed. The originals of both have never been found.[24]

The absence of sound meant a heavier reliance on intertitles, but the silent version of *Three Songs of Lenin* not only includes title cards explaining both the structure of the film and the historical events, but it is a completely new edit of the film, that starts and ends in an entirely different place than any of the sound versions. Instead of the famous opening shots of Gorki as the place where "Lenin died," the silent variant opens with shots of N. Ivanov, the worker who on August 30, 1918, apprehended Lenin's shooter, Fanya Kaplan. This is followed by a new edit of the First Song, focusing more on women and children—longer shots of the blind woman, now stumbling toward us instead of being filmed in profile, are repeated several times, as are the shots of different young women lifting the veil (and one putting on a gas mask). Missing is the shot of Gasanova looking out the window, while new and extended shots of young Pioneers get their own refrain: *krasnyi galstuk na grudi, my rastem, my razvivaemsia* (a red tie around our neck, we are growing, we are maturing). Also included are shots of children in school marching and singing, a boy arranging wooden blocks into Lenin's name, and a new photograph of Lenin as a young boy that seems to echo the general shift of this version toward childhood and motherhood, similar to Vertov's 1937 *Lullaby*. There are repeated shots of Lenin speaking from the tribune of the monument to labor and shots of Stalin waving from the mausoleum. Only at the end of the First Song do we see the sequence in Gorki, underscoring the fact that Lenin is dead.

The Second and Third Songs are structurally unchanged (with the exception of the very final shot, which changes from variant to variant), but one notes that familiar shots come in a different order, new shots replace

Figure 5.3a. "We are growing, we are maturing" (*Three Songs of Lenin*, 1938 silent variant, frame capture)

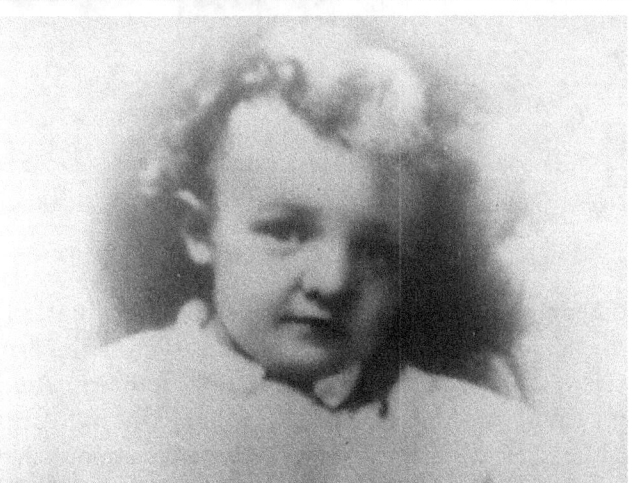

Figure 5.3b. Portrait of a young Lenin (*Three Songs of Lenin*, 1938 silent variant, frame capture)

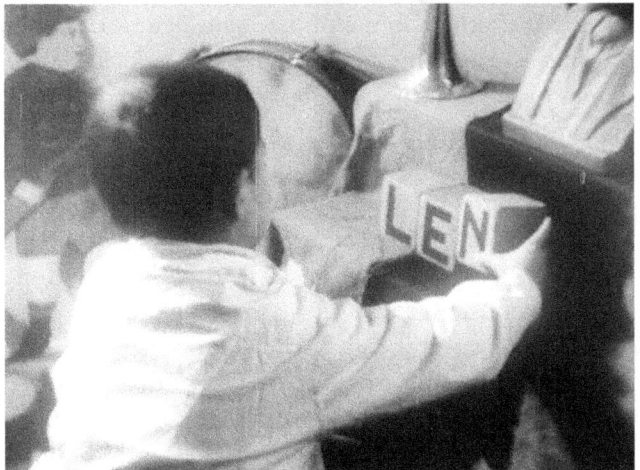

Figure 5.3c. Lenin's name spelled out in blocks (*Three Songs of Lenin*, 1938 silent variant, frame capture)

Figure 5.4a. Lifting the veil (*Three Songs of Lenin*, 1938 silent variant, frame capture)

other similar ones, there are added or altered intertitles, and even shots that appeared in earlier Vertov films, such as the 1929 *Man with a Movie Camera*. Thus, for example, the change from "And *Russians* called him simply Ilych," to "And *we* called him simply Ilych," marks a different form of address, as the silent variant removes the famous shot of Gasanova looking out the window in the First Song and replaces it with shots of Stalin waving from the tribune of the mausoleum in the Third. The funeral sequence restores some of the original *Lenin Kino-Pravda* titles, giving us the names of the mourners, and names are also provided for the figures who appear at the end of the film (Thälmann, Ibarruri), carrying on Lenin's work abroad.[25] And throughout, but in particularly, in the Third Song, there are many more shots of Stalin, either walking or waving from the top of the mausoleum. Indeed, in the silent variant of *Three Songs of Lenin*, Stalin's gaze organizes the visual field, with Vertov repeatedly coming back to Stalin on the tribune of the mausoleum, intercut with other, more familiar shots, such as the female combatants from the Spanish Civil War, who now seem to be looking up and saluting Stalin himself. The ending is different for every version, and therefore it is difficult to say which variant may have been Vertov's original intent. The 1938 silent variant ends

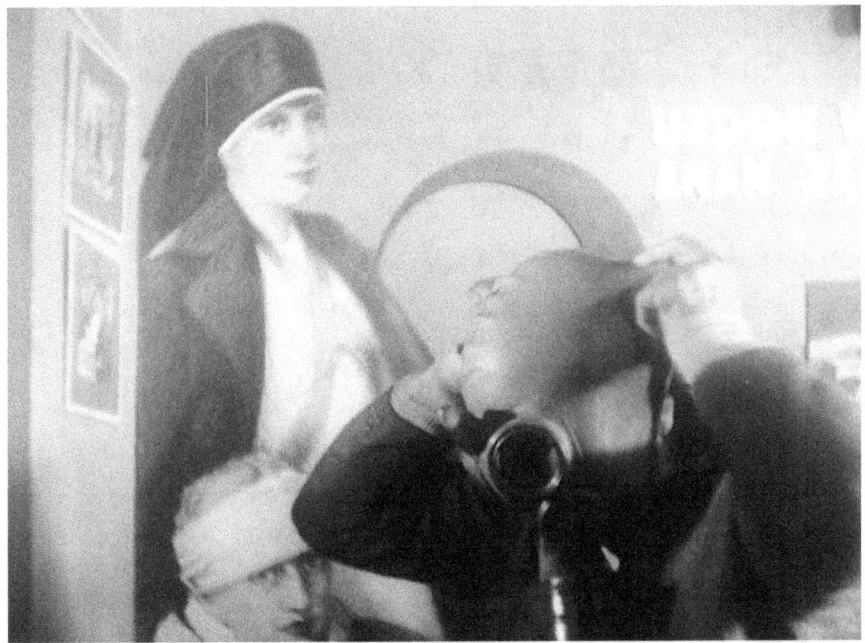

Figure 5.4b. and putting on the gas mask (*Three Songs of Lenin*, 1938 silent variant, frame capture)

with a composite shot of Lenin's profile superimposed over a neon sign ("October") and columns of soldiers marching past the mausoleum. The restored Gosfil'mofond copy of *Three Songs of Lenin* ends with the double set of revolving titles, with Lenin's commandment to "Stand firm.... Stand together.... Forward, bravely against the foe," followed by the lyric of one of the Turkic folk songs, "Centuries will pass / and people will forget the names of the countries in which their ancestors lived / but they will never forget the name Lenin / the name Ilych Lenin."[26] The final image of the film is of the words "Ilych Lenin." The 1970 restoration follows this with a shot of Lenin in the Kremlin courtyard, smiling.[27]

These radically different endings speak to the overall instability of this filmic text, the impossibility of making definitive claims about its content or meaning. That is not to say that all attempts at interpretation are futile, but only that we must be aware of the degree to which every variant of this film is incomplete and marked by the moment in which it was produced, edited, and released. The fact that Vertov continued working on this film throughout the 1930s, creating new and different versions—not only silent and sound, but also, responding to different ideological pressures—means

Figure 5.5a. Final shot of the 1938 silent variant (*Three Songs of Lenin*, 1938 silent variant, frame capture)

Figure 5.5b. Final shot of the full sound variant (*Three Songs of Lenin*, Gosfilmofond, frame capture)

Figure 5.5c. Final shot of the 1970 variant (*Three Songs of Lenin*, 1970, frame capture)

that the film remained forever a work-in-progress, and that is perhaps why Vertov returned to it again and again throughout the 1940s, using it as an example of the kind of cinema that was no longer possible in the USSR.

We might be tempted to say that watching the silent version of *Three Songs of Lenin* is like watching again a *kinok* film, a film made by the "old" Vertov, an avant-garde film that firmly continues the tradition set by the *Lenin Kino-Pravda* of 1925, by *A Sixth Part of the World* (Shestaia chast' mira, 1926), and even by *Man with a Movie Camera*, where rhythmic montage, false eye-line matches, loop printing, sped up and slowed down time, and the tension between stillness and motion produce a unified whole, a musical composition written in images. We might note that the "five minutes of motionlessness" in the Second Song are not five minutes of "silence," and that choice underscores the primacy of the moving image rather than the sound image in this film. But the sound version challenges all that. The tightly composed sound track, with its variety of musical fragments, with its different kinds of sound recordings, including Lenin's voice, including the direct-sound interviews, and—in the 1938 version—including the live recording of Stalin's speech (that brings the movement of the entire film to a halt in a way that is completely different from the five minutes of stopped time), takes the film in a radically different direction from the silent variants. This is not an avant-garde film made by the "constructivist" Vertov, but neither is it Socialist Realism. It is, indeed, a "third composition," one that cannot be found on either the image or the sound track, but "exists only through the constant interaction of the phonogram and the visual image."

A Film Without Words

Commenting on his *Three Songs of Lenin* the year of its original release in 1934, Vertov wrote,

> This film translates poorly into verbal language, though in its image-language it is easily accessible to any popular audience.
>   It is, on the one hand, a group of film documents on Lenin's death, on his last forty kilometers, on Lenin's final route from Gorki to Moscow; it is, on the other, Lenin in motion on film, a compendium of the film documents of Lenin that have been preserved, our film heritage of Lenin.
>   From still another perspective, it is an interior monologue proceeding from the old to the new, from the past to the future, from slavery to the free and civilized life of the man liberated by the revolution.[28]

Three Songs was not Vertov's first attempt to make a film about Lenin. Vertov's (or, the *kinoks*'s) first attempt to organize filmic material on Lenin was the "Lenin calendar" (Leninskii kalendar'), released while Lenin was still alive. Next came the 1925 *Lenin Kino-Pravda* (Leninskaia Kino-Pravda / Kino-Pravda # 21), an almost full feature film divided into three parts, moving from Lenin's work and deeds, to his illness and death, and finally, to the millions of people who continued his work after his death—anticipating the final composition of *Three Songs*. This was followed by *Kino-Pravda* #22: "Lenin Is Alive in the Heart of the Peasant" (V serdtse krest'ianina Lenin zhiv, 1925). Finally, for the ten-year anniversary of Lenin's death, under commission from Mezhrabpom-fil'm, Vertov and his assistant editor Elizaveta Svilova embarked on the process of collecting, examining, restoring, and rerecording audio and visual documents of Lenin, to which they added new documentary footage that likewise collected and preserved the folk songs of the Far East dedicated to the memory of Lenin.[29]

A variant of the scenario (written no later than 1933) used Lenin's voice as the starting point of the film, before moving on to film documents of "the living Lenin," "Lenin's death," "the Party," "the Plan," and concluding with "a word from comrade Stalin."[30] According to Vertov's plans in this early version of the scenario, "The Cinematic Heritage of Lenin" (Kinonasledstvo o Lenine), the film would open with Lenin's voice (Reel 1) and conclude with Stalin's (Reel 6). In between, we would see a series of documents of the "living Lenin" (Reel 2): Lenin in his office, Lenin in the Kremlin, Lenin in front of the memorial for Karl Marx, etc., all followed by more excerpts from his speeches; documents on the death of Lenin (Reel 3), beginning with his illness and concluding with the five minutes of silence and stopped motion; Lenin's call and the 100,000 new members who have joined the Party since his death (Reel 4); and the Five-Year Plan as Lenin's plan (Reel 5), including footage of Magnitogorsk and Dneprostroi, and ending with the "voice of the Party, the voice of the leader—the call of the immortal [*neumershego*: literally, undead] Lenin" repeating the speech from the opening reel, "Stand firm.... Stand together.... Forward, bravely against the foe."

Thus, already in 1933, the film was meant to conclude with a "word from Comrade Stalin," though we have no record of what Vertov intended to include in this segment. We can see the way the use of sound in general, and the reproduction of the voice, more specifically, was for Vertov the driving force behind the organization of his film about Lenin. Indeed, we might say that the central trauma of the film is not Lenin's death, which can be overcome by the transformation of Lenin into the Soviet Union itself—into the "woman who has thrown off the chador," into "water that has come to the desert," into Soviet industry and the like, or even his immobility, which can be counteracted by the "magic" of cinema, by loop-printing (the immediate repetition of shots, exactly and without variation) and other techniques meant to reanimate the body, by the moving masses, by the superimposition of Lenin on rapidly moving water—but his *silence*. "Lenin—but doesn't speak" is the lack that the film attempts, but ultimately fails to overcome.

In its 1934 version, according to Vertov, *Three Songs* included "Lenin's final voyage from Gorki to Moscow, the funeral procession, moments from the Civil War, and the song, 'The Great Pupil of the Great Lenin, Stalin, has Led Us to Battle' (Velikii uchenik velikogo Lenina—Stalin—povel nas v boi)," given both as image and sound.[31] Over 10,000 words of song texts, remarks, monologues, speeches by Lenin and others were recorded on tape; and after editing, the film contained around thirteen hundred words (1,070 in Russian and the rest in other languages). Despite the number of words spoken in the film, H. D. Wells claimed that the film would have been perfectly understandable without them: "The thoughts and nuances of the film all reached me and act upon me without the help of words [*pomimo slov*]."[32] According to Vertov, this sentiment was echoed by other foreign viewers—Japanese, Americans, English, German, Swedish, and French—who, for technical reasons, watched the film without translation.

Trying to account for the power of his film to affect the viewer even when that viewer could not understand any of the film's 1,300 words, Vertov insisted that the film in fact *did not* translate—not from Russian to English, which would be unimportant—but from cinema language into verbal speech. For Vertov, the words on the screen performed a "contrapuntal" function and the film was a "symphony orchestra of thoughts," where "an accident to a violin or a cello does not put an end to the concert." The "electrical current" of thought is not interrupted, but "continues even if one of the interconnecting wires is broken."[33] Not being able to understand Russian did not impede an understanding of the film itself, since it was the combination of all the elements of the film that made it into an organic, coherent whole.

The contents of *Three Songs*, wrote Vertov,

> develop in a spiral fashion, now in the sound, now in the image, now in a voice, now in an intertitle, now through facial expression alone—with no music or words—now through movement within the shot, now in the collision of one group shot with another, now smoothly, now by jolts from dark to light, from slow to fast, from the tired to the vigorous, now through noise, now through silent song, a song without words, through thoughts that fly from screen to viewer without the viewer-listener having to translate thought into words.[34]

The film, as Vertov called it, is an "interior monologue," meant to progress in a spiral fashion (that is to say, dialectically), from image to sound to graphic to title, bypassing verbal speech.

In the forties, Vertov railed against the imposition of the "voice-of-God" narration that became standard practice for Soviet documentary (and documentary cinema, more generally), particularly, for newsreel and other documentary films made during the Second World War. Voice-of-God narration ensured that the message of the film came through clearly and was never left to the discretion or interpretation of the viewer.[35] For Vertov, a well-made film would never need a narrator's voice-over to explain the content of the image. *Three Songs of Lenin*, he notes, did not need a narrator. If we added a narrator, "the film would speak through words." Thoughts would be mediated through the invisible off-screen voice; they would not reach the viewer directly from the screen. The narrator would become a "translator"; the film would be perceived as a "radio-monologue," all of its richness transferred over to the accompanying audio track. The viewer would cease to be a viewer and become a "listener" (*slushatel'*). This might be needed, suggests Vertov, in cases where the film is assembled from random and fragmented bits that require a verbal narration to bring them all together. But it is unnecessary if "life speaks directly from the screen, without the need for assistants, teachers, or mentors [*bez pomoshchnika, bez ukazchika, bez nastavnika*], who assertively explain how and what the viewer should see, hear, and understand."[36]

And yet, as Oksana Bulgakowa points out, there is something odd about the overall *silence* of *Three Songs of Lenin*. "Song—the very title of the film," she writes, "implies voice, but voice is transferred in the film to a different plane: the graphic, the title."[37] Vertov, who by the end of the 1920s had abandoned the use of titles, taking a polemical stance against them in the prologue to *Man with a Movie Camera*, returns to intertitles in *Three Songs*, using them again in the graphic manner of his earlier films. Contrary to Vertov's own assertions, Nikolai Izvolov has argued that Vertov was above all a man of verbal, not visual culture: "He was always interested in the *expressive word* instead of the *expressive image*." As Izvolov suggests, upon closer examination, the structure of Vertov's montage is somewhat bewildering. It seems that he was not at all concerned with the laws of joining two frames—which was the subject of Kuleshov's montage theories and his students Sergei Eisenstein and Vsevolod Pudovkin. He did not need the exact, filigree adjustment of adjacent images, the creation of a united spatial and temporal continuum. The closest comparison of his creative method may be that of collage and photomontage—and, indeed,

Figure 5.6a. Gasanova studying Alexander Rodchenko's photomontage, "The Death of Lenin" (1924) (*Three Songs of Lenin*, Gosfilmofond, frame capture)

in *Three Songs of Lenin* we see a shot of Gasanova pouring over Alexander Rodchenko's photomontage commemorating Lenin's death, which reproduces many of the same images and elements (Lenin in his coffin in Gorki, Lenin's funeral, the mausoleum, Lenin's call [*Leninskii prizyv*], Lenin's deeds live on, etc.) of Vertov's film. Vertov includes a shot of Rodchenko's photomontage in the film and draws our attention to it through Gasanova's intensive look, signaling, as he often does, the intermediality of his films, their influence by and reference to other forms of art.

To achieve the expressive word on the screen, Vertov resorted to graphic means as a way to "materialize" the word, to make it from the same material as the image. Izvolov notes that if we compare the inscriptions of *Kinopravda* with Vertov's previous film journal *Kinonedelia* (Film-week, 1918–1919), the difference in style is immediately noticeable. In *Kinonedelia* the titles are always set in identical font and typed in a typographical style. In *Kinopravda* Vertov's title words are always different; they are "materialized, they are man-made in the most direct sense." Thus, *Kinopravda* also differs from the *State Film Studio Calendar* (Goskinokalendar', 1923), made by Vertov at the same time, but looking much more conventional

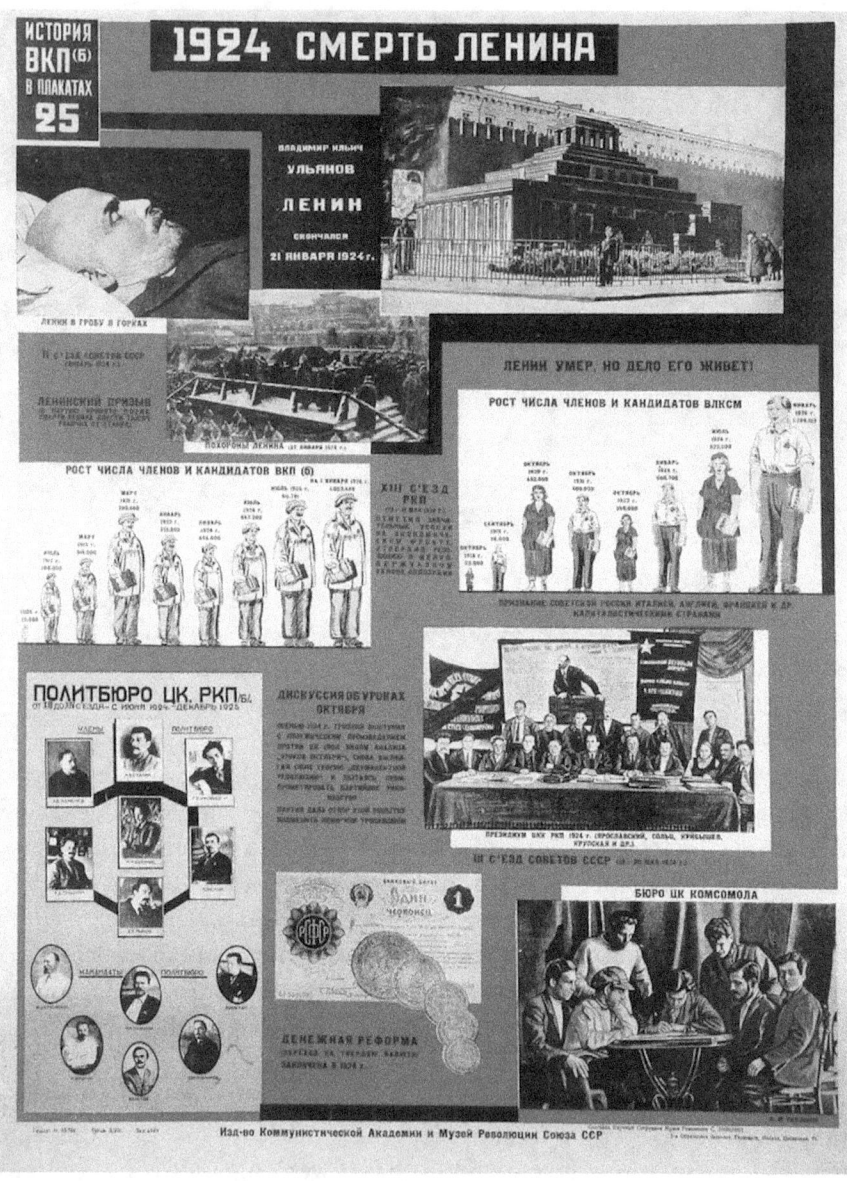

Figure 5.6b. Alexander Rodchenko, "The Death of Lenin" (1924), from *The History of KPSS in Posters* [Istoriia VKP(b) v plakatakh]; photomontage

and "typographical." *Kinopravda* was meant to look different from all the newsreels of that time. The intertitles turn into a moving image, on par with the other shots. They are "objects of the material world captured on film." They cannot even be called just "intertitles"; "they are already something completely different."[38]

Kinopravda 19 used the constructivist font we have come to associate with Rodchenko, and with Vertov's films from this point forward, including his 1924 first feature film, *Kino-Eye* (Kino-glaz). The inscriptions are "expressive, rhythmically perfected, and accentuated through various sizes," and this is true for the intertitles of *Kino-Eye, Stride, Soviet!* (Shagai, Sovet!, 1926) and *A Sixth Part of the World*; all of them are made with Rodchenko's "chopped constructivist font."[39] The first change to this comes with the film *The Eleventh Year* (Odinadtsadtyi, 1928), made in Ukraine, where only the opening credits are connected to constructivism and poster-style, while the remainder are replaced with "standard, faceless 'typographical' inscriptions."[40] These same standard, faceless, "typographical" inscriptions will reappear in *Three Songs of Lenin*, as Vertov attempts to get away from accusations of formalism and to conform to the new precepts of Socialist Realism. And yet, the reference to Rodchenko will remain; the constructivist photomontage included into the First Song underscores the assembly-like nature of Vertov's "narrative-hostile films."[41] Despite the anticonstructivist turn, we are still dealing here with a "film thing"; film facts are like bricks and you can make different things out of them, so we can have three (or even five) different films made from the same film facts.[42]

Three Songs of Lenin brings back the intertitle (barely used in *The Eleventh Year*, abandoned in *Man with a Movie Camera*, and mostly forgotten about in *Enthusiasm*), but in a way that avoids the "authorial word," presenting the film instead from the perspective of the "liberated" Turkic women. It is their voices, their songs, their gaze that organizes the film. At the same time, however, these "song-documents" of the Far East are from the beginning marked as anonymous and not belonging to the women who sing them, and they are fragmented into separate registers. Some are recorded "on the sound track, some are expressed in the images, still others are reflected in the intertitles."[43] Just as the women's voices are never matched to bodies, the songs are never given in sync-sound, and Russian translations stand in for their authentic speech. And while Vertov avoids voice-over commentary in favor of silent-style intertitles, a choice, as Jeremy Hicks suggests, clearly "motivated by the desire not to disturb the visual integrity of the film by making voice the generator of meaning," the substitution of anonymous women's voices for the authorial voice leaves this film without a clear speaker, a gap that Vertov tries to suture by giving us, for the first time, Lenin's voice on film.[44]

LA VOIX

In all of his accounts of the filmmaking process, Vertov stressed the preservation of Lenin's voice, the acquisition and transfer of the sound material that matched the 100,000 meters of archival footage examined by Svilova in order to produce a new cinematic portrait of the "living Lenin":

> Work on *Three Songs of Lenin* lasted through almost all of 1933. During that time our group accomplished the following:
>
> 1. A group member (my assistant), Comrade Svilova, by tirelessly sifting and studying archival footage in Moscow, Tiflis, Kiev, Baku, and other cities, accomplished what we had been unable to accomplish during the nine years following Lenin's death. During these nine years, only one new film document of Lenin was discovered (in America). While in 1933 for the tenth anniversary of Lenin's death we were able to report that Comrade Svilova had located ten new film-documents.
>
> 2. We had tried to transfer Lenin's voice to film in Leningrad back in 1931. The results were not very satisfactory. Our work was considerably more successful in 1933 when the soundman Shtro managed not only to preserve the quality of the recording but actually obtain a better result than that of a phonograph record. We are thus able to hear Lenin speaking on film, addressing the soldiers of the Red Army.[45]

And again:

> During work on our previous film in Leningrad our group attempted to transfer Lenin's voice to film. Because of the imperfection of the sound camera, the results obtained were not very satisfactory.
>
> Work in 1933 (done by sound engineer Shtro) turned out more successfully. Lenin's voice came out better on film than on the phonograph record. From Lenin's address to members of the Red Army the following words, clearly audible and easy to make out, went into the film: "Stand firm.... Stand together.... Forward, bravely against the foe.... Victory shall be ours. ... The power of the landowners and capitalists, crushed here in Russia, shall be defeated throughout the entire world!" In this way we found it possible to preserve Lenin's voice on film and to present Vladimir Ilych speaking from the screen.[46]

For the Soviets, the preservation of Lenin's voice on film took on almost mystic qualities. "Science and technology," wrote E. Yaroslavsky in 1932, using nearly the same language as Vertov, "have preserved Lenin in motion on film.... Science and technology have preserved Lenin's voice: eighteen gramophone records, eighteen Lenin speeches." Yaroslavsky calls on all the workers' clubs and reading rooms to save these records, so that Lenin's voice will sound its call from "beyond the grave.... And then, Lenin's words, the voice of the long dead leader will sound like a military command from the far past: do not stop! Continue working, perfecting, making life better!"[47] Celebrating the advances in science and technology, Yaroslavsky nevertheless bemoans the fact that sound film technology did not come soon enough: "What an immense impression we would have now, if the development of sound cinema had not come too late."[48]

Three Songs of Lenin contains three distinct recordings of the "real human voice": the songs of the Turkic women in the First Song, the reproduction of Lenin's speech in the Second Song, and the live interviews with workers/farmers in the Third Song. These three different recordings—the anonymous voices of Turkic women forming part of the film's score along with Wagner, Chopin, and Shaporin; the disembodied voice of Lenin projected over images of his public speaking and revolving titles repeating his words: "Stand firm.... Stand together.... Forward, bravely against the foe"; and the embodied voice of the "worker" recorded live and anticipating *cinéma vérité* of the 1960s[49]—represent three distinct sound practices and three distinct consequences for the production and reproduction of the voice on film.

As Vertov argued, the sync-sound interviews in *Three Songs* and *Lullaby* were a continuation of his earlier practices of "catching life unawares," but now, with the methods of sound film.[50] Vertov's Soviet biographer N. P. Abramov noted that it was specifically the mistakes, the genuine, unrehearsed speech of the interviewees, with their grammatical errors and mispronunciations, that made these recordings so valuable, and captured, as Vertov would say, the "living person" on screen. Writing about *Three Songs of Lenin* in 1962, Abramov stressed Vertov's vanguard role in documentary *sound* cinematography: "Dziga Vertov was the first documentary film maker in the world to include in his film the authentic, simultaneously recorded speech of a person (the story of the female cement-work, the story of the old collective farmer) ... authentic, unrehearsed speech ... with pauses, with irregular accents ... sounded from the screen for the first time, giving credibility and expression to the image of a living person in documentary film."[5]

As Bill Nichols points out, with the coming of sound, the central point of identification for documentary becomes the spoken word and the commentator who delivers it. It is the "literal voice of the film," writes Nichols,

Figure 5.7a. Cement worker Maria Belik (*Three Songs of Lenin*, Gosfilmofond, frame capture)

Figure 5.7b. ZAGES engineer (*Three Songs of Lenin*, Gosfilmofond, frame capture)

"and it arrives in the form of 'He Who Already Knows,' a voice that marshals sounds and images in support of a carefully crafted perspective known from the outset."[52] The spoken word stands for the "disembodied, omniscient, invulnerable filmmaker who retains full control over the assembly of images and the rhythm of the film."[53] Made more pronounced with the arrival of sound in documentary in the 1930s, this position of He Who Already Knows shifts dramatically in the 1960s with the invention of portable cameras and tape recorders, capable of recording sync-sound on actual locations. With new technology enabling a different stance toward the subject, the documentary filmmaker is now able to "adopt an embodied, situated, and often highly visible position as one among many—albeit

Figure 5.7c.
Communal farmer
(*Three Songs of Lenin*,
Gosfilmofond,
frame capture)

Figure 5.7d.
Chairwoman of the
Collective Farm
named after Lenin
(*Three Songs of Lenin*,
Gosfilmofond,
frame capture)

the one with the movie camera." The image track is no longer a collage of shots that build "a mood or attitude"; it is instead "the visible counterpart to the voice of the speaking subject." The filmmaker now holds his or her camera "on the one who speaks, in sync." The image as caught serves to "anchor spoken words to individual bodies."[54]

Vertov, always ahead of his time, does precisely this with the sync-sound interviews in *Three Songs of Lenin*, anchoring the spoken words to individual bodies. He remains off-screen, while "impromptu, spontaneous speech" prevails over the well-polished commentaries of standard (Soviet and otherwise) documentary cinema.[55] At the time of the film's 1934 release, Vertov linked the success of the sync-sound interviews in *Three Songs* to his notion of the *kino-eye*, singling out specifically the interview with Maria Belik because it accomplished what he had always striven for, "complete synchrony between words and thoughts," stressing that this is "more than simply a synchronization of sound and image, it is the synchronization of words and thoughts."[56] And he frequently returns to the "smile of Belik" as a moment of clarity and simplicity captured on film.[57] In "About [My] Love for the Living Person" (O [moei] liubvi k zhivomu cheloveku), an article published in *Iskusstvo kino* (Art of Cinema) in 1958, but written in the 1940s, Vertov quotes in full the sync-sound interviews from both *Three Songs* and *Lullaby* to demonstrate the way documentary cinema can capture the "living person."[58] Speaking about the interview with the female parachutist in *Lullaby*, he underscores the "absolute, genuine sincerity, the 100 percent synchronization" of thoughts, words, and images. It is as if we are "seeing the invisible—seeing thoughts on the screen," he concludes.[59]

The interview with the cement worker Maria Belik certainly remains one of the best known moments in *Three Songs of Lenin* and one to which Vertov himself returns to in his writings. But it may actually be the interview with the chairwoman of the collective farm that provides a key to understanding Vertov's film, by allowing us to see the transformations that led from a script where Lenin's voice and his "living" presence predominated (as they had in the original *Lenin Kino-Pravda* from 1925) to a film in which Lenin's death becomes the primary object of reflection, while cinema is powerless to bring back that which has been lost forever.

The chairwoman of the collective farm named after Lenin recounts in her own words the speeches of the First All-Union Conference of collective farm shock workers and, specifically, Stalin's speech to the kolkhoz workers from February 19th, with injunctions against turning back, against choosing the wrong path (back toward capitalism), against keeping women down, and the like.[60] Yet, what emerges from her narrative is less a parroting of an official party line and more of a profound consideration of the traumatic effects of the past:

> [As Comrade Stalin says],[61] a woman on a collective farm is a great force, and women cannot be kept down. . . . I'm the president of the Lenin collective farm here. . . . We have three women on the administrative board, and two are group leaders. We carry on merciless work, despite the fact that we have no men. (Pause) . . . And I feel where I've come to . . . and what our leaders are saying. Those are golden words they are saying. You should write them down . . . and put them in your head . . . and when you come home, you've got to tell them . . . and you want to do as the leaders say . . . you want to get things organized on the collective farm . . . !? And you think to yourself . . .

you remember what's behind you, but the Bolsheviks say don't turn back [*po-zadi-to ty pomnish', no bol'sheviki ne veliat nazad vertat'sia*]; forget the hard times you've gone through and march ahead [*vpered shagai*]! ... so you think it's like that, but maybe it's ... you need to live through it, you need to reach it, you need to figure out how to approach it.... Well, you get all that into your head, and the tears well up all by themselves.⁶²

The delivery of the speech makes all the difference in this episode, because it is the expression and the pauses, even more than the content, that turn this from mere reproduction of official ideology into a compulsive repetition signifying the work of trauma. Indeed, as Andrei Shcherbenok notes, it is particularly the lack of clarity and logical coherence of this speech that marks it as a product of trauma.⁶³ As with Belik, whose account of falling into liquid cement shocks us not because of the accident, which can happen anywhere, but by her drive to immediately return to work to finish her shift, the traumatic content of the chairwoman's speech is alluded to in passing—the absence of men, the "merciless" (*bezposhchadno*) call to work, the unnamed events of the past that "must not be remembered but cannot be forgotten," and the command to "march ahead," despite the fact that the path forward remains unclear. We might particularly underscore the desire and yet, clearly, the inability to "stride forward" (*shagat' vpered*), a direct reference to Vertov's own *Stride, Soviet!* (Shagai, Sovet!) as symptomatic of the workings of trauma.

The traumatic events of the past are superseded by the demand to keep going, but their repression is marked here precisely by the inability to bring together the two types of speech—the authorial (Bolshevik, Stalinist) word and the unauthorized, halting speech of the "living person"—by the inability to fully answer the call of the state. That call of the state is underscored not only by references to Stalin (excised in the 1970 version of *Three Songs*), but by the voice of Lenin that comes to us as an *acousmêtre*, twice repeating the demand to "Stand firm.... Stand together.... Forward, bravely against the enemy." In *Three Songs of Lenin*, Lenin's free-floating voice is figured as a *Leninskii prizyv* (Lenin's call to arms), and it marks the absent presence of the Leader, now "more alive than anyone" (*Lenin i teper' zhivee vsekh zhivykh*) issuing directives from beyond the grave.⁶⁴ Lenin's absent presence disturbs the standard binary opposition of life and death, marking the place of slippage between the two states. Like Paul de Man's understanding of the figure of *apostrophe*, Lenin's disembodied voice issuing from the screen alters the relation between the dead and the living. As de Man suggests, when we address the dead, we do so at our own risk: "when the dead speak, the living fall silent."⁶⁵

The disembodied voice relies on sound cinema's ability to produce the effect of "truth" through the disengagement of voice from body. For voice-overs in documentary films, the free-floating male voice, unanchored to a specific body, takes on the attributes of omniscience and omnipotence. As Mary Ann Doane has put it, the voice's "radical otherness with respect to the diegesis," the fact that it is not produced by a body that we can *see*, allows it to assume superhuman or extrahuman status—the status of a pure signifier of power:

> As a form of direct address, it speaks without mediation to the audience, bypassing the "characters" and establishing a complicity between itself and the spectator—together they understand and *place* the image. It is precisely because the voice is not localizable, because it cannot be yoked to a body, that it is capable of interpreting the image, producing its truth. Disembodied, lacking any specification in space or time, the voice-over is, as [Pascal] Bonitzer points out, beyond criticism—it censors the questions "Who is speaking?," "Where?," "In what time?," and "For whom?"[66]

Doane goes on to quote from Pascal Bonitzer: "This is not, one suspects, without ideological implications. The first of these implications is that the voice-off represents a power, that of disposing of the image and of what it reflects, from a space absolutely *other* with respect to that inscribed in the image-track. *Absolutely other and absolutely indeterminant.* Because it rises from the field of the Other, the voice-off is assumed to know: this is the essence of its power.... The power of the voice is a stolen power, an usurpation."[67] We can see precisely this form of power at work in *Three Songs*, in which Lenin's "free floating" and "unanchored" voice "haunts" the film, taking on the "attributes of omniscience and omnipotence," particularly when compared to the anonymous songs of the Turkic women or the "authentic, unrehearsed speech" of the sync-sound interviewees.

Indeed, when we compare the disembodied voice of Lenin to the partially embodied voices of the Turkic singers or the fully embodied voices of the workers, we can see the way the disembodied voice speaks with an authority that the embodied voice lacks, because its power is located elsewhere, outside the film proper, yet still with "one foot" in the image.[68] The Turkic women, the shock workers, and the collective farmers have nothing "uncanny" about them; they speak without authority, merely recounting the story of their own lives, their bodies worn out from work, their speech incorrect, ungrammatical, foreign, or accented. In contrast, Lenin's voice remains precisely "un-anchored" and "free floating." It "rises from the field of the Other," speaking its demands from beyond the grave, while the image of Lenin remains deliberately *not* synchronized with the recording of his voice.

In many ways, this is an odd choice. As Nichols argues, sometimes important events occur when a camera is not present to record them. Reenactment or reconstruction is a "logical solution" to the paradoxical quandary a documentary filmmaker often confronts: how to film an actual event that occurred before a camera could record it so that it once again appears as it might have appeared at the time it originally occurred. As long as the filmmaker's intentions were deemed honorable (as long as viewers shared the apparent intentions of the maker), argues Nichols, these "ways of giving creative shape to reality were readily accepted." Moreover, "music, sound effects, and speech could all be plausibly added to a reenactment. . . . In a reenactment the creative use of sound can heighten what it might feel like to witness a given event for which the camera was not initially present."[69] Documentary cinema, in other words, is always a convention, a pact made between the viewer and the filmmaker to suspend certain kinds of disbelief in order to bring us a historical event or a series of facts. It is always "creative treatment of actuality," to use John Grierson's famous definition.[70] This is precisely the kind of montage that Vertov had always championed, writing famously in 1923, "I make the viewer see in the manner best suited to my presentation of this or that visual phenomenon. . . . You are walking down a Chicago street today in 1923, but I make you greet Comrade Volodarsky, walking down a Petrograd street in 1918, and he returns your greeting."[71] In his writings about *Three Songs*, Vertov stresses the preservation of Lenin's voice, the acquisition and transfer of the sound material that matches the 100,000 meters of archival footage examined by Svilova in order to produce a new cinematic portrait of the "living Lenin." And yet, he chooses to leave Lenin's voice separate from the image.

Matching Lenin's voice to an image of Lenin speaking would have been precisely the kind of permissible "reenactment" that the majority of Vertov's viewers would have expected and accepted. But for Vertov, the knowledge that the sound camera had indeed arrived "too late" meant that a "sync"-sound recording of the leader issuing commands from the screen could not be sustained. Even more vitally, perhaps, Vertov's decision *not* to synchronize image and sound here speaks to the inability to overcome a certain kind of trauma—a "break in the mind's experience of time," in which the threat from outside is recognized "*one moment too late*"—that the film as a whole attempts to undo.[72] The loss of Lenin, and the loss of Lenin's *voice*, marks a break in the Soviet experience of time. By the time the sound camera arrives in 1928, it is too late and no amount of archival research can restore what has been permanently lost. The image track and the sound track must remain forever out of sync.

Death 18x a Second

Indeed, the reproduction of Lenin's voice in the film acts to underscore rather than amend that break. Lenin's voice issuing from the screen makes palpable the silences of the film, the silence of the masses, brought once again before the immobile corpse of their leader.

Writing about Vertov in 1982, Soviet critic Lef Rochal spends some time trying to lay out the construction of the 1925 *Lenin Kino-pravda*, the original source for the Second Song of *Three Songs of Lenin*, in an attempt to reveal its thematic and cinematic techniques. He is particularly attentive to the moment of Lenin's funeral, when the film introduces the titles:

66. LENIN—
67. does not move.
68. LENIN—
69. is silent.
70. The masses
71. moving
72. The masses
73. are silent

ЛЕНИН
а не движется
ЛЕНИН
а молчит
МАССЫ
движутся
МАССЫ
молчат

What draws Rochal's attention is the lack of punctuation in these statements. A period, he speculates, would have been a statement of tragedy (*tochka [by] konstatirovala tragediiu*), an exclamation point would have shown raw emotion, a question mark would have demonstrated the inability to comprehend the full force of the catastrophe.[73] Without punctuation, Roshal believes, Vertov makes it possible for all three responses to coexist, allowing the public and the private to merge and to reflect simultaneously general and individual suffering.

I want to suggest, however, that there is something else strange about this set of titles, which are carried over unchanged into the Second Song of *Three Songs of Lenin*. What looks at first to be a chiasmus, or in any case, a reversal of terms (Lenin is immobile, but the masses move), becomes an equivalence (Lenin is silent, the masses are silent). Made uneasy by the first premise—Lenin should be moving and speaking (or this is not Lenin)—we are unsure how to interpret the second: the masses move and yet they are silent. Indeed, this segment relies on one of Vertov's favorite devices, the stopping of cinematic time. At first, as Roshal points out, Lenin and the masses are shown in constant motion, when suddenly—everything comes to a halt: "After the black film leader and the lines from the obituary, we saw immobile (literally immobile!) shots of Lenin in his coffin" (*vsled za chernoi prokleikoi i strokami iz nekrologa, stoiali [imenno stoiali!] kadry Lenina v grobu*).[74] The sudden stoppage of movement is picked up again a few moments later when the entire country observes its minute of silence: among the shots of men, women, and machines paused in the middle of work, we see a shot of a train stopped in midmotion. But this minute of silence is filmed as five minutes of motionlessness, a disruption in the flow of both historical and cinematic time. Vertov is relying on cinema's ability to stop time to communicate the impossibility of Lenin's immobility. On the screen, Lenin is as alive as he was when the image was made; moreover, film projected at 24x (or 18x) frames per second creates movement out of immobility, so even the dead Lenin continues to move, impervious to his own death. After shots of the funeral, writes Roshal, "columns of young pioneers marched in front of the wooden mausoleum. . . . And over the mausoleum, over the teeth of the Kremlin, appeared (with the help of a double exposure) the living Lenin." This, he concludes, "was the beginning of immortality." Not only in terms of device, "but also in terms of its meaning, this shot was built on the principles of double exposure."[75]

Techniques of stopped time and double exposure have a "chiasmic" capacity in the same way that de Man's *apostrophe* and *prosopopeia* do; that is, Lenin's immortality already troubles the living—the masses are silent—the mechanized reproduction of his speech giving voice to the dead, while "the living fall silent."[76] It may be an obvious statement to say that *Three Songs of Lenin* is about death, yet it may not be as obvious in what ways it is about death—that is to say, the ways in which this film demonstrates cinema's "privileged" relationship to death, "the co-presence of movement and stillness, continuity and discontinuity" that constitutes, as Laura

Mulvey suggests, cinema's "eternal paradox."⁷⁷ Vertov's desire for new, never-before-seen footage of Lenin, the desire to reproduce Lenin's voice on film, the desire to show "the living Lenin," "Lenin in motion" on the screen, gives us the central paradox of filmmaking: turning life into death, and then reanimating, reproducing, ventriloquizing, and galvanizing the dead.

We recall Mayakovsky's tirade against the depiction of Lenin in Eisenstein's *October*, promising that "at the most solemn moment . . . I shall hiss and pelt this fake Lenin with rotten eggs."⁷⁸ In his *Three Songs*, Vertov wanted to show a different, "real" (*zhivoi*) Lenin, to hear his voice for the first time issuing from the screen. The description of the lengths the camera crew had to go to find new documentary footage, the desire for Lenin's "real voice" to be recorded on film—all this points to a desire for the representation of "truth" on film. Not "kino-eye for its own sake, but the truth through kino-eye, that is, kino-pravda."⁷⁹ Instead, as Dragan Kujundzic has noted, *Three Songs* reproduces the "endless, long shots of the cadaverized body, infinitely identical with itself . . . the dead specter of the sclerotized gaze."⁸⁰ What *Three Songs* wants to capture is life (movement, voice—we recall Vertov's formulations: "Lenin in motion on film. The preserved film-documents of the living Lenin; our film heritage of Lenin"). What it captures instead is death:

> 15.—"We never beheld him. . ."
> 16.—"We never heard his voice. . ."
> 66. LENIN—
> 67. does not move.
> 68. LENIN—
> 69. is silent.
> (Ленин—а не движется . . . Ленин—а молчит . . .)

The original 1924 recording of Lenin's funeral registered the death of Lenin as an event, and in that, through the miracle of cinema, provided the images with an immortality (by removing them from the flow of historical time). By the time the footage is repeated in *Three Songs* ten years later, however, we are no longer witnessing the registration of an event, but its traumatic reenactment. Hysterics, Freud famously wrote, "suffer from reminiscences," and Vertov's film reproduces at the site of its "body" (i.e., on the level of its enunciation) the "truth" that can no longer be spoken, the truth that Lenin is dead.

Vertov's *Lenin Kino-Pravda* was made at the height of the Lenin cult and released in 1925 to mark the one-year anniversary of his death. His

Three Songs of Lenin was made ten years later, when the cult of Lenin was not merely waning, but had already waned, when *Pravda* published a photograph not of the Leader in movement and action but as an old, sick man sitting on a bench in Gorki, a "helpless icon."[81] The cult of Lenin, as Nina Tumarkina has argued, did not survive the ten-year anniversary of his death. In this way, *Three Songs* marks Lenin's "second death"—symbolic rather than actual—by showing us Lenin alive and then dead, frozen on the screen.

Once Lenin is immobilized ("Lenin—but doesn't move"), once cinema is powerless to create movement from or between still images, the entire project of trying to make a film about the "living Lenin" comes to a halt. Indeed, the film itself comes to a standstill in the five minutes of motionlessness (rather than five minutes of *silence*, which is perhaps what we were expecting). If the frozen-time sequence in *Man with a Movie Camera* shocked the viewer by breaking down the film into its component parts in order to demonstrate the power of the moving/movement-image, of cinema as "more than" a series of stills, here instead, we are confronted by cinema's very powerlessness. Cinema, the vehicle of movement and time, has no means by which to conquer the one event that cannot be reversed or undone—no matter how hard it tries (via sound, metaphor, camera movement, superimposition, optical printing, the image's infinite reproducibility), it cannot bring Lenin back, make him "alive" on the screen.

It is perhaps for this reason that the Third Song, while ostensibly transforming Lenin into the industrial dynamism of the Second Five-Year Plan (signaled most clearly by the shot of the bust of Lenin superimposed over the Dniepr Hydroelectric Dam), gives us instead the Leader frozen in time—in "eternal poses" or with "immobile sections," as Gilles Deleuze would have it.[82] The cadaverized body of Lenin lying in state from the Second Song is here solidified into a monument, with time-lapse photography used to counter through the movement of nature behind him (sky, clouds, water) the trauma of Lenin's immobility. This is particularly evident in the shots of Ivan Shadr's eleven-meter-high bronze monument to Lenin at ZAGES (the Zemo-Avchal'skaia Hydro-Electric Station named after V. I. Lenin) in Georgia, erected in 1927 (and disassembled in 1991). This was one of the first Soviet monuments to Lenin, and one of Shadr's most significant works.[83] For his inspiration, Shadr (pseudonym for I. Ivanov) used photo- and film-documents of Lenin to try to capture Lenin's movement and gestures, finally settling on a photograph of Lenin speaking on Red Square at the celebration of Vsevobuch in 1919 (which we see earlier in *Three Songs of Lenin*). The odd gesture of Lenin pointing down was initially criticized as

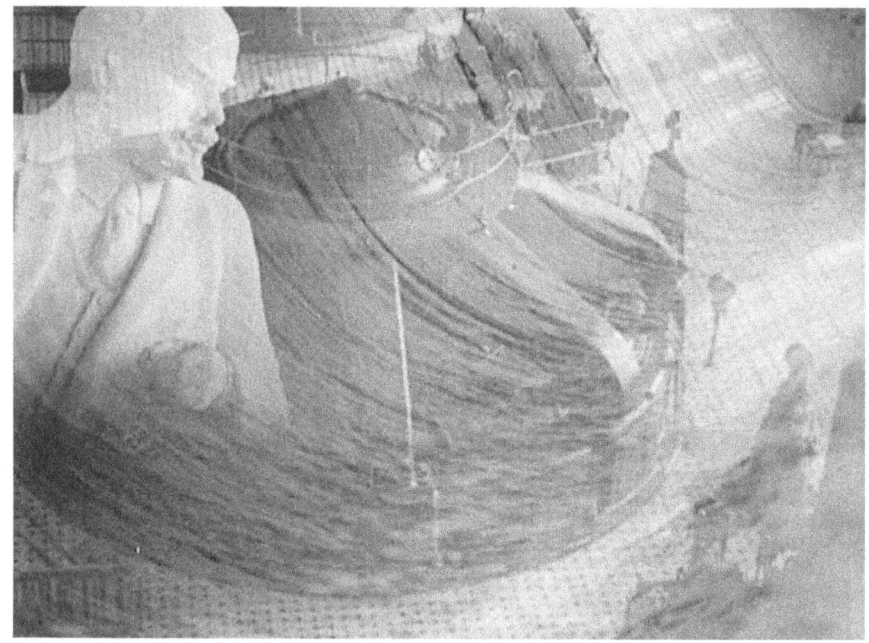

Figure 5.8a. Movement of energy (*Three Songs of Lenin*, Gosfilmofond, frame capture)

chosen at random, but made sense once the monument was placed in relation to the hydro-electric station, with Lenin pointing down at the rushing water generating energy, below. As Michelson puts it, noting the way the process of historicization transforms "document into monument": "The function of the monumental is not only to commemorate, but definitively to inter and block the return of the dead (the stone set over the grave to impede the corpse's resurrection)."[84]

In the silent variant of the film, the camera placed on rails tracks past another Lenin monument, producing the illusion that the monument itself is moving. Yet, these efforts to overcome Lenin's "eternal pose" do nothing to bring him back to life. Similarly, the repetition in the final frames of the film of Lenin's commandment to "stand firmly, stand together, forward bravely against the foe," produces an uncanny effect. The titles, no longer supported by a recording of Lenin's voice or intercut with images of the speaking Lenin, are merely a mechanical reproduction, an echo, no longer capable of bringing the "living Lenin" on screen.[85]

I think that in *Three Songs* Vertov may have been attempting to halt the infinite reproducibility of the photographic image, to stop time, to enshrine Lenin in a (cinematic) mausoleum that would preserve him, that

Figure 5.8b. Monument to Lenin at ZAGES, Ivan Shadr, 1927
(*Three Songs of Lenin*, Gosfilmofond, frame capture)

would be the "truth" of Lenin. This is one way in which we can read the "freeze frame" that marks the moment of silence. Vertov's team (and in particular, Svilova) scoured the archives for new, never-before-seen footage of Lenin, for the recorded voice of the "living Lenin" (*zhivogo Lenina*), underscoring the desire to renew and refresh the images that had already grown old and familiar through over use. Yet, the central device of the film (the Second Song) is not "original" but a repetition, a new assembly of the footage Vertov showed in his *Lenin Kino-Pravda*. Filmed in 1924, this footage recorded a real event—Lenin's funeral and the masses—now, in 1934, this footage performs another task: it marks the passage of time between events, it marks the distance between 1924 and 1934 (an enormous, unbridgeable gap, as Sheila Fitzpatrick has argued[86]), and it marks the end of the Lenin cult, its "death at 18x per second."

The Silences of the Voice

While the 1925 *Lenin Kino-Pravda* focused on Lenin in motion—walking in the Kremlin after being shot by Fanya Kaplan, giving speeches, smiling, shaking hands, speaking to great crowds—we open the 1934 *Three*

Figure 5.9a. Pine trees in Gorki, opening shot (*Three Songs*, Gosfilmofond, frame capture)

Figure 5.9b. Pine trees in Gorki, closing shot (*Three Songs*, Gosfilmofond, frame capture)

Songs with Lenin dead. From the beginning, it is not his presence, but his absence that structures our vision, from the uncanny low-angle shots of swaying trees, to the Gorki residence reflected in the pool of water, to the bench "familiar from photographs" standing empty in the gardens. Intertitles underscore Gorki not as the place where Lenin lived but rather as the place where Lenin died; we are told that the room "where Lenin died faces onto a garden," and a "reverse" shot from inside the house gives us the perspective Lenin would have had on the garden, briefly placing us in the position of the dead leader.[87] A second shot now outside that same room, framed on both sides by two white columns, centers on a path that Lenin may have taken, suggesting that the camera has stepped out of Lenin's room the way he himself might have done. The final shot of this prologue returns us to the swaying trees (still low-angle, but now captured from a slightly different vantage point), but this time we can better understand the trees' uncanny effect: we are looking at them through "Lenin's eyes," while knowing full well that Lenin is dead.[88]

"We never saw him ... we never heard his voice," the intertitles tell us, and indeed, there are barely any images of Lenin in the First Song. Instead, we are reminded of Lenin's sacrifice as a form of dismemberment: "He gave us everything that he had: his brain, his blood, his heart." We then return to shots of the house and park in Gorki, cross-cut with images of a printing press printing copies of the dust jacket of Lenin's *Die Bilanz der Revolution 1905* (Lecture on the 1905 Revolution).[89] There is again the "famous bench," now shown from the back; the dust jacket with a picture of a younger Lenin; the trees in Gorki, and black out, while a sound bridge of Chopin's funeral march carries us over to the Second Song—"the central panel of the triptych," as Annette Michelson calls it—the song of loss.[90]

Here shots of grieving women are intercut with shots of Lenin in his coffin (still and immobile, as Roshal would have it) and with other documentary footage, such as shots of the park in Gorki now in deep winter, shots of the train carrying Lenin's body the last forty kilometers, Lenin speaking, and Lenin's funeral. Once again, like in the First Song, our vision is guided by a subjective POV. Newsreel footage of Lenin's funeral familiar to viewers from *Lenin Kino-Pravda* and other newsreels is intercut with close-ups of faces of women from Central Asia and intertitles that suggest that we are seeing Lenin's death through their eyes, that this is their memory of Lenin. But it is also *our* memory of Lenin; the reuse of footage from *Kino-Pravda* #21 creates the effect of remembrance. Then, the "backward glance" is itself halted. In the five minutes of motionlessness, the film alternates between freeze frames and still shots, between loop printing and time slowed to a halt.[91] As Bulgakowa suggest, "Vertov uses the freeze-frame in order to halt moving objects—cars, machines, the movement of a film print through a projector, and finally—the camera itself: the film shot is replaced with a photograph and finally—with a drawing of the mausoleum."[92] And while the dynamism of the Third Song and the achievements of the Second Five-Year Plan are meant to counteract this moment of immobility, we are never quite free of the feeling that time is "out of joint." Like the chairwoman of the collective farm named after Lenin, we can only obey the command to "stride forward" if we don't

Figure 5.10a. "I, a worker at the factory" (*Lenin Kino-Pravda*, 1925, frame capture)

Figure 5.10b. N. Ivanov (*Lenin Kino-Pravda*, 1925, frame capture)

look back, if we forget where we have come from. But any backward glance reveals a "break in the mind's experience of time," underscoring cinema's inability to suture our loss.

Nowhere is this "backward glance" made more clear than in the silent variants (both 1935 and 1938) of *Three Songs*, whose opening shots mark a radical departure from the sound versions of the film.[93] The absence of sound meant a heavier reliance on intertitles, but the silent variant not only includes new title cards explaining both the structure of the film (*vstuple-nie*/prologue) and the historical events ("30th of August 1918, in this factory Lenin gave a speech"), but also begins in a completely different place than the sound version. Instead of opening with shots of the park at Gorki,

Figure 5.10c. "I, a worker at the factory" (*Three Songs of Lenin*, 1938 silent variant, frame capture)

Figure 5.10d. N. Ivanov (*Three Songs of Lenin*, 1938 silent variant, frame capture)

the silent version returns instead to the opening of the 1925 *Lenin Kino-Pravda*, and to N. Ivanov, the worker who on August 30, 1918, arrested Lenin's shooter, Fanya Kaplan. Yet, what appears at first glance to be a return to the original source (the 1925 film), turns out in fact to be a reconstruction. Instead of the constructivist intertitles used in the 1925 *Lenin Kino-Pravda*, we have plain intertitles that match those of the 1934 *Three Songs of Lenin*; instead of the original footage of Ivanov from the 1920s, we have new footage of him filmed a decade later; instead of shots showing us the factory square where the assassination attempt took place and the 1922 monument

Figure 5.11a. Monument marking the place where Lenin was shot (*Lenin Kino-Pravda*, 1925, frame capture)

Figure 5.11b. Vladimir Pchelin, "The Attempt on Lenin's Life" [Pokushenie na Lenina, 1927] (*Three Songs of Lenin*, 1938 silent variant, frame capture)

Figure 5.11c. Vladimir Pchelin, "The Attempt on Lenin's Life" [Pokushenie na Lenina, 1927] (*Three Songs of Lenin*, 1938 silent variant, frame capture)

that was erected to mark the spot where Lenin fell, we have close-ups of Vladimir Pchelin's 1927 painting, "The Attempt on Lenin's Life" (Pokushenie na Lenina).[94]

As a whole, this sequence is longer than the original from 1925, and its purpose is no longer to document a historical fact, but to underscore the degree to which the historical event can only be reproduced as a fiction. This is made evident by the change from the pure documentary shot of the empty factory square that showed us the exact place where the assassination attempt took place to shots of a painting depicting the same event, but now in a romantic realist fashion. The same intertitle, "Pokushenie proizoshlo zdes'" (The assassination attempt took place here) introduces both sequences, but in the 1938 silent version, the empty snow-covered factory square with its lonely monument marking the place where Lenin fell is replaced with a close-up of Pchelin's painting. The painting is first seen in the background behind the speaking Ivanov; Vertov then moves in on Ivanov's face, superimposing it over the painting and finally dissolving the close-up to show us the painting behind him. Panning across distraught faces and rushing bodies depicted on the large canvass behind Ivanov, the camera stops when we see the small figure of Lenin lying in the street. A tight close-up shows us Lenin lying on the ground, followed by a medium shot that continues the pan from right to left until we reach the edge of the canvass. The superimposition and dissolve serve to give us Ivanov's "memories" of the event, while the narrative painting and the mobile camera bring them to "life." The excision of the shot of the Browning pistol used by Kaplan (included in the original *Kino-Pravda* #21) underscores the idea that we are no longer interested in facts, but in something else altogether. The indexical sign—"*zdes'*" [here]—no longer locates us in a specific place or moment in time. Like the drawing of the mausoleum noted by Bulgakowa, the documentary fact has been replaced by its representation; history has become myth.

As Papazian argues, in the 1920s, Vertov sought the possibility of unfettering film art from the bonds of verbal language, of creating a new language based on properties inherent in film—most importantly, its ability to represent sensory "facts" to the viewer. For Vertov, the special "indexical" relationship between the photographed object and its image on film (in which the photograph registers the actual existence of the object in real life) "seemed to offer the possibility of circumventing not only verbal language, but representation itself as an artistic operation: specifically, the mediation of an authoring presence." The kino-eye would present life as it was, without the interference of any kind of artistic "vision."[95] This is why Vertov considered his sync-sound interviews in *Three Songs* as a form of the "kino-eye"—a direct recording of "life as it really was" without an authoring presence. But here, in this substitution of a narrative painting (and a *romantic* realist painting) for the basic factual shot that registered "the actual existence of the object in real life," Vertov is doing the opposite. In a quiet and unobtrusive way, in a version of the film playing outside of the urban centers of Moscow or Leningrad or London, he bares the device of *Three Songs of Lenin*, underscoring not its faithfulness to fact, but its romantic fictionalization. Like the refusal to sync Lenin's voice with his image, Vertov's move is melodramatic; it is the admission of the "too late," of documentary cinema's inability to record events as they happen, of its fundamentally fictive nature.[96]

This is particularly evident in the nonuse of Lenin's recorded voice as a match for the image. Vertov's voice recordings (which had to be carefully worked on to achieve a decent quality of sound) are superimposed on the images but are in themselves asynchronous. The difference in location between body and voice is underscored by the unavailability of synchronized sound and image recordings during Lenin's lifetime. Cinema grants us the illusion of unity, and this illusion is what makes cinema possible (and enjoyable). But this illusion returns us to cinema's central paradox: the copresence of movement and stillness, of continuity and discontinuity. As Stephen Heath has argued, cinema functions via the erasure of difference: still shots are projected at a speed that obscures their individual identity and difference from each other and yet the illusion of movement is constituted precisely via that difference.[97] Like photography, cinema records the moment of registration, the "moment extracted from the continuity of historical time."[98] We might recall Jean-Luc Godard's answer to the question, "What is cinema?" Cinema, he said, echoing Vertov, is "truth at 24x a second." But only if we understand that "truth" to be the truth of the recorded moment, the registration of the "fact" of existence torn from historical time. In all other ways, cinema is an untruth, a mechanical operation that endlessly reproduces images outside of their historical place, reanimates the dead, and tricks us into seeing what is not there.

As Nichols has noted, a central aspect of the early fascination with cinema was based on our ability to recognize the world we already inhabit. "The extraordinary power of the photographic camera to take slices of reality and freeze them within an illusionistic frame," he writes, "rises exponentially in this breathtaking succession of cinematographic images that restores motion, and life, to the frozen image." The living, "seemingly embalmed on a strip of film," suddenly come back to life, repeating actions and restoring events that had, until that moment, belonged to the domain of the irretrievable: the historical past.⁹⁹ This is precisely what Vertov is playing with in *Kino-Eye* where the "kino-eye turns time back" (unbutchering a bull and unbaking the bread), or in *Man with a Movie Camera* when the film suddenly freezes, turns back into the series of still photographs that are the "truth" of cinema. Yet, in *Three Songs of Lenin*, despite all of Vertov's assurances to the contrary, there is a clear refusal to use the power of cinema to bring Lenin back to "life," and every choice—from the opening prologue consciously marking his absence to the nonsynchronized speech, underscoring the fact that "Lenin—is silent"—mitigates against cinema's ability to turn back time. Michelson points out that among the many special effects used by Vertov in *Three Songs*, the one he does not use is the reversal of motion: "To the [list] we must add one, whose significance and significant absence from *Three Songs* we will want to note: that of the reversal of motion deployed by Vertov as a heuristic strategy in an unequaled manner beginning with his earliest feature (*Kino-Glaz*, 1925)."¹⁰⁰ Michelson leaves this thought unfinished. Why doesn't this film use reverse motion? Because the one thing it cannot do is reverse time to when Lenin was alive. Compared to the 1925 *Lenin Kino-Pravda* that went back to 1919 and forward to Lenin's funeral, *Three Songs* seems stuck in a kind of loop/stretch printing. Time is halted, stretched, looped, frozen; despite what the film wants to claim, it can neither go back nor move forward.

Three Songs is the first film in which Vertov does not move time backward. Like the chairwoman of the Third Song, he tries not to look back at the earlier trauma, but neither can he obey the command to move forward. Instead, and despite the rapid montage that concludes the Third Song, the film seems to be stuck in place, particularly, in its 1938 sound version where Stalin's speech, given to us in full, as one static shot filmed with an immobile camera, uncut and unincorporated into the fabric of the film, concludes the film. *Three Songs of Lenin* registers Vertov's resistance to the imposition of any authorial voice, resistance to "the voice of the Party, the voice of the leader," resistance even to "the call of the immortal Lenin." It is a refusal to reduce meaning to a single unified message to be delivered either via voice-over or explanatory titles. The film does not translate into words, and it privileges incorrect, halting speech over the "golden words" of Soviet leaders. In his diaries, Vertov called the 1937 *Lullaby* his "first sound film," perhaps because there, unlike in *Three Songs of Lenin*, he no longer had any choice but to allow the voice of power, ideology, and the State to speak for him.¹⁰¹

Notes

Note on sources: most of the archival materials cited here are from RGALI f. 2091 (Vertov). A Soviet edition of Vertov's articles, notes, and diaries was published in 1966 as *Dziga Vertov: Stat'i, dnevniki, zamysly*, ed. Sergei Dobrashenko (Moscow: Iskusstvo, 1966), hereafter referred to as SDZ. This was the source for the 1984 English edition, *Kino-Eye: The Writings of Dziga Vertov*, ed. Annette Michelson, trans. Kevin O'Brien (Berkeley: University of California Press, 1984). In 2004, a new edition and translation of Vertov texts from the twenties was published as *Lines of Resistance: Dziga Vertov and the Twenties*, ed. Yuri Tsivian, trans. Julian Graffy (Pordenone: Le Giornate del Cinema Muto, 2004). In 2008, a complete publication in Russian of Vertov's articles, notes, and diaries based on available archival material was published as a two-volume set, *Dziga Vertov. Iz naslediia* (Moscow: Eizenshtein-tsentr, 2008).

1. See Vertov, "O moei bolezni," SDZ, 188–196; "On My Illness," in *Kino-Eye*, 188–195; and "Shest' udarov po fil'me o Lenine" (1934), *Iz naslediia*, 2: 259–260.

2. Gosfil'mofond preserves a memo from Soiuzdetfilm to GURK (Glavnoe upravlenie po kontroliu za zrelishchami i repertuarom), dating January 7, 1937, stating that all copies of the original film have been returned for reediting, and no prints of the original version remain in circulation. A return memo on January 10, 1937, from the GURK allows the demonstration of the reedited film; and on January 21, 1938, the GURK approves the reedited sound version of *Three Songs of Lenin* for indefinite release in the USSR. The document specifies that they are approving a third edit of the film (Gosfil'mofond, section I, f. 7, op. 1, ed. khran. 121).

3. Even the lengths of the different versions are disputed: the official film reference to Soviet films, *Repertuarnyi ukazatel'. Kinorepertuar*, gives the length of the 1934 version at 1,874 meters, while the film archive Gosfil'mofond preserves a document that gives the length as 1,813 meters. A montage list for the 1938 sound version found at Gosfil'mofond lists the length at 1,888 meters and seven parts. Similarly, Glavrepertkom (the censorship body) recorded the original length of the silent version at only 1,650 meters in a document dated December 7, 1934, though most modern filmographies give the length of the 1935 silent version as either 2,045 or 2,100. For details, see Adelheid Heftberger, "The Same Thing from Different Angles," DVD notes to the 2014 release of *Three Songs of Lenin* by the Österreichisches Filmmuseum in Vienna.

4. On this see John MacKay, "Allegory and Accommodation: Vertov's *Three Songs of Lenin* (1934) as a Stalinist Film," *Film History* 18, no. 4 (2006): 376–391.

5. For the 1938 edit, new documents were inserted, while images of people who had fallen out of favor with the regime were removed. Pictures of Nikolai Yezhov, Nikita Khrushchev, Georgii Dimitrov, Nikolai Shvernik, and even Lenin at the Second Congress of the Communist International were eliminated, while a speech by Stalin was added, as were "seven hundred meters of footage at the end of the film showing Stalin's continuation of Lenin's policies" (Dziga Vertov, *Tagebücher—Arbeitshefte*, ed. Thomas Tode and Alexandra Gramatke [Konstanz: UVK, 2000], 235, n. 16).

6. Jeremy Hicks has written on the problem of textology in his *Dziga Vertov: Defining Documentary Film* (London: I. B. Tauris, 2007), 100–105.

7. MacKay, "Allegory and Accommodation: Vertov's *Three Songs of Lenin* (1934) as a Stalinist Film," 377.

8. The film exists in the RGAKFD in two versions, silent and sound, released on DVD by the Österreichisches Filmmuseum in Vienna in 2014.

9. Most critics agree that while *Three Songs of Lenin* is as rich and complex as the earlier Vertov films, it nevertheless "marks a crucial turning point in Vertov's artistic career—specifically, the turning point between the 'avant-garde' 1920s and the 'Stalinist' 1930s." See, for example, MacKay, "Allegory and Accommodation: Vertov's *Three Songs of Lenin* (1934) as a Stalinist Film," 378.

10. Tsivian, *Lines of Resistance*, 25.

11. See "Protokol N. 11 otkrytogo partiinogo sobraniia Tsentral'noi studii dokumental'nykh fil'mov ot 14–15 marta 1949 goda" (Record #11: Minutes of the Open Party Meeting of the Central Studio of Documentary Films, from March 14–15, 1949), published in *Iskusstvo kino* 12 (1997): 128–133.

12. Martin Stollery, "Three Songs About Lenin," *Encyclopedia of the Documentary Film*, ed. Ian Aitken (New York: Routledge, 2006), 1319–1321.

13. Oksana Bulgakowa, "Spatial Figures in Soviet Cinema of the 1930s," in *The Landscape of Stalinism*, ed. Evgeny Dobrenko and Eric Naiman (Seattle: University of Washington Press, 2003), 51–76; here 56.

14. Annette Michelson, "The Kinetic Icon in the Work of Mourning: Prolegomena to the Analysis of a Textual System," *October* 52 (Spring 1990): 16–39; here: 20.

15. While the biblical reference might seem distant at first, the Song of Songs celebrates the union of man and woman (or Jews and Israel, or man and God, or the Virgin Mary and God) that underlies Vertov's film. Lenin is the husband that comes to the women/people; he is spring; the celebration of the harvest after years of struggle, of different kinds of exile and imprisonment ("my face was a dark prison"), exodus from Egypt; transformation of the world. The marriage ceremony is here replaced by the funeral, the spectacle that brings the whole country together.

16. Elizabeth A. Papazian, "Literacy or Legibility: The Trace of Subjectivity in Soviet Socialist Realism," in *The Oxford Handbook of Propaganda Studies*, ed. Jonathan Auerbach and Russ Castronovo (Oxford: Oxford University Press, 2013), 63–86; here: 72. English translations of the title, such as "Three Songs about Lenin" or "Three Songs dedicated to Lenin," miss this nuance.

17. Collected and recorded in Turkmenistan, Uzbekistan, Azerbaijan, and elsewhere.

18. Vertov, "Lenin," *Iz naslediia* 2: 260–261; here 261. Unpublished.

19. This sequence is omitted in the 1938 silent variant.

20. Katheryn Kalinak notes that in the early sound period, composers in the Soviet Union, such as Shaporin and Dmitrii Shostakovich, treated the score as an element of montage (influenced by the 1928 "Statement on Sound"). She specifically gives the example of Vsevolod Pudovkin's *Deserter*, in which the despair and suicide of the starving worker caught stealing bread is "alarmingly at odds" with the jazzy melody and the Latin-inflected rhythms of Shaporin's score (Katheryn Kalinak, *Film Music: A Very Short Introduction* [Oxford: Oxford University Press, 2010], 59).

21. Vertov, Diary entry (O fil'me "Tebe Front!"), 1942, SDZ, 242.

22. Robert Robertson, *Cinema and the Audiovisual Imagination: Music, Image, Sound* (London: I. B. Tauris, 2015), 118.

23. Robertson, *Cinema and the Audiovisual Imagination*, 119–120.

24. The 1938 silent version was screened at the Locarno Film Festival (Soviet retro) on August 4, 2000, with a running time of 57 min. See Deborah Young, "Review: *Three Songs About Lenin*," *Variety* (August 21, 2000); accessed at: http://variety.com/2000/film/reviews/three-songs-about-lenin-1200463721/.

25. Ernst Thälmann was the leader of the Communist Party of Germany (KPD) during much of the Weimar Republic. He was arrested by the Gestapo in 1933 and held in solitary confinement for eleven years, before being shot in Buchenwald on Adolf Hitler's orders in 1944. Isidora Dolores Ibárruri Gómez—known as "La Pasionaria"—was a Spanish Republican heroine of the Spanish Civil War and communist politician of Basque origin, known for her famous slogan "¡No Pasarán!" (They shall not pass!) during the Battle for Madrid in November 1936.

26. In his study of the literature of Central Asia, Soviet literary scholar Arshaluis Arsharuni provides a partial text of this folk song, "We'll Never Forget Lenin's Name" (Ne zabudem my imeni Lenina):

> ... Пусть сравняются с землей вершины Памира,
> Пусть океан зальёт это место,

> Пусть на этом месте вырастут новые горы,
> Величиной превосходящие первые в десять раз.
> За это время железной стопой пройдут века по земле,
> И люди забудут названия стран, где жили раньше предки,
> Люди забудут язык предков,
> Но имя Ленина не забудут они

(Arshaluis Arsharuni, *Khudozhestvennaia literatura Srednei Azii*, partially published in *Krasnaia niva* 16 [1929]: 10–11).

27. It is clear from the sound track, which comes to a climactic end and then restarts again, that the order of the final shots of the film has been altered (probably more than once) from the original composition. We have no way of knowing which of the shots in the final sequence was in fact used as the final concluding image of the film in 1934.

28. Vertov, "Bez slov," *Iz naslediia*, 2: 262–263; here 263. Original publication: *Rot-fil'm*, August 14, 1934. Translated as "Without Words," in *Kino-Eye*, 117–119. Translation modified.

29. Mezhrabpom-fil'm was the last privately run Soviet production company; it was liquidated in 1936.

30. Vertov, "Kinonasledstvo o Lenine (Vtoroi variant [stsenarnogo plana])," *Iz naslediia*, 1: 139–140.

31. Vertov, "Kak my delali fil'm o Lenine," 262. The reference to Stalin is missing from SDZ, and, consequently, the 1984 translation, "How We Made Our Film About Lenin," in *Kino-Eye*, 115–117. It is present in the draft of the program of the Film Society for the UK screening of *Three Songs of Lenin* (Igor Montagu Collection, Item # 181: "*Three Songs of Lenin* title & synopsis," BFI National Film Archive).

32. Vertov, "Bez slov," *Iz naslediia*, 2: 262–263; here 262. "Without Words," in *Kino-Eye*, 117–119; here: 117.

33. «Ток мыслей продолжается даже в том случае, если оборван один из сплетенных между собой проводов.» Vertov, "Bez slov," 262; "Without Words," 118. Translation modified.

34. Vertov, "Bez slov," 263; "Without Words," 118.

35. As Bill Nichols has argued, the voice-of-God commentary is associated specifically with the expository mode of documentary filmmaking, in which "there is a commentary directed toward the viewer; images serve as illustration or counterpoint." The expository mode can incorporate elements of interviews, but "the voices of others are woven into a textual logic that subsumes and orchestrates them.... The voice of authority resides with the text itself, rather than with those recruited to it" (Bill Nichols, *Representing Reality: Issues and Concepts in Documentary* [Bloomington: Indiana University Press, 1991], 32, 37). On alternative forms of narration in Soviet documentary films, see Jeremy Hicks, "Challenging the Voice of God in World War II–Era Soviet Documentaries," in *Sound, Speech, Music in Soviet and Post-Soviet Cinema*, ed. Lilya Kaganovsky and Masha Salazkina (Bloomington: Indiana University Press, 2014), 129–144; and Hicks, *Dziga Vertov*, 100–105.

36. Vertov, Diary entry (Povtorenie—edinstvenno nevozmozhnaia veshch' na zemle), September 17, 1944, SDZ, 258.

37. Bulgakowa, "Spatial Figures in Soviet Cinema of the 1930s," 56.

38. Nikolai Izvolov, "Dziga Vertov and Aleksandr Rodchenko: The Visible Word," *Studies in Russian and Soviet Cinema* 10, no. 1 (2016): 2–14; here: 5.

39. Izvolov, "Dziga Vertov and Aleksandr Rodchenko," 8.

40. For Izvolov this partly reflects the fact that Beliakov, the chief designer of the inscriptions after Rodchenko, had stayed in Moscow. Izvolov, "Dziga Vertov and Aleksandr Rodchenko," 9.

41. I am grateful to John MacKay for his thoughts on Vertov's uses of photomontage and for the accompanying image of Rodchenko's collage.

42. Elizabeth Astrid Papazian, *Manufacturing Truth: The Documentary Moment in Early Soviet Culture* (DeKalb: Northern Illinois University Press, 2009), 81.

43. Vertov, SDZ, 181; *Kino-Eye*, 178, translation modified (see Hicks, *Dziga Vertov*, 159, n. 40).

44. Hicks, *Dziga Vertov*, 111.

45. Vertov, Diary entry (Desiat' let ne byl v dome otdykha), May 26, 1934, SDZ, 179–181; *Kino-glaz*, 176–177.

46. Vertov, "Kak my delali fil'm o Lenine" (1934), *Iz naslediia*, 2: 261–262; here 261; "How We Made Our Film about Lenin," 115–117, translation modified.

47. «И тогда эти слова Ленина, этот голос давно умершего вождя будет звучать как боевой приказ из далекого прошлого: не останавливаться, продолжать работу, совершенствовать, улучшать жизнь!» E. Iaroslavskii, quoted in: "Lenin v kino" (1932), RGALI 2091–1–91.

48. «Какая же была бы сила впечатления, если бы звуковое кино не опоздало со своим развитием ... » Iaroslavskii, quoted in: "Lenin v kino" (1932), RGALI 2091–1–91.

49. Which was itself, of course, a French translation of Vertov's own *kino-pravda*. *Cinéma vérité* ("truthful cinema") is a style of documentary filmmaking, invented by Jean Rouch, inspired by Vertov's theory of Kino-Pravda and influenced by Robert Flaherty's films. It is sometimes called "observational cinema," if understood as pure direct cinema: mainly without a narrator's voice-over.

50. Vertov, "O liubvi k zhivomu cheloveku," *Iskusstvo kino* 6 (1958): 95–99.

51. N. P. Abramov, *Dziga Vertov* (Moscow: Izdat. Akademii nauk SSSR, 1962), 142–143.

52. Bill Nichols, "Documentary Film and the Coming of Sound," *Speaking Truths with Film: Evidence, Ethics, Politics in Documentary* (Berkeley: University of California Press, 2016), 66.

53. Nichols, *Speaking Truths with Film*, 66.

54. Nichols, *Speaking Truths with Film*, 71.

55. Nichols, *Speaking Truths with Film*, 71.

56. Vertov, "Tri pesni o Lenine i Kino-glaz" (1934), SDZ, 138; "*Three Songs of Lenin* and Kino-eye," in *Kino-Eye*, 124. He says something similar in "Kak rodilsia i razvivalsia kino-glaz," *Iz naslediia*, 2: 295.

57. Vertov, "Poslednii opyt" (1935), SDZ, 143–145; here: 144; "My Latest Experiment," in *Kino-Eye*, 132–137; here: 135.

58. Originally published in *Iskusstvo kino* 6 (1958). A censored version, removing all references to Stalin and *Lullaby*, was republished in SDZ ("O liubvi k zhivomu cheloveku," 154–160) and translated in *Kino-Eye* ("About Love for the Living Person," 147–157). The original ms of the article is dated May 16, 1940. See: "O moei liubvi k zhivomu cheloveku," *Iz naslediia*, 2: 324–329 and 570.

59. Vertov, "O moei liubvi k zhivomu cheloveku," *Iz nasledia*, 2: 325.

60. See Stalin's speech delivered at the First All-Union Congress of Collective Farm Shock Workers (Pervyi vsesoiuznyi s"ezd kolkhoznikov-udarnikov), February 15–19, 1933.

61. Audible in the 1938 sound version and was most likely part of the original recording, although it is not transcribed in the 1933 scenario variant (RGALI op. 2, ed. khran. 49, l. 4–11), nor in Vertov's article "O liubvi k zhivomu cheloveku" (first published in *Iskusstvo kino* 6 [1958]: 95–99). The previous interview with the male farmer similarly ends with a reference to Stalin, so that we in fact get a double invocation of his name: "And as Comrade Stalin says ..." / "Comrade Stalin says ..."

62. «[Товарищ Сталин сказал, что] женщина у колхозе большая сила, и женщину под спудом держать нельзя. Вот я председатель колхоза, колхоз имени Ленина ... У нас, у колхозе, три женщины у управления и два управВода. Мы ведем работу ... беспощадную, несмотря, что у нас нет мужчин ... А я-ж чувствую, куды я приехала, и что наши вожди говорят. Ведь они все таки золотые слова говорят. И надо записать. И надо в голову взять. И дома приехать и надо рассказать. И хочется так и сделать, как вожди говорят, хочется же в колхозе так поставить. А и думаешь ... Из зади-то, ты помнишь ... Но большевики не велят назад вертаться. Что трудности прошли, это не напоминай! А

уперед шагать, думаешь что так, а оно так и может быть... надо это пережить еще, надо достигнуть еще... Надо уметь подойдить еще... Вот тут-та вот и вопрос... И вот ето все в голову возьмешь, и нявольно слезы пойдут.» For a variant of this speech, see "Tri pesni o Lenine" (variant stsenariia, written in 1933), *Iz naslediia* 1: 161–176; here: 175–176.

63. Andrei Shcherbenok, "'Vzgliani na Lenina, i pechal' tvoia razoidetsia kak voda.' Estetika travmy v fil'me Dzigi Vertova," in *Travma: Punkty*, ed. Sergei Ushakin and Elena Trubinaia (Moscow: Novoe literaturnoe obozrenie, 2009), 704–723.

64. "Lenin" and "Death"—
these words are enemies.
"Lenin" and "Life"—
are comrades...
Lenin—
lived.
Lenin—
lives.
Lenin—
will live.

as Vladimir Mayakovsky famously put it in his 1924 poem, "Komsomol'skaia," published in the journal *Molodaia gvardiia* (Vladmir Maiakovskii, "Komsomol'skaia," *Molodaia gvardiia* 2–3 (1924): 10–14). The cult, which preceded Lenin's actual death, and which so clearly distinguished between the "king's two bodies" ("Lenin, the leader, is dead. Lenin, the leader, lives. He lives in the heart of his people." *Three Songs*, 40, 41), made Lenin infinitely reproducible: his image, his writings, and his words all took on the attributes of the "living Lenin."

65. "The dominant figure of the epitaphic or autobiographical discourse is, as we saw, the *prosopopeia*, the fiction of the voice-from-beyond-the-grave... chiasmic figures, crossing the conditions of death and of life with the attributes of speech and of silence... [this] cannot fail to evoke the latent threat that inhabits *prosopopeia*, namely that by making the dead speak, the symmetrical structure of the trope implies, by the same token, that the living are struck dumb, frozen in their own death" (Paul De Man, "Autobiography as De-Facement," *The Rhetoric of Romanticism* [New York: Columbia University Press, 1984], 67–81; here: 77–78). On the relationship "between the dead and the living," and "the confrontation of the direct interviews with the spectral voice" in *Three Songs of Lenin*, see also Oksana Bulgakova, *Sovetskii slukhoglaz: kino i ego organy chuvstv* (Moscow: Novoe literaturnoe obozrenie, 2010), 90–91.

66. Mary Ann Doane, "The Voice in Cinema: The Articulation of Body and Space," *Yale French Studies* 60 (1980): 33–50.

67. Pascal Bonitzer, "Les Silences de la voix," *Cahiers du cinéma* 256 (February–March 1975): 25; translated as: "The Silences of the Voice," in *Narrative, Apparatus, Ideology*, ed. Philip Rosen (New York: Columbia University Press 1986), 319–334.

68. For Chion, the uncanny power of the *acousmêtre* is fueled by the fact of its simultaneous presence and absence within the film, its having *"one foot in the image."* The *acousmêtre* "must haunt the borderlands that are neither the interior of the filmic stage nor the proscenium," which is what gives it the ability "to be everywhere, to see all, to know all, and to have complete power" (Michel Chion, *The Voice in Cinema*, trans. Claudia Gorbman [New York: Columbia University Press, 1999], 24). Emphasis in the original.

69. Nichols, *Speaking Truths with Film*, 69.

70. John Grierson, "First Principles of Documentary" (1932–1934), in *Nonfiction Film Theory and Criticism*, ed. Richard Barsam (New York: E. P. Dutton & Co, 1976), 19–30.

71. Vertov, "Kinoki. Perevorot" (1923), SDZ, 50–58; here: 54; "Kinoks: A Revolution," in *Kino-Eye*, 11–21; here: 16–17.

72. Cathy Caruth, *Unclaimed Experience: Trauma, Narrative, and History* (Baltimore: Johns Hopkins University Press, 1996), 61–62.

73. Lev Roshal', *Dziga Vertov* (Moscow: Iskusstvo, 1982), 122.

74. Roshal', *Dziga Vertov*, 121.

75. «Вслед за кадрами похорон перед деревянным мавзолеем проходили колонны пионеров, а над мавзолеем, над зубцами Кремля появлялся (с помощью двойной экспозиции) живой Ленин... начиналось—бессмертие... Не только по приему, но и смыслу кадр действительно строился на принципах двойной экспозиции». Roshal', *Dziga Vertov*, 122–123.

76. De Man, "Autobiography as De-Facement," 77–78.

77. Laura Mulvey, *Death 24x a Second: Stillness and the Moving Image* (London: Reaktion Books 2006), 12.

78. Vladimir Mayakovsky, "Speech in Debate on 'The Paths and Policy of Sovkino'" (October 15, 1927), in *The Film Factory: Russian and Soviet Cinema in Documents 1896–1939*, ed. Richard Taylor and Ian Christie (London: Routledge, 1994), 171–174; here: 173. (Source: V. V. Maiakovskii, *Polnoe sobranie sochinenii*, vol. 12 [Moscow: Gos. izd-vo khudozh, 1959], 353–359.)

79. Vertov, "Kinopravda" (1934), SDZ, 139–143; here: 143; "Kinopravda," in *Kino-Eye*, 126–132; here: 132.

80. Dragan Kujundzic, "Dziga Vertov or the Return of the Sight (Five Intervals)," in *Apparatur und Rhapsodie: Zu den Filmen des Dziga Vertov*, ed. Natascha Drubek-Meyer and Jurij Murasov (Frankfurt am Main: Peter Lang, 2000), 171–199; here: 197.

81. See Nina Tumarkina, *Lenin Lives! The Lenin Cult in Soviet Russia* (Cambridge, MA: Harvard University Press, 1983), 250.

82. Deleuze writes, "there is no cinema without movement, no way of breaking it down into its constituent parts. To recompose movement with *eternal poses* or with *immobile sections* is to miss movement and instead to construct a Whole—one assumes that 'all is given', whilst movement only occurs if the whole is neither given nor giveable. As soon as a whole is given to one in the eternal order of forms or poses... then either time is no more than the image of eternity, or it is the consequence of a set; there is no longer room for real movement" (Gilles Deleuze, *Cinema 1: The Movement-Image*, trans. Hugh Tomlinson (Minneapolis: University of Minnesota Press, 1986), 7. Emphasis in the original.).

83. See T. G. Koloskova and O. V. Kitashova, "Lenin v rabotakh skul'ptora Ivana Shadra," accessed at: http://propagandahistory.ru/2343/Lenin-v-rabotakh-skulptora-Ivana-SHadra/. Among Shadr's most famous and most characteristic works are sculptures *The Cobblestone Is the Weapon of the Proletariat* (Bulyzhnik—oruzhee prolitariata, 1927) and *The Girl with an Oar* (Devushka s veslom, 1936).

84. Michelson, "The Kinetic Icon in the Work of Mourning," 38.

85. As Tumarkina notes, "under Stalin's rule, the cult of Lenin grew as cold and lifeless as the stone mausoleum. It glorified the dead, not the living Lenin" (Tumarkina, *Lenin Lives!*, 206).

86. Sheila Fitzpatrick, *Everyday Stalinism: Ordinary Life in Extraordinary Times: Soviet Russia in the 1930s* (Oxford: Oxford University Press, 1999).

87. This is a point-of-view shot from inside Lenin's bedroom, with the camera placed at what might have been Lenin's bed or chair—neither of these are pictured, but the angle and direction all speak to us occupying the space formerly occupied by him. The POV shot appears to be the second shot of a shot/counter shot sequence, but without the first, "establishing" shot (in this case, a medium shot of the house from the garden, or even a close-up shot of the windows of Lenin's bedroom, looking from outside in).

88. The low angle shot of the swaying trees is another reference to Rodchenko, this time to his 1927 photograph series, "Pine Trees in Pushkino" ("Sosny. Pushkino." Originally published in *Novyi Lef* 7, 1927). As Bernd Stiegler puts it, "The prologue [to *Three Songs of Lenin*] opens with a shot that is so similar to one of the photographs from Rodchenko's pine tree series that it might be mistaken for it.... By the fact that, in a film about Lenin, Vertov includes a reference to Rodchenko's controversial photographs of pine trees and even goes so far as to emphasize that

reference by using the photographs twice to frame the entire opening sequence, Vertov documents (in this documentary) an aesthetico-political position and makes it possible to decipher his dual support for Lenin and for a visual revolution through film and photography.... *Three Songs about Lenin* turns out to be a pointed instance of the politics of image and montage as well as a visual memory bank and a mnemonic pictorial archive." See Bernd Stiegler, "When a Photograph of Trees Is Almost like a Crime (Rodchenko, Vertov, Kalatozov)," trans. James Gussen, Études photographiques 23 (May 2009), accessed at: http://etudesphotographiques.revues.org/2668.

89. First published in *Pravda*, no. 18, January 22, 1925. Written in German before January 9 (22), 1917. Signed: N. Lenin. Vertov is giving us the German dust jacket here.

90. Michelson, "The Kinetic Icon in the Work of Mourning," 20.

91. For a shot-by-shot description of the minutes of silence, see Seth R. Feldman, *Dziga Vertov: A Guide to References and Sources* (Boston: G. K. Hall & Co., 1979), 119–120.

92. Bulgakova, *Sovetskii slukhoglaz*, 89.

93. The shooting script for *Three Songs of Lenin*, marked 1934/1935 "silent version," held at Gosfil'mofond, shows that it had the same opening prologue as the 1938 silent version (Gosfil'mofond, section I, f. 7, op. 1, ed. khran. 121).

94. While we know that the 1935 version opens with the speech by N. Ivanov, we do not know if Vertov is reusing footage from the 1925 *Lenin Kino-Pravda* or substituting that footage with new shots.

95. Papazian, *Manufacturing Truth*, 71.

96. I am referring to Linda Williams's formulation that melodrama is the genre of the "too late": Linda Williams, "Film Bodies: Gender, Genre, and Excess," *Film Quarterly* 44, no. 4 (1991): 2–13.

97. See Stephen Heath, *Questions of Cinema* (Bloomington: Indiana University Press, 1982).

98. Mulvey, *Death 24x a Second*, 13.

99. Nichols, *Speaking Truths with Film*, 63.

100. Michelson, "The Kinetic Icon in the Work of Mourning," 22.

101. RGALI 2091-2-55, l. 3. According to Graham Roberts, *Lullaby* was taken away from Vertov and "re-edited by the Party's censors" (Graham Roberts, *Forward Soviet! History and Non-fiction Film in the USSR* [London: I. B. Tauris, 1999], 129); Feldman similarly notes that the film was "badly mutilated by Soiuzkinokhronika before its release" (Feldman, *Guide to References*, 124).

Conclusion

SOCIALIST REALIST SOUND

"How obvious it becomes that the material of the sound-film is not dialogue. The true material of the sound-film is, of course, the monologue."
 —S. Eisenstein, after a meeting with James Joyce in Paris

IN HIS CONCLUDING CHAPTER TO *Cinema 2: Time-Image*, Gilles Deleuze offers a counter narrative to the standard understanding of the coming of sound as a disruption or break in cinema history.¹ While most histories and theorists (including Soviet ones) have often described the addition of sound to the visual image as a secondary—and, at first glance, unnecessary—supplement to the moving image, for Deleuze, sound cinema is the fulfillment of the promises of silent cinema. As he points out, cinema was never truly silent, but only "noiseless" (as Jean Mitry has suggested) or "deaf" (as Michel Chion has argued). Indeed, as Rick Altman has shown, silent cinema was always accompanied by sound, and there was no time that films would have been shown either without a musical accompaniment, or without people talking, etc.² It is only with the coming of sound that theaters became quiet; it is only with the coming of sound that movies were, for the first time, able to give us true silence, the total absence of sound issuing from the screen. Moreover, movies before 1927 anticipated sound and sound effects—from intertitles that delivered lines of dialogue (as in standard bourgeois pictures) or graphically reproduced speech (as in avant-garde practices by Dziga Vertov, for example), to rapid montage meant to reproduce sound visually (rapid gunfire in Sergei Eisenstein's *October*, for example). The coming of sound, in other words, while it produced a series of massive changes at the level of technology and industry (the need for new equipment, new acting styles, new plots, new ways of "hearing" films), and resistances on the part of filmmakers who had developed a set of techniques for overcoming the *lack* of sound, at the same time fulfilled the promise of cinema, finally creating a true "audio-visual" art.

But Deleuze insists on yet another difference that characterizes silent and sound film, the difference in the components of the silent image with that of the talking image. For Deleuze, the silent image is composed from the seen image and the intertitle, which is read. The intertitle includes, among other elements, "speech acts." Being scriptural, those speech acts passed into an indirect style (thus, the intertitle "I'm going to kill you" is read in the form "He says he's going to kill him") and they thereby took on "an abstract universality and expressed in some sense a law." While the image developed in a different direction—toward naturalness, a kind of "innocent physical nature" which has no need of language—the intertitle or piece of writing showed us "the law, the forbidden, the transmitted order." In order to intertwine the seen image and the read image, silent cinema needed to form "real blocs with the intertitle" (in the style of Vertov and Alexander Rodchenko), or to make particularly important scriptural elements pass into the visual (such as the repetition of the word "Brothers," whose letters grow larger in *Battleship Potemkin*).[3]

But "what happens in the talking cinema?" The speech-act is no longer connected with the "second function of the eye"; it is no longer read but heard. In contrast to the intertitle, the sound film is heard, but as *"a new dimension of the visual image, a new component."*[4] When sound cinema makes itself heard, it is "as if it makes something new visible, and the visible image, de-naturalized, begins to become readable in turn, *as* something visible or visual."[5] For Deleuze, what sound cinema ultimately makes visible is the "out-of-field"—that space just beyond the frame that cinema always both denies and brings into play. Sound does not "invent" the out-of-field, but "dwells in it," filling the visual "not-seen" with a specific presence. (The noise of boots is all the more interesting, writes Deleuze, when they are not seen.) Its full realization is "at the level of the voice in the voice-off, whose source is not seen."[6] With sound, speech, and music, the circuit of the movement-image achieves a different figure. The talkie perfects the silent film by constituting "an immense 'internal monologue' which constantly internalizes and externalizes itself: not a language, but a visual material which is the utterable of language."[7] In sound cinema, the Big Other moves into the off-screen space, into the "out-of-field," into the position of the *acousmêtre*. And, as I have been arguing throughout this book, this is precisely what happens in early Soviet sound film. In early Soviet sound cinema, we hear it, and we see it (loudspeaker, record player, radio, Lenin's voice)—it is made visible by being made audible.

"The First Russian Sound Film—an Artistic Achievement"

In their 1981 article on Nikolai Ekk's *The Road to Life* (Putyovka v zhizn', 1931), titled, "The Origin of the Hero" (Proiskhozhdenie geroia), Evgeny Margolit and Viktor Filimonov emphasize Nikolai Ekk's original use of sound in order to make their case for the film's historic and cinematographic importance.[8] They argue that the "jealousy of [Ekk's] cinematographic brethren" has kept hidden the fact that "the problem [of synchronized sound] that stumped world-renowned directors was solved without much effort by an unknown debutant."[9] Moreover, the 1971 volume *20 Directors' Biographies* (20 Rezhisserskikh biografii), which supplements an earlier edition of *The Masters of Soviet Cinema* (Mastera sovetskogo kino) with a list of Soviet "firsts," introduces Nikolai Ekk as part of "the pleiad of talented and unusual directors who stood at the cradle of the Soviet cinema [*u kolybeli sovetskogo kino*] and with their effort helped formulate the principles of the new art, which became the method of Socialist Realism."[10] In this way, Ekk's *The Road to Life* achieves the status of a precursor to Socialist Realism, a film that was able to point the Soviet film industry in the proper ideological and methodological direction. Ekk is the first to "shock the world" not just with sound, but with the "new cinematographic aesthetic" that will "establish itself victoriously in *Chapaev* and *The Youth of Maxim*." Unlike the experimental formalist films of the twenties, *The Road to Life* obeys "the newly formed sensibility of the real spectator," moving Soviet cinema away from director-driven to "hero"-driven film.[11]

However, probably the most interesting description of the film's significance for Soviet cinema comes from the Soviet Academy of Science's *Notes on the History of Soviet Film* (Ocherki istorii sovetskogo kino), published in 1956. Here we find the following analysis of the introduction of sound and the role played by *The Road to Life* in its success. While the editors single out three films as the first Soviet sound features—*The Road to Life*, *Golden Mountains* (Zlatye gory, dir. Yutkevich, 1931), and *Counterplan* (Vstrechnyi, dir. Ermler and Yutkevich, 1932)—they begin their account with *The Road to Life*, because (first) this film was completed before the others and released June 1, 1931; second, it was "the first film in which the quality of sound registration met with the highest acoustic requirements"; and finally, this was a film that "met with the warmest response of the general audience."[12] It is enough to say, the editors stress, "that in a single Moscow theater, 'Koloss,' *The Road to Life* played non-stop for over a year," while at the same time, being shown in all existing and just opening sound theaters in Moscow, Leningrad, and other cities of the USSR."

Figure 6.1. "The First 100-Percent Soviet Talkie"
(*The Road to Life* / Putevka v zhizn', 1931)

Moreover, they argue, sound in *The Road to Life* is organically and integrally woven into the fabric of the film. Both natural sounds (of the city or of nature) and human speech play a vital dramatic role in the deepening of the film's characters and in its "realism." For the first time, the editors tell us, "the viewer saw protagonists who had earned the right to speak."[13]

Similarly, looking at the American reception of the film, we note that *The Road to Life*—a "startling drama of Russia's 'Wild Children'"—was heralded as the first Soviet sound film by the Amkino Corporation that distributed the film in the United States in 1932.[14] Writing for the *Partisan Review* in 1938–1939, Dwight McDonald calls *The Road to Life* "a 100 per cent all-talking film."[15] And a biographical note by Audio Brandin Films also marks *The Road to Life* as "the first Soviet film conceived for sound."[16] In his 1960 seminal work *Kino: A History of the Russian and Soviet Film*, Jay Leyda is a little more circumspect: "Between the releases of *The Earth Thirsts* and *Alone* appeared the film sometimes regarded as the first Soviet sound-film, *The Road to Life*, released on June 1, 1931. True, it was the first Soviet sound-film to have been conceived and written in that form, despite its superfluity of sub-titles."[17] And when Catherine de la Roche, writing on Soviet cinema in 1972, provides a brief history of the introduction of sound, she singles out *Alone* as "the first sound feature film," though she specifies that "It was made as a silent film and had music and effects added subsequently."[18] Meanwhile in 1976, Alexander S. Birkos refers to *The Road to Life* as "the first true Soviet sound film, having been conceived, written, and filmed as such."[19] Similarly, Richard Taylor and Ian Christie, under the bibliographical citation for Ekk in *The Film Factory* (1988) write simply, "directed the first Soviet sound film, *The Path to Life*, 1931," though Taylor himself, in an earlier article on Soviet Socialist Realism and film comedy, lists the film third among the first sound features completed in 1931, giving credit first to Kozintsev and Trauberg's *Alone*, followed by Yutkevich's *Golden Mountains*.[20]

In other words, not unlike *The Jazz Singer* (Crosland, 1927), the place of Nikolai Ekk's 1931 *The Road to Life* in Soviet cinematic history as the first sound picture remains somewhat disputed and attenuated by considerations beyond mere production or release. The first experimental sound-on-film program—excerpts from the film *Women from Ryazan* (Baby riazanskie)—was demonstrated on October 5, 1929, in Leningrad in the Sovkino Cinema, specially equipped with Shorin's sound-on-film system. A few months later, on March 5, 1930, the first sound theater, *Khudozhestvennyi* (The Art), opened in Moscow, with a demonstration of a *Combined Sound Program No. 1* (Zvukovaia sbornaia programma N1), which included four films: a speech by Anatoly Lunacharsky about the significance of cinema; *March* by Sergei Prokofiev from the opera *The Love for Three Oranges* (Liubov' k trem apel'sinam, Op. 33); Abram Room's documentary *The Plan for Great Works* (Piatiletka. Plan velikikh rabot); and the animated film *Tip Top*. Kozintsev and Trauberg's *Alone* was put into production in June of 1929, and *Letopis' rossiiskogo kino 1930–1945* lists October 3, 1930, as the date that Kozintsev and Trauberg began work on the sound version of film. Dziga Vertov's *Enthusiasm: Symphony of the Donbass* was completed in November 1930, but not released until April 1931. As Seth Feldman puts it, "The production of *Enthusiasm* took approximately six months. There were considerable difficulties with the Ukrainfil'm (the name adopted by VUFKU in 1930) labs. This, along with problems in post-production, delayed the preview of *Enthusiasm* until November 1, 1930. The official premiere of the film was delayed even further, until April 2, 1931. Even so, the film was released to the public some two months before Nikolai Ekk's *Road to Life*, the work often regarded as the first Soviet talkie."[21]

This, then, is the first moment of uncertainty that faces a historian attempting to trace some kind of lineage for early Soviet sound film. Depending on which thread one chooses to follow, *The Road to Life* becomes either one in a series of early experiments in sound, or the very first Soviet sound film. The archival material sheds some light on this confusion. A look at Soviet advertisements for the film from 1931 reveals that *The Road to Life* was distributed simultaneously as a silent and as a "new exemplar of sound film" (novyi ekzempliar khudozhestvennoi fil'my).[22] In film reviews, however, it was discussed only as a sound film—the first to utilize the new sound technology created by director Ekk, cameraman Pronin, and sound-operator Nesterov. For example, a contemporary review of the film in the journal *Pioner* (Pioneer) is equally excited by the technical achievement of the film as it is by the film's content. *The Road to Life* was filmed, they write, "by cameramen Pronin and Nesterov with the Soviet [sound] camera, Tagafon."[23] What is promoted here, in other words, is not so much the artistic merits of the film as its technical breakthrough. *The Road to Life* was filmed with *Soviet* equipment; it represents not simply an achievement in sound but an achievement in *Soviet* sound. Similarly, for Amkino's release of the film in the United States, the primacy of Ekk's achievement also proves vital to the selling of the film and its likelihood to do well at the box office. It is unclear why precisely this film, and not in fact Kozintsev and Trauberg's *Alone* or Yutkevich's *Golden Mountains*, gets picked up by the American distributor, but once it does, the historical significance of its technological achievement is highlighted by the advertisement. "The First Russian Sound Film—an Artistic Achievement," announces Amkino's press release.

Because the arrival of sound-on-film technology in the USSR coincided with such great industrial changes in the Soviet film industry, suggests Jay Leyda in *Kino*, it is "natural to consider the sound-film as a 'reason' for the obvious change that took place in the artistic character of the Soviet cinema." But the full reason must be sought in all the changes that took place at this time: "The emphasis of the first Five-Year Plan on the development of heavy industry gave a new propaganda job to the comparatively light film industry, and geared film-making to the basic industrial programme.... The changed film industry centralized its financial structure and acquired a new industrial administrator, Boris Shumyatsky, whose primary task was to develop the Soviet film industry as an industry."[24] Thus, the turn away from NEP, the industrial revolution, and the First Five-Year Plan, all have an influence on the promotion of *The Road to Life* as "the first Soviet sound film."

Indeed, sound is an important component of the aesthetic effect of the film. De la Roche and others have commented on the night scene on the railway—the climax of the film—as "an early example of the possibilities of sound effects... the metallic noise of wheels and Mustafa's carefree song, as he rides alone in a rail hand-cart; further along the line, the stillness of the night, broken only by croaking frogs and the light clinking of tools while the murderer loosens a rail; then Mustafa's distant song becoming louder and louder as he approaches danger."[25] The Pacific Film Archive's advertising of the film provides a similar formulation: "Often cited as the first Soviet sound film, *The Road to Life* uses many titles but also experiments with sound to produce emotional effect. (In a memorable instance, the sound of steam from a locomotive expresses the grief of hundreds of onlookers)."[26] It is curious again how much these observations seem to rely on early Soviet accounts of the film. "This is a sound picture," writes Evgenii Simonov in *Pioner*, "it not only shows, but tells. The silent cinema screen smacks the lips of its loudspeakers, it now sings and screams, and the celluloid track of the film stock pulls with it the sounds of trams and of frogs' song."[27] *The Road to Life* is therefore not only a technological and an ideological achievement but it is also an artistic achievement—its "first" use of sound proving vital for all three categories.

It is worth noting the rhetoric that comes to characterize *The Road to Life*'s entrance onto the sound stage. The audience is present for a birth, and even the projector that allows the new technological miracle to take place has become human: it smacks its lips, it "sings and screams," it mimics the sounds of the outside world. This description suggests that at stake in the critical reception of the film is the notion of materiality, but in a different sense than was the case for Vertov's *Enthusiasm*—Ekk's film not only touches its audience, but it does so because in some sense cinema has become "human," has learned to talk via its mechanical apparatus. Presented in this way, *The Road to Life* assumes the status of the first film of a new era, an era that had its own requirements of realism and mass entertainment.

The film's technological achievement (synchronized sound) combined with its ideological achievement (reaching the masses) to bring Soviet cinematography to a new level, well on the road to Socialist Realism. As Maya Turovskaya suggests, *The Road to Life* was the first to achieve the new paradigm, "ideology plus profitability plus sound," the first to outline the "specific relationships being established in the 1930s between the mass audience and cinema."[28] The new decade was inaugurated by the introduction of speech; the positive hero could now be heard as well as seen.[29]

Cinema for the Millions

In 1935, the All-Union Creative Conference on Cinema Affairs adopted the principles of Socialist Realism as set out for literature, with sound cinema now ready to furnish a form "intelligible to the millions."[30] Accusing Soviet filmmakers of "creative atavism," Shumyatsky, the new head of the cinema industry, maintained that "they have not yet got used to the discipline of the concrete tasks that our mass audience is setting them." As Richard Taylor notes, without a plot, no film could be entertaining. He quotes Shumyatsky: "A film and its success are directly linked to the degree of entertainment in the plot in the appropriately constructed and realistic artistic motivations for its development. That is why we are obliged to require our masters to produce works that have strong plots and are organized around a storyline. Otherwise they cannot be entertaining, they can have no mass character, otherwise the Soviet screen will not need them."[31] By 1935, Soviet cinema had produced around twenty sound films, two of which became instant classics of Socialist Realism: the civil war film *Chapaev* and the musical comedy *Jolly Fellows* (Veselye rebiata, dir. Aleksandrov, 1934). And although the Soviet Union continued to release silent variants of films until at least 1938, the era of avant-garde experimentation, as well as the era of silent cinema, had come to an end. This was also underscored by the publication, also in 1935, of Shumyatsky's *A Cinema for the Millions* (Kinematografiia millionov), which became a blue print for Soviet cinema.[32]

In his book, Shumyatsky praises Soviet cinema for finally becoming a cinema of the masses, resonating with millions of viewers. He mentions specifically the unprecedented *Chapaev* as well as other instant classics of Socialist Realism, including *The Peasants* (Krest'iane, dir. Ermler, 1934), *The Youth of Maxim* (Iunost' Maksima, dirs. Kozintsev and Trauberg, 1934), and *The Pilots* (Letchiki, dir. Raizman, 1935). These films, he notes, are characterized by Bolshevik party-mindedness (*partiinost'*) and by Socialist Realism. They are an art "truly penetrated by the class struggle of the proletariat," showing the viewer the "*truth* of our picturesque life."[33] He notes that in all these films, we have not only high quality directorial work and realistic performances by the actors, but we also have a high level of technology, in particular—of sound.³⁴ Indeed, Shumyatsky's whole book is dedicated to sound film; it is a systematic analysis of the years 1932–1935 when sound films first appear on Soviet screens.

For Shumyatsky, sound is directly tied to Socialist Realism as the technology that makes Socialist Realism possible in the cinema. He notes, for example, that after watching *Alone, Golden Mountains,* and *The Road to Life,* Stalin gives the express command to Soviet cinema to develop sound, seeing in the elements of sound a "large, supplementary force to the artistic expression of our ideas."³⁵ He finds that Alexander Dovzhenko's *Ivan,* while a failure (*neudacha*), nevertheless reflects the filmmaker's complete transformation from "socialist romanticism" to Socialist Realism.³⁶ Shumyatsky dismisses *The Accordion* (Garmon', dir. Savchenko, 1934) as an "ugly" film ("osobenno urodlivaia . . . rabota rezhissera Savchenko"), noting only in passing that, like the much more successful *Peasants,* this film too is characterized by a slow tempo (*zamedlennost'*), which plagues many films of the period. (Shumyatsky is particularly intolerant of close-ups and musical interludes as devices that interfere with narrative progress and slow down the film, and even criticizes the "Moonlight Sonata" sequence of *Chapaev* for the same problem—the slowing down of the tempo of an otherwise pitch-perfect film.³⁷) But he devotes an entire chapter to *Jolly Fellows,* arguing that it is good precisely because there is "nothing arid or pretentious in it." Even its critics cannot deny the good things there are in the film, including "its cheerfulness, its joie-de-vivre and its laughter."³⁸ Both *Chapaev* and *Jolly Fellows* are fully entitled to exist within the framework of Soviet cinema, he argues: "both films are the necessary and regular work of Soviet masters."³⁹

Coming to *Three Songs of Lenin* (Tri pesni o Lenine, dir. Vertov, 1934), Shumyatsky notes that the film is "good and significant" precisely because Vertov has "renounced documentalism" and produced a film of "organized, connected and ideologically molded artistic material."⁴⁰ The famous bench, "well-known from the photographs, the tops of the trees against the autumn sky, the house in Gorki: all these shots tell us sorrowfully of Lenin who is no longer among the living."⁴¹ Responding to criticism of the film, he writes that some detractors who "completely fail to understand the irresponsibility of their statements," maintain that *Three Songs of Lenin* has "rehabilitated the genre of documentary films." Rather, this film "bears witness to the transition by even the ideologists of the factographic documentary film to the positions of Socialist Realism." The film does have some shortcomings, though. In contrast to the depiction of the East, which is vivid, rich, and graphic, the remaining parts of the Soviet Union are depicted very weakly and half-heartedly in unsuccessful photographic montages (Dneprostroi), in the long monologues by the farm-girl (*batrachka*: hired-hand) who has been awarded the Order of Lenin. He notes that "in themselves these shots are good but they are too drawn out (*zatianuty*)." Despite its shortcomings, this film nevertheless proves that "the transition to the positions of Socialist Realism is a fact common to all (with very few exceptions) of our artists." "Soviet cinema marches forward together in lock step," he writes, "ascending to the next level."[42]

Thus, for example, in 1934, "the best film produced by Soviet cinema in the whole period of its existence was released: *Chapaev* as a film represented the real summit of Soviet film art." The film, notes Shumyatsky, is distinguished by its *exceptional* simplicity: "This simplicity, which is a characteristic only of high art, is so organic to *Chapaev*, it constitutes such a striking contrast to every Formalist device that in the first period after the film's release a number of 'critics' were unable to explain the reasons for its success to their own satisfaction." The strength of *Chapaev*, he concludes, lies in the "profound *vital truth* of the film."[43] He praises the camerawork, which "contains nothing superfluous or obtrusive, no admiration of nature for nature's sake, and harmonizes beautifully with the content of the film," and likewise, the work of the composer, Popov, who incorporates folk songs into his film in a way that provides depth to the character or scene, without being a distracting musical number.[44]

Finally, turning to an analysis of film music and the sound track in Soviet sound films, Shumyatsky particularly praises those—*Counterplan* (Vstrechnyi, composer Shostakovich, sound operator Arnshtam, 1932), *Lieutenant Kizhe* (Poruchik Kizhe, composer S. Prokofiev, 1934), and *Ankara—Heart of Turkey* (Ankara—serdtse Turtsii, sound director Arnshtam, composers Osman Zeki Üngör, Erkem Zeki, and Cemal Reşit Rey, 1934)—in which sound is "tightly" linked with the visual image, in which there is no experimentation, no unnecessary sound effects, in which music "does not create its own sound-objects, but simply adds to the visual image." He contrasts these successful uses of sound with several particularly unsuccessful examples: *Deserter* (Dezertir, dir. Pudovkin, composer Shaporin, 1933), *Revolt of the Fishermen* (Vosstaniie rybakov, dir. E. Piskator, composers Vladimir Fere, N. Chemberdski, and Ferenc Szabó), and Dovzhenko's *Ivan* (composers Meitus and Liatoshinsky), where the sound is disjointed from the visual image.[45] Quoting from Eisenstein, Pudovkin, and Aleksandrov's 1928 "Statement on Sound," Shumyatsky argues that the three filmmakers were wrong in their ideas about sound and that the first Soviet sound films have disproved their theories. Sound can be organized in such a way that it provides a *"realistic* image," he writes, creating a unified audio-visual field.[46] Beyond the obviously strong ideological inflection, Shumyatsky is also voicing a standard criticism of early/transition-era sound films (both in the USSR and abroad) in which sound experimentation and sound effects overwhelmed viewers not yet accustomed to hearing films. Conventional sound cinema (both Soviet and Hollywood) strives for a "marriage" of sight and sound, naturalizing the process of synchronized recording to present us with a world we can easily recognize. Indeed, from the first years of sound cinema, film sound has been operating under a kind of erasure. As Donald Crafton points out, almost immediately following the coming of sound, Hollywood studios found themselves in a curious position: sound effects that the year before had seemed impressive and new, viewers now found distracting, intrusive, and unnecessary. Crafton suggests that already by the end of the 1928–1929 Hollywood movie "season," American journalists were reacting against flamboyant insertions of sound effects: "Like overly garish Technicolor, they felt, sound should not call attention to itself as a supplement."[47]

Everywhere, and not just in the Soviet Union, integration of sound and image, coherence, and "naturalness" were prized for sound film. In 1929–1930, writes Crafton, American audiences could still see movies that "emphasized the newly discovered screen voice," but they could also "observe film styles which played down formal expression and novel effects to construct an illusion of unified audiovisual space." Meanwhile, sound engineers were making their technology "inaudible."[48] Rather than foregrounding sound, directors and engineers were learning to make sound disappear, to erase its presence from the consciousness of the audience. The viewer was becoming desensitized to sound, and this happened both through diffusion (that is to say, the more sound films audiences watched, the less attuned to sound they became) and through the conscious efforts of the sound engineers, directors, and producers. Most audiences, and not just Boris Shumyatsky, wanted a unified filmic space, in which there was no disjunction between sound and image. Realism, if not Socialist Realism, became the guiding principle for sound in film.

The transition to sound in the USSR came to play a major role in the implementation of Socialist Realism, but not, perhaps, precisely in the way we might have anticipated. By the late thirties, when the transition to sound was complete, the Soviet film industry really had become a cinema "intelligible to the millions," with sound seamlessly synchronized to the moving image and serving as its ideological support, with an emphasis on dialogue and song and dance numbers, and no contrapuntal, or dialogic, or other formalist tricks. But the new sound technology brought with it an extradiegetic element: the "out-of-field" voice now audible from the screen. As "an Ideological State Apparatus" whose function was to naturalize the transmission of ideology, early Soviet sound films transmitted ideological messages directly, in their undisguised form, structuring the viewer as a *citizen-to-be-addressed*.[49] But as the products of a period of instability and transition, as films made directly before the implementation of Socialist Realism as the official method of all Soviet art, early Soviet sound films also registered the resistance to the voice-of-ideology they were now meant to communicate.

Writing about the simultaneous birth of the horror film genre with Hollywood's transition to sound, Robert Spadoni has suggested that the coming of sound produced, for the second time in film history, the "media sensitive viewer."[50] Spadoni borrows the notion of media sensitivity from Yuri Tsivian, who argued that the early film viewer was particularly sensitized (aware, watchful) to the film-viewing experience, and to his/her role as a *viewer*.[51] The early viewer was always aware that s/he was watching a film, which meant at once the "miracle" of the moving image and sensitivity to everything that the moving image still lacked. (Thus Maxim Gorky's famous 1896 description of the Lumière Cinématographe as a "kingdom of shadows," as well as O. Winter's similar formulations a few months later.[52]) Spadoni argues that we can see something similar happen with early film sound: the coming of sound to cinema reproduced that original sense of the "uncanny," reminding the audience that they were watching a mechanically reproduced shadow play, only now, with sound, whose source and reproduction were still troubling, in particular if the sound went out of sync with the moving image. According to Spadoni, early sound films marked the "return of the repressed" of early cinema; in his formulation, this was "the perception of realism mixed with the unreal, bodies that seemed more alive but also dead." The heightened awareness of the medium produced medium-sensitive viewers; people would go to the movies to *hear a voice* (not see a picture).[53]

Commenting on the "elocution vogue" in Hollywood, Crafton similarly suggests that it revealed "a specific anxiety about the voice." The supposition that the voice can be isolated and altered, he writes, suggests that it was "something extra," apart from the personality or physical being of the actor. Like the sound track, which was at the time conceived of as a supplement to the silent film, the actor's voice was being treated as a separate commodity, and the debate over who controlled the "disembodied film voice" had repercussions in the realm of labor, "increasing the executives' anxiety about actors." The producers "quickly appended riders to the Standard Agreement that legally recognized the separation of the voice from the body and established their right to exploit it."[54]

We might agree therefore that the transition to sound was indeed a period of crisis for Soviet cinema, but this crisis had perhaps less to do with the difficulties of mastering new technology and more to do with the difficulties of succumbing to new ideological directives. How does Soviet cinema imagine its relationship to sound when the historical moment of "joining"—which should have been experienced as a kind of organic wholeness or reparation of a broken system now made whole, vision and hearing together—coincided with the rise of Stalinism and the end of the revolutionary avant-garde? In psychoanalytic film theory, sound has been variously described either as a maternal "blanket" and "sonorous envelope" that surrounds the child, or as an "umbilical net" which the mother weaves around the child, and in which the infant is hopelessly trapped.[55] The paternal voice that reaches the infant from outside this "sonorous envelope" or "umbilical net" is the voice of the *other*, taken for the voice of the Other (Law, prohibition). The coming of sound to Soviet cinema coincided not only with the First Five-Year Plan, with policies of "industrialization" and "collectivization," and with the centralization of the cinema and the creation of a massive bureaucratic apparatus of censorship and oversight, but also with the shift from avant-garde experimentation to the ideological demands of Socialist Realism. With uncanny visibility, early Soviet sound cinema (re)produced not just *any* voice, but the acousmatic voice of state power—"unanchored" and "free-floating"—that addressed the viewer directly from the screen.

As Alan Williams notes, "It is too rarely remarked that the shape of the transition to sound in the rest of the world seems to have been rather different from what happened in the United States."[56] In Europe, the coming of sound brought relative stylistic uniformity to a diverse set of textual strategies produced by a "remarkable variety of art movements, tendencies, and stubborn individualists." In France, the period of the transition to sound coincides with the death of the "Impressionist" and other avant-garde art movements; in Germany, with the end of Expressionism. And in the USSR, writes Williams, "the first sound feature—Ekk's *The Road to Life*—is also the first manifestation of Soviet Socialist Realism (or classical Hollywood style in the service of the Party)." On the one hand, he writes, there is no "immediate, local connection," between the final stage of the basic mechanization of the cinema and "the consolidation of Stalin's state power in the Soviet Union, which finds expression (among many other places) in the adoption of Socialist Realism as the only sanctioned method of filmmaking."[57]

And yet, the new medium clearly offered a powerful pretext for imposing uniform adherence to a new "line," in part because it made film production more capital-intensive and thus a more pressing target for administrative centralization. "Everywhere," Williams concludes, "the coming of sound appears to have reduced diversity and acted against those who would oppose the classical Hollywood cinema with an alternative of their own."[58] The "liberation of speech" brought with it the "repression of the body" (both the actor's body and the film body) and neither would become free again until world cinema reinvented itself in the 1960s, producing new techniques, new technologies, new bodies, new voices, and new ways of seeing and hearing films.

Notes

1. Gilles Deleuze, *Cinema 2: The Time Image*, trans. Hugh Tomlinson and Robert Galeta (Minneapolis: University of Minnesota Press, 1989).
2. Rick Altman, *Silent Film Sound* (New York: Columbia University Press, 2004).
3. Deleuze, *Cinema 2*, 225–226.
4. Deleuze, *Cinema 2*, 226. Emphasis in the original.
5. Deleuze, *Cinema 2*, 229. Emphasis in the original.
6. Deleuze, *Cinema 2*, 235.
7. Deleuze, *Cinema 2*, 241.
8. E. Ia. Margolit and V. P. Filimonov, "Proiskhozhdenie geroia (*Putevka v zhizn'* i iazyk narodnoi kul'tury)," *Kinovedcheskie zapiski* 12 (1991): 74–98. *The Road to Life* was released by Mezhrabpomfil'm in 1931 and re-sounded by the Gorkii Studio (Kinostudiia im. Gor'kogo) in 1957. For archival materials, see RGALI 2794-1-49 (N. Ekk); 2794-1-228 (materialy k podgotovke *Putevki v zhizn'*); and 2639-1-60 (Regina Ianushevskaia). Materials on the American reception of the film, including John Dewey's introduction of the American release, are located at the Pacific Film Archive, Berkeley, Calif. File: *The Road to Life*.
9. Margolit and Filimonov, "Proiskhozhdenie geroia," 74.
10. I. N. Vladimirtseva, et al., ed., *20 rezhisserskikh biografii* (Moscow: Iskusstvo, 1971), 5–6.
11. Margolit and Filimonov, "Proiskhozhdenie geroia," 75.
12. Iu. S. Kalashnikova, et al., ed., *Ocherki istorii sovetskogo kino v trekh tomakh* (Moscow: Iskusstvo, 1956), 280.
13. *Ocherki istorii sovetskogo kino*, 280–281. The editors use the term "sound realism" to describe the new technological breakthrough.
14. Pacific Film Archive. File: *The Road to Life*.
15. As Taylor and Christie point out, McDonald's memory is not to be trusted, since he characterizes *Alone* as a "conventional talkie," and *Enthusiasm* as "just a silent film, with realistic 'sound effects.'" See Richard Taylor and Ian Christie, "Introduction," *The Film Factory: Russian and Soviet Cinema in Documents 1896–1939*, ed. Taylor and Christie (London and New York: Routledge, 1994), 9.
16. Pacific Film Archive. File: *The Road to Life*.

17. Jay Leyda, *Kino: A History of Russian and Soviet Film* (Princeton: Princeton University Press, 1983), 284.
18. Thorold Dickinson and Catherine de la Roche, *Soviet Cinema* (London: The Falcon Press Ltd., 1948), 40.
19. Alexander S. Birkos, ed., *Soviet Cinema: Directors and Films* (Hamden, CT: Archon Books, 1976), 52.
20. Taylor and Christie, *The Film Factory*, 438; Richard Taylor, "'A Cinema for the Millions': Soviet Socialist Realism and the Problem of Film Comedy," *Journal of Contemporary History* 18, no. 3 (July 1983): 439–461; here: 450.
21. Seth R. Feldman, *Dziga Vertov: A Guide to References and Sources* (Boston: G. K. Hall & Co., 1979), 13–14.
22. RGALI 2794-1-261, ll. 19–24.
23. RGALI, f. 2794 (Ekk), op. 1, ed. 261.
24. Leyda, *Kino*, 278. Shumyatsky was removed from his post in 1938 and arrested and shot in 1939. (See G. Ermolaev, "Chto tormozit razvitie sovetskogo kino?" *Pravda* [January 9, 1938]: 4; translated as: "What is Holding Up the Development of Soviet Cinema?," *The Film Factory*, 386–389; and "Fashistskaia gadina unichtozhena," *Iskusstvo kino* no. 2 [February 1938]: 5–6; translated as: *Iskusstvo kino* Editorial, "The Fascist Cur Eradicated," *The Film Factory*, 387–389.) Shumyatsky's replacement as head of the new State Cinema Committee for Cinema Affairs was Semyon Dukelsky, who lasted in his post from 1938–1939. He was in turn replaced by Ivan Bolshakov.
25. Dickinson and de la Roche, *Soviet Cinema*, 41.
26. Pacific Film Archive, calendar of events, November 26, 1986.
27. *Pioner* 22 (RGALI, f. 2794 (Ekk), op. 1, ed. 261).
28. Maya Turovskaya, "The 1930s and 1940s: Cinema in Context," in *Stalinism and Soviet Cinema*, ed. Richard Taylor and Derek Spring (New York: Routledge, 1993): 34–53; here: 45.
29. For a full analysis of Ekk's *The Road to Life*, including its resistance to the mechanisms of state power, see Kaganovsky, "Forging Soviet Masculinity in Nikolai Ekk's *The Road to Life*," in *Gender and National Identity in Twentieth-Century Russian Culture*, ed. Helena Goscilo and Andrea Lanoux (Dekalb: Northern Illinois Press, 2006), 146–175.
30. The resolution of the December 1928 Conference of Soiuzkino workers deemed that an essential part of any experimental work was to be "artistic expression that is intelligible to the millions." It was Shumiatsky's 1935 *Kinematografiia millionov* (A Cinema for the Millions, Moscow, 1935), however, that used the phrase "cinema for the millions" to describe the main goal of Soviet cinematography.
31. Boris Shumyatsky, "Tvorcheskie zadachi templana," *Sovetskoe kino* 12 (December 1933): 1–15; here: 6–7; quoted in Richard Taylor, "Boris Shumyatsky and the Soviet Cinema in the 1930s: Ideology as Mass Entertainment," *Historical Journal of Film, Radio and Television* 6:1 (1986): 43–64; here: 51. A
32. Boris Shumiatskii, *Kinematografiia millionov* (Moscow: Kinofotoizdat, 1935). Partially translated as Boris Shumyatsky, "A Cinema for the Millions," in *The Film Factory*, 358–369.
33. Shumiatskii, *Kinematografiia millionov*, 16, 17.
34. Shumiatskii, *Kinematografiia millionov*, 18.
35. Shumiatskii, *Kinematografiia millionov*, 121.
36. Shumiatskii, *Kinematografiia millionov*, 125.
37. Shumiatskii, *Kinematografiia millionov*, 132, 156, 157.
38. Shumiatskii, *Kinematografiia millionov*, 249; "A Cinema for the Millions," 369. For a detailed analysis of the making of and reception of *Jolly Fellows*, see Rimgaila Salys, *The Musical Comedy Films of Grigorii Aleksandrov: Laughing Matters* (Bristol: Intellect Press, 2009), 19–120.
39. Shumiatskii, *Kinematografiia millionov*, 241; "A Cinema for the Millions," 368.
40. Shumiatskii, *Kinematografiia millionov*, 173; "A Cinema for the Millions," 365.

41. Shumiatskii, *Kinematografiia millionov*, 174; "A Cinema for the Millions," 365.

42. Shumiatskii, *Kinematografiia millionov*, 175–176; "A Cinema for the Millions," 365–367. This perhaps explains why Denise Youngblood, in her account of Vertov's *Three Songs of Lenin*, accuses it of being "fascistic" (Denise Youngblood, *Soviet Cinema in the Silent Era, 1918–1935* [Ann Arbor: UMI Research Press, 1985], 230).

43. Shumiatskii, *Kinematografiia millionov*, 148; "A Cinema for the Millions," 358. Emphasis in the original.

44. Shumiatskii, *Kinematografiia millionov*, 156–157; "A Cinema for the Millions," 361. On music in Chapaev, see Julian Graffy, *Chapaev*, KINOfiles Film Companion 12 (London: I. B. Tauris, 2010).

45. Shumiatskii, *Kinematografiia millionov*, 222–223.

46. Shumiatskii, *Kinematografiia millionov*, 225.

47. Donald Crafton, *The Talkies: American Cinema's Transition to Sound, 1926–1931* (Berkeley: University of California Press, 1997), 311.

48. Crafton, *The Talkies*, 311.

49. Playing off Laura Mulvey's idea of "to-be-looked-at-ness," in her "Visual Pleasure and Narrative Cinema" (*Screen* 16.3 [1975]: 6–18)—I am grateful to Joshua Malitsky for this formulation.

50. Robert Spadoni, *Uncanny Bodies: The Coming of Sound Film and the Origins of the Horror Genre* (Berkeley: University of California Press, 2007).

51. Yuri Tsivian, *Early Cinema in Russia and its Cultural Reception* (Chicago: The University of Chicago Press, 1991).

52. See Rick Altman, *Silent Film Sound* (New York: Columbia University Press, 2005), 89.

53. Spadoni, *Uncanny Bodies*, 6, 18. We can see an example of this with Dziga Vertov's *Three Songs of Lenin*: a front-page article in the newspaper *Pravda*, from 1934, shows a photo of the working masses on their way, as the caption tells us, "to hear" *Three Songs of Lenin* (*Pravda* n. 303, November 2, 1934).

54. Crafton, *The Talkies*, 456.

55. In *The Voice in Cinema*, Michel Chion writes, "In the beginning, in the uterine darkness, was the voice, the Mother's voice. . . . We can imagine the voice of the Mother weaving around the child a network of connections it's tempting to call the *umbilical web*. A rather horrifying expression to be sure, in its evocation of spiders—and in fact, this original vocal connection will remain ambivalent" (Michel Chion, *The Voice in Cinema*, trans. Claudia Gorbman [New York: Columbia University Press, 1999], 61). For a feminist reading of the maternal voice, see Kaja Silverman, *The Acoustic Mirror: The Female Voice in Psychoanalysis and Cinema* (Bloomington: Indiana University Press, 1988).

56. Alan Williams, "Historical and Theoretical Issues in the Coming of Recorded Sound to the Cinema," in *Sound Theory / Sound Practice*, ed. Rick Altman (New York: Routledge, 1992), 126–137; here: 135.

57. Williams, "Historical and Theoretical Issues in the Coming of Recorded Sound to the Cinema," 135.

58. Williams, "Historical and Theoretical Issues in the Coming of Recorded Sound to the Cinema," 136.

WORKS CITED

Archival Sources

British Film Institute National Archive (BFI):
Collection: Film Society
Item 15: Performance 49; Seventh Season 1931–1932; *Entuziazm* (Su, 1931); Performance 81; Eleventh Season 1935–1936; *Tri Pesni o Lenine* (Su, 1934)
Item 12: Theatres: New Gallery Kinema and The Tivoli, Strand; Correspondence Regarding the Use of Theatres for Performances, 1929–1939
Collection: Ivor Montagu
Item 181: *Tri Pesni o Lenine* (Three Songs of Lenin) (Su, 1934); English presentation and titles for Film Society show, plus synopsis
Item 182: Manuscript by W. H. Auden of English versions of the first Two Songs

Gosudarstvennyi fond kinofil'mov Rossiiskoi Federatsii (Gosfil'mofond):
Ed. khran. 968 ("Piatiletka"); Section I, fond 7, op. 1, ed. khran. 1 ("K.Sh.E"); Section I, fond 3, op. 1, ed. khran. 327 ("Vozvrashchenie Neitana Bekkera"); Section I, fond 3, op. 1, ed. khran. 429 ("Garmon'"); Section I, fond 7, op.1, ed. khran. 121 ("Tri Pesni o Lenine"); Section V, fond 7, op. 1, ed. khran. 4543 ("Ivan")

Museum of Modern Art Film Study Center (MoMA):
Collection: Artkino
Box 1: #937 (Aerograd); 939 (Arsenal); 942 (Chelovek s Kinoapparatom); 946 (Dela i lyudi); 957 (The Five Year Plan); 960 (Gorizont)
Box 2: #968 (Koliivshchina); 981 (Odna); 982 (Okraina)
Box 4: #1015 (Tri Pesni o Lenine); 1027 (Zemlia Zhazhdyet)

Pacific Film Archive, Berkeley, California (PFA):
File: *The Road to Life* (1931)

Rossiiskii gosudarstvennyi arkhiv literatury i iskusstva (RGALI):
f. 279 (Lunacharskii); f. 631 (Soiuz pisatelei SSSR (Moscow, 1932–1991); f. 645 (Glaviskusstvo NKP RSFSR); f. 966 (Gos. lit. izdat. literatury po voprosam kino); f. 1847 (Aduev); f. 1923 (Eisenstein); f. 1976 (Kurikhin); f. 1992 (Savchenko); f. 2502 (Popov); f. 2081 (Dovzhenko); f. 2048 (Shostakovich); f. 2091 (Vertov); f. 2450 (Glav. upravlenie po proizvodstvu khud. fil'mov Ministerstva kinematografii SSSR (Moscow, 1936–1953); f. 2453 (Mosfil'm); f. 2456 (Ministerstvo kinematografii SSSR); f. 2494 (ARRK, 1923–1932); f. 2495 (ODSK); f. 2620 (ARK, 1926–1930); f. 2627 (Tsekhanovskii);

f. 2639 (Ginsburg); f. 2653 (Ianushkevich); f. 2690 (Tager); f. 2698 (Morskoi); f. 2734 (Aleinikov); f. 2794 (Ekk); f. 3016 (Trauberg); f. 3035 (Shub); f. 3070 (Iutkevich); f. 3107 (Sutyrin)

University of Illinois Archives:
Joseph T. Tykociner Papers, 1900–1969
Box 3: Outgoing Correspondence, 1921–1937; Box 4: Jacob Chaitkin, 1931–1933 (Letters regarding J. T. Tykociner's Inventions, June, September, 1931); Box 7: Florence and Milward Pick, 1923–1959 (material about sound on film); Box 11: Newspaper File, 1922–1969 and Biographical Material Collected by Joseph T. Tykociner (On Research, Sound on film, et al.); Box 18: First experimental talking film, 1921–22 and related audio and video recordings; Biographical Tape Recordings—May 3, 1965, interview by M. J. Brichford; Box 20: Sound on Film (including Tykociner's lectures, publications, etc.)

Published Sources

Abramov, N. P. *Dziga Vertov*. Moscow: Izdatel'stvo Akademii nauk SSSR, 1962.
Avraamov, Arsenii. "Sinteticheskaia muzyka." *Sovetskaia muzyka* 8 (1939): 67–75.
Aleksandrov, Grigorii. *Epokha i kino*. Moscow: Izdatel'stvo politicheskoi literatury, 1976.
———. *Gody poiskov i truda*. Moscow: Soiuz kinematografistov SSSR, 1975.
———. "Velikii drug sovetskogo kino." *Iskusstvo kino*. (December 1939).
Althusser, Louis. *Lenin and Philosophy and Other Essays*. Translated by Ben Brewster. New York: Monthly Review Press, 1971.
Altman, Rick. *The American Film Musical*. Bloomington: Indiana University Press, 1988.
———. *Silent Film Sound*. New York: Columbia University Press, 2004.
———. ed. *Sound Theory / Sound Practice*. New York: Routledge, 1992.
Anderson, Barbara A., and Brian D. Silver. "Equality, Efficiency, and Politics in Soviet Bilingual Education Policy: 1934–1980." *American Political Science Review* 78 (December, 1984): 1019–1039.
Anderson, K. M. *Kremlevskii kinoteatr. 1928–1953: Dokumenty*. Moscow: Rosspen, 2005.
Balázs, Béla. "Novye fil'my—novoe zhiznesohchushchenie." *Sovetskoe kino* 3–4 (1933).
———. *Theory of the Film: Character and Growth of a New Art*. Translated by Edith Bone. London: Denis Dobson, 1952. Originally published as *Filmkultúra (a film muveszetfilozofiaja)*. Budapest: Szikra Kiadas, 1948.
Balina, Marina, Evgeny Dobrenko, and Yury Murashov, eds. *Sovetskoe bogatstvo. Stat'i o kul'ture, literature i kino*. Petersburg: Akademicheskii proekt, 2002.
Balio, Tino. *United Artists, the Company Built by the Stars*. Madison: University of Wisconsin Press, 2009.
Barker, Jennifer M. *The Tactile Eye: Touch and the Cinematic Experience*. Berkeley: University of California Press, 2009.
Barrios, Richard. *A Song in the Dark: The Birth of the Musical Film*. Oxford: Oxford University Press, 2010.
Baudry, Jean-Louis. "Ideological Effects of the Basic Cinematographic Apparatus." *Film Quarterly* 28, no. 2 (Winter 1974–75): 39–47.
Belodubrovskaya, Maria. *Not According to Plan: Filmmaking under Stalin*. Ithaca: Cornell University Press, 2017.
Belton, John. "Awkward Transitions: Hitchcock's *Blackmail* and the Dynamics of Early Film Sound." *Musical Quarterly* 83, no. 2 (1999): 227–246.

Bennett, Jane. *Vibrant Matter: A Political Ecology of Things*. Durham: Duke University Press, 2010.
Beskin, Osip. "Editorial." *Sovetskoe kino* 1 (1928): 1.
Beumers, Birgit. *A History of Russian Cinema*. Oxford: Berg, 2009.
Birkos, Alexander S., ed. *Soviet Cinema: Directors and Films*. Hamden, CT: Archon Books, 1976.
Bohlinger, Vincent. "The Development of Sound Technology in the Soviet Union during the First Five-Year Plan." *Studies in Russian and Soviet Cinema* 7, no. 2 (Summer 2013): 189–205.
Bonitzer, Pascal. "The Silences of the Voice." In *Narrative, Apparatus, Ideology*, edited by Philip Rosen, 319–334. New York: Columbia University Press, 1986. Originally published as "Les Silences de la voix." *Cahiers du cinéma* 256 (Feb–March 1975): 22–33.
Bordwell, David, Janet Staiger, and Kristin Thompson. *The Classic Hollywood Cinema: Film Style and Mode of Production to 1960*. New York: Columbia University Press, 1985.
Bourke-White, Margaret. *Eyes on Russia*. New York: Simon and Schuster, 1931.
———. *Sovetskii slukhoglaz: kino i ego organy chuvstv*. Moscow: Novoe Literaturnoe Obozrenie, 2010.
———. "Spatial Figures in Soviet Cinema of the 1930s." In *The Landscape of Stalinism: The Art and Ideology of Soviet Space*, edited by Evgeny Dobrenko and Eric Naiman, 51–76. Seattle: University of Washington Press, 2003.
Bulgakowa [Bulgakova], Oksana. "The Ear against the Eye: Vertov's Symphony." *Kieler Beiträge zur Filmmusikforschung* 2 (2008): 142–158.
———. *Golos kak kul'turnyi fenomen*. Moscow: Novoe Literaturnoe Obozrenie, 2015.
Butler, Judith. *Bodies That Matter: On the Discursive Limitations of "Sex."* London: Routledge, 1993.
Butovskii, Iakov. "'Odna' na perekrestkakh obshchikh problem rossiiskogo kinovedeniia." *Kinovedcheskie zapiski* 77 (2006): 310–319.
Caruth, Cathy. *Unclaimed Experience: Trauma, Narrative, and History*. Baltimore: Johns Hopkins University Press, 1996.
Cavandish, Philip. *The Men with the Movie Camera: The Poetics of Visual Style in Soviet Avant-Garde Cinema of the 1920s*. Oxford: Berghahn Books, 2013.
———. "*Zemlia / Earth*." In *The Cinema of Russia and the Former Soviet Union*, edited by Birgit Beumers, 57–60. London: Wallflower Press, 2007.
Chadaga, Julia Bekman. *Optical Play: Glass, Vision, and Spectacle in Russian Culture*. Evanston: Northwestern University Press, 2014.
Chion, Michel. *The Voice in Cinema*. Translated by Claudia Gorbman. New York: Columbia University Press, 1999. Originally published as *La voix au cinéma*. Paris: Editions de l'Etoile, 1982.
Chomentowski, Gabrielle. "Du cinéma muet au cinéma parlant. La politique des langues dans les films soviétiques." *Cahiers du monde russe* 55, no. 3 (2014): 295–320.
Christie, Ian. "Soviet Cinema: Making Sense of Sound." *Screen* 23, no. 2 (1982): 34–49; republished as "Making Sense of Soviet Sound." In *Inside the Film Factory: New Approaches to Russian and Soviet Cinema*, edited by Richard Taylor and Ian Christie, 176–192. London: Routledge, 1991.
Clark, Katerina. "'Chtoby tak pet', dvadtsat' let uchit'sia nuzhno: Sluchai *Volgi-Volgi*." In *Sovetskoe bogatstvo. Stat'i o kul'ture, literature i kino*, edited by Marina Balina, Evgeny Dobrenko, and Yury Murashov, 371–390. St. Petersburg: Akademicheskii proekt, 2002.
———. *The Soviet Novel: History as Ritual*. Chicago: Chicago University Press, 1981.
Cohan, Steven, ed. *Hollywood Musicals: The Film Reader*. London: Routledge, 2001.

———. *Incongruous Entertainment: Camp, Cultural Value, and the MGM Musical*. Durham: Duke University Press, 2005.
Cooke, Mervyn, ed. *The Hollywood Film Musical Reader*. Oxford: Oxford University Press, 2010.
Crafton, Donald. *The Talkies: American Cinema's Transition to Sound, 1926–1931*. Berkeley: University of California Press, 1997.
De Man, Paul. "Autobiography as De-Facement." In *The Rhetoric of Romanticism*, 67–81. New York: Columbia University Press, 1984.
Deleuze, Gilles. *Cinema 1: The Movement-Image*. Translated by Hugh Tomlinson. Minneapolis: University of Minnesota Press, 1986. Originally published as *L'Image-mouvement. Cinéma 1*. Paris: Les Éditions de Minuit, 1983.
———. *Cinema 2: The Time Image*. Translated by Hugh Tomlinson and Robert Galeta. Minneapolis: University of Minnesota Press, 1989. Originally published as *L'Image-temps. Cinéma 2*. Paris: Les Éditions de Minuit, 1985.
Deleuze, Gilles, and Félix Guattari. *A Thousand Plateaus: Capitalism and Schizophrenia*. Translated by Brian Massumi. Minneapolis: University of Minnesota Press, 1987. Originally published as *Mille Plateaux*. Paris, Les Éditions de Minuit, 1980.
Deriabin, A. S. *Letopis' rossiiskogo kino 1863–1929*. Moscow: Materik, 2004.
———. *Letopis' rossiiskogo kino 1930–1945*. Moscow: Materik, 2007.
———. "Poteria i obretenie nemoty." *Kinovedcheskie zapiski* 23 (1994): 181–185.
Derrida, Jacques. *Of Grammatology*. Baltimore: The Johns Hopkins University Press, 1976.
Dickinson, Kay, ed. *Movie Music, the Film Reader*. London: Routledge, 2003.
Dickinson, Thorold and Catherine de la Roche. *Soviet Cinema*. London: The Falcon Press Ltd., 1948.
Doane, Mary Ann. "The Voice in Cinema: The Articulation of Body and Space." *Yale French Studies* 60 (1980): 33–50.
Dobrenko, Evgeny. *Political Economy of Socialist Realism*. New Haven: Yale University Press, 2007.
Dovzhenko, Aleksandr. *Aleksandr Dovzhenko. Sobranie sochinenii v chetyrekh tomakh*. Vols. 1–4. Moscow: Iskusstvo, 1969.
Dovzhenko, Alexander. *Alexander Dovzhenko: The Poet as Filmmaker: Selected Writings*. Edited and translated by Marco Carynnyk. Cambridge, MA: MIT Press, 1973.
Drubek-Meyer, Natascha. "Zvuki muzyki. (Anti-)medium v sovetskikh muzykal'nykh komediiakh." In *Sovetskaia vlast' i media*, edited by Hans Günther and Sabine Hänsgen, 578–592. St. Petersburg: Akademicheskii proekt, 2006.
———. "Zvukomontazh v fil'me 'Garmon'' (1934) Igoria Savchenko." In *Welt der Slaven, Schwerpunkt: "Stumm oder vertont. Krisen und Neuanfänge in der Filmkunst um 1930,"* edited by D. Zakharine. Vol. 54, 2009. 2: 309–325.
Ďurovičová, Nataša. "Translating America: The Hollywood Multilinguals 1929–1933." In *Sound Theory / Sound Practice*, edited by Rick Altman, 138–153. New York: Routledge, 1992.
Dyer, Richard. "Entertainment and Utopia." In *Only Entertainment*, 19–35. London: Routledge, 1992; 2002, 2nd ed.
———. "White." *Screen* 29, no. 4 (October 1, 1988): 44–65.
Dzhulai, Liudmila. *Dokumental'nyi illiuzion*. Moscow: Materik, 2005.
Eikhenbaum, Boris. "Problemy kino-stilistiki." In *Poetika kino*, edited by Boris Eikhenbaum, 13–52. Moscow: Kinopechat', 1927. Translated as Ejxenbaum, B. "Problems of Cinema Stylistics." In *Russian Formalist Film Theory*, edited by Herbert Eagle, 55–80. Ann Arbor: Michigan Slavic Publications, 1981.

Eisenstein, Sergei. *Film Form: Essays in Film Theory*. Edited and translated by Jay Leyda. New York: Harcourt Brace Jovanovich, 1949.

———. *Memuary*. Vol. 2. Moscow: Redaktsiia gazety "Trud," 1997.

Eisenstein, S., W. Pudowkin, and G. Alexandrow [Alexandrov]. "Achtung! Goldgrube! Gedanken uber die Zukunft des Horfilms." *Die Lichtbildbuehne* (July 28, 1928); and "Tonender Film: Montage und Kontrapunkt. Gedanken uber die Zukunft der Filmkunst." *Vossische Zeitung* (July 29, 1928).

Eisenstein, S. M., W. I. Pudowkin [Pudovkin], and G. V. Alexandroff [Alexandrov]. "The Sound Film. A Statement from USSR." *Close Up* (October 1928).

Eisenstein [Eizenshtein], Sergei, Vsevolod Pudovkin, and Grigorii Aleksandrov [Alexandrov]. "Zaiavka (Budushchee zvukovoi fil'my)." *Zhizn' iskusstva* (August 5, 1928); and *Sovetskii ekran* (August 7, 1928). Translated as "Statement on Sound." In *The Film Factory: Russian and Soviet Cinema in Documents 1896–1939*, edited by Richard Taylor and Ian Christie, 234–235. London: Routledge, 1994.

Elektronnaia evreiskaia entsiklopediia. "Esfir' Shub," accessed at http://www.eleven.co.il/article/14953.

Ermolaev, G. "Chto tormozit razvitie sovetskogo kino?" *Pravda* (January 9, 1938): 4. Translated as: "What is Holding Up the Development of Soviet Cinema?" In Taylor and Christie, *The Film Factory*, 386–387.

Erofeev, Vladimir. "Uroki zvukovogo kino." *Sovetskoe iskusstvo* 29 (January 1931).

Eyman, Scott. *The Speed of Sound: Hollywood and the Talkie Revolution, 1926–1930*. New York: Simon and Schuster, 1997.

"Fashistskaia gadina unichtozhena." *Iskusstvo kino* 2 (February 1938): 5–6. Translated as: *Iskusstvo kino* Editorial, "The Fascist Cur Eradicated." In Taylor and Christie, *The Film Factory*, 387–389.

Feldman, Seth R. "'Cinema Weekly' and 'Cinema Truth': Dziga Vertov and the Leninist Proportion." In *Show Us Life! Toward a History and Aesthetics of the Committed Documentary*, edited by Thomas Waugh, 3–20. London: The Scarecrow Press, Inc., 1984.

———. *Dziga Vertov: A Guide to References and Sources*. Boston: G. K. Hall & Co., 1979.

Feuer, Jane. *The Hollywood Musical*. Bloomington: Indiana University Press, 1982.

Fielding, Raymond, ed. *A Technological History of Motion Pictures and Television*. Berkeley: University of California Press, 1967.

Fisher, Lucy. "*Enthusiasm*: From Kino-Eye to Radio-Eye." *Film Quarterly* 31, no. 2 (Winter 1977–78): 25–34.

Fitzpatrick, Sheila. *Everyday Stalinism: Ordinary Life in Extraordinary Times: Soviet Russia in the 1930s*. Oxford: Oxford University Press, 1999.

Foucault, Michel. *Discipline and Punish: The Birth of the Prison*. Translated by Alan Sheridan. New York: Pantheon Books, 1977. Originally published as *Surveiller et punir: Naissance de la prison*, Paris: Gallimard, 1975.

Freiberg, Freda. "The Transition to Sound in Japan." In *History on/and/in Film*, edited by T. O'Regan and B. Shoesmith, 76–80. Perth: History & Film Association of Australia, 1987.

Freud, Sigmund. *The Standard Edition of the Complete Psychological Works of Sigmund Freud*. Edited and translated by James Strachey. London: Hogarth Press, 1986.

Gillespie, David C. "The Sounds of Music: Soundtrack and Song in Soviet Film." *Slavic Review* 62, no. 3 (Autumn, 2003): 473–490.

Glinsky, Albert. *Theremin: Ether Music and Espionage*. Urbana: University of Illinois Press, 2000.

Goldmark, Daniel, Lawrence Kramer, and Richard Leppert, eds. *Beyond the Soundtrack: Representing Music in Cinema*. Berkeley: University of California Press, 2007.
Gomery, Douglas. *The Coming of Sound: A History*. London: Routledge, 2005.
———. "The Coming of Sound: Technological Change in the American Film Industry." In *Film Sound: Theory and Practice*, edited by Elizabeth Weis and John Belton, 5–24. New York: Columbia University Press, 1985.
Gorham, Michael S. *Speaking in Soviet Tongues: Language Culture and the Politics of Voice in Revolutionary Russia*. DeKalb: Northern Illinois University Press, 2003.
Graffy, Julian. *Chapaev*. KINOfiles Film Companion, 12. London: I. B. Tauris, 2010.
Grierson, John. "First Principles of Documentary" (1932–1934). In *Nonfiction Film Theory and Criticism*, edited by Richard Barsam, 19–30. New York: E. P. Dutton & Co, 1976.
Groys, Boris. *The Total Art of Stalinism: Avant-Garde, Aesthetic Dictatorship, and Beyond*. Princeton: Princeton University Press, 1992.
Gukasian, F. G. *Kinooperator Andrei Moskvin: ocherk zhizni i tvorchestva; vospominaniia tovarishchei*. Leningrad: Iskusstvo, 1971.
Günther, Hans and Sabine Hänsgen, eds. *Sovetskaia vlast' i media*. St. Petersburg: Akademicheskii proekt, 2006.
Gurko, S. L. "Fonogramma fil'ma *Zemlia*." *Kinovedcheskie zapiski* 23 (1994).
Hänsgen, Sabine. "'Audio-Vision': O teorii i praktike rannego sovetskogo zvukovogo kino na grani 1930x godov." In *Sovetskaia vlast' i media*, edited by H. Günther and S. Hänsgen, 350–364. St. Petersburg: Akademicheskii proekt, 2006.
Hass, David. *Leningrad's Modernists: Studies in Composition and Musical Thought, 1917–1932*. New York: Peter Lang, 1998.
Heath, Stephen. *Questions of Cinema*. Bloomington: Indiana University Press, 1982.
Hicks, Jeremy. "Challenging the Voice of God in World War II-Era Soviet Documentaries." In *Sound, Speech, Music*, edited by Kaganovsky and Salazkina, 129–144. Bloomington: Indiana University Press, 2014.
———. *Dziga Vertov: Defining Documentary Film*. London: I. B. Taurus, 2007.
Hubbert, Julie. "Eisenstein's Theory of Film Music Revisited: Silent and Early Sound Antecedents." In *Composing for the Screen in Germany and the USSR*, edited by Robynn J. Stilwell and Phil Powrie, 125–147. Bloomington: Indiana University Press, 2008.
Iezuitov, N. *Pudovkin*. Moscow: Iskusstvo, 1937.
Iukov, K. "Novyi etap (K voprosu o 'krizise' v kino)." *Kino* 51 (1928): 2–3.
Izvolov, Nikolai. "Dziga Vertov and Aleksandr Rodchenko: The Visible Word." *Studies in Russian and Soviet Cinema* 10, no. 1 (2016): 2–14.
———. "From the History of Graphic Sound in the Soviet Union; or, Media without a Medium." In *Sound, Speech, Music*, edited by Kaganovsky and Salazkina, 23–37. Bloomington: Indiana University Press, 2014.
———. "Moment ozhivleniia spiashchei idei." *Kinovedcheskie zapiski* 15 (1992): 290–296.
Jacobs, Lea. *Film Rhythm After Sound: Technology, Music, and Performance*. Berkeley: University of California Press, 2015.
James, Richard S. "Avant-Garde Sound-on-Film Techniques and Their Relationship to Electro-Acoustic Music." *The Musical Quarterly* 72, no. 1 (1986): 74–89.
Kaganovsky, Lilya. "Forging Soviet Masculinity in Nikolai Ekk's *The Road to Life*." In *Gender and National Identity in Twentieth-Century Russian Culture*, edited by Helena Goscilo and Andrea Lanoux, 146–175. Dekalb: Northern Illinois Press, 2006.
———. *How the Soviet Man Was Unmade: Cultural Fantasy and Male Subjectivity under Stalin*. University of Pittsburgh Press, 2008.

———. "The Voice of Technology and the End of Soviet Silent Film: On Grigorii Kozintsev and Leonid Trauberg's *Alone*." *Studies in Russian and Soviet Cinema* 1, no. 3 (2007): 265–281.
Kaganovsky, Lilya, and Masha Salazkina, eds. *Sound, Speech, Music in Soviet and Post-Soviet Cinema*. Bloomington: Indiana University Press, 2014.
Kalashnikova, Iu. S. et al., ed. *Ocherki istorii sovetskogo kino v trekh tomakh*. Moscow: Iskusstvo, 1956.
Kalinak, Katheryn. *Film Music: A Very Short Introduction*. Oxford: Oxford University Press, 2010.
Kavina, Lydia. "Therminvox." In *Electrified Voices*, edited by Dmitri Zakharine and Nils Meise, 187–200. Göttingen: Vandenhoeck & Ruprecht, 2012.
Kenez, Peter. *Cinema and Soviet Society: From the Revolution to the Death of Stalin*. London: I. B. Tauris, 2001.
Kepley Jr., Vance. "The First 'Perestroika': Soviet Cinema under the First Five-Year Plan." *Cinema Journal* 35, no. 4 (1996: Summer): 31–53.
———. *In the Service of the State: The Cinema of Alexander Dovzhenko*. Madison: The University of Wisconsin Press, 1986.
Khersonskii, Khrisanf. "Garmon'." *Iskusstvo* 138 (June 15, 1934).
Kittler, Friedrich A. *Gramophone, Film, Typewriter*. Translated by Geoffrey Winthrop-Young and Michael Wutz. Stanford: Stanford University Press, 1999.
Kokhno, Leonid. "Poeziia truda." In *Dovzhenko v vospominaniiakh sovremennikov*, edited by Liudmila Pazhitnova and Iulia Solntseva, 79–85. Moscow: Iskusstvo, 1982.
Kostiuk, Hryhorii. *Okaianni roky: Vid Luk'ianivs'koi tiurmy do Vorkuts'koi trahedii (1935–1940 rr.)*. Toronto: Diialoh, 1978.
Kozintsev, Grigorii. "Iz pisem kinematografistam." *Iskusstvo kino* 7 (1995): 112–121.
———. *Sobranie sochinenii v piati tomakh*. Vol. 1. Leningrad: Iskusstvo 1984.
Krzhizhanovskii, Gleb. *10 let GOELRO*. Moscow: Ogiz, 1931.
Kujundzic, Dragan. "Dziga Vertov or the Return of the Sight (Five Intervals)." In *Apparatur und Rhapsodie: Zu den Filmen des Dziga Vertov*, edited by Natascha Drubek-Meyer and Jurij Murasov, 171–199. New York: Peter Lang, 2000.
———. *The Returns of History: Russian Nietzscheans After Modernity*. Albany: SUNY Press, 1997.
Lastra, James. *Sound Technology and the American Cinema: Perception, Representation, Modernity*. New York: Columbia University Press, 2000.
Le Foll, Claire. "A la recherche de l'introuvable film juif-biélorusse? Politique des nationalités et cinéma en BSSR dans les années 1920 et 1930." In *Kinojudaica: Les représentations des Juifs dans le cinéma de Russie et d'Union soviétique des années 1910 aux années 1980*, edited by Valérie Pozner and Natacha Laurent, 79–109. La Cinémathèque de Toulouse / Nouveau Monde Editions, 2012.
Leaming, B. *Grigori Kozintsev*. Boston: Twayne Publishers, 1980.
Lemberg, Aleksandr G. "Dziga Vertov prikhodit v kino." In *Iz istorii kino: materialy i dokumenty*, edited by S. Ginzburg et al., 39–49. Vol. 13. Moscow: Akademiia nauk SSSR, 1958–1962.
Leyda, Jay. *Kino: A History of the Russian and Soviet Film*. Princeton: Princeton University Press, 1960.
Liber, George O. *Alexander Dovzhenko: A Life in Soviet Film*. London: British Film Institute, 2002.
Łotysz, Sławomir. "Contributions of Polish Jews: Joseph Tykocinski-Tykociner (1877–1969), Pioneer of Sound on Film." *AAPJS Gazeta* 13, no. 3 (Winter–Spring 2006).

Lovell, Stephen. "Broadcasting Bolshevik: The Radio Voice of Soviet Culture, 1920s–1950s." *Journal of Contemporary History* 48, no. 1 (2013): 78–97.

———. "How Russia Learned to Listen: Radio and the Making of Soviet Culture." *Kritika: Explorations in Russian and Eurasian History* 12, no. 3 (2011): 591–615.

———. *Russia in the Microphone Age: A History of Soviet Radio, 1919–1970.* Oxford: Oxford University Press, 2015.

Luchina, Nina and Tat'iana Derevianko. *Igor' Savchenko. Sbornik statei i vospominanii.* Kiev: Mistetstvo, 1980.

Lunacharskii, Anatolii. "Zadachi gosudarstvennogo kinodela v R.S.F.S.R." Translated as Lunacharsky, Anatoly. "The Tasks of the State Cinema in the RSFSR." In Taylor and Christie, *The Film Factory*, 47–49.

Kinematograf. Sbornik statei. Moscow: Gos Izd-vo, 1919.

MacKay, John. "Allegory and accommodation: Vertov's *Three Songs of Lenin* (1934) as a Stalinist Film." *Film History* 18, no. 4 (2006): 376–391.

———. "Disorganized Noise: Enthusiasm and the Ear of the Collective." *KinoKultura* 7 (January 2005), accessed at: http://www.kinokultura.com/articles/jan05-mackay.html.

———. "Film Energy: Process and Metanarrative in Dziga Vertov's *The Eleventh Year* (1928)." *October* 121 (Summer 2007): 41–78.

Mayakovsky [Maiakovskii], Vladimir. "Komsomol'skaia." *Molodaia gvardiia* 2–3 (1924): 10–14.

———. "Speech in Debate on 'The Paths and Policy of Sovkino'" (October 15, 1927). In Taylor and Christie, *The Film Factory*, 171–174. Originally published in *Polnoe sobranie sochinenii.* Vol. 12, "Stat'i, zametki i vystupleniia, Noiabr' 1917–1930." Moscow: Gos. izdat. khudozh, 1959.

———. "Vladimir Il'ich Lenin." *Polnoe sobranie sochinenii v trinadtsati tomakh.* Moscow: Gos. izdat. khud. lit., 1957.

Malitsky, Joshua. *Post-Revolution Nonfiction Film: Building the Soviet and Cuban Nations.* Bloomington: Indiana University Press, 2013.

Margolit, Evgenii. "Problema mnogoiazychiia v rannem sovetskom zvukovom kino (1930–1935)." In *Sovetskaia vlast' i media*, edited by H. Günther and S. Hänsgen, 378–386. Translated as Margolit, Evgeny. "The Problem of Heteroglossia in Early Soviet Sound Film." In *Sound, Speech, Music*, edited by Kaganovsky and Salazkina, 119–128. Bloomington: Indiana University Press, 2014.

———. "Zaklinanie eposom. *Garmon'* Igoria Savchenko i genezis sovetskoi muzykal'noi komedii." *Kinovedcheskie zapiski* 13 (1992): 120–133.

———. *Zhivye i mertvoe. Zametki k istorii sovetskogo kino 1920-kh—1960-kh godov.* St. Petersburg: Seans, 2012.

Margolit, Evgenii, and V. P. Filimonov, "Proiskhozhdenie geroia (*Putevka v zhizn'* i iazyk narodnoi kul'tury)." *Kinovedcheskie zapiski* 12 (1991): 74–98.

Mar'iamov, A. *Dovzhenko. Zhizn' zamechatel'nykh liudei.* Moscow: Izd. TsK VLKSM "Molodaia gvardiia," 1968.

Marks, Laura U. *The Skin of the Film: Intercultural Cinema, Embodiment, and the Senses.* Durham: Duke University Press, 2000.

Martin, Terry. *Affirmative Action Empire: Nations and Nationalism in the Soviet Union, 1923–1939.* Ithaca: Cornell University Press, 2001.

Massumi, Brian. *Parables for the Virtual: Movement, Affect, Sensation.* Durham: Duke University Press, 2002.

Michelson, Annette. "The Kinetic Icon in the Work of Mourning: Prolegomena to the Analysis of a Textual System." *October* 52 (Spring 1990): 16–39.
Miller, Jamie. *Soviet Cinema: Politics and Persuasion under Stalin*. London: I. B. Tauris, 2010.
Morton, David. *Sound Recording: The Life Story of a Technology*. Baltimore: Johns Hopkins University Press, 2006.
Mulvey, Laura. *Death 24x a Second: Stillness and the Moving Image*. London: Reaktion Books, 2006.
———. "Visual Pleasure and Narrative Cinema." In *Visual and Other Pleasures*, 14–28. Bloomington: Indiana University Press, 1989.
Murashov, Iurii. "Elektrifitsirovannoe slovo. Radio v sovetskoi literature i kul'ture 1920–30kh godov." In *Sovetskaia vlast' i media*, edited by Hans Günther and Sabine Hänsgen, 17–38. St. Peterburg: Akademicheskii Proekt, 2006.
Murav, Harriet. *Music from a Speeding Train: Jewish Literature in Post-Revolution Russia*. Stanford: Stanford University Press, 2011.
Nichols, Bill. *Representing Reality: Issues and Concepts in Documentary*. Bloomington: Indiana University Press, 1991.
———. *Speaking Truths with Film: Evidence, Ethics, Politics in Documentary*. Berkeley: University of California Press, 2016.
Nisnevich, Anna. "Ear of the Beholder: Listening in Muzykal'naia Istoriia (1940)." In Kaganovsky and Salazkina, *Sound, Speech, Music in Soviet and Post-Soviet Cinema*, 193–211.
Nusinova, N. "'Odna', SSSR (1931)." *Iskusstvo kino* 12 (1991): 162–164.
Ostrovskii, Nikolai. *Kak zakalialas' stal'. Molodaia gvardiia* (1932–1934). Translated as Ostrovsky, Nikolai. *How the Steel Was Tempered*. Translated by R. Prokofieva. Moscow, 1959.
Papazian, Elizabeth Astrid. "Literacy or Legibility: The Trace of Subjectivity in Soviet Socialist Realism." In *The Oxford Handbook of Propaganda Studies*, edited by Jonathan Auerbach and Russ Castronovo, 63–86. Oxford: Oxford University Press, 2013.
———. *Manufacturing Truth: The Documentary Movement in Early Soviet Culture*. DeKalb: Northern Illinois Press, 2009.
Pervyi vsesoiuznyi s"ezd sovetskikh pisatelei: Stenograficheskii otchet. Moscow: Khudozhestvennaia literatura, 1934. Partially translated as Scott, H. G. *Problems of Soviet Literature: Reports and Speeches at the First Soviet Writers' Congress*. Moscow: Cooperative Publishing Society of Foreign Workers in the U.S.S.R., 1935.
Petric, Vlada. "Esther Shub: Film as a Historical Discourse." In *Show Us Life! Toward a History and Aesthetics of the Committed Documentary*, edited by Thomas Waugh, 21–46. London: The Scarecrow Press, Inc., 1984.
Petrov, Petre. *Automatic for the Masses: The Death of the Author and the Birth of Socialist Realism*. Toronto: University of Toronto Press, 2015.
Petrov-Bytov, Pavel. "U nas net sovetskoi kinematografii." *Zhizn' iskusstva* (April 21, 1929). Translated as Petrov-Bytov, Pavel. "We Have No Soviet Cinema." In Taylor and Christie, *The Film Factory*, 259–262.
Piotrovskii, Adrian. "Est' li krizis v sovetskom kino?" *Zhizn' iskusstva* (November 25, 1928): 6–7. Translated as Piotrovsky, Adrian. "Is There a Crisis in Soviet Cinema?" In Taylor and Christie, *The Film Factory*, 239–241.
———. "Kinofikatsiia muzyki." *Zhizn' iskusstva* 9 (1929).
———. "Tonfil'ma." *Zhizn' iskusstva* 30 (1929): 4–5.

Pozner, Valérie. "Shklovskii / Eizenshtein—dvadtsatye gody. Istoriia plodotvornogo ne-ponimaniia." *Kinovedcheskie zapiski* 46 (2000), accessed at http://www.kinozapiski.ru/ru/article/sendvalues/586/.

———. "To Catch Up and Overtake Hollywood: Early Talking Pictures in the Soviet Union." In *Sound, Speech, Music*, edited by Kaganovsky and Salazkina, 60–80. Bloomington: Indiana University Press, 2014.

"Protokol N. 11 otkrytogo partiinogo sobraniia Tsentral'noi studii dokumental'nykh fil'mov ot 14–15 marta 1949 goda." *Iskusstvo kino* 12 (1997): 128–133.

———. "K voprosu zvukovogo nachala v fil'me." *Kino i kul'tura* 5–6 (1929).

Pudovkin, Vsevolod. *Akter v filme*. Leningrad: Gos. Akademiia Iskusstvoznaniia, 1934.

———. *Film Technique and Film Acting*. Translated by Ivor Montagu. New York: Lear, 1949.

———. *Sobranie sochinenii v trekh tomakh*. Moscow: Iskusstvo, 1974–1977.

———. *Vsevolod Pudovkin: Selected Essays*. Edited and translated by Richard Taylor. London: Seagull Books, 2006.

Puti kino. Vsesoiuznoe partiinoe soveshchanie po kinematografii. Edited by B. S. Ol'khovyi. Moscow: Tea-kino-pechat', 1929.

Radek, Karl. "Dve fil'my." *Izvestiia*. (April 23, 1931).

Richards, Rashna Wadia. *Cinematic Flashes: Cinephilia and Classical Hollywood*. Bloomington: University of Indiana Press, 2013.

Riley, John. *Dmitri Shostakovich: A Life in Film*. London: I. B. Taurus, 2005.

Roberts, Graham. "Esfir Shub: A Suitable Case for Treatment." *Historical Journal of Film, Radio and Television* 11, no. 2 (1991): 149–159.

———. *Forward Soviet! History and Non-fiction Film in the USSR*. London: I. B. Tauris, 1999.

Robertson, Robert. *Cinema and the Audiovisual Imagination: Music, Image, Sound*. London: I. B. Tauris, 2015.

Robin, Régine. *Socialist Realism: An Impossible Aesthetic*. Translated by Catherine Porter. Stanford: Stanford University Press, 1992.

Ronnel, Avital. *The Telephone Book: Technology, Schizophrenia, Electric Speech*. Lincoln: University of Nebraska Press, 1989.

Roshal', Lev. *Dziga Vertov*. Moscow: Iskusstvo, 1982.

Roth, Mark. "Some Warners' Musicals and the Spirit of the New Deal." *The Velvet Light Trap* 77 (Winter 1977): 1–7.

Rutherford, Anne. "Cinema and Embodied Affect." *Senses of Cinema* 25 (March 2003), accessed at http://sensesofcinema.com/2003/feature-articles/embodied_affect/.

Ryabchikova, Natalie. "ARRK and the Soviet Transition to Sound." In Kaganovsky and Salazkina, *Sound, Speech, Music*, 81–99.

———. "The Flying Fish: Sergei Eisenstein Abroad, 1929–1932." Ph.D. dissertation, 2016.

Salys, Rimgaila. *The Musical Comedy Films of Grigorii Aleksandrov: Laughing Matters*. Bristol: Intellect Press, 2010.

Sargeant, Amy. *Vsevolod Pudovkin: Classic Films of the Soviet Avant-Garde*. London: I. B. Tauris, 2000.

Savchenko, Igor'. *Kak ia stal rezhisserom*. Moscow, 1946.

———. "Pravo zapet'." *Sovetskoe kino* 5 (1934): 57–61.

Sazhin, Petr. Review of *Enthusiasm*. *Kino-front* (March 1930).

Shcherbenok, Andrei. "'Vzgliani na Lenina, i pechal' tvoia razoidetsia, kak voda.' Estetika travmy v fil'me Dzigi Vertova." In *Travma: Punkty*, edited by Sergei Ushakin and Elena Trubinaia, 704–723. Moscow: Novoe literaturnoe obozreniie, 2009.

Shklovskii, Viktor. "Iskusstvo kak priem." *Sborniki po teorii poeticheskogo iazyka*, 2nd ed., 3–14. Petrograd, 1917.

———. *Za sorok let*. Moscow: Iskusstvo, 1965.
Shub, Esfir'. *Zhizn' moia—kinematograf*. Moscow: Iskusstvo, 1972.
Shumiatskii, Boris. "'A driani podobno 'Garmon'' bol'she ne stavite? . . . 'zapiski besed B. Z. Shumiatskogo s I. V. Stalinym posle kinoprosmotrov. 1934 g." *Kinovedcheskie zapiski* 61 (2002): 281–346.
———. *Kinematografiia millionov: Opyt analiza*. Moscow: Kinofotoizdat, 1935. Partially translated as Boris Shumyatsky, "A Cinema for the Millions." In Taylor and Christie, *The Film Factory*, 358–369.
———. "Tvorcheskie zadachi templana." *Sovetskoe kino* 12 (December 1933): 1–15.
Silverman, Kaja. *The Acoustic Mirror: The Female Voice in Psychoanalysis and Cinema*. Bloomington: Indiana University Press, 1988.
Skvortsov-Stepanov, Ivan. *Elektrifikatsiia RSFSR v sviazi s perekhodnoi fazoi mirovogo khoziaistva*. Moscow: Gosizdat, 1922.
Slezkine, Yuri. "The USSR as a Communal Apartment, Or How a Socialist State Promoted Ethnic Particularism." *Slavic Review* 53, no. 2 (Summer 1994): 414–452.
Slowik, Michael. *After the Silents: Hollywood Film Musicals in the Early Sound Era, 1926–1934*. New York: Columbia University Press, 2014.
Smirnov, Andrey. "Graphical Sounds." http://asmir.info/graphical_sound.htm.
———. *Sound in Z: Experiments in Sound and Electronic Music in Early 20th Century Russia*. London: Koenig Books, 2013.
Smith, Michael G. *Language and Power in the Creation of the USSR, 1917–1953*. Berlin: Mouton de Gruyter, 1998.
Sobchack, Vivian. *The Address of the Eye: A Phenomenology of Film Experience*. Princeton: Princeton University Press, 1992.
Sobolev, R. *Aleksandr Dovzhenko*. Moscow: Iskusstvo, 1980.
Sokolov, I. "Vtoraia programma tonfil'm." *Kino i zhizn'* 27 (October 1930): 11. Translated as Sokolov, I. "The Second Sound Film Programme." In Taylor and Christie, *The Film Factory*, 308–309.
"Sovetskoe kino dolzhno zazvuchat'." *Vecherniaia Moskva* (March 26, 1930): 3; and *Vecherniaia Moskva* (April 2, 1930): 2.
Spadoni, Robert. *Uncanny Bodies: The Coming of Sound Film and the Origins of the Horror Genre*. Berkeley: University of California Press, 2007.
Sponable, E. I. "Historical Development of Sound Films," *Journal of the Society of Motion Picture Engineers*, vol. 48, nos. 4–5 (April/May 1947).
Stalin, I. V. "God velikogo pereloma: k XII godovshchine Oktiabria." *Pravda* (November 3, 1929).
———. "O nedostatkakh partiinoi raboty i merakh likvidatsii trotskistskikh i inykh dvurushnikov." *Pravda* (March 29, 1937).
Stiegler, Bernard. *Technics and Time 2: Disorientation*. Trans. Stephen Barker. Stanford: Stanford University Press, 2009.
Stiegler, Bernd. "When a Photograph of Trees Is Almost like a Crime (Rodchenko, Vertov, Kalatozov)." Trans. James Gussen. *Études photographiques* 23 (May 2009), accessed at: http://etudesphotographiques.revues.org/2668.
Stollery, Martin. "Three Songs About Lenin." *Encyclopedia of the Documentary Film*, edited by Ian Aitken, 1319–1321. New York: Routledge, 2006.
Taylor, Richard. "Boris Shumyatsky and the Soviet Cinema in the 1930s: Ideology as Mass Entertainment." *Historical Journal of Film, Radio and Television* 6, no. 1 (1986): 43–64.
———. "A Cinema for the Millions: Soviet Socialist Realism and the Problem of Film Comedy." *Journal of Contemporary History* 18, no. 3 (July 1983): 439–461.

———. "K topografii utopii v stalinskom miuzikle." In *Sovetskoe bogatstvo*, edited by Marina Balina, Evgeny Dobrenko, and Yury Murashov, 358–370. St. Petersburg: Akademicheskii proekt, 2002.

———. "Singing on the Steppes for Stalin: Ivan Pyr'ev and the Kolkhoz Musical in Soviet Cinema." *Slavic Review* 58, no. 1 (Spring, 1999): 143–159.

Taylor, Richard, and Ian Christie, eds. *The Film Factory: Russian and Soviet Cinema in Documents 1896–1939*. London and New York: Routledge, 1994.

———. *Inside the Film Factory: New Approaches to Russian and Soviet Cinema*. London: Routledge, 1991.

Thompson, Kristin. "Early Sound Counterpoint." *Yale French Studies* 60, Cinema/Sound (1980): 115–140.

Titus, Joan. *The Early Film Music of Dmitry Shostakovich*. Oxford: Oxford University Press, 2016.

Tseitlin, Boris. "Simfoniia Donbassa." *Kino i zhizn'* 14 (May 11, 1930): 19.

Tsekhanovskii, Mikhail. "O zvukovoi risovannoi fil'me." *Kino i zhizn* 34–35 (1930): 14.

Tsivian, Yuri. "Dziga Vertov and the Soviet Avant-Garde." Accessed January 31, 2015. http://hcl.harvard.edu/hfa/films/2008marchapril/soviet.html.

———. *Early Cinema in Russia and its Cultural Reception*. Chicago: The University of Chicago Press, 1991.

———. ed. *Lines of Resistance: Dziga Vertov and the Twenties*. Translated by Julian Graffy. Pordenone: La Giornate del Cinema Muto, 2004.

Tumarkina, Nina. *Lenin Lives! The Lenin Cult in Soviet Russia*. Cambridge, MA: Harvard University Press, 1983.

Turovskaya, Maya. "The 1930s and 1940s: Cinema in Context." In *Stalinism and Soviet Cinema*, edited Richard Taylor and Derek Spring, 34–53. New York: Routledge, 1993.

Uvralov, V. A. and E. N. Shoshkov. *Aleksandr Fedorovich Shorin*. Moscow: Nauka, 2008.

Vertov, Dziga. *Iz naslediia*. 2 Volumes. Moscow: Eisenstein Center, 2004–2008.

———. *Kino-Eye: The Writings of Dziga Vertov*. Edited by Annette Michelson. Translated by Kevin O'Brien. Berkeley: University of California Press, 1985.

———. "Mart Radio-glaza." *Kino i zhizn'* 20 (1930): 14.

———. *Stat'i, dnevniki, zamysly*. Edited by S. Dobrashenko. Moscow: Izd. Iskusstvo, 1966.

———. *Tagebücher—Arbeitshefte*. Edited by Thomas Tode and Alexandra Gramatke. Konstanz: UVK, 2000.

Vladimirtseva, I. N., et al., ed. *20 rezhisserskikh biografii*. Moscow: Iskusstvo, 1971.

Weis, Elisabeth, and John Belton, eds. *Film Sound: Theory and Practice*. New York: Columbia University Press, 1985.

Widdis, Emma. "Making Sense without Speech: The Use of Silence in Early Soviet Sound Film." In *Sound, Speech, Music*, edited by Kaganovsky and Salazkina, 100–118. Bloomington: Indiana University Press, 2014.

———. *Socialist Senses: Film, Feeling and the Soviet Subject*. Bloomington: Indiana University Press, 2017.

———. *Visions of a New Land: Soviet Film from the Revolution to the Second World War*. New Haven: Yale University Press, 2003.

Williams, Alan. "Historical and Theoretical Issues in the Coming of Recorded Sound to the Cinema." In *Sound Theory / Sound Practice*, edited by Rick Altman, 126–137. New York: Routledge, 1992.

Williams, Linda. "Film Bodies: Gender, Genre, and Excess." *Film Quarterly* 44, no. 4 (1991): 2–13.

Winter, Marian Hannah. "The Function of Music in Sound Film." *The Musical Quarterly* 27, no. 2 (April 1941): 146–164.
Wurtzler, Stephen. *Electric Sounds: Technological Change and the Rise of Corporate Mass Media*. New York: Columbia University Press 2008.
Yakubinskii, Lev. "Russkii iazyk v epokhu diktatury proletariata." *Literaturnaia ucheba* 9 (1931): 66–76.
Yampolsky, Mikhail. "Reality at Second Hand." Translated by Derek Spring. *Historical Journal of Film, Radio and Television* 11, no. 2 (1991): 161–171.
Yekelchuk, Serhy. *Stalin's Empire of Memory: Russian Ukrainian Relations in the Soviet Imagination*. Toronto: University of Toronto Press, 2004.
Youngblood, Denise. *Soviet Cinema in the Silent Era, 1918–1935*. Ann Arbor: UMI Research Press, 1985.
Zak, Mark, L. Parfenov, and O. Iakubovich-Iasnyi, eds. *Igor' Savchenko*. Moscow: Iskusstvo, 1959.
Zakharine, Dmitri, and Nils Meise, eds. *Electrified Voices: Medial, Socio-Historical and Cultural Aspects of Voice Transfer*. Göttingen: V & R Press, 2013.
Zizek, Slavoj. *Looking Awry: An Introduction to Jacques Lacan through Popular Culture*. Cambridge, MA: The MIT Press, 1992.
———. *The Sublime Object of Ideology*. London: Verso, 1989.
Zorkaya, Neya. *The Illustrated History of the Soviet Cinema*. New York: Hippocrene Books, 1989.
——— [Zorkaia, Neia]. "'Odna' na perekrestkakh." *Kinovedcheskie zapiski* 74 (2005): 143–158.

INDEX

Page numbers in italics refer to figures.

"About [My] Love for the Living Person" (Vertov article), 202
Abramov, N. P., 199
Accordion, The (Savchenko film), 112–149; accordion in, *113*, 114, 118, 127–128, 130; bodily discipline in, 116, 125, 127, 132–133, 136n22; Bolshevik ear in, *129*, 130; Bolshevik ideology in, 130, 133; chorus in, 117–118; as cinema for the millions, 31–32, 117; collectivization as theme of, 114, 116, 118, 126–128, 132; communists vs. kulaks in, 114, 116, 127–128; debates over genre terminology of, 117; Freudian psychic agencies in, 130–132; vs. Hollywood musicals, 31; ideological mechanisms in, 31–32, 116, 127–128; kulaks in, *115*, 119, *119*, 127–129, *129*, 130–131, 136n22; labor non-mechanized in, *123*; Marusya in, 114, *114*, 125, 127; men with guns in, *128*, *129*; musical/rhythmic structure of, 31, 112–113, 116, 118–120, 123–225, 132–133; music privileged over speech in, 118–120; as operetta, 117–118; plot lines of, 114, 127–128; pulled from Soviet screens, 31, 114, 135n19; revolutionary development in, 32; Russian folk music and dance in, 117–118; Savchenko in/on, 117, 119; Shumyatsky on, 235; Socialist Realism and, 31–32, 130, 134; as Stalinist musical comedy, 31–32, 117; Stalin's disapproval of, 112, 135n18; synchronized sound in, 116; Timosha/Timofei Vasil'evich Dudin in, *113*, 114, 125, 127–128, 130, *131*, 132–133, *132*, 136n30; Tosklivyi in, 127–129, *129*, 136n34; utopia portrayed in, 31–32, 118, 124, 127, 132, 134
acousmêtre. See disembodied voice (*acousmêtre*)

Aduev, Nikolai, 133
Aerograd (Dovzhenko film), 162–172; airplanes in, 154, *171*, 176n49; ambiguities in, 167; characters' ideological positions indicated in, 163; collective farms in, 167; critics'/audiences' responses to, 162, 172; direct address in, 154, 163, 165–167, 169–170, 177n73; Dovzhenko on language in, 171; Dovzhenko's lyrical visual sensibilities in, 163; Dovzhenko's political silence in, 170; Hlushak the guide in, 163, 166–167, *168*, 169–170; Japanese enemies in, 162, *165*, 166–170, *168*; Khudiakov the traitor in, 167, *168*, 169–170, 177n79; Madonna and Child in, *164*; modernity in, 140; musical score of, 166, 169, 176n49, 177n70; New Soviet Man in, *164*; Old Believer in, *165*; plot lines of, 163, 166–167, 169–170; Russian language in, 162; Socialist Realism and, 142; Soviet expansion into the Far East and, 162–167, 169–170; Soviet paranoia reflected in, 162–163; Stalin and, 141, 167; the taiga in, 163–166, 169–170; titles in, 163–165; us vs. them dichotomies in, 165–166; voice of the State privileged over the individual in, 163
Aleksandrov, Grigori: *Circus*, 117, 157; counterpoint dialectical sound advocated by, 14–15; *The Epoch and the Cinema*, 15–16; European sound technology studied abroad by, 13, 34n10, 36n44, 37n57; "The Great Friend of Soviet Cinema," 13, 36n44; *Jolly Fellows*, 29–30, 112, 117, 234–235; montage/sound concepts of, 183; multilingualism in films of, 157; music serving ideology in films of, 134; realistic sound opposed by, 66n19; *The Sentimental*

257

Romance, 15; *Sonny Boy*'s effect on, 15; on Soviet sound film, 15; Stalin and, 36n44. *See also* "Statement on Sound, A"
All-Union Combine of the Movie-Photo Industry. *See* Soiuzkino (Soviet film-industry organization)
All-Union Communist Party of the Bolsheviks, 46
All-Union Congress of Soviet Writers (First, 1934), 28–29, 33n2, 137n57
All-Union Congress on Cinema Affairs (1928), 8, 29, 46, 111, 144
All-Union Creative Conference on Cinema Affairs (1935), 29, 137n57, 234
All-Union Leninist Young Communist League. *See* Komsomol (Young Communist League)
All-Union Party Conference on Collective Farm Shock Workers, 202, 223n60
Alone (Kozintsev and Trauberg film), 40–69; airplane in, 62, 63–64; alarm clock in, 41, 42, 48, 55, 63; answerability demanded in, 48, 50–53, 60–61, *61*, 62, 63, 67n43; dialogue reduced to single line in, 30, 43, 48, 66n25; direct address in, 42–43, *49*; disembodied voice in, 51, 54–55, 67n32, 152; as first Soviet sound film, 30, 40–41, 64, 65n4, 122, 231; horse's flayed skin in, 55, 56, 57, 59, 63; "How Good Life Will Be!" in, 30, 43, *44*, 55, 57–58, 122; ideological content in, 41–42, 47, 51, 53–55, 60–63; internal speech in, 48; intertitles in, 63; Kuzmina in, *49*, 58–59, *61*, 62, 66n25, 122–123, 149; as last silent avant-garde film, 64; Lenin and, 42, 51, 53–54, 62; loudspeakers in, 24, 30–31, 41, 48–54, *49*, 51, 62, 151–152; McDonald on, 240n15; Moskvin as cameraman for, 57–60; plot lines of, 40–41, 48, 51, 53–55; production of, 11, 41, 43, 57–60, 63, 66n25, 68n49, 231; radios in, 30–31, 45; Shostakovich's musical scoring in, 30, 43, 55, 57–58, 64, 68n50, 122; silence used in, 149; sixth reel of, destroyed, 59–60; as Socialist Realist film, 234; sound/image relationships in, 30, 43, 62–64; State power projected in, 40–41, 45–46, 49, 53–56, 57–60, 62–64; subjective camerawork in, 57–61, 68n47; synchronized sound in, 51, 67; as talkie, 240n15; technology privileged over human subjects in, 45, 47, 51, 52, 53, 63;

67n38, 151; telephones/telephone booth in, 30, 42, 45, 51, *52*, 53, 64, 67n38; titles in, 53, 66n25; whiteness in, 55–63, *58*, 69n62
Althusser, Louis, 50, 107n100, 112–113, 116
animated film, 3, 19–21, 38n76, 68n56, 231
Ankara—Heart of Turkey (Yutkevich film), 236
Arnshtam, Lev, 111, 236
ARRK (Association of Workers in Revolutionary Cinematography), 10–11, 28, 38n73, 143
assemblages models, 95–96
Astaire, Fred, 116
"Asynchronism as a Principle of Sound Film" (Pudovkin), 18, 34n11, 37n63
asynchronous sound/music, 18, 32, 75–76, 180
Atlantik (Dupont film), 35n21
"Attempt on Lenin's Life, The" (Pchelin painting), *216*, 217
avant-garde film. *See* Soviet avant-garde film
Avraamov, Arseny, 3, 19–21, *20*, 38n73, 38n76, 174n31

Balázs, Béla, 5, 34n13, 66n21, 154–155
Barker, Jennifer, 31, 81, 92
Barnet, Boris, 4, 156
Barrios, Richard, 108, 120
Battleship Potemkin (Eisenstein film), 37n51, 228
Belgoskino film production organization, 11, 143, 176n61
Belton, John, 65n7
Bely, Andrei, 85
Benjamin, Walter, 110
Bennett, Jane, 94–95
Bentham, Jeremy, 153
Berkeley, Busby, 117
Beskin, Osip, 143
Bezhin Meadow (Eisenstein film), 167
Birkos, Alexander, 231
Blackmail (Hitchcock film), 35n21
Bleiman, Mikhail, 172
Blue Angel, The (von Sternberg film), 15–16
Bogdan Khmelnitsky (Savchenko film), 113
Bogdanov-Berezovsky, Valerian, 110
Bonitzer, Pascal, 204
Bordwell, David, 6
Bourke-White, Margaret, 16
Brik, Osip, 84
British sound film, 6–7, 35n21, 161

"Budushchee zvukovoi fil'my–Zaiavka." See "Statement on Sound, A"
Bukharin, Nikolai, 29
Bulgakowa, Oksana, 83, 181, 194, 213, 217
Burliuk, David, 85
Butler, Judith, 54
Butovsky, Yakov, 65n4

Caché (Haneke film), 71
Case, Theodore, xviii
Cavandish, Philip, 140
Central Committee of the All-Union Communist Party of the Bolsheviks (TsK VKPb), 46
Chapaev (Vasil'ev brothers film), 11, 29, 229, 234–236
Chaplin, Charlie, 67n38, 80
Chion, Michel: on the disembodied voice, 26, 130, 152, 175n42, 175n44, 224n68; on the loudspeaker's all-seeing voice, 152; on the maternal voice, 242n55; opinions on silent film cited by, 1; on silent film, 39n86, 227; vococentrism concept of, 83
Chomentowski, Gabrielle, 143
Chopin, Frédéric, 182, 185, 199, 213
Christie, Ian, 3, 30, 47, 112, 231, 240n15
cinema for the millions, 30, 32–33, 65n5, 112, 117, 229–230, 234–240, 241n30
Cinema for the Millions, A (Shumyatsky book), 30, 32–33, 234–235, 241n30
cinéma vérité film making, 199, 223n49. See also Kinopravda (Vertov newsreel series)
Circus (Aleksandrov film), 117, 157, 176n58
civil war, 29, 139–140, 179, 188, 221n25, 193, 234
Clair, René, 15, 109, 121
Clark, Katerina, 173n9
"Close-Ups in Time" (Pudovkin essay), 17
collective farms (kolkhozy), 112. See also Accordion, The (Savchenko film); Dovzhenko, Alexander; Last Crusaders, The (Dolidze and Shvelidze film); Three Songs of Lenin (Vertov film)
Combined Sound Program No. 1 (sound-film demonstration), 3, 231
Constructivism, 94, 105n50, 191, 196–197, 215
Conveyer Belt of Death, The (Pyr'ev film), 28
Cooper, Hugh, 102
Council of People's Commissars, 46, 135n19
Counterplan (Ermler and Yutkevich film), 88, 155, 229, 236

Crafton, Donald, 6–7, 237–238
"Creative Goals of Thematic Planning" (Shumyatsky tract), 112
Crosland, Alan, 5, 121, 231
Cultural Revolution, 7, 27, 41, 45–46, 156

Dalsky, Dmitry, 22
de Forest, Lee, xviii
de la Roche, Catherine, 231, 233
Deleuze, Gilles, 69n62, 95, 209, 225n82, 227–228
de Man, Paul, 51, 203, 207
Demutsky, Danylo, 140, 149–150, 162, 174n29, 175n38
Demy, Jacques, 137n40
Deserter (Pudovkin film), 16–18, 24, 148–149, 151, 221n20, 236
Dickinson, Thorold, 80
disembodied voice (acousmêtre): characteristics of, 26, 130, 152, 175n42, 222n35; compulsion created by, 68n44; of the documentary filmmaker, 200–201; as a film production commodity, 239; ideological demands of, 53–55, 63; individuals transformed into subjects by, 55–56; life/death relationships altered by, 51, 54, 203; presence in/absence from film, 175n44, 194, 224n68, 228; vs. realistic sound, 67n32; as truth, 51, 204; as voice of God commentary, 107n99, 194, 222n35; as voice of power/ideology, 18, 27, 45, 54, 57, 63, 133, 142, 163, 204, 219, 239; voice-over as partial disembodiment, 67n42. See also Alone (Kozintsev and Trauberg film); Chion, Michel; Enthusiasm: Symphony of the Donbass (Vertov film); Ivan (Dovzhenko film); Lenin, Vladimir; loudspeakers; radio; telephones; Three Songs of Lenin (Vertov film)
Dniepr Hydroelectric Station (Dneprostroi/DneproGES). See Enthusiasm: Symphony of the Donbass (Vertov film); Ivan (Dovzhenko film); K.Sh.E. (Komosomol: Patron of Electrification) (Shub film); Three Songs of Lenin (Vertov film)
documentary film: avant-garde documentaries in, 181; cinéma vérité film making and, 199, 223n49; compilation documentaries, 84, 87; as creative treatment of actuality, 205; developing before feature films, 70–71; disembodied filmmaker's voice in,

200–201; facts replaced by myth in, 217; *Kino-Pravda* (see also *Lenin Kino-Pravda* [*Kino-Pravda #21*; Vertov newsreel]); recording previous events, 205; sound recordings in, 31–32, 70–72, 75–79, 88, 107n86, 179, 199–200; Soviet sound film beginning in, 21; spoken work/speaker's authenticity in, 199–201, *200*, *201*; Stalinist/Social Realist documentaries, 181, 194; time issues in, 205, 207–214, 217–219; Vertov as first to record unrehearsed speech in, 199–201; voice of God narration in, 222n35; voice-overs in, 51, 204. See also *Eleventh Year, The* (Vertov film); *Enthusiasm: Symphony of the Donbass* (Vertov film); *Fall of the Romanov Dynasty* (Shub film); *Great Road, The* (Shub film); *K.Sh.E.* (Komosomol: Patron of Electrification) (Shub film); *Lullaby* (Vertov film); *Maybe Tomorrow* (Dalsky and Snezhinskaya film); *Olympics of the Arts, The* (Erofeev film); *Plan for Great Works, The* (Room film); *Three Songs of Lenin* (Vertov film)

Dolidze, Siko, 32, 106n64, 158–159

Dovzhenko, Alexander: ambiguities in films by, 140, 155, 162–163, 167; authorial voice of, 142; vs. Bolshevism, 139; as cinematic modernist pioneer, 140; as diplomat, 139; *Earth*, 140, 171–172; family expelled from collective farm, 162; human body in films by, 150; as Kiev Film Studio founder, 138; language used by, 171–172; loudspeakers in films by, 24; lyrical visual sensibilities of, 140–142, 163–164; nervous breakdown of, 154; photo of, *146*; *A Poem of the Sea*, 138; political silence of, 170; profile of, 138–141; as a revolutionary filmmaker, 140; *Shchors*, 140–142; silence in sound films of, 146–148; silent films of, 140; as a Socialist Realist, 138, 140, 142; sound film's early impressions on, 144–145; sound film studied abroad by, 145; sound film transitions by, 4, 23; Stalin and, 138, 141–142, 162, 172n1; Tissé as cameraman of, 166; Ukraine and, 32, 138–139, 142; *Ukraine in Flames*, 138; Vertov and, 146; voice of power and, 142; in VUFKU, 139–140, 143; western reception of, 140–41. See also *Aerograd* (Dovzhenko film); *Ivan* (Dovzhenko film)

drawn sound, 19–21, *20*. See also optical sound tracks

Dr. Mabuse (*Gilded Mold*) (Lang film), 87

Drubek-Meyer, Natascha, 119, 125, 132

dubbing, 11–12, 32, 66n25, 89, 142, 144, 173n13

Dunaevsky, Isaak, 134

Ďurovičová, Nataša, 11–12

Dyer, Richard, 118, 124, 161, 166

Earth (Dovzhenko film), 140, 171–172

Earth Thirsts, The (Raizman film), 11, 231

Edison, Thomas, xv, xvii, xviii–xixn1

Ego and the Id, The (Freud), 130

Eikhenbaum, Boris, 46–47, 66n20

Eisenstein, Sergei: *Battleship Potemkin*, 37n51, 228; *Bezhin Meadow*, 167; as contrapuntal theory practitioner, 16; counterpoint dialectical sound advocated by, 14; European sound technology studied abroad by, 13, 34n10, 36n44, 37n57; *General Line*, 158; on *Ivan*, 145; as latecomer to sound film, 4; Mayakovsky's tirade against *October*, 208; montage/sound concepts of, 183; on music in silent films, 108; *October*, 208, 227; Popov congratulated by, 89; realistic sound opposed by, 66n19; *Sentimental Romance, The*, 15; Shub's collaboration with, 87; *Sonny Boy's* effect on, 15; on sound film, 227; sound reproduced visually by, 227; Tissé as cameraman of, 13, 34n10, 36n44, 166; travels abroad, 19, 28; von Sternberg and, 15–16; on watching movies, 47; as writer of film theory and practice, 4–5. See also "Statement on Sound, A"

Eisler, Hans, 1, 37n63

Ekk, Nikolai. See *Road to Life, The* (Ekk film)

Electrification of the Russian Socialist Federated Soviet Republic (Skvortsov-Stepanov book), 98–99

Eleventh Ukrainian Party Congress, 76

Eleventh Year, The (Vertov film), 74, 84, 95–96, 104n19, 107n83, 197

End of St. Petersburg, The (Pudovkin film), 16

Enthusiasm: Symphony of the Donbass (Vertov film), 72–84; *Alone* and, 43, 45; biomechanics in, 82; bodies and machines in, 77; critics'/audiences' responses to, 81–84; din of machinery in,

78; direct sound recorded at its source in, 75, 77–79; disembodied sounds in, 79–80, 83; Dniepr Hydroelectric Station in, 23, 72; film-making as subject in, 89, 90–93; First Five-Year Plan in, 72; among the first Soviet sound films, 43; haptic relationships in, 31, 71, 92; human voice in, 83–84, 93; intertitles lacking in, 197; kino-eye in, 90; *K.Sh.E.* and, 96; London screening of, 80; loudspeakers in, 22, 43, 84, 125; materiality of sound in, 83, 233; mobile energy in, 95–96; music in, 78, 83, 104n25, 109; physical interactions of sounds in, 80; production of, 11, 76–79, 103n14, 232; radio-ear in, 90; radios in, 22, 26, 75; release of, 232; screening difficulties with, 83; vs. Shub's presentation of sound recording, 93; sound as embodied perception mechanism in, 81; sound dominating images in, 79–80; sound editing in, 78; sound experimentation in, 76, 181; sound recording as subject in, 93; sound/spectator physical interactions in, 80–83; sound's physicality in, 72, 80–81; sound/voice hierarchies absent in, 83–84, 93; structure of, 77–78; synchronized sound in, 89; vs. *Three Songs of Lenin*, 181; Timartsev's Mikst camera used in, 77, 104n22; Vertov's defense of, 82; Vertov's personal enthusiasm about, 76; visual sound track of, *91*
Epoch and the Cinema, The (Aleksandrov book), 15–16
Ermler, Fridrikh, 88, 155, 229, 234–235
Erofeev, Vladimir, 89

Fadeev, Aleksandr, 162, 177n65
Fall of the Romanov Dynasty (Shub film), 84, 87
Fanon, Frantz, 161
FEKS (Factory of the Eccentric Actor) (theater/film artists group), 4, 40, 65n2, 110
Feldman, Seth, 103n14, 226n101, 232
Filimonov, Viktor, 229
Fischinger, Oskar, 21
Fisher, Lucy, 79–80
Five-Year Plan (First): Cultural Revolution in, 41, 45–46; in *Enthusiasm*, 72; film production and, 7–9; film's importance to, 45–46; films portraying, 31, 41; industrialization in, 5, 233, 239; in *Ivan*, 161–162; in *K.Sh.E.*, 72, 93; language policies of, 144; Lenin and, 192; vs. nationalism, 144; production films in period of, 23; in *The Return of Nathan Bekker*, 159; *The Road to Life* and, 233
Five-Year Plan (Second), 209, 213
Flaherty, Robert, 223n49
formalism: *Chapaev* as example against, 236; *The Road to Life* and, 229; Shostakovich accused of, 111; Shub accused of, 99, 101; Socialist Realism vs., 27, 46; in Soviet avant-garde film, 27; Soviet sound film vs., 238; Vertov accused of, 82, 181, 197
Foucault, Michel, 116, 153, 169, 175n45
Fox Movietone sound system, xviii, 39n95, 176n48
Fox, William, xviii
France, xviii–xixn1, 6–7, 12, 15, 35n21, 239
Freud, Sigmund, 68n44, 130, 132, 208
futurism (Russian futurism), 23

Gan, Aleksei, 87, 105n50
General Line (Eisenstein film), 158
Gerasimov, Sergei, 43, 55, 60, 65n2, 68n45
Germany: *Atlantik* as first talking feature of, 35n21; commercially driven sound film in, 6; Eisenstein group in, 15–16; Expressionism in, 239; Nazism in, 162, 167; sound film in, 2, 6–7, 10, 21; Tobias-Klangfilm company of, 7, 36n27
Glinsky, Albert, 98
Godard, Jean-Luc, 218
GOELRO (State Electrification commission), 96, 97, 98
Gomery, Douglas, 6–7, 35n23
Gorki (place of Lenin's death). See *Three Songs of Lenin* (Vertov film)
Gorky, Maxim, 29, 151, 238
Gosinprom Gruzii (Georgian film production organization), 143–144, 158–159
Goskino (Soviet State Cinema), 87
gramophones, 22, 26, 109–110, 152, 199. See also *K.Sh.E.* (Komosomol: Patron of Electrification) (Shub film)
Gramsci, Antonio, 116
"Great Friend of Soviet Cinema, The" (Aleksandrov article), 13, 36n44
Great Road, The (Shub film), 87, 99
Great Turn/Turning Point, 5. See also Soviet film industry
Gres, S., 109–110, 135n4

Grieg, Edvard, 122
Grierson, John, 205
Gruziia film production studio, 11, 158
Guattari, Felix, 95
Gukasian, F. G., 57–58

Haneke, Michael, 71
Hänsgen, Sabine, 23
haptic film theory and criticism, 71–72, 81. See also *Enthusiasm: Symphony of the Donbass* (Vertov film); *Ivan* (Dovzhenko film); *K.Sh.E.* (Komosomol: Patron of Electrification) (Shub film)
Heath, Stephen, 133–134, 218
Hicks, Jeremy, 79, 89, 104n30, 197–198
Hitchcock, Alfred, 35n21
Hollywood/United States transition to sound film: *The Accordion* vs., 31; advertisement for, *xvi*; automatic sound perception in, 14, 37n48; background music vs. sound synchronization in, 65n7; commercial uses of, xviii, 4, 6, 13, 240; de Forest credited with, xviii; dominance of, 33, 35n17; early sound-film developments in, xv–xix, *xvi*; Edison and, xv, xvii, xviii–xixn1; and electrical industry development, 6; first demonstration of, xv, xvii; Fox Movietone in, xviii; gangster films of, 117; human voice privileged in, 22; ideology in, 116–117; independent development of, 10; *The Jazz Singer* as first talking feature, xviii; language issues in, 11; musicals in, 116–118, 120–121, 123, 137n44; optical sound track system in, xviii; patents for, xvii–xviii; Phonofilm sound system and, xviii; reactions against, xvii–xviii, 14, 37n51, 237; sound becoming unobtrusive in, 237; sound cameras developed for, xviii; vs. sound development elsewhere, 239–240; sound's functions in, 6, 237; speech liberation as body repression in, 240; stock market crash and, 7, 35n24; as talkies, 7, 14; in transition, 6–7, 31, 35n23, 237, 239–240; Tykocinski-Tykociner as inventor of, xv, xviii; at the University of Illinois, xv, xviii; utopia portrayed in, 118; Vitaphone sound system in, xviii

Honegger, Arthur, 108
Horsemen (Savchenko film), 113
"How Good Life Will Be!" (Shostakovich song). See *Alone*

Hubbert, Julie, 108, 121–122
Hugon, André, 35n21
Hydrocentral (Shaginian book), 93–94

Ibarruri Gomez, Isodora Dolores, 179, 188, 221n25
ideology. See *Accordion, The* (Savchenko film); *Aerograd* (Dovzhenko film); Aleksandrov, Grigori; *Alone* (Kozintsev and Trauberg film); disembodied voice (*acousmêtre*); Dovzhenko, Alexander; Eisenstein, Sergei; Hollywood/United States transition to sound film; Komsomol (Young Communist League); *K.Sh.E.* (Komosomol: Patron of Electrification) (Shub film); Lenin, Vladimir; loudspeakers; *Lullaby*; multilingualism; Pudovkin, Vsevolod; Pyr'ev, *Ivan* (Dovzhenko film); radios; Shub, Esfir; Shumyatsky, Boris; Socialist Realism; Soviet film industry; Stalin, Joseph; telephones; *Three Songs of Lenin* (Vertov film); Vertov, Dziga
"Ideology and Ideological State Apparatuses" (Althusser essay), 50
Iezuitov, Nikolai, 17
indigenization of non-Russian populations, 156, 174n20
internal speech/monologues, 30, 46–48, 228
Internationale, the, 174n31, 182
"In the Hall of the Mountain King" (Grieg musical composition), 122
ISA (Ideological State Apparatus), 31–32, 50, 116, 127–128, 238. See also Althusser, Louis
Iskusstvo kino (Soviet film journal), 141–142, 202
Italian Fascism, 162, 167
Italian sound film, 6, 11–12, 35n21
Ivan (Dovzhenko film), 144–157, 161–164; airplanes in, 154, 176n49; ambiguities in, 155, 162–163; compositional simplicity of, 145; construction site ballet in, *150*; contrapuntal sound in, 151; critics'/audiences' responses to, 154–155, 161–162, 172; cuts made to, 155; direct address in, 154; disciplinary power in, 153; Dniepr Hydroelectric Station in, 23, 145–146, 149–150, *149*, 155, 161, 175n38; Eisenstein's praise of, 145; female chorus in, 145–146, 164; First Five-Year Plan in, 161–162; haptic relationships in, 150; Huba the shirker in,

151, 152, 153, 167; human body in, 149–151, 149, 150; industrial sounds in, 146–148; Komsomol in, 154; language issues in, 32; loudspeakers in, 24, 151–154, 153; lyrical visual sensibilities in, 140–142; modernity in, 140; montage slowed in, 145, 150; mother's grief in, 148, 149, 151; multilingualism in, 154; musical score in, 152; plot lines of, 145, 147–148, 147, 148, 151–154; production of, 145–146, 146; propaganda in, 172; radios in, 151, 154; screenings of, 155; Shumyatsky on, 234–237; silence used in, 146–148, 151; as silent film with sound effects, 240n15; Socialist Realism and, 142, 154, 234; sonorous landscape in, 145–146; telephones in, 165; Ukraine and, 145–146, 155–156, 161–162, 165, 170, 176n52; unheroic hero of, 145; voice/body privileged over technology in, 149–151, 175n39; voices competing in, 154; worker's death in, 147, 149–151

Ivanov, N. See *Three Songs of Lenin* (Vertov film)

Izvolov, Nikolai, 19–21, 194–195, 222n40

Japanese film, 3–4, 33n5
Japanese Imperialism, 162, 167. See also *Aerograd* (Dovzhenko film)
Jazz Singer, The (Crosland film), xviii, 5, 7, 14, 121, 124, 231
Jolly Fellows (Aleksandrov film), 29–30, 112, 117, 234–235
Jolson, Al, 14–15, 88, 121, 124

Kalinak, Katheryn, 221n20
Kalinin, Mikhail, 102
Kaplan, Fanya. See *Three Songs of Lenin* (Vertov film)
Kaufman, Mikhail, 87
Kenez, Peter, 1–2, 167
Kepley, Vance, Jr., 8–9, 139, 143–144, 177n73
Kheifits, Iosif, 156–157
Khersonsky, Khrisanf, 117, 120, 125
Khlebnikov, Velimir, 85
Khudozhestvennyi sound theater (Moscow), 3, 231
Kiev Film Studio, 138
Kino: A History of the Russian and Soviet Film (Leyda), 231
kino-eye (Vertov concept), 74–75, 90, 184, 202, 208, 217–219
Kino-Eye (Vertov film), 85, 136n22, 197, 219

Kino-Eye: The Writings of Dziga Vertov (Michelson, ed.), 220 (in note on sources)
kinoks (Vertov's film-production crew), 74–78, 191
Kinonedelia (Vertov film journal), 195
Kinopravda (Vertov newsreel series), 73, 195, 197. See also *Lenin Kino-Pravda* (*Kino-Pravda #21*; Vertov newsreel)
Kirov, Sergey, 141–142, 162, 177n66
Kokhno, Leonid, 174n29, 175n38
Kolli, Nikolai, 97
Komsomol (Young Communist League): in *The Accordion*, 128; establishment of, 135n20; film conferences organized by, 45–46; film industry centralization and, 28; in *Ivan*, 154; *K.Sh.E.* and, 88, 95, 99–100, 102; Zharov as member of, 31, 135n20
"Komsomol'skaia" (Mayakovsky poem), 224n64
Kopalin, Ilya, 179
korenizatsiia (indigenization), 156, 174n20
Kostiuk, Hryhory, 172
Kovalsky, Konstantin, 91–92, 102
Kozintsev, Grigori: among FEKS founders, 65n2; as first Soviet sound film-maker, 30; loudspeakers in films by, 24; Moskvin as cameraman for, 57; *New Babylon*, 43, 110; as Socialist Realist, 69n63; transitioning to sound, 4, 41; Vachnadze and, 106n64; *The Youth of Maxim*, 229. See also *Alone*
Kruchenykh, Aleksei, 23
Krupskaya, Nadezhda, 53
Kryzhitsky, Leonid, 65n2
Krzhizhanovsky, Gleb, 97
K.Sh.E. (Komsomol: Patron of Electrification) (Shub film): assemblage in, 96; critics'/audience's responses to, 99, 101; direct voice recording in, 93; Dniepr Hydroelectric Station in, 23, 31, 72, 88, 94–98, 101–102; electrical energy as subject of, 92–103, 97, 100; *Enthusiasm* and, 96; film/world interactions in, 94–96; First Five-Year Plan in, 72, 93; gramophones in, 88, 93; haptic relationships in, 31, 71, 102; human voice privileged in, 93; individual/collective interactions in, 96; invisible made visible in, 102; Komsomol in, 157–158; Lenin in, 94; lightbulbs in, 100, 101–102; matter-movement and matter-energy in, 96; montage in, 94, 96, 99, 103; multilingualism in, 157; music in, 89–93,

98–99, 101, 103, 105n60; objects speaking for themselves in, 87; organic relationships in, 94–96, 99, 101; radio broadcasts in, 26; Shaginian in, 93–94, 101; Shub on, 88, 99, 101; sound/image relationships in, 72, 94, 101; sound/spectator physical interactions in, 92; sound synchronization in, 89, 93, 101; Stalin in, 101; synchronized sound in, 88–91, 93–94, 99, 101, 103; telephones/telephone operators in, 93; theremin in, *90*, 91–93, 98

Kujundzic, Dragan, 208

Kuleshov, Lev, 87, 194

Lang, Fritz, 87, 121–122

Last Crusaders, The (Dolidze and Shvelidze film), 32, 158–159, 162

Lastra, James, 6

Lemberg, Aleksandr, 72–73

"Lenin calendar" (Vertov newsreel), 192

Lenin in October (Romm film), 12

"Lenin Is Alive in the Heart of the Peasant" (*Kino-Pravda #22*; Vertov newsreel), 192

Lenin Kino-Pravda (*Kino-Pravda #21*; Vertov newsreel): Ivanov in, *214*, 215; "Lenin calendar" and, 192; Lenin in motion in, 211; "Lenin Is Alive in the Heart of the Peasant" and, 192; Lenin's death as subject of, 202, 208–209; Lenin's funeral in, 188, 206, 211, 213, 219; Lenin's obituary in, 68n56; monument marking Lenin's assassination attempt in, *216*; titles in, *214*, *215*, 226n94. See also *Three Songs of Lenin* (Vertov film)

Lenin, Vladimir: chart announcing vital signs of, 68n56; on communism as electrified Soviet power, *97*, 98–99; cult of, 180, 209, 225n85; "The Death of Lenin" (Rodchenko photomontage), 196; disembodied voice of, 32, 51, 54, 66n27, 182, 199; electrical power and, 94, 98–99; in GOLERO Plan poster, *97*; "The Great Pupil of the Great Lenin, Stalin, Has Led Us to Battle" (*Three Songs of Lenin* film), 193; "Lenin calendar," 192; "Lenin Is Alive in the Heart of the Peasant," 192; mausoleum of, 91, 94, 195; photos of, *187*, *190*; *prizyv* (calls to action by), 42, 48, 51, 65n9, 195, 203; returning from exile, xvii, xixn3; Stalin vs., 225n85; theremin and, 98; Vertov's various documents on, 192; "Vladimir Ilych Lenin," 51; voice of, recorded, 192. See also *Alone* (Kozintsev and Trauberg film); *Three Songs of Lenin* (Vertov film)

Leyda, Jay, 1, 13, 28, 34n11, 231–232

Liber, George, 139, 155–156

Lieutenant Kizhe (Prokofiev film score), 236

Life Is Good! (*A Simple Case*) (Pudovkin film), 16–18, *16*, 37n59

Lorre, Peter, 121–122

loudspeakers: answerability demands of, 50; as content in sound film, 22, 24, 26–27, 48–55, *49*; disembodied voice from, 26–27; in *Ivan*, 151; in "Press stand with Radio-speaker," *25*; in sound film projection, xviii, 20–21; State ideology broadcast through, 26–27; in *Stride, Soviet!* 70; visible made audible by, 228; voice of authority projected by, 151–55. See also *Alone* (Kozintsev and Trauberg film); *Enthusiasm: Symphony of the Donbass* (Vertov film); non-human sounds/voices;

Love for Three Oranges, The (Prokofiev musical composition), 3, 231

Lovell, Stephen, 24, 39n87, 151

Lullaby (Vertov film): censored, 226n101; childhood/motherhood themes in, 186; Stalinist ideology in, 182, 233; sync-sound interviews in, 199, 202; as Vertov's first sound film, 219

Lumière brothers, 39n86, 238

Lunacharsky, Anatoly, 3, 144, 231, 232

M (Lang film), 121–122

Macheret, Aleksandr, 23–24, 45, 157, 159

MacKay, John, 90, 95–96, 104n22, 179, 220n9, 222n41

Malitsky, Joshua, 90, 92–93, 99, 106n65, 242n49

Man with a Movie Camera (Vertov film), 90, 182, 209, 219. See also *Three Songs of Lenin* (Vertov film)

March (Prokofiev musical composition), 3, 231

"March of the Shock Workers" (Shaporin musical composition), 182

Marconi, Gugliemo, xv

Margolit, Evgeny, 21–22, 24, 71, 136n30, 156–157, 229

Mariamov, Alexander, 163

Marks, Laura, 71

Martin, Terry, 174n20
materiality of sound, 70–109
Mayakovsky, Vladimir, 28, 51, 65n2, 85, 208, 224n64
Maybe Tomorrow (Dalsky and Snezhinskaya film), 22
McDonald, Dwight, 231, 240n15
McLaren, Norman, 19, 21
media sensitive viewer, 238
"Melody for a Street Organ" (Muratova film), 71–72
Men and Jobs (Macheret film), 23–24, 45, 157, 159
Meyerhold, Vsevolod, 65n2, 85
Mezhrabpom–fil'm (Mezhrabpom-Rus') studio, 143, 192, 222n29, 240n8
Michelson, Annette, 220 (in note on sources)
Mikhoels, Solomon, 160, 176n61
Milman, Mark, 32, 159
Mitry, Jean, 1, 227
Modern Times (Chaplin film), 67n38
Molotov, Vyacheslav, 135n19, 141–142
montage film-making: in *The Accordion*, 125; of Eisenstein, 183, 194; end of, 1; in *K.Sh.E.*, 87, 96, 99, 103; Kuleshov's theories of, 194; music as montage in, 125, 221n20; of Pudovkin, 183, 194, 221n20; in silent films, 5; sound as counterpoint dialectic in, 13–27; sound film vs., 3, 15, 45, 88–89; in Soviet sound film, 109; in *Three Songs of Lenin*, 182; of Vertov, 74, 77–78, 84, 96, 194; viewer's role in, 47
Moscow Sound Factory, 11, 90, 106n63
Mosfilm production organization, 106n63, 139, 142, 162, 173n12
Moskvin, Andrei, 57–58, 60, 64, 65n2, 68n49, 68n60
Mother (Pudovkin film), 16
movement of energy, 90, 92, 95–96, 99, 103, 106n65, 210
multilingualism, 18, 155–162, 165–67. See also *Ivan* (Dovzhenko film)
Mulvey, Laura, 123–124, 207–208, 242n49
Muratova, Kira, 71–72, 101
musicals as film genre, 29–31, 108, 137n40, 137n44. See also *Accordion, The* (Savchenko film); Hollywood/United States sound film
music in sound film (general): as accompaniment to images, 4, 30, 37n51, 39n86;

Clair on, 109; extraneous sounds mixed into, 78; in film-sound hierarchy, 22; industrialization of, 109–110; in *M*, 122; mechanical recording and, 109–110; moods created by, 108; music as asynchronous element in, 18; music recorded on separate tracks in, 12; performerless music, 19; synchronized sound and, 110; unified with images, 108
music in Soviet sound film, 108–137; as accompaniment to images, 108; industrialization of, 109; intelligibility of, 110–111; justification for, 124–125; as montage, 109, 125, 221n20; Shumyatsky on, 236–237; technical developments in, 19–21, 30. See also *Accordion, The* (Savchenko film); *Aerograd* (Dovzhenko film); *Enthusiasm: Symphony of the Donbass* (Vertov film); *Ivan* (Dovzhenko film); *K.Sh.E.* (Komosomol: Patron of Electrification) (Shub film); *New Babylon*; Popov, Gavril; Prokofiev, Sergei; Rimsky-Korsakov, Georgy; *Road to Life, The* (Ekk film); Shaporin, Yuri; Sholpo, Evgeny; Shostakovich, Dmitri; theremin; *Three Songs of Lenin* (Vertov film); Timofeev, Nikolai; Wagner, Richard
My Native Land (Kheifits and Zarkhi film), 156, 159

Narkompros (People's Commissariat of Education), 49, 51–52, 58–59, 67n37, 85, 144
New Babylon (Kozintsev and Trauberg film), 43, 110–111
New Deal (Roosevelt-era economic initiative), 116–117
New Economic Policy (NEP), 8, 35n15, 143–144, 233
Nichols, Bill, 70, 102, 107n99, 199–200, 205, 218, 222n35
NIKFI (Cinema-Photo Research Institute), 12, 173n13
Nisnevich, Anna, 134
non-fiction film. See documentary film
non-human sounds/voices, 22, 24, 26–27, 84, 151. See also disembodied voice (*acousmêtre*)

October (Eisenstein film), 208, 227
October/Russian Revolution, xvii, xixn3, 35n15, 66n27, 139–140, 174n31

ODSK (Society of Friends of Soviet Cinema), 28, 45–46
Olympics of the Arts, The (Erofeev film), 89
optical sound tracks, xviii, 81, 91–92. *See also* drawn sound
Oram, Daphne, 21
organicity/organicist models, 94–96, 173n9
"Origin of the Hero, The" (Margolit and Filimonov article), 229
Outskirts, The (Barnet film), 156
Overcoat, The (Kozintsev and Trauberg film), 57–58

Papazian, Elizabeth, 182, 217
Partisans in the Ukrainian Steppes (Savchenko film), 113
The Party Card (Pyr'ev film), 167
Pchelin, Vladimir, 216, 217
The Peasants (Ermler film), 234–235
Peer Gynt Suite No. 1 (Grieg musical composition), 122
Petrov-Bytov, Pavel, 111–112
Pfenninger, Rudolf, 21
Phonofilm (de Forest/Case sound system), xviii
phonographs, xv, xviii–xixn1, 6, 26, 101–102, 125, 175n42, 198
Pilots, The (Raizman film), 234
"Pine Trees in Pushkino" (Rodchenko photo series), 225n88
Piotrovsky, Adrian, 14, 22–23, 109
Piskator, E., 236
Plan for Great Works, The (Room film), 3, 13, 19, 76, 104n19, 231
Popov, Gavril, 89–91, 101, 103, 105n60, 236
"Press stand with Radio-Speaker" (Rodchenko photo), 25
prizyv (a call to arms/action), 48, 50–51, 54, 63, 65n9, 66n27. *See also* Lenin, Vladimir
"Problem of Cinema Stylistics" (Eikhenbaum essay), 46–47
Prokofiev, Sergei, 3, 231, 236
public address media/technologies. *See* loudspeakers; radio (general); radio in Soviet cinema
Pudovkin, Vsevolod: "Asynchronism as a Principle of Sound Film," 18; contrapuntal sound advocate and, 14, 16–18; *The End of St. Petersburg*, 16; European sound technology studied abroad by, 37n57; loudspeakers in films by, 24; montage/sound concepts of, 183; *Mother*, 16; music as montage in films by, 221n20; photo of, 16; realistic sound opposed by, 66n19; silence in sound films of, 148–149; sound/image relationships in, 63–64; on Soviet's sound-theory advancement over the West, 18; transitioning to sound, 4; as writer of film theory and practice, 4–5. *See also Deserter; Life Is Very Good!;* "A Statement on Sound"
Pumpianskaia, Semiramida, 179
Pushkin, Alexander, 182
Pyr'ev, Ivan, 12, 28, 134, 167

Queen's Necklace, The (Lekain and Ravel film), 35n21

Radek, Karl, 29, 82
radio (general), xv–xvii, 6, 9–10
radio (in Soviet cinema): as content in sound film, 22; disembodied voice from, 26–27, 154; music in, 109; State ideology broadcast through, 26–27; voice of authority projected by, 151–52. *See also Alone* (Kozintsev and Trauberg film); *Enthusiasm: Symphony of the Donbass* (Vertov film); *Ivan* (Dovzhenko film)
Raizman, Yuli, 11, 234
RAPP (Russian Association of Proletarian Writers), 178, 181
Return of Nathan Bekker, The (Shpis and Milman), 32, 159–162, 159, 160, 176n61
Revolt of the Fishermen (Piskator film), 236
Richards, Rashna Wedia, 39n95, 65n7
Rich Bride, The (Pyr'ev film), 12
"Right to Sing, The" (Savchenko article), 124–125
Riley, John, 37n51, 43, 66n19
Rimsky-Korsakov, Georgy, 3, 21
Road to Life, The (Ekk film): as all-Soviet production, 232; critics'/audiences' responses to, 229–233; First Five-Year Plan and, 233; among first Soviet sound films, 11, 43, 103n14, 231–232; as first Soviet talking feature, 4, 26, 32–33, 122, 156, 230, 231–234; vs. formalism, 229; Mari language in, 156; materiality of sound in, 233; music in, 122; Mustafa the thief in, 156; radios in, 26; Socialist Realism and, 229, 234; synchronized sound in, 229–230, 233, 240n13; Tager sound camera and, 11; titles used in, 233; U. S. distribution of, 230–232
Roberts, Graham, 226n101

Robertson, Robert, 185
Rodchenko, Alexander, 25, 85, 105n50, 195, 195, 196, 197, 225n88, 228
Rogers, Ginger, 116
Romm, Mikhail, 12
Ronnel, Avital, 48, 50
Room, Abram, 3, 13, 19, 76, 104n19, 231
Roshal, Lev, 76, 206–207, 213
Roth, Mark, 116–117
Rouch, Jean, 223n49
Russia of Nicholas II and Lev Tolstoy, The (Shub film), 87

Sargeant, Amy, 17
Savchenko, Igor, 31, 113, 124–125, 134. See also *The Accordion* (Savchenko film)
Sazhin, Petr, 81
Sentimental Romance, The (Aleksandrov and Eisenstein film), 15
Shadr, Ivan (pseudonym for I. Ivanov), 209–210
Shaginian, Marietta, 93–94, 101–102
Shaporin, Yuri, 182, 185, 199, 221n20, 236
Shaw, George Bernard, 154, 176n48
Shcherbenok, Andrei, 203
Shchors (Dovzhenko film), 140–142
Shchors, Nikolai, 139
Shklovsky, Viktor, 37n48, 84, 140
Shkurat, Stepan, 151, 152, 167–168
Sholpo, Evgeny, 19, 21, 38n76
Shorin, Alexander: Central Laboratory of Wire Communication and, 19; foreign technological mistakes avoided by, 13; optical sound track patterns of, 94; sound camera of, 2, 3, 9, 11, 76, 106n65, 231; Vertov's collaboration with, 76; *Women from Ryazan* and, 3, 231
Shostakovich, Dmitri, 30, 43, 64, 65n2, 68n50, 110–111, 221n20, 236
Shpis, Boris, 32, 159
Shub, Esfir: as editor, 87; Eisenstein's collaboration with, 87; documentary authenticity in films of, 84–85; *The Fall of the Romanov Dynasty*, 87; as first compilation documentarian, 84; as first user of sync-sound in the USSR, 93; *The Great Road*, 87, 99; in *K.Sh.E.*, 94, 96; on mastering sound in film, 88; as montage expert, 87, 96; as objective documentarian, 72; photos of, 85, 86; profile of, 85, 87; radio in films by, 26; *The Russia of Nicholas II and Lev Tolstoy*, 84–85, 87;

sound film's early impressions on, 88, 144; *Today*, 95; Vertov's friendship with, 84, 87. See also *K.Sh.E.* (Komosomol: Patron of Electrification) (Shub film)
Shumyatsky, Boris: on *The Accordion* as musical operetta, 117; *The Accordion* pulled from screens by, 135n19; arrest and execution of, 241n24; Bolshevik ideology of, 29, 112; *A Cinema for the Millions*, 229–230; cinema for the millions, concept of, 30, 32–33, 65n5, 234; "Creative Goals of Thematic Planning," 112; film genres stressed by, 112; sound/image unity demanded by, 237; Soviet film industrialization overseen by, 233; as Soviet film industry commissar, 27–29, 46, 112, 233
Shvelidze, Vakhtang, 32, 106n64, 158–159
silent film (general): bodily emphasis in, 133; characteristics of, 5; deafness of, 1, 26, 39n86, 227; as Great Silent/Mute film, 45, 110, 144–145; images in vs. talking images, 228; as an international language, 142–143; *The Jazz Singer* as the end of, 121; as noiseless vs. silent, 227; silence as integral to, 5; silent/sound divide, 42, 64; sound as accompaniment to, 227, 238–239; sound film fulfilling the promises of, 227; speech acquisition and, 110; titles in, 39n86. See also Soviet sound film
Simba (Hurst film), 161, 166
Simonov, Evgenii, 233
Simple Case, A (Pudovkin). See *Life is Very Good!*
Singing Fool, The (Jolson singing in), 88
Singin' in the Rain (Donon and Kelly film), 7
Sixth Part of the World, A (Vertov film), 74, 191
Skin of the Film, The (Marks book), 71
Skvortsov-Stepanov, Ivan, 98
Smirnov, Andrey, 2–3, 19–20
Snezhinskaya, Liudmila, 22
Sobolev, Ramil, 146, 175n39
Socialist Realism: avant-garde film-making and, 21, 27–33; characteristics of, 29, 33n2; cinema for the millions as principle of, 112, 234–240, 241n30; Dovzhenko and, 138; vs. formalism, 27, 46; hero-driven films in, 229; ideological demands of, 239–240; Kozintsev and Trauberg and, 69n63; in literature, 29; as official Soviet art doctrine, 1, 27–28, 33n2, 134, 137n57, 238, 240; principles of, established,

234; Socialist Realist sound, 227–242; Soviet sound film development slowed by, 19; State power voiced through, 5–6, 21, 24, 33, 154; synchronized sound and the advent of, 134; transition to, 4–6; as utopian, 134; Vertov conforming to, 197. See also *Accordion, The* (Savchenko film); *Aerograd* (Dovzhenko film); *Alone* (Kozintsev and Trauberg film); *Chapaev* (Vasil'ev brothers film); Dovzhenko, Alexander; Ekk, Nikolai; *Jolly Fellows* (Aleksndrov film); *Road to Life, The* (Ekk film); Shumyatsky, Boris

Soiuzkino (Soviet film-industry organization): foreign technical advice solicited by, 9; language issues in, 144; and the Moscow Sound factory, 106n63; as oversight authority, 9; in possession of Shorin's sound camera, 76; renamed, 173n11; silent to sound transition overseen by, 144; Sovkino replaced by, 28, 45–46, 144

Sokolov, Ippolit, 27

Solntseva, Yulia, 138, 155

Sonny Boy (Mayo film), 15

Sovetskoe kino (Soviet film journal), 28, 143

Soviet avant-garde film: *Alone* as last example of, 64; cinema for the millions and, 111–112; documentaries as, 181; early sound developments in, 2–3; end of, 1, 30, 234, 239; formalism in, 27; Golden Age of, 1, 6; materiality of, 71; Socialist Realism vs., 21, 27–33; Soviet film industry and, 227; *Three Songs of Lenin* and, 181, 220n9; Vertov's titles and, 227; vs. Western commercial constraints, 4

"Soviet Cinema: Making Sense of Sound" (Christie essay), 3

Soviet film industry: antisemitism in, 181; backwardness of, 1–4, 7–8; bureaucratization of, 9; censorship in, 27–28; centralization of, 5, 8–9, 27–28, 144, 234, 239–240; cinema for the millions and, 8–9, 111–112; Great Turning Point and, 5, 8, 35n15, 47; ideological nature of, 45, 47; industrialization of, 5, 41, 232–233, 239–240; as national in form but socialist in content, 143, 156, 173n18; native production industry lacking in, 7; under NEP, 8; production organizations in, 11–12, 143, 173n17; purges in, 12, 45–46; Socialist Realism in, 27–33, 45; transitioning from avant-garde film, 45; US/European developments vs., 2, 4; Vertov ostracized from, 181. See also Cultural Revolution; Shumyatsky, Boris; Soiuzkino (Soviet film-industry organization); Sovkino (Soviet film-industry organization)

Soviet film journals, 14, 28, 109–111, 141–143, 195, 202

Soviet silent film: as deaf, 26; Dovzhenko and, 138; end of, 13, 64, 234; as Great Silent/Mute, 45, 110; internal speech in, 46–47; silent versions of sound films, 13, 30 (see also *Three Songs of Lenin* [Vertov film]); vs. sound film, 2, 46–47. See also silent film (general)

Soviet sound film (general): counterpoint dialectics in, 13–27, 30–31, 66n19; silence in, 18, 23–24; vs. Stalinism, 239; State power voiced through, 30–31

Soviet sound film (as new apparatus): as alternative future, 30, 39n95; audiences trained in watching, 133; as cinema for the millions, 30, 32–33, 65n5, 112, 117, 234; direct address in, 42–43, 47, 49; documentary films as beginning of, 21, 71; vs. formalism, 238; homogenous thinking subject in, 130–134; industrial content of, 109; language issues in, 32, 143; montage in, 109; multilingualism in, 154–162; music privileged over speech in, 118–120; *Road to Life* as first talking film, 26; silent/sound divide in, 42, 64, 178–226; simultaneity of speech and sound in, 110; State ideologies resisted in, 238–239; as utopian, 134; utopia portrayed in, 118; visible made audible in, 228; as the voice of ideology, 238. See also disembodied voice (*acousmètre*); music in sound films (general); Socialist Realism; synchronized sound

Soviet sound film (transition to), 1–40; active vs. passive approaches to, 13–14; alternative future for, 30, 39n95; Avraamov's hand-drawn music tracks, 19–21, 20; counterpoint dialectics to images in, 14; as a crisis, 239; equipment lacking in, 11; facial expressions augmented in, 5, 34n13; feelings generated by sound in, 14, 37n49; home-grown nature of, 9–10; independent development of, 10; industrial content of, 8, 23–24; language issues in, 11–12; late development of, 7–9, 13, 18, 19; materiality and texture of sound, 14; as montage counterpoint, 14; non-human sound in, 21–24, 26–27; radio in, 22–24, 26, 30, 39n87; reactions against, 46–47, 66n19, 66n21, 237; as revolution in film-making, 5; silence used in, 18, 23–24, 146–149; silent versions of, 13; Socialist Realism's development and, 237–238; sound experimentation in, 13; Soviet cultural chaos and, 1, 5, 9, 12–13; State power voiced through, 5, 12, 24, 26; technological innovations in, 13, 19; theory leading practice in, 18–19; as turning point in Soviet film history, 3; vs. Western films and film production, 9, 14. *See also* music in Soviet sound film

Sovkino (Soviet film-industry organization), 3, 8, 11, 27–28, 45–46, 143–144

Spadoni, Robert, 238

Speaking Truths with Film (Nichols book), 102

Sponable, E. I., xviii

Staiger, Janet, 6

Stalin, Joseph: *The Accordion* and, 31–32, 112, 117, 135n18; *Aerograd* and, 141, 167; Aleksandrov and, 36n44; *Chapaev* and, 29; *Cinema for the Millions* and, 30; Dovzhenko and, 138, 141–142, 162, 172n1; film industry centralization by, 5; Great Family and, 173n9; in *K.Sh.E.*, 101; vs. Lenin, 225n85; light films preferred by, 112; repression by, 167, 176n64; sound film's importance to, 13. *See also* Five-Year Plan (First); *Three Songs of Lenin* (Vertov film)

"Statement on Sound, A" (Eisenstein, Pudovkin, Aleksandrov manifesto), 13–15, 34n11, 37n51, 66n19, 75, 89, 221n20, 236–237

Stiegler, Bernard, 178, 225n88

stock market crash (1929), 7, 34n10, 35n24, 116

Stollery, Martin, 181

Stride, Soviet! (Vertov film), 70, 99, 197, 203

subtitles, 12, 39, 39n86. *See also* titles (intertitles)

Svilova, Elizaveta, 74, 179, 192, 198, 205, 211

"Symphony of the Sirens" (Avraamov musical composition), 146

synchronized sound (sync-sound): in *The Accordion*, 113, 116; vs. background sound in silent films, 65n7; disembodied voice and (see also *Alone* [Kozintsev and Trauberg film]); First Five-Year Plan and, 134, 182–183; interviews in, 199, 201–202, 204, 218; in *The Jazz Singer*, 121; in *Lullaby*, 199, 202; music in films and, 110, 120; as natural vs. studio-engineered, 75; Socialist Realism and, 45; sound/talking cinema as goal of, 110; technological limitations of, 110–11. *See also Enthusiasm: Symphony of the Donbass* (Vertov film); *K.Sh.E.* (Komosomol: Patron of Electrification) (Shub film); *Road to Life*; *Three Songs of Lenin* (Vertov film)

Tactile Eye, The (Barker book), 31, 81, 92
Tagafon sound camera, 232
Tager, Pavel, 2–3, 9–11, 10, 13, 16, 106n65
Taras Shevchenko (Savchenko film), 113
Taylor, Richard, 1, 112, 137n44, 231, 234, 240n15
telephones, 6, 26–27, 48, 152, 154, 175n42. *See also Alone* (Kozintsev and Trauberg film); *Ivan* (Dovzhenko film); *K.Sh.E.* (Komosomol: Patron of Electrification) (Shub film)
Terminator (Cameron film), 63, 68n58
Tesla, Nikola, xv
Thälmann, Ernst, 188, 221n25
Theory of the Film (Balás), 34n13
theremin (musical instrument), 68n50, 89, 90, 91–93, 98, 102, 106n69
Theremin, Lev, 93, 98, 106n69
Thompson, Kristin, 6, 19, 63–64, 148–149
Thousand Plateaus, A (Deleuze book), 95
Three Songs of Lenin (Vertov film), 178–226; 1934/35 versions of, 178–181, 191, 193, 214, 220nn2–3, 226n93; 1938 silent version of, 183, 185–186, 187, 188, 191, 210, 214, 220n8, 221n19; 1938 sound version of, 179–180, 182–188, 184, 188, 220nn8, 222n27, 223n61; 1970 restoration of, 179–180, 189, 190, 203; avant-garde traces in, 181, 220n9; chairwoman of the collective farm in, 201, 202–203, 213–214, 219; collage/photomontage methods in, 194–195, 195; collective farms in, 182, 199, 201, 202–204, 213; compilation elements in, 182; critics'/audiences' responses to, 178, 181, 193; disembodied voice of power/ideology in, 199, 204–205; Dniepr Hydroelectric Station in, 107n83, 192, 209–210, 210, 236; vs. *Enthusiasm*, 181; Fanya Kaplan in, 186, 211, 215, 217; fictionalization of, 217–218;

269

Index

First Song of, 185–186, 188, 197, 213; Gasanova in, 186, 188, 195, *195*; gas masks in, 186, *189*; Gorki in, 185–186, 191, 193, 195, 209, 212–215, *212*, 235; ideology undercut in, 202–203; as interior monologue, 191, 194; interviews recorded in sync-sound in, 32, 182, 199, 201–203, 218; Ivanov in, 186, 214, 215, *215*, 217, 226n94; Lenin cult and, 180, 209, 225n85; Lenin in motion in, 211; *Lenin Kino-Pravda* footage and, 188, 191–193, 211, 213, *214*, 215, 216; Lenin removed from, 220n5; Lenin's assassination attempted, 186, 215–217, *216*, 225n87; Lenin's funeral in, 184, 188, 195, 206–209, 219; Lenin's immortality attempted/failed in, 203–219, 224nn64–65; Lenin's mausoleum in, 94, 195, 207, 217; Lenin's name spelled in blocks, *187*; Lenin's photos in, *187*, *190*; Lenin's speeches in, 185–186, 188, 199; Lenin's Stand Firm exhortation in, 189, 198–199, 203; Lenin's statue in, 209–210, *211*; Lenin's voice absent from, 192–193, 218–219; Lenin's voice in, 32, 182, 199, 202–208; *Man with a Movie Camera* and, 184, 191, 194, 197, 209; Maria Belik in, 200, *201*, 203; materialization of words in, 195; mobility vs. immobility in, 206–209, 213, 217, 225n82; montage in, 182; movement of energy in, 209, *210*; movement privileged over sound in, 191; music in, 182, 184–185, 199, 213; photomontage and, 194–195, *195*, *196*, 197, 222n41, 236; pine trees in, 212–213, *212*, 225n88; politics of image and montage in, 225n88; pulled from Soviet screens, 178; Second Song of, 182, 185, 188, 191, 199, 206–207, 209, 211, 213; shooting scripts for, 226n93; Shumyatsky on, 235–236; as Socialist Realist film, 235–236; soldiers marching to, *180*; Song of Songs in, 182, 221n15; sound as fundamental component of, 181–183; sound/image relationships in, 191; sound/image/voice unities in, 179–180, 182–185, 191, 193; sound limitations in, 182; Stalin in, 179–180, *183*, *184*, 188, 192, 202–203, 220n5, 220n9, 223n61; Stalin removed from, 203, 221n19, 222n31, 223n58, 223n61; Stalin's victims removed from, 186; synchronized sound in, 180, 182–183, 186, 197, 199, 201–202, 205–206, 218; Third Song of, 182, 185, 188, 199, 209, 213; time issues in, 207–213, 219; titles in, 182, 185–186, 188–189, *190*, 194–195, 197, 199, 206–207, 210, 212–215, *214*, *215*, 219; Turkic songs and women in, 182, 185, 189, 199, 204, 221n26; veil lifted in, 186, *188*; Vertov as editor of, 185–186; Vertov on, 191; Vertov's kino-eye and, 217–218; voice of authority rejected by, 219; voice of God narration absent from, 194; voice recordings in, 199; voices silenced in, 211–219; "We are growing, we are maturing" song in, 186, *187*

Timartsev, Nikolai, 77, 104n22

Timofeev, Nikolai, 78

Tip Top (Soviet animated film), 3, 231

Tissé, Eduard, 13, 15, 34n10, 36n44, 166, 177n70

titles (intertitles): abandoned, 11, 14, 74, 231; changeability of, 143; as dialogue, 227; experienced as a law, 228; fused with images, 228; in *Lenin Kino-Pravda*, 215; literacy and, 12, 39; multilanguage issues in, 11, 39n86, 144; read aloud, 143; as reproduced speech, 227; universality of, 228; in Vertov's avant-garde films, 227. See also *Alone* (Kozintsev and Trauberg film); *Road to Life, The* (Ekk film); *Three Songs of Lenin* (Vertov film)

Titus, Joan, 110–111

Tobis-Klangfilm company, 7, 36n27

Today (Shub film), 95

To You, Front! (Vertov film), 184

Trauberg, Ilya, 123

Trauberg, Leonid: among FEKS founders, 65n2; as first Soviet sound film-maker, 30; Moskvin as cameraman for, 57; *New Babylon*, 43, 110; as Socialist Realist, 69n63; transitioning to sound, 4, 41; *The Youth of Maxim*, 229. See also *Alone* (Kozintsev and Trauberg film)

Tretyakov, Sergei, 84

Tsekhanovsky, Mikhail, 19

Tsivian, Yuri, 70, 181, 238

Tumarkina, Nina, 209, 225n85

Turovskaya, Maya, 234

Tykocinski-Tykociner, Joseph, xv–xix, *xvi*

Tynyanov, Yury, 57, 65n2, 66n21

Ukraine, 76, 139, 155–156, 163–164, 170, 174n20, 176n64. See also Dovzhenko, Alexander; *Enthusiasm: Symphony of the Donbass* (Vertov film); *K.Sh.E.* (Komosomol: Patron of Electrification) (Shub film); Vertov, Dziga; VUFKU (All-Ukrainian Film Studio)

Ukraine in Flames (Dovzhenko film), 138
Umbrellas of Cherbourg, The (Demy film), 137n40
Under the Rooftops of Paris (Clair film), 15, 121
United States sound film. *See* Hollywood/United States transition to sound film
University of Illinois, Urbana, xv, xvii
utopia, 118, 162. *See also Accordion, The* (Savchenko film)

Vachnadze, Nato, 90–92, 106n64
Vainkop, Yulian, 111
VAPLITE (Free Academy of Proletarian Literature) (Ukrainian literary organization), 139
Vasil'ev brothers. *See Chapaev* (Vasil'ev brothers film)
Vertov, Dziga: "About [My] Love for the Living Person," 202; accused of formalism, 82, 181, 197; cameras used by, 76, 104n22; Chaplin on, 80; contrapuntal sound used by, 16, 73; Dovzhenko and, 146; electrical power in films of, 99; film as thing/object for, 197; on film as truth at 24x a second, 218; as first to record unrehearsed speech in film, 199; futurist influences on, 23, 35n21; industrial sound as interest of, 73; intertitles abandoned by, 194; kino-eye concept of, 74–75, 90, 184, 202, 208, 217–219; *Kinonedelia* newsreels of, 195; *Kinopravda* newsreels of, 73, 195, 197; in Laboratory of Hearing, 73; "Let's Discuss Ukrainfilm's First Sound Film," 78; on mobile energy, 95–96; montage editing pace of, 87; natural vs. studio-engineered sound demanded by, 75; non-human sound in films of, 22–23; ostracized by Soviet film industry, 181; photo of, 74; radio-ear and, 74, 90, 125; radio-film vs. audio-visual film concepts of, 184; *radiopravda* concept of, 73; Shorin's collaboration with, 76; Shub's friendship with, 84, 87; silent/talking/sound categories rejected by, 76; *A Sixth Part of the World*, 191; Socialist Realism and, 197; sound as early interest of, 72–73; sound clichés rejected by, 183; *Stride, Soviet!* 70, 99, 203; as subjective documentarian, 72; synchronous and asynchronous sound as used by, 75–76; title/image fusion in, 228; titles in avant-garde films of, 227; transitioning to sound, 4; VUFKU films made by, 178; as writer of film theory and practice, 4–5; *To You, Front!* 184. *See also Eleventh Year, The* (Vertov film); *Enthusiasm: Symphony of the Donbass* (Vertov film); *Lullaby*; *Man with a Movie Camera*; *Three Songs of Lenin* (Vertov film)
Vesnin, Viktor, 97
Vibrant Matter (Bennett book), 94–95
Vishnevsky, Vsevold, 172
Vitaphone sound system, xviii
"Vladimir Ilych Lenin" (Mayakovsky poem), 51
Voice in Cinema, The (Chion book), 1
Voinov, Nikolai, 21
von Sternberg, Joseph, 15–16
Voroshilov, Kliment, 141–142
Vostokkino film production studio, 11, 173n17
VUFKU (All-Ukrainian Film Studio), 76, 103n14, 139–140, 143–144, 178, 232
Vuskovich, Igor, 65n2

Wagner, Richard, 182, 184, 199
Warner Brothers, xviii, 116–117
Wells, H. D., 193
Western Electric, xviii, 36n27
"White" (Dyer essay), 161
Widdis, Emma, 23, 97–99, 164–165
Williams, Alan, 239–240
Williams, Linda, 226n96
Winter, Marian Hannah, 37n51
Winter, O., 238
Women from Ryazan (Pravov and Preobrazhenskaya film), 3, 231

Yampolsky, Mikhail, 87
Yankovsky, Boris, 21, 38n76
Youngblood, Denise, 1–2, 12–13, 36n45, 43, 66n21, 67n32, 242n42
Youth of Maxim, The (Kozintsev and Trauberg film), 229, 234
Yutkevich, Sergei, 43, 65n2, 155, 229, 231

Zak, Mark, 114, 128
Zarkhi, Aleksandr, 156–157
Zeldovych, Hryhory, 155
Zharov, Aleksandr, 31, 114, 118, 135n20
Zhdanov, Andrei, 29
Zhizn' iskusstva (Soviet art journal), 14, 109–111
Zizek, Slavoj, 68n59
Zorkaya, Neya, 41, 65n4, 66n25

LILYA KAGANOVSKY is Professor of Slavic, Comparative Literature, and Media & Cinema Studies at the University of Illinois, Urbana–Champaign. She is author of *How the Soviet Man Was Unmade* and is editor (with Lauren M. E. Goodlad and Robert A. Rushing) of *Mad Men, Mad World: Sex, Politics, Style, and the 1960s* and (with Masha Salazkina) of *Sound, Music, Speech in Soviet and Post-Soviet Cinema* (IUP).

www.ingramcontent.com/pod-product-compliance
Lightning Source LLC
Chambersburg PA
CBHW052046220426
43663CB00012B/2465